The 2010s

ISBN 978-1-5400-8987-8

Visit Hal Leonard Online at
www.halleonard.com

Contact us:
Hal Leonard
7777 West Bluemound Road
Milwaukee, WI 53213
Email: info@halleonard.com

In Europe, contact:
Hal Leonard Europe Limited
42 Wigmore Street
Marylebone, London, W1U 2RN
Email: info@halleonardeurope.com

In Australia, contact:
Hal Leonard Australia Pty. Ltd.
4 Lentara Court
Cheltenham, Victoria, 3192 Australia
Email: info@halleonard.com.au

The 2010s

CONTENTS

from Sam Hunt - *Southside*

Body Like a Back Road

Words and Music by Sam Hunt, Josh Osborne, Shane McAnally and Zach Crowell

Verse

Gtrs. 2 & 3 tacet

N.C. C Dm B♭

Oo. 1. Got a girl from the south side, got braids in her hair. First time I seen her

End Rhy. Fig. 1

let ring

Gtr. 1: w/ Rhy. Fig. 1 (last 2 meas.)

F C F N.C.

walk by, oo, man, I 'bout fell off of my chair. Had to get her

Gtr. 1: w/ Rhy. Fig. 1

F C

num - ber, it took me like six

Dm B♭ F C F N.C.

weeks. Now me and her go way back, like Cad - il - lac seats. Bod - y like a

Gtr. 4 (slight dist.)

Fill 1

mf

let ring

Chorus

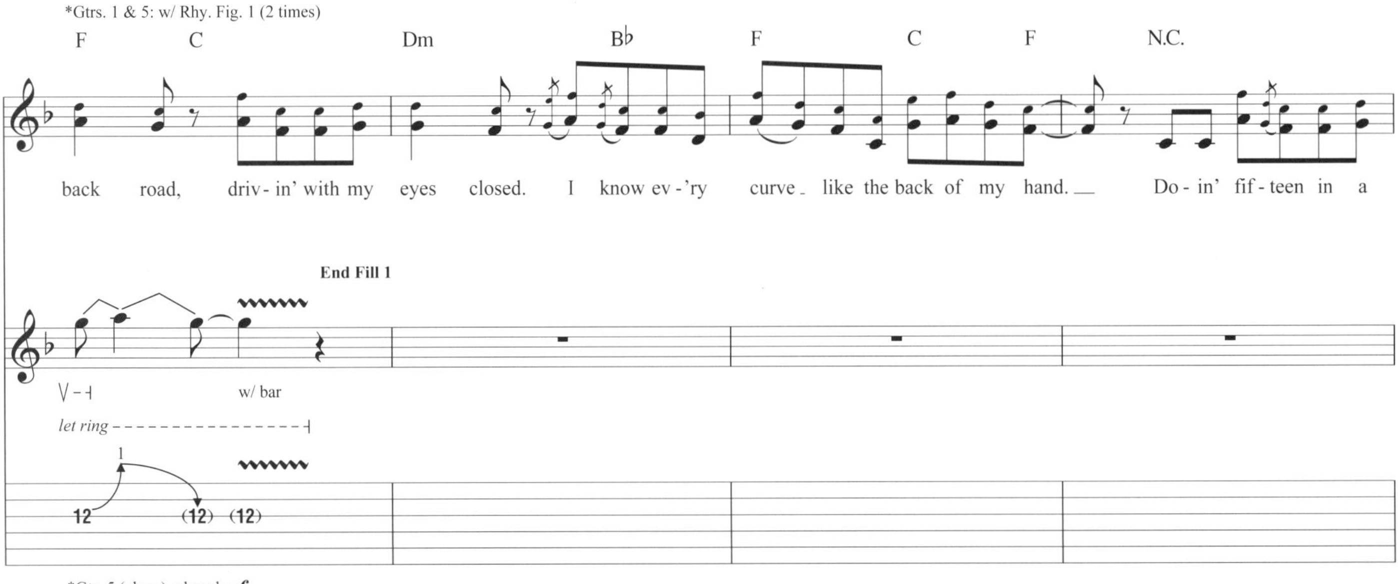
*Gtrs. 1 & 5: w/ Rhy. Fig. 1 (2 times)
F C Dm B♭ F C F N.C.
back road, driv - in' with my eyes closed. I know ev - 'ry curve like the back of my hand. Do - in' fif - teen in a
End Fill 1
w/ bar
let ring
1
12 (12) (12)
*Gtr. 5 (clean), played mf.

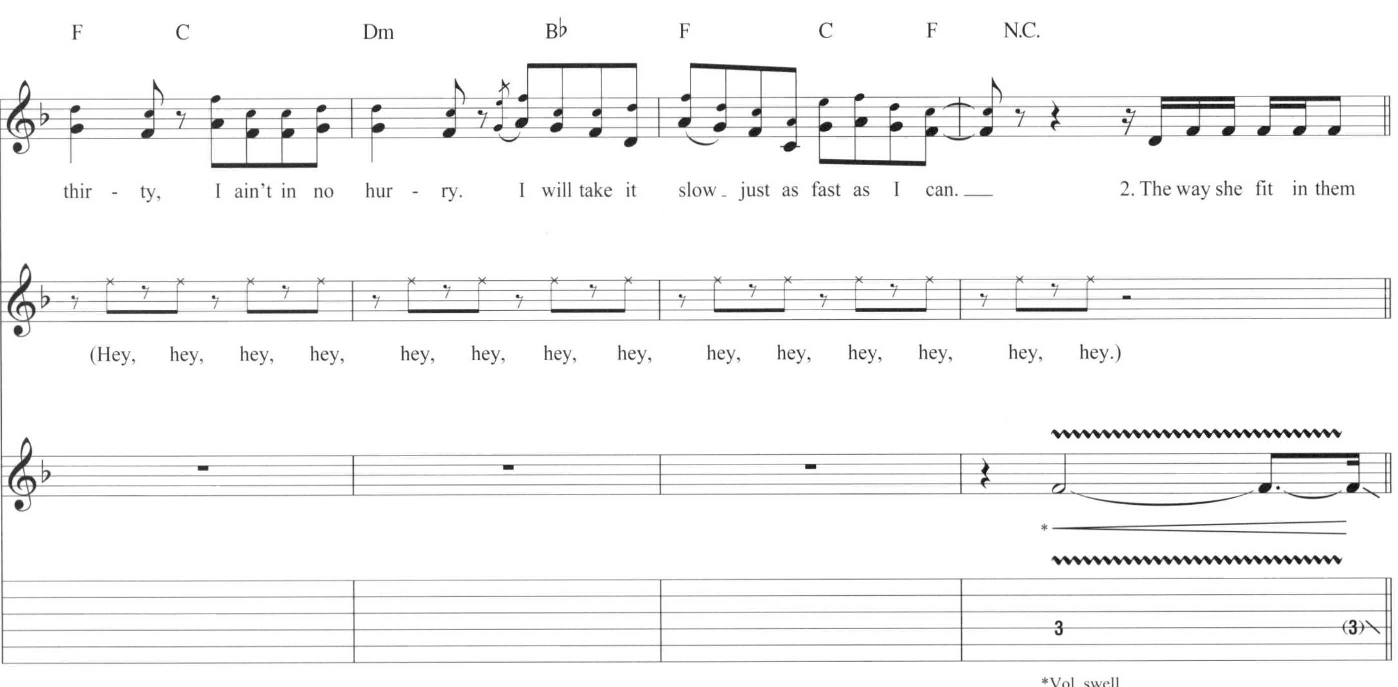
F C Dm B♭ F C F N.C.
thir - ty, I ain't in no hur - ry. I will take it slow just as fast as I can. 2. The way she fit in them
(Hey, hey, hey, hey, hey, hey, hey, hey, hey, hey, hey, hey, hey, hey.)
3 (3)
*Vol. swell

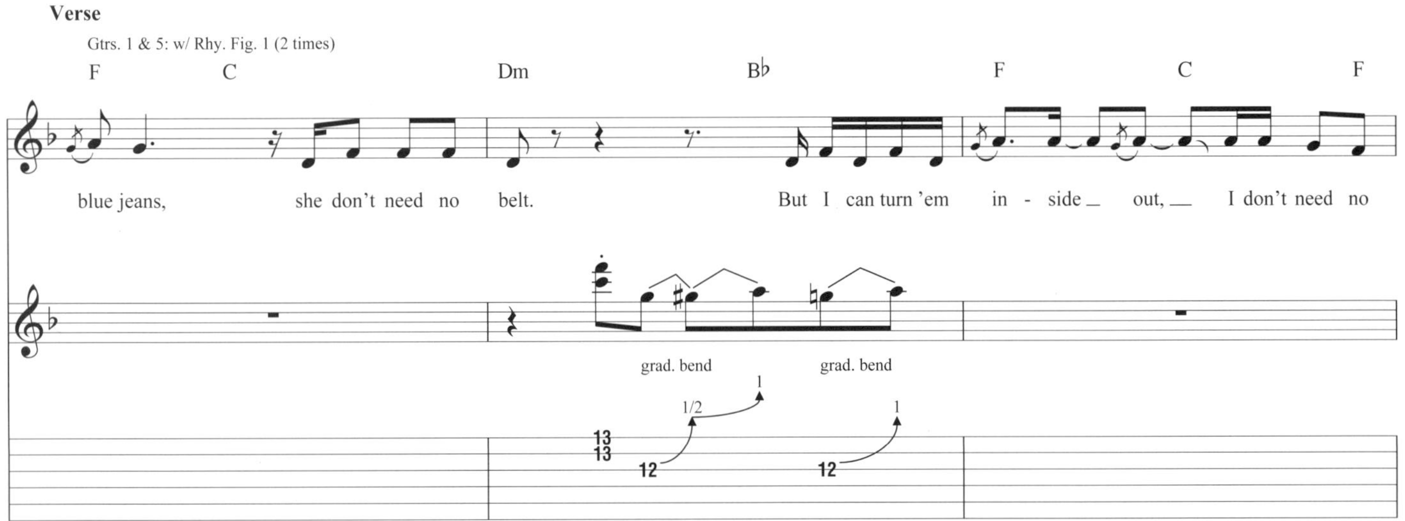
Verse
Gtrs. 1 & 5: w/ Rhy. Fig. 1 (2 times)
F C Dm B♭ F C F
blue jeans, she don't need no belt. But I can turn 'em in - side out, I don't need no
grad. bend grad. bend
1/2 1 1
13
13
12 12

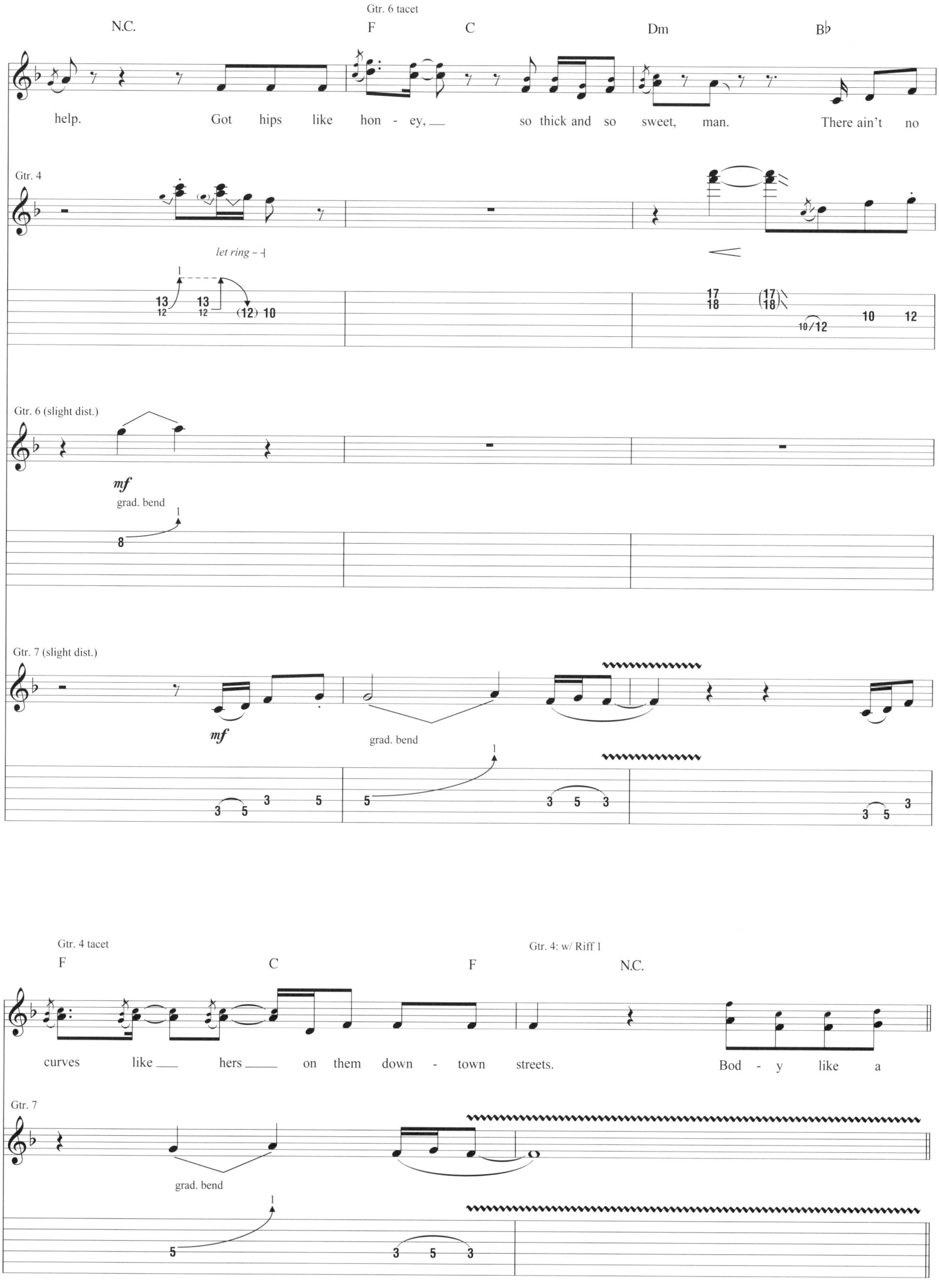

N.C.
Gtr. 6 tacet
F
C
Dm
B♭
help. Got hips like hon - ey, so thick and so sweet, man. There ain't no
Gtr. 4
let ring
1
13 12 13 12 (12) 10
17 18 (17 18) 10/12 10 12
Gtr. 6 (slight dist.)
mf
grad. bend
1
8
Gtr. 7 (slight dist.)
mf
grad. bend
1
3 5 3 5
5 3 5 3
3 5 3
Gtr. 4 tacet
Gtr. 4: w/ Riff 1
F
C
F
N.C.
curves like hers on them down - town streets. Bod - y like a
Gtr. 7
grad. bend
1
5 3 5 3

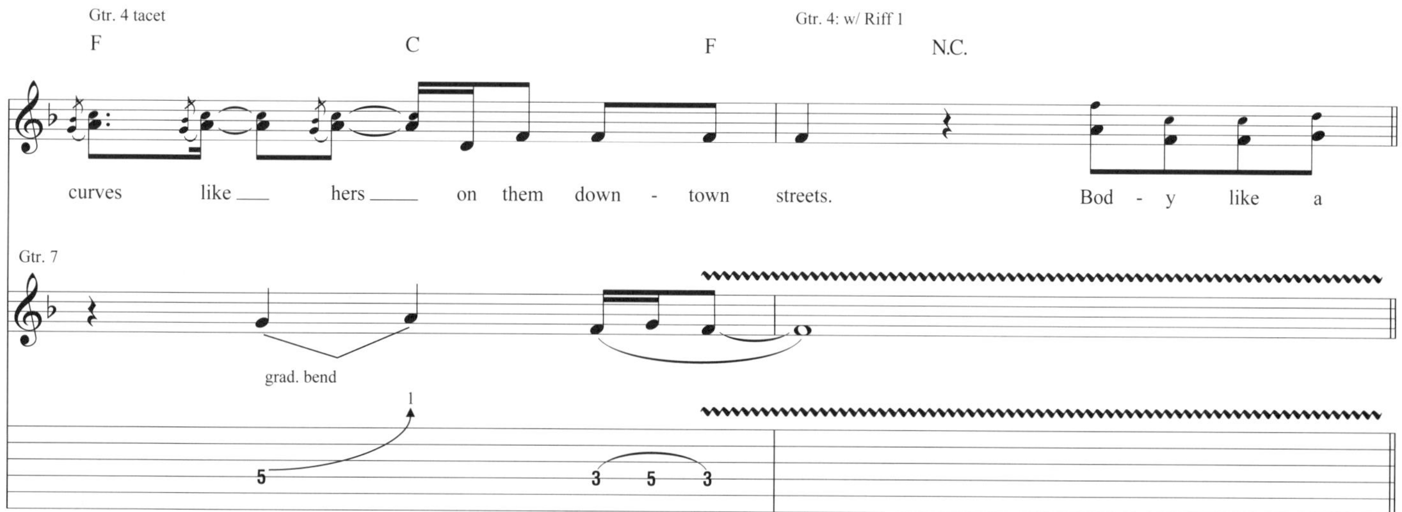

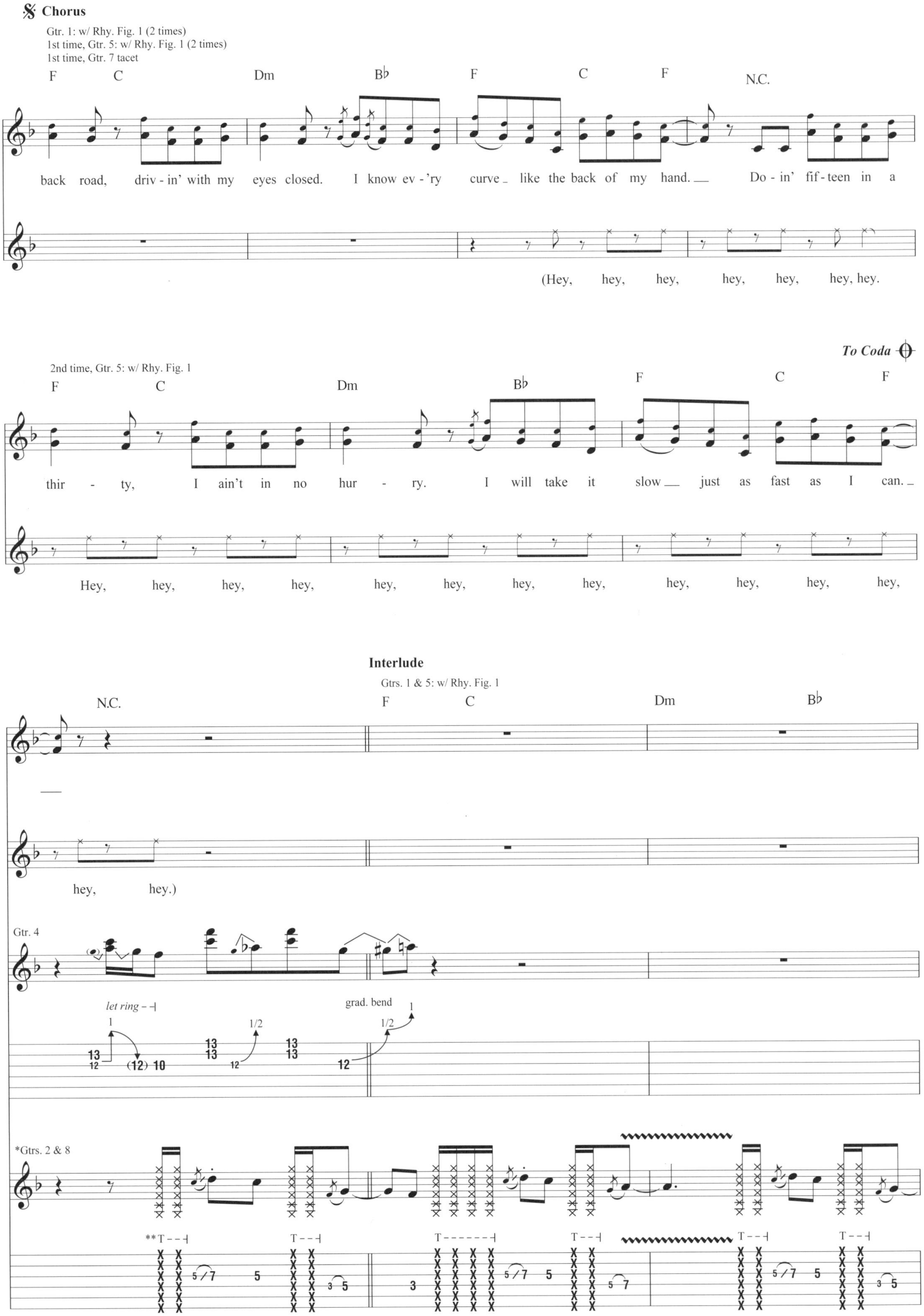

Chorus

Gtr. 1: w/ Rhy. Fig. 1 (2 times)
1st time, Gtr. 5: w/ Rhy. Fig. 1 (2 times)
1st time, Gtr. 7 tacet

Interlude

Gtrs. 1 & 5: w/ Rhy. Fig. 1

N.C. F C Dm B♭

hey, hey.)

Gtr. 4

let ring grad. bend

*Gtrs. 2 & 8

**T = Thumb on 6th string

*Gtr. 8 (dist.), played ***mf***.
Composite arrangement

Verse

*Kybd. arr. for gtr.

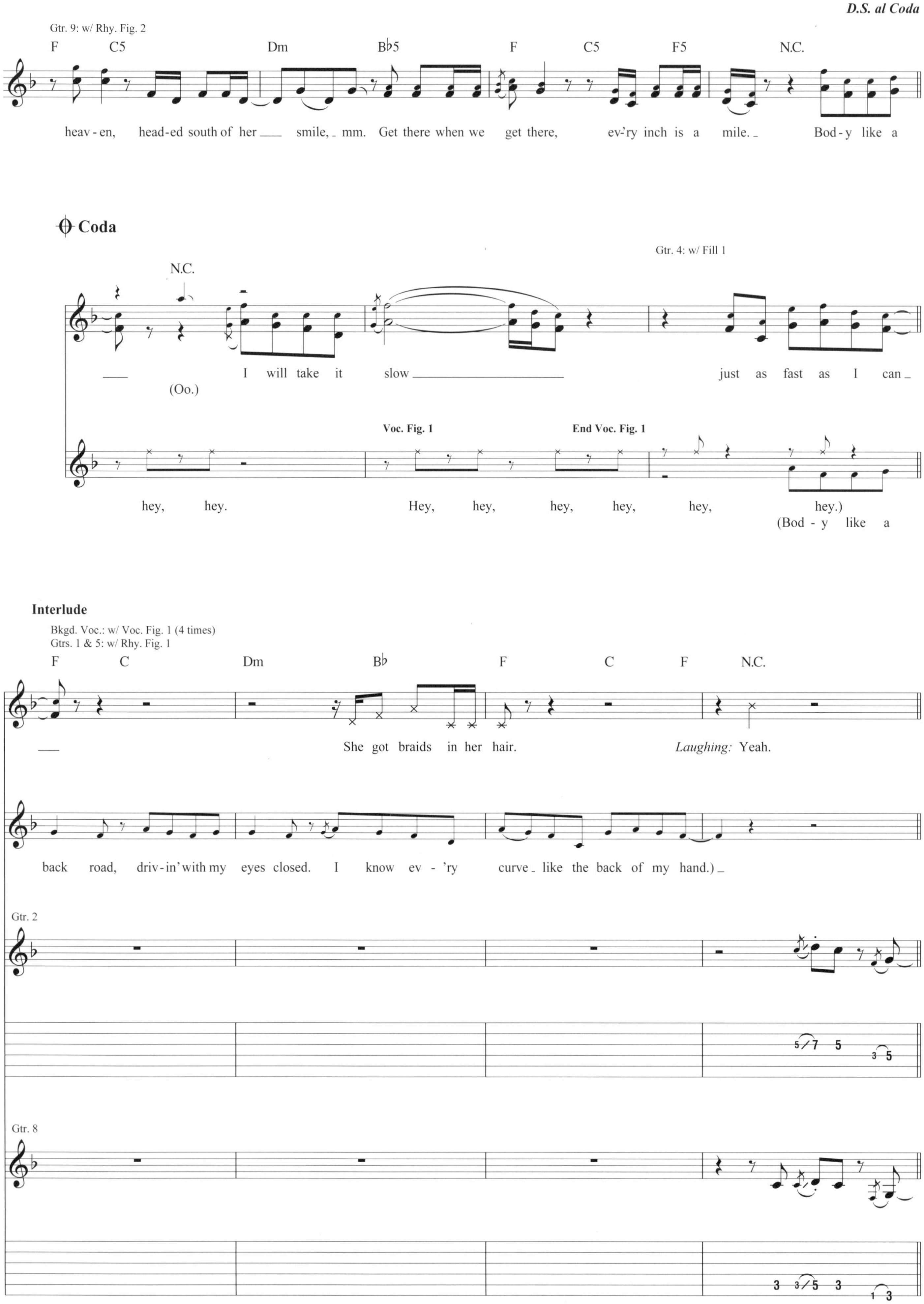

D.S. al Coda

Interlude

Bkgd. Voc.: w/ Voc. Fig. 1 (4 times)
Gtrs. 1 & 5: w/ Rhy. Fig. 1

F C Dm B♭ F C F N.C.

She got braids in her hair. *Laughing:* Yeah.

back road, driv-in' with my eyes closed. I know ev - 'ry curve like the back of my hand.)

Gtr. 2

5 7 5 3 5

Gtr. 8

3 3 5 3 1 3

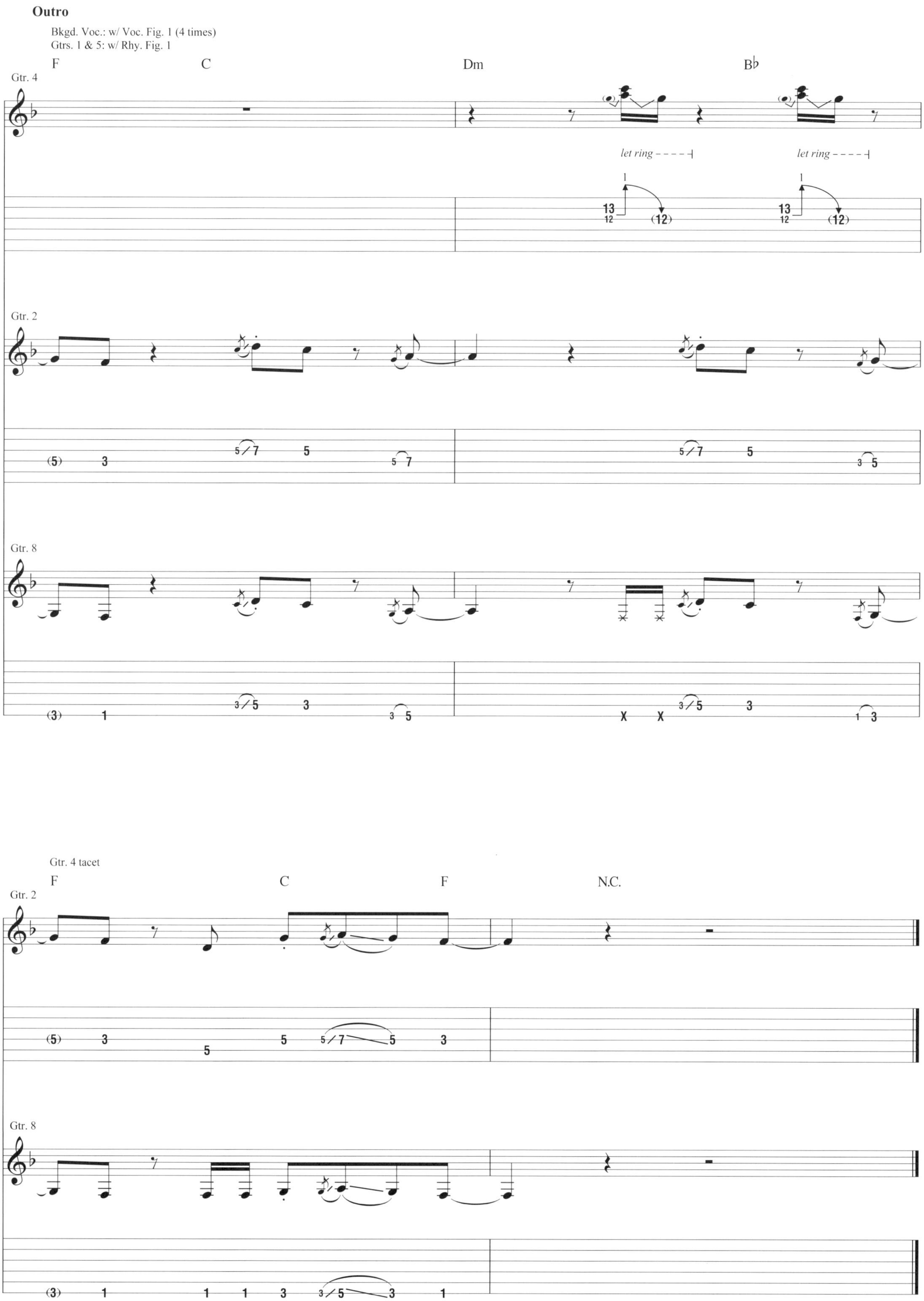

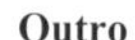

Outro
Bkgd. Voc.: w/ Voc. Fig. 1 (4 times)
Gtrs. 1 & 5: w/ Rhy. Fig. 1
F
C
Dm
B♭
Gtr. 4
let ring
let ring
Gtr. 2
Gtr. 8
Gtr. 4 tacet
F
C
F
N.C.
Gtr. 2
Gtr. 8

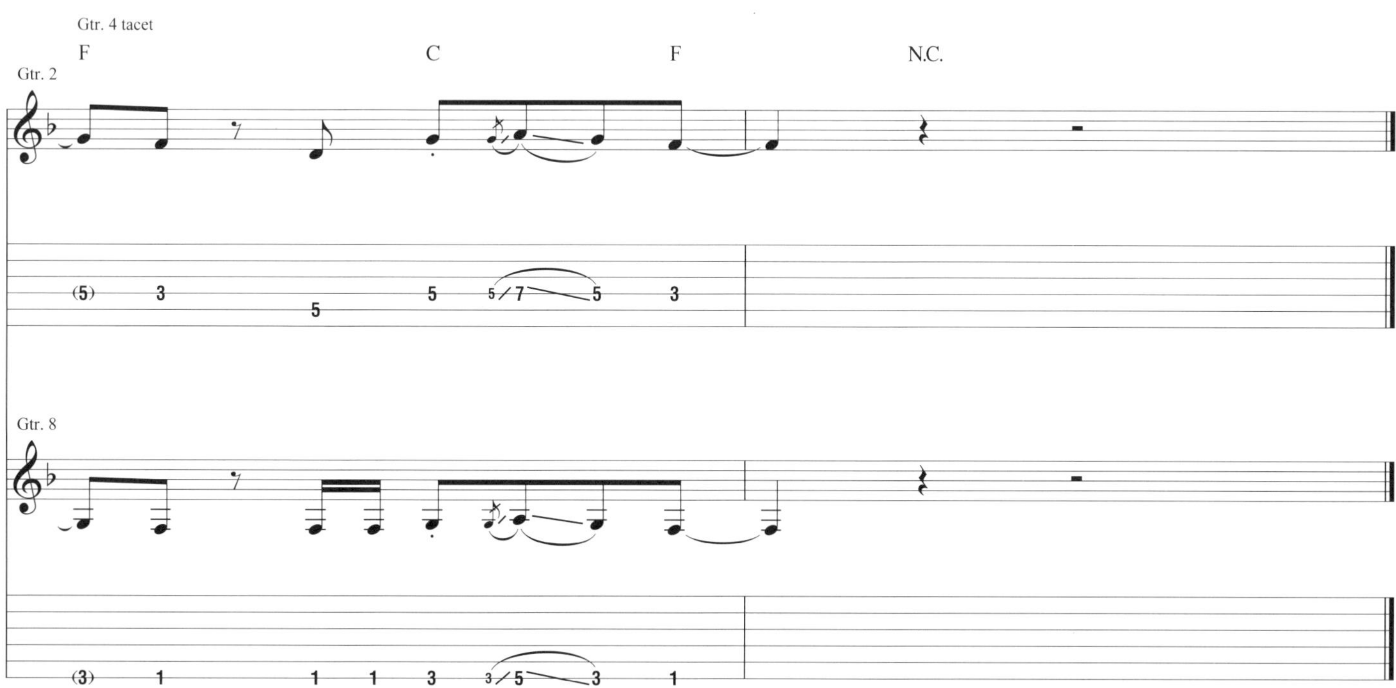

from DNCE - *DNCE*

Cake by the Ocean

Words and Music by Joseph Jonas, Justin Tranter, Robin Fredriksson and Mattias Larsson

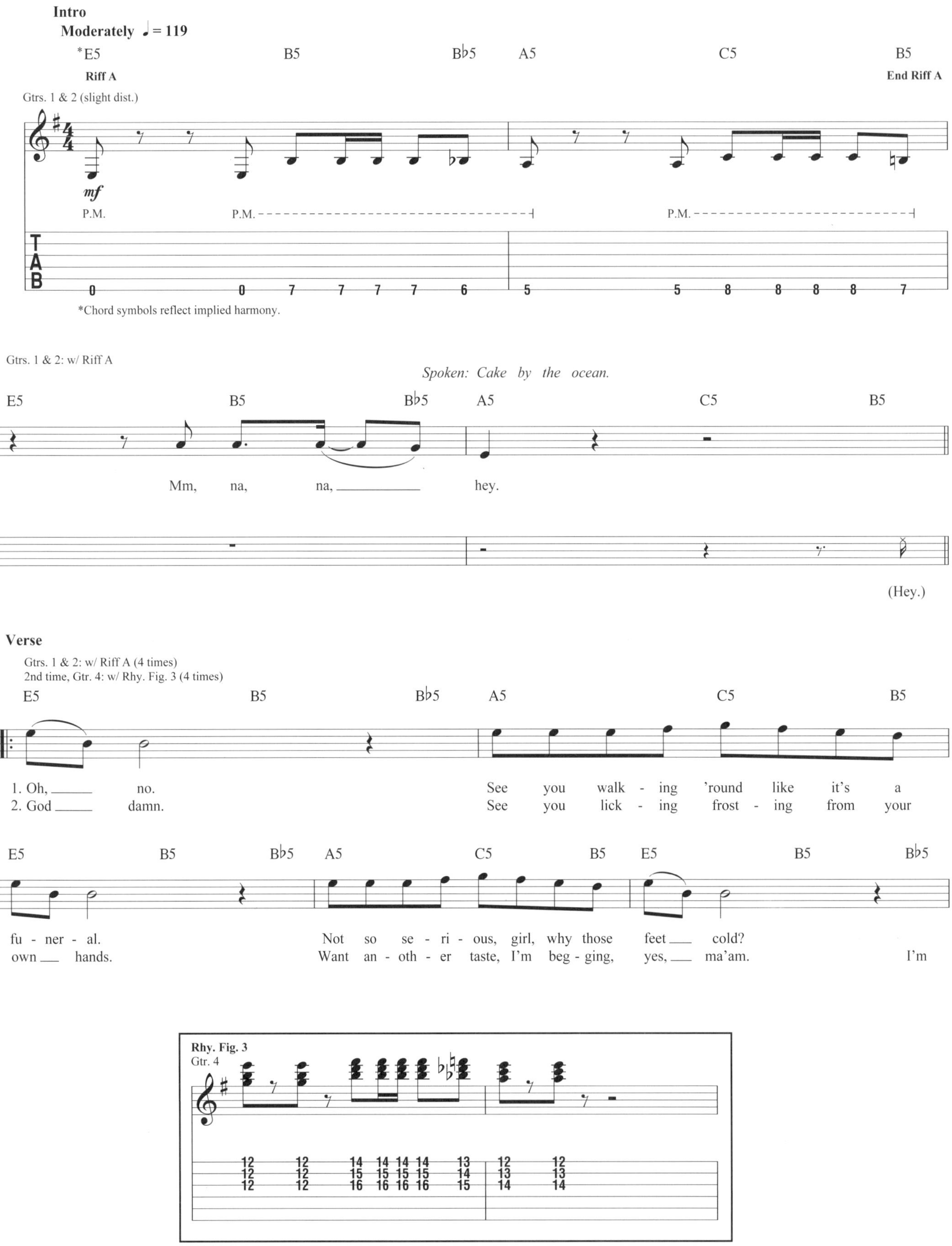

Intro

Moderately ♩ = 119

*E5 B5 B♭5 A5 C5 B5

Riff A ... End Riff A

Gtrs. 1 & 2 (slight dist.)

mf

P.M. P.M. P.M.

*Chord symbols reflect implied harmony.

Gtrs. 1 & 2: w/ Riff A

Spoken: Cake by the ocean.

E5 B5 B♭5 A5 C5 B5

Mm, na, na, hey.

(Hey.)

Verse

Gtrs. 1 & 2: w/ Riff A (4 times)
2nd time, Gtr. 4: w/ Rhy. Fig. 3 (4 times)

E5 B5 B♭5 A5 C5 B5

1. Oh, no. See you walk - ing 'round like it's a
2. God damn. See you lick - ing frost - ing from your

E5 B5 B♭5 A5 C5 B5 E5 B5 B♭5

fu - ner - al. Not so se - ri - ous, girl, why those feet cold?
own hands. Want an - oth - er taste, I'm beg - ging, yes, ma'am. I'm

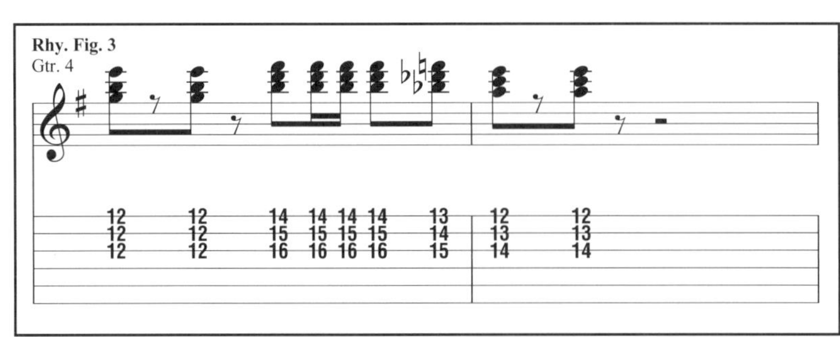

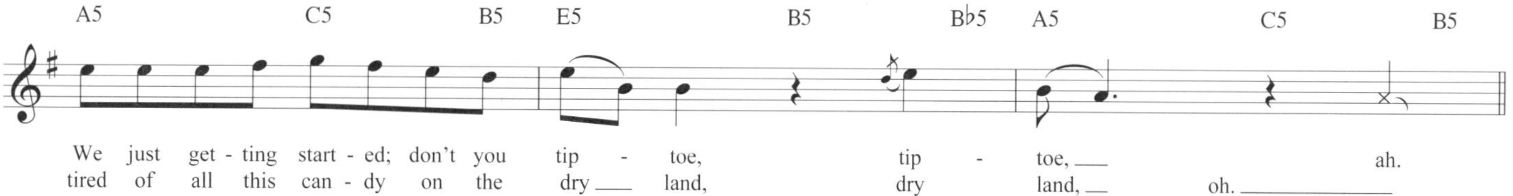
A5 C5 B5 E5 B5 B♭5 A5 C5 B5
We just get - ting start - ed; don't you tip - toe, tip - toe, ah.
tired of all this can - dy on the dry land, dry land, oh.

Pre-Chorus

Gtrs. 1 & 2: w/ Riff A (3 1/2 times)
2nd time, Gtr. 4: w/ Rhy. Fig. 3 (3 times)
2nd time, Gtr. 5: w/ Rhy. Fig. 1 (3 times)
Em Bm Am C B
Waste time with a mas - ter - piece, don't waste time with a mas - ter - piece.
(Huh!)
Rhy. Fig. 1
Gtr. 3 (clean)
End Rhy. Fig. 1
mf

Gtr. 3: w/ Rhy. Fig. 1 (2 times)
Em Bm Am C B Em Bm
You should be roll - ing with me, oh, you should be roll - ing with me, ah. You're a real - life fan - ta - sy, you're a

2nd time, Bkgd. Voc.: w/ Voc. Fig. 1
Am C B E5 B5 N.C.
real - life fan - ta - sy. But you're mov - ing so care - ful - ly; let's start liv - ing dan - ger - ous - ly.
(Huh!)

Voc. Fig. 1
(Whoa, oh.)

Chorus

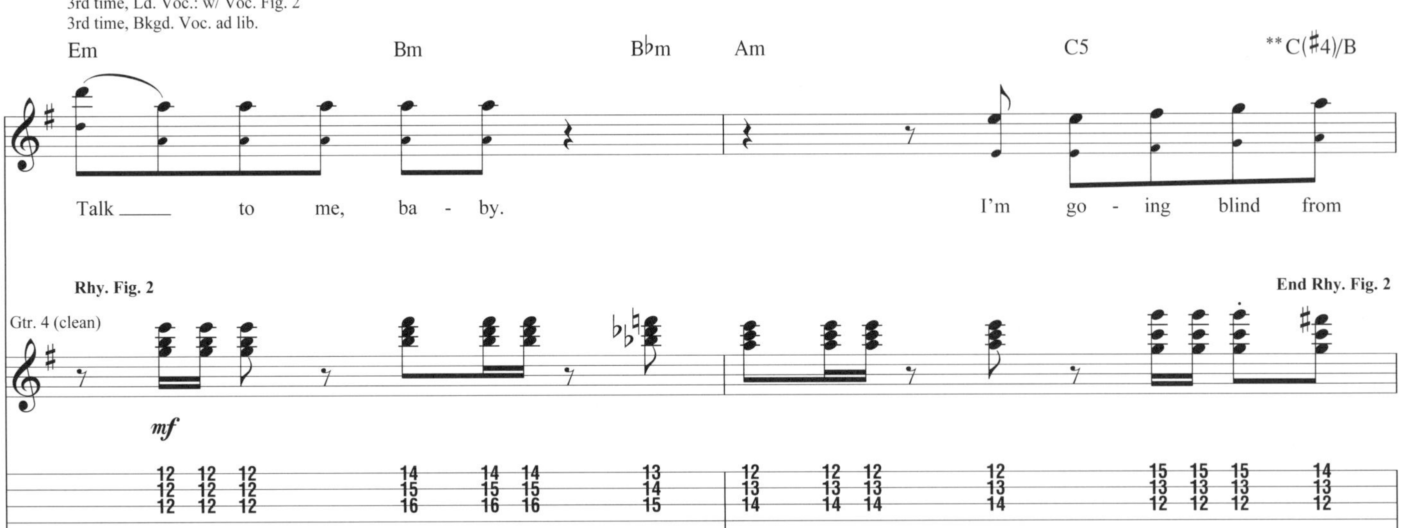

Gtrs. 1 & 2: w/ Riff A (8 times)
*Gtrs. 3 & 5: w/ Rhy. Fig. 1 (8 times)
3rd time, Ld. Voc.: w/ Voc. Fig. 2
3rd time, Bkgd. Voc. ad lib.
Em Bm B♭m Am C5 **C(♯4)/B
Talk to me, ba - by. I'm go - ing blind from
Rhy. Fig. 2
End Rhy. Fig. 2
Gtr. 4 (clean)
mf
*Gtr. 5 (clean), played mf.
**Bass plays B.

Gtr. 4: w/ Rhy. Fig. 2 (7 times)
Em Bm B♭m Am C5 C(♯4)/B Em Bm B♭m
this sweet, sweet crav - ing, whoa, oh. Let's lose our minds and go fuck - ing cra - zy.
(Whoa, oh.)

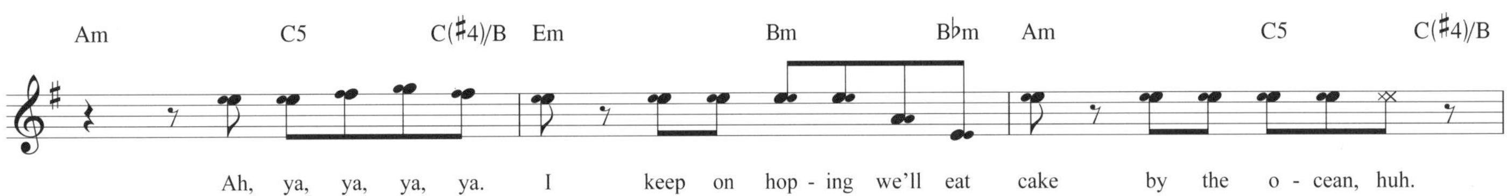

Am C5 C(♯4)/B Em Bm B♭m Am C5 C(♯4)/B
Ah, ya, ya, ya, ya. I keep on hop - ing we'll eat cake by the o - cean, huh.

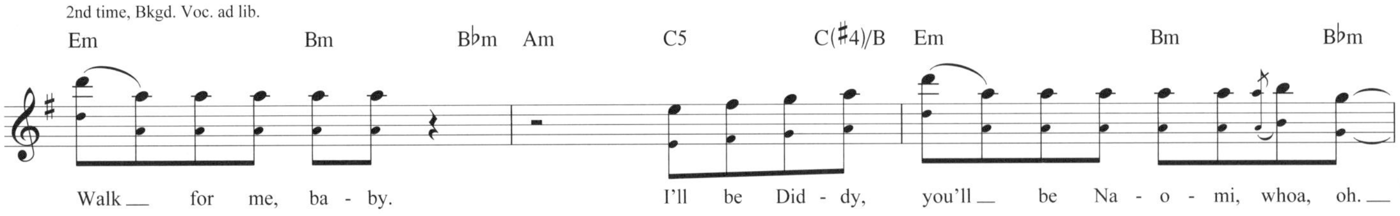

2nd time, Bkgd. Voc. ad lib.
Em Bm B♭m Am C5 C(♯4)/B Em Bm B♭m
Walk for me, ba - by. I'll be Did - dy, you'll be Na - o - mi, whoa, oh.

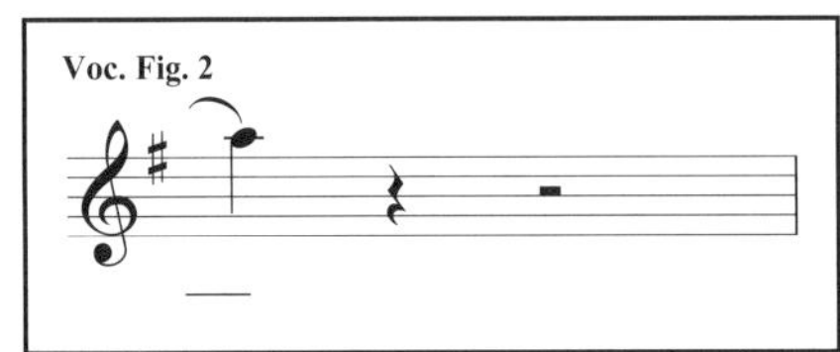

Voc. Fig. 2

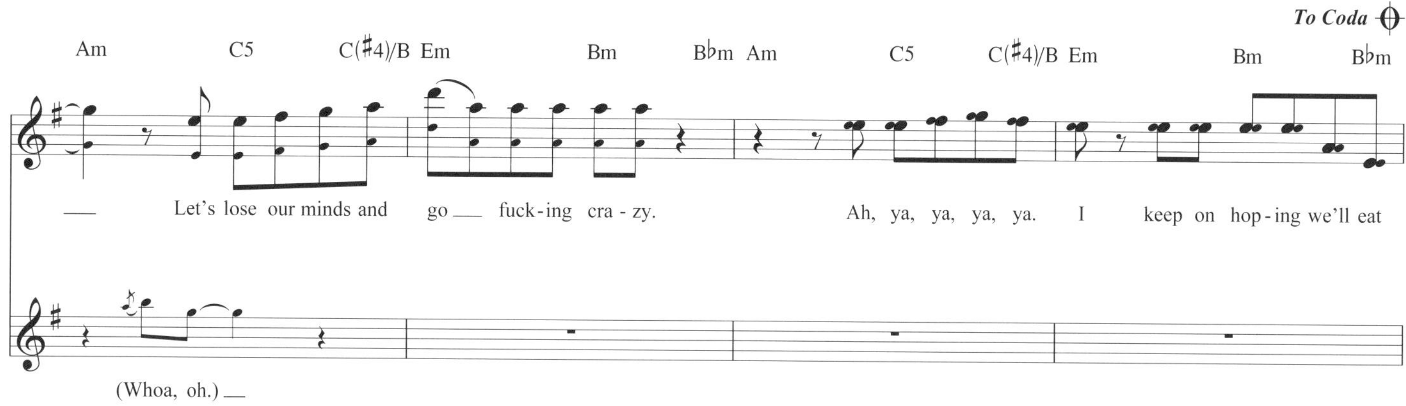
To Coda
Am C5 C(♯4)/B Em Bm B♭m Am C5 C(♯4)/B Em Bm B♭m
Let's lose our minds and go fuck-ing cra-zy. Ah, ya, ya, ya, ya. I keep on hop-ing we'll eat
(Whoa, oh.)

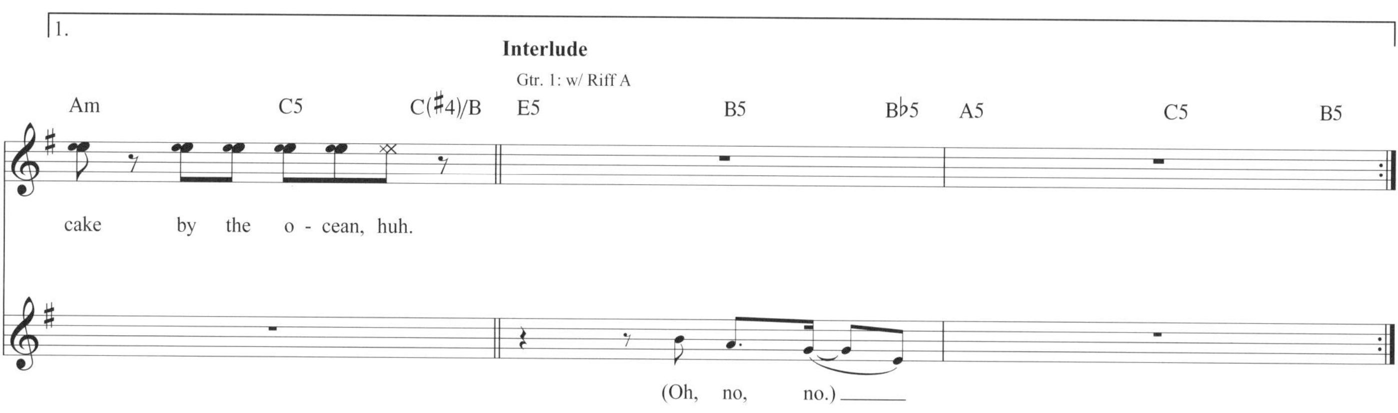
1.
Interlude
Gtr. 1: w/ Riff A
Am C5 C(♯4)/B E5 B5 B♭5 A5 C5 B5
cake by the o-cean, huh.
(Oh, no, no.)

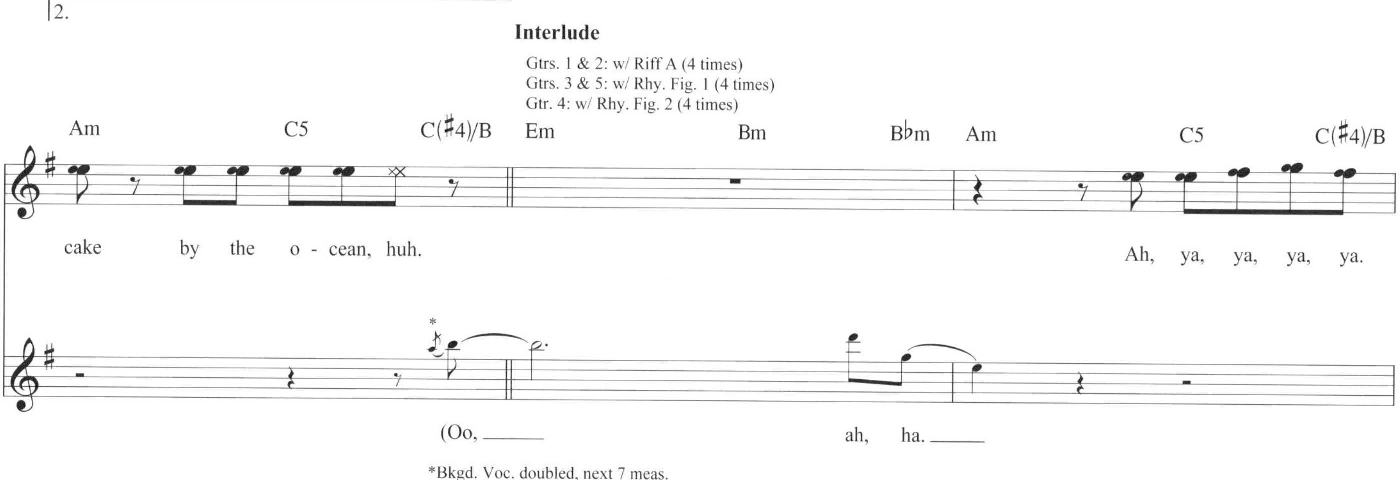
2.
Interlude
Gtrs. 1 & 2: w/ Riff A (4 times)
Gtrs. 3 & 5: w/ Rhy. Fig. 1 (4 times)
Gtr. 4: w/ Rhy. Fig. 2 (4 times)
Am C5 C(♯4)/B Em Bm B♭m Am C5 C(♯4)/B
cake by the o-cean, huh. Ah, ya, ya, ya, ya.
(Oo, ah, ha.
*Bkgd. Voc. doubled, next 7 meas.

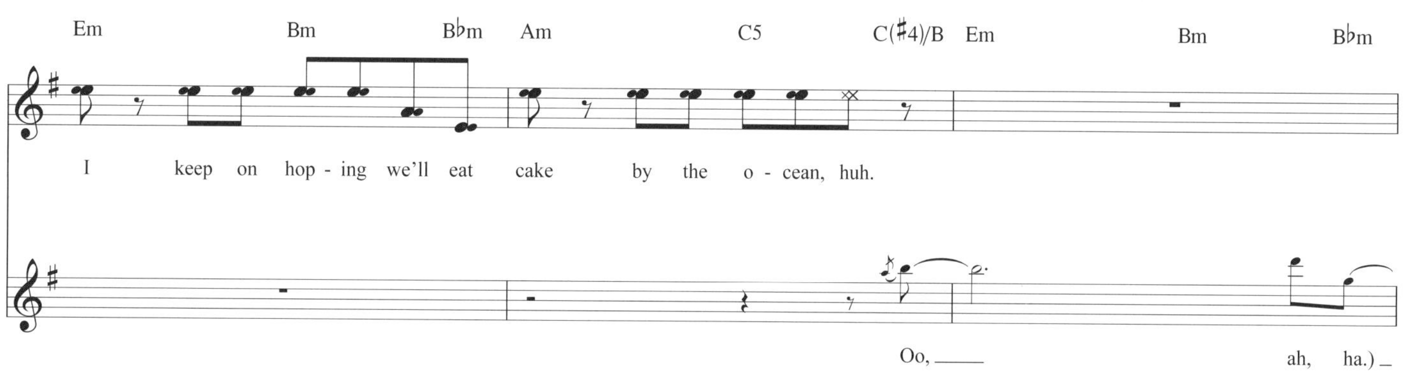
Em Bm B♭m Am C5 C(♯4)/B Em Bm B♭m
I keep on hop-ing we'll eat cake by the o-cean, huh.
Oo, ah, ha.)

Am C5 C(♯4)/B Em Bm B♭m Am C5 C(♯4)/B
Ah, ya, ya, ya, ya. I keep on hop - ing we'll eat cake by the o - cean, huh.

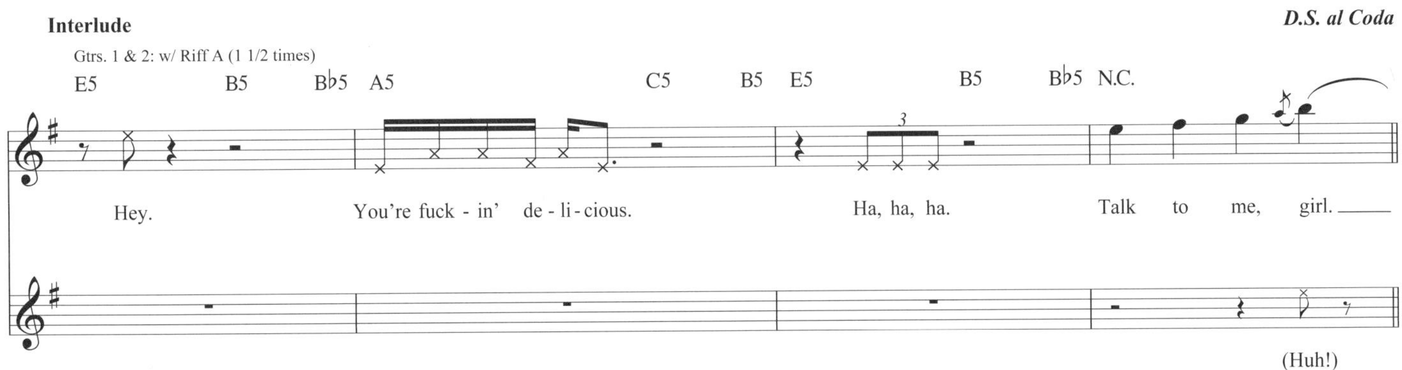
Interlude
D.S. al Coda
Gtrs. 1 & 2: w/ Riff A (1 1/2 times)
E5 B5 B♭5 A5 C5 B5 E5 B5 B♭5 N.C.
Hey. You're fuck - in' de - li - cious. Ha, ha, ha. Talk to me, girl.
(Huh!)

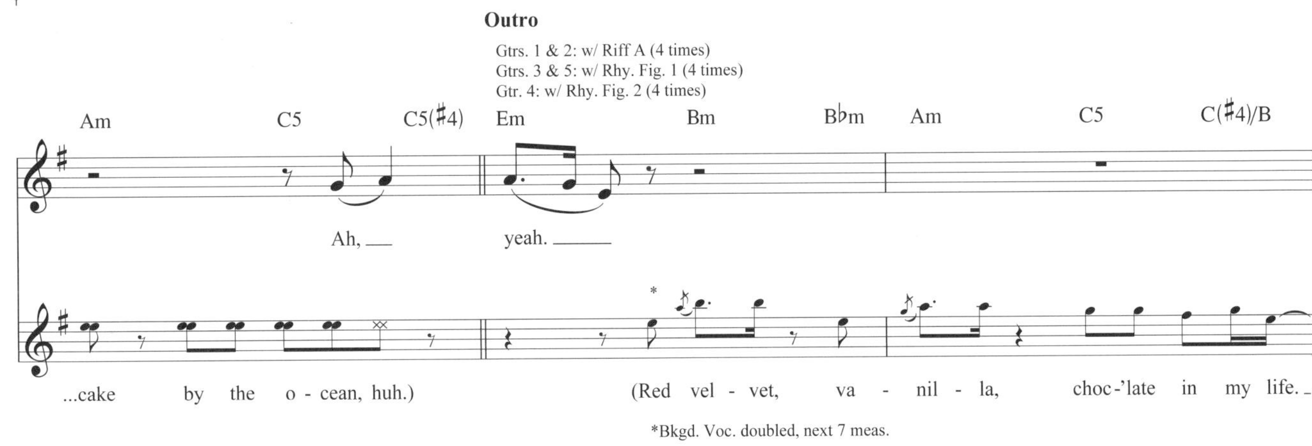
Coda
Outro
Gtrs. 1 & 2: w/ Riff A (4 times)
Gtrs. 3 & 5: w/ Rhy. Fig. 1 (4 times)
Gtr. 4: w/ Rhy. Fig. 2 (4 times)
Am C5 C5(♯4) Em Bm B♭m Am C5 C(♯4)/B
Ah, yeah.
...cake by the o - cean, huh.) (Red vel - vet, va - nil - la, choc-'late in my life.
*Bkgd. Voc. doubled, next 7 meas.

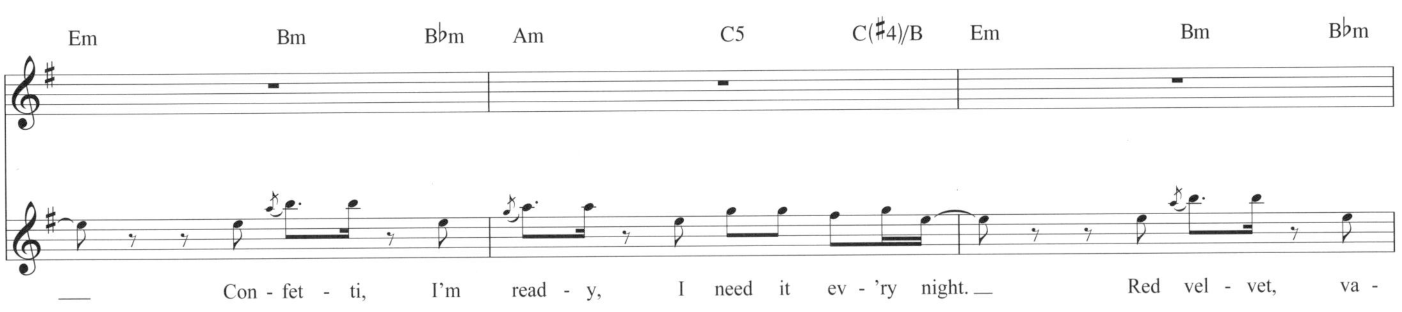
Em Bm B♭m Am C5 C(♯4)/B Em Bm B♭m
Con - fet - ti, I'm read - y, I need it ev - 'ry night. Red vel - vet, va -

Am C5 C(♯4)/B Em Bm B♭m Am C5 C(♯4)/B
Ah, ya, ya, ya, ya. I keep on hop - ing we'll eat cake by the o - cean, huh.
nil - la, choc-'late in my life.)

from Ed Sheeran - *Divide*

Castle on the Hill

Words and Music by Ed Sheeran and Benjamin Levin

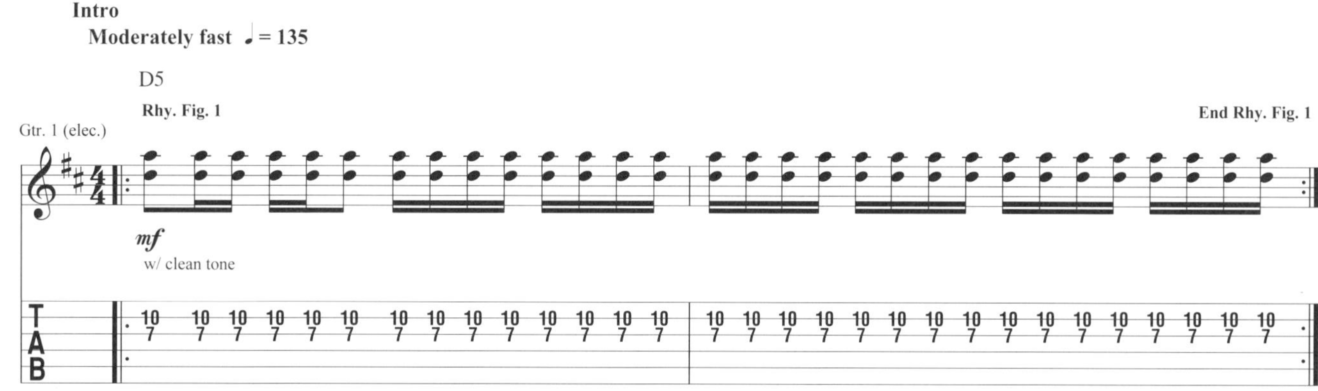

D/F♯
G5
B5
A5
A/C♯
D5
And tast - ed the sweet per - fume of the moun - tain grass I rolled down.
Riff B

D/F♯
G5
B5
A5
A/C♯
D5
I was young - er then.
Take me back to when I
End Riff B

Pre-Chorus
Gtr. 1: w/ Rhy. Fig. 1 (5 times)
G
A
G
found my heart and broke it here, made friends and lost them through the years.
week - end jobs and when we got paid, we'd buy cheap spir - its and drink them straight.
Voc. Fig. 1
(Oo.
Gtr. 2

A
D
G
And I've not seen the roar - ing fields in so long. I
Me and my friends have not thrown up in so long. Oh,
Oo.
A5
know I've grown,
how we've grown,
but I can't wait to go home.
End Voc. Fig. 1
Oo.)
Chorus
1st time, Gtr. 1: w/ Rhy. Fig. 1 (8 times)
2nd time, Gtr. 1: w/ Rhy. Fig. 1 (12 times)
Gtr. 2: w/ Riff A
2nd time, Bkgd. Voc.: w/ Voc. Fig. 2
D
Dadd4/F♯
G5
Bm7
A5
A7sus4
I'm on my way,
driv - in' at nine - ty down those
Rhy. Fig. 2
Gtr. 3 (dist.)
End Rhy. Fig. 2
Voc. Fig. 2
(Oh, oo.)

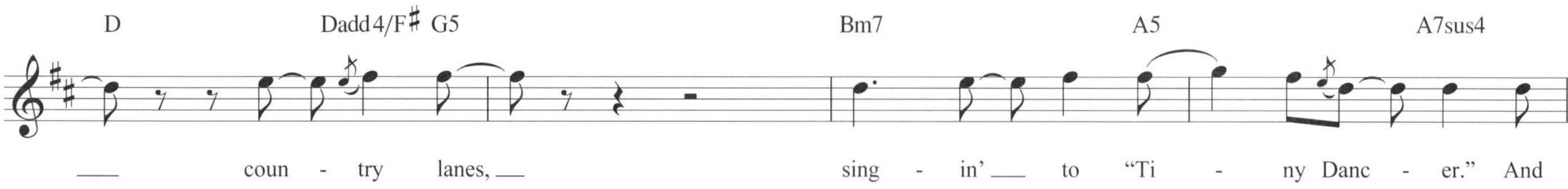

1st time, Gtr. 2: w/ Riff B
2nd time, Gtr. 2: w/ Riff B (1st 7 meas.)
D Dadd4/F♯ G5 Bm7 A5 A7sus4
I miss the way you made me feel, and it's real when

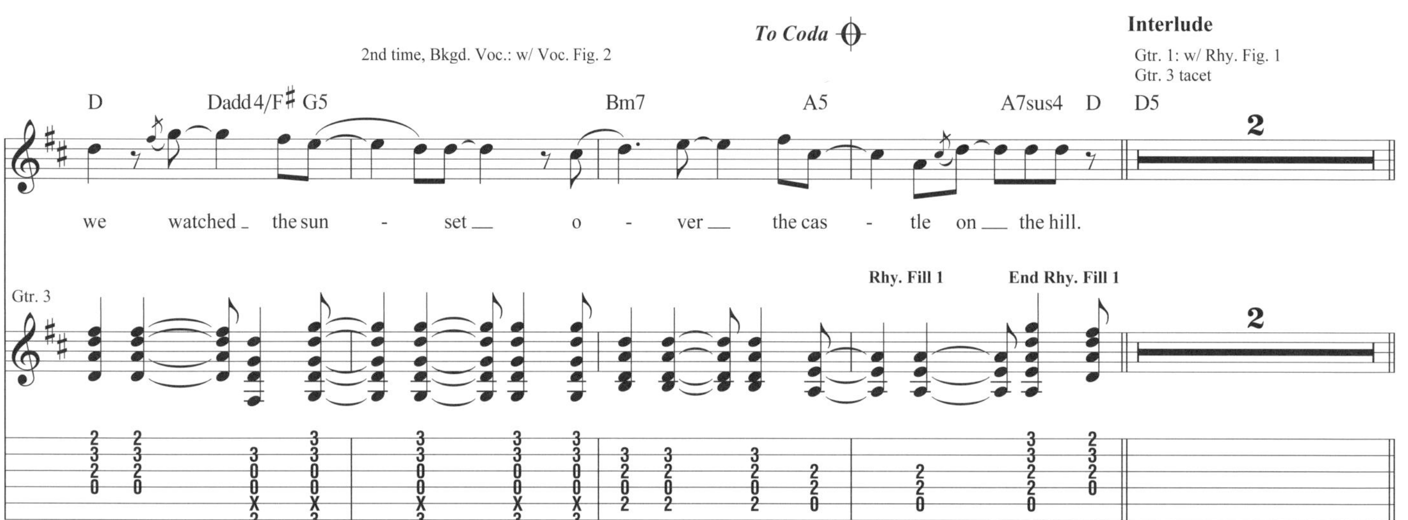

Verse

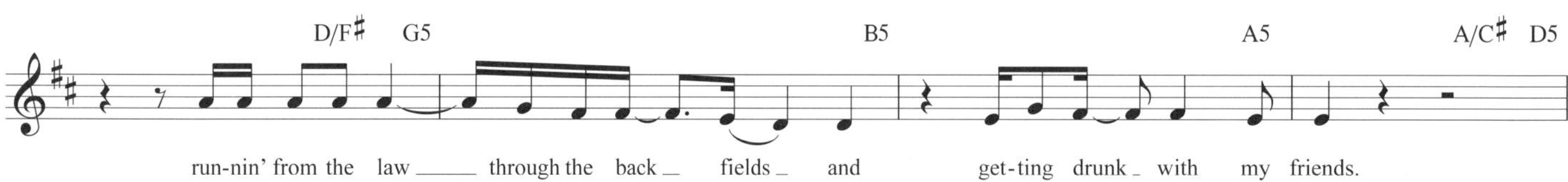

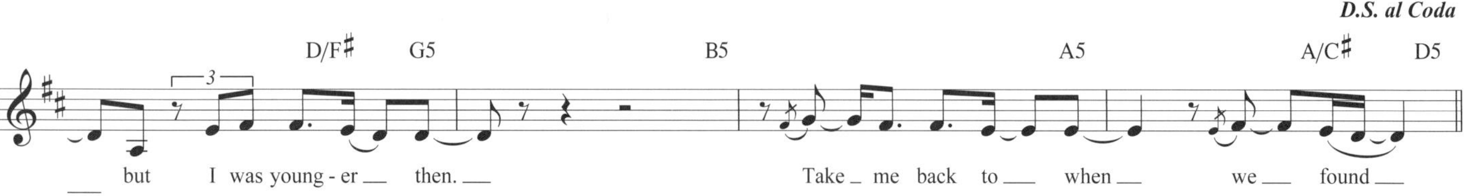

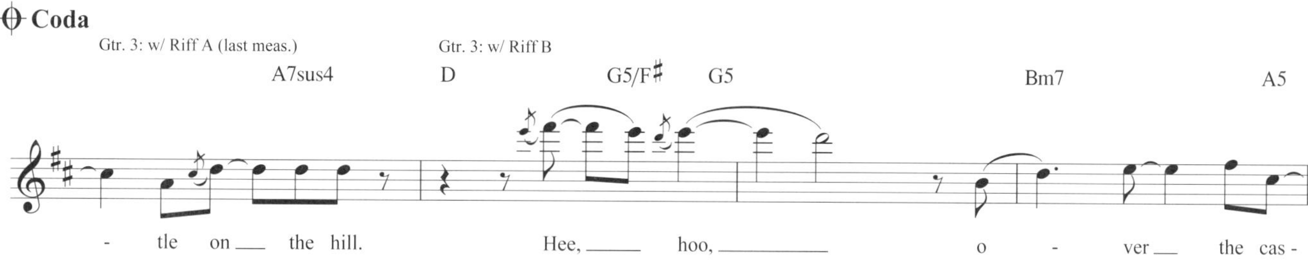

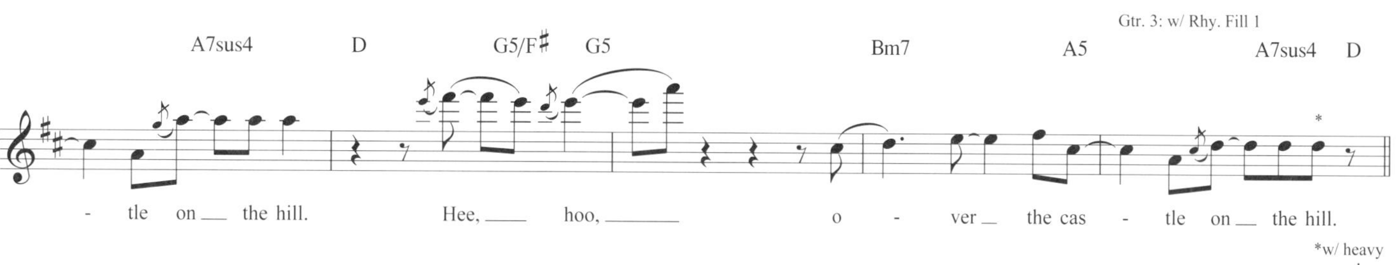

Interlude

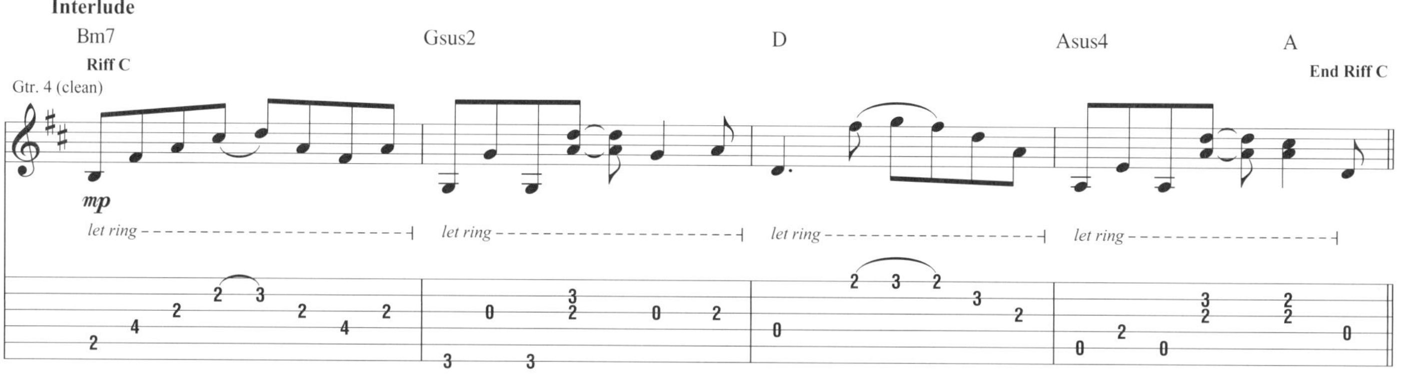

Bridge

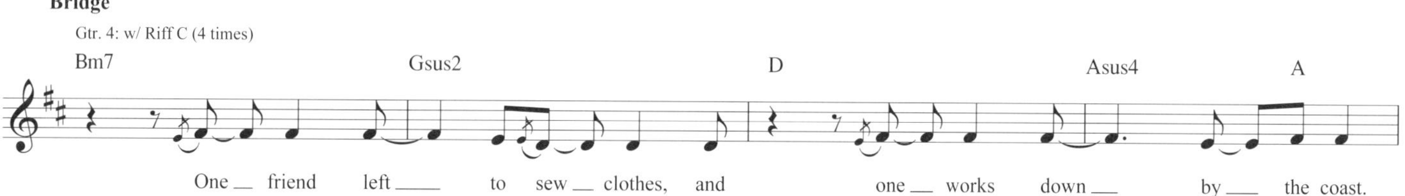

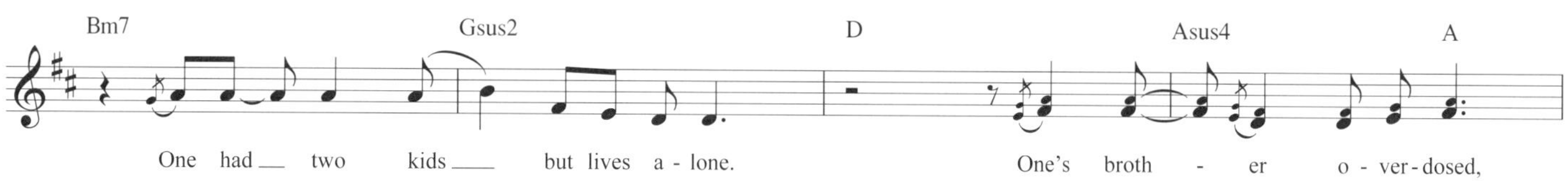

Chorus
D5 Dmaj7/F♯ G Bm7 A5 Asus4
I'm on my way. I still re - mem - ber these old
*Gtr. 6
Rhy. Fig. 3
End Rhy. Fig. 3
mf
w/ fingers
let ring
*Piano arr. for gtr.
Gtr. 6: w/ Rhy. Fig. 3
*Gtr. 1: w/ Rhy. Fig. 1 (1st meas.)
Gtr. 1: w/ Rhy. Fig. 1 (8 times)
Gtr. 2: w/ Riff A
Gtr. 3: w/ Rhy. Fig. 2 (3 3/4 times)
D5 Dmaj7/F♯ G Bm7 A5 Asus4 D Dadd4/F♯ G5
coun - try lanes when we did not know the an - swers. And I miss the way
*Fade in.
Bkgd. Voc.: w/ Voc. Fig. 2
Bm7 A5 A7sus4 D Dadd4/F♯ G5
you made me feel, and it's real when we watched the sun -
Bkgd. Voc.: w/ Voc. Fig. 2
Gtr. 3: w/ Riff A (last meas.)
Gtr. 2: w/ Riff B (1st 7 meas.)
Bm7 A5 A7sus4 D Dadd4/F♯ G5
- set o - ver the cas - tle on the hill. Hee, hoo, o -
Bm7 A5 A7sus4 D Dadd4/F♯ G5 Bm7 A5
- ver the cas - tle on the hill. Hee, hoo, o - ver the cas -
Outro
Begin fade
Fade out
Gtr. 1: w/ Rhy. Fig. 1 (2 times)
D5
- tle on the hill.
Gtr. 3
Gtr. 2
divisi
*Gtr. 3 to left of slash in tab.

from Luke Bryan - *Tailgates & Tanlines*

Country Girl (Shake It for Me)

Words and Music by Luke Bryan and Dallas Davidson

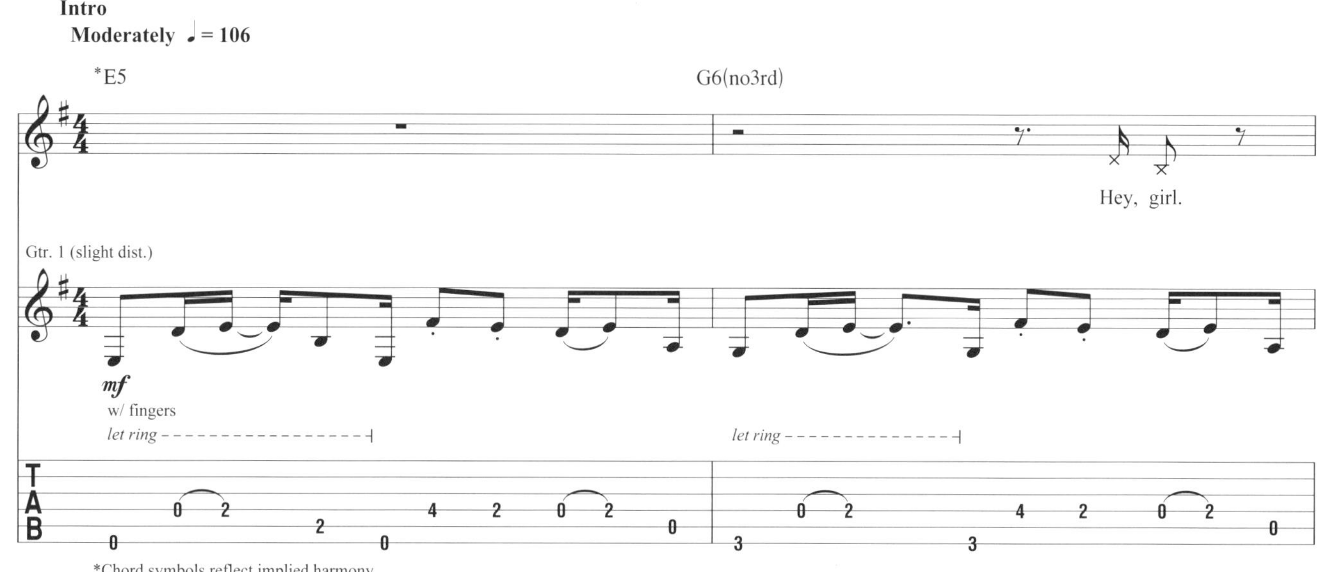

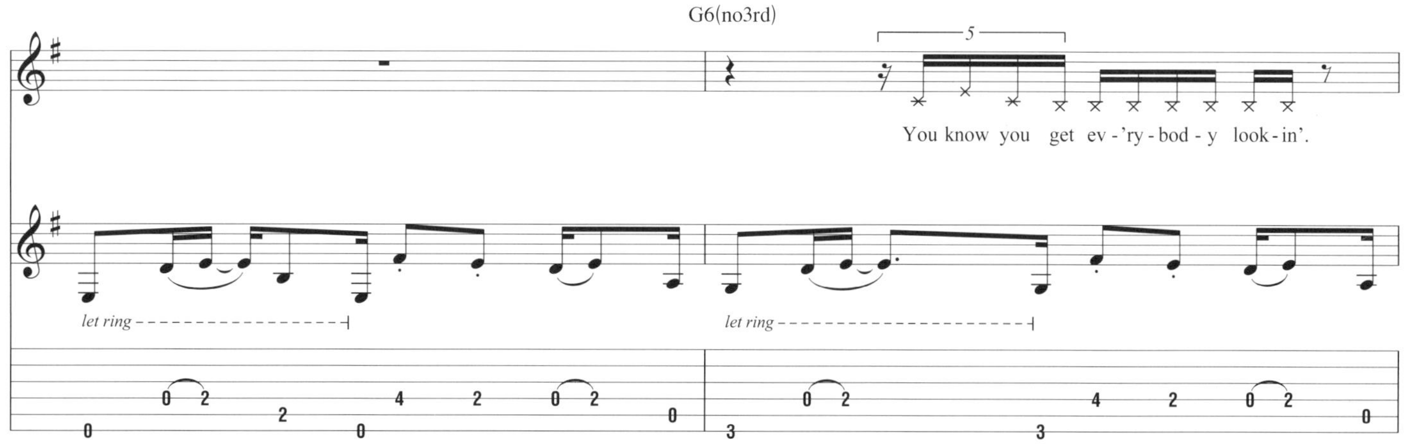

D/F#
G5
E5
1. I
let ring
1/4

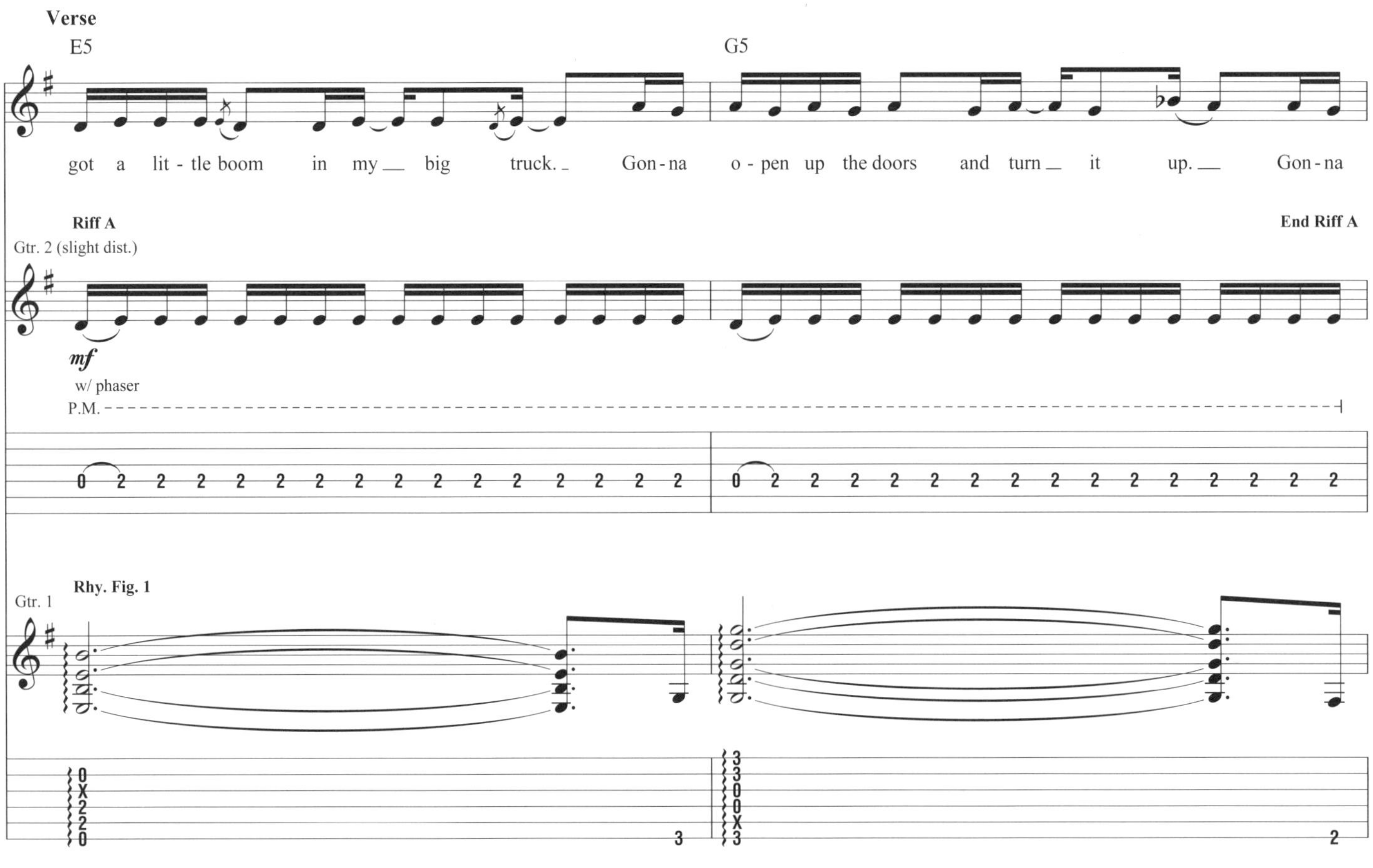
Verse
E5
G5
got a lit - tle boom in my big truck. Gon - na o - pen up the doors and turn it up. Gon - na
Riff A
End Riff A
Gtr. 2 (slight dist.)
mf
w/ phaser
P.M.
Rhy. Fig. 1
Gtr. 1

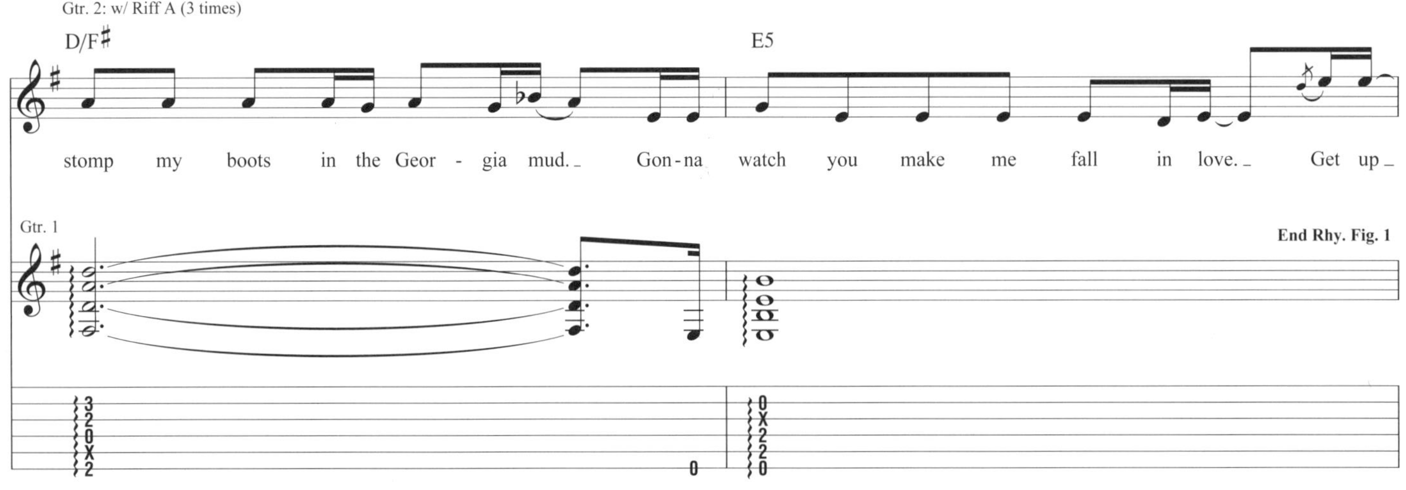
Gtr. 2: w/ Riff A (3 times)
D/F#
E5
stomp my boots in the Geor - gia mud. Gon - na watch you make me fall in love. Get up
Gtr. 1
End Rhy. Fig. 1

Gtr. 1: w/ Rhy. Fig. 1
G5
on the hood of my dad - dy's trac - tor. Up on the tool box, it don't mat - ter. Down

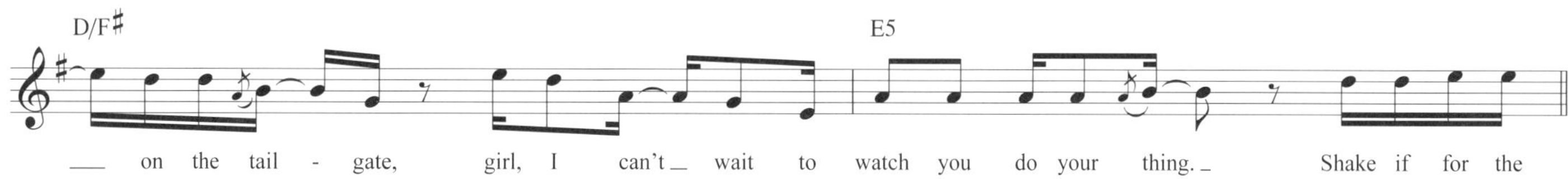
D/F♯
E5
on the tail - gate, girl, I can't wait to watch you do your thing. Shake if for the

Pre-Chorus

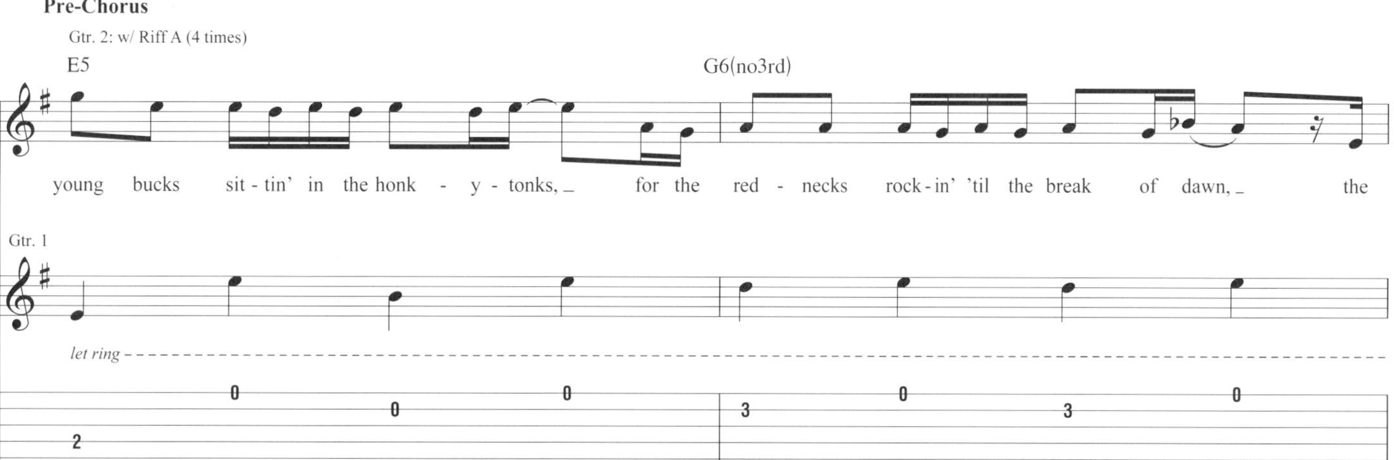
Gtr. 2: w/ Riff A (4 times)
E5
G6(no3rd)
young bucks sit - tin' in the honk - y - tonks, for the red - necks rock - in' 'til the break of dawn, the
Gtr. 1
let ring

D/F♯
E5
d. j. spin - nin' that coun - try song. Come on, come on, come on. Shake it for the
let ring

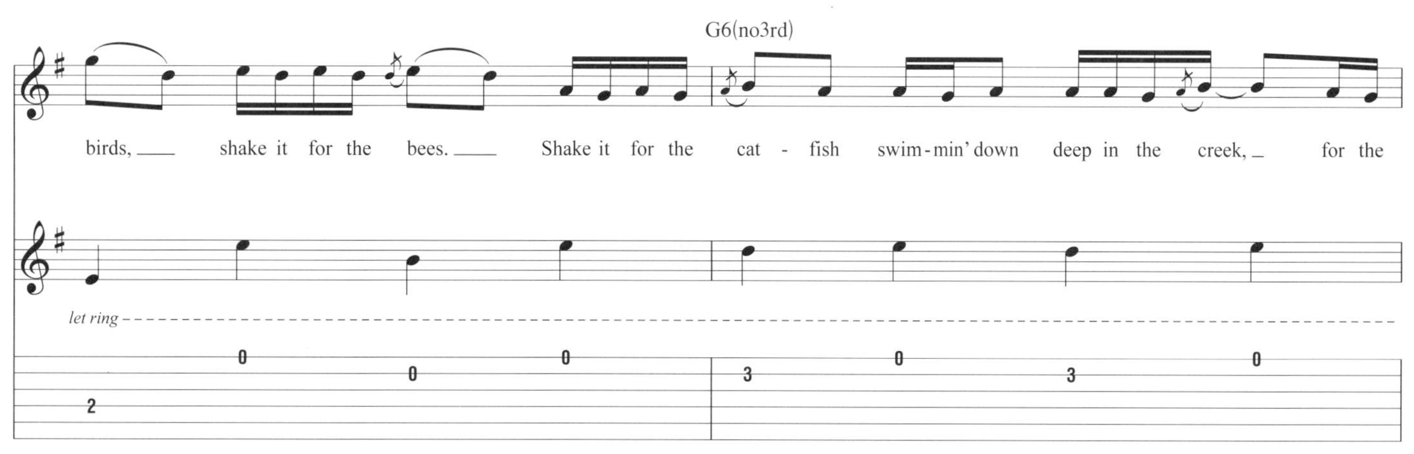
G6(no3rd)
birds, shake it for the bees. Shake it for the cat - fish swim - min' down deep in the creek, for the
let ring

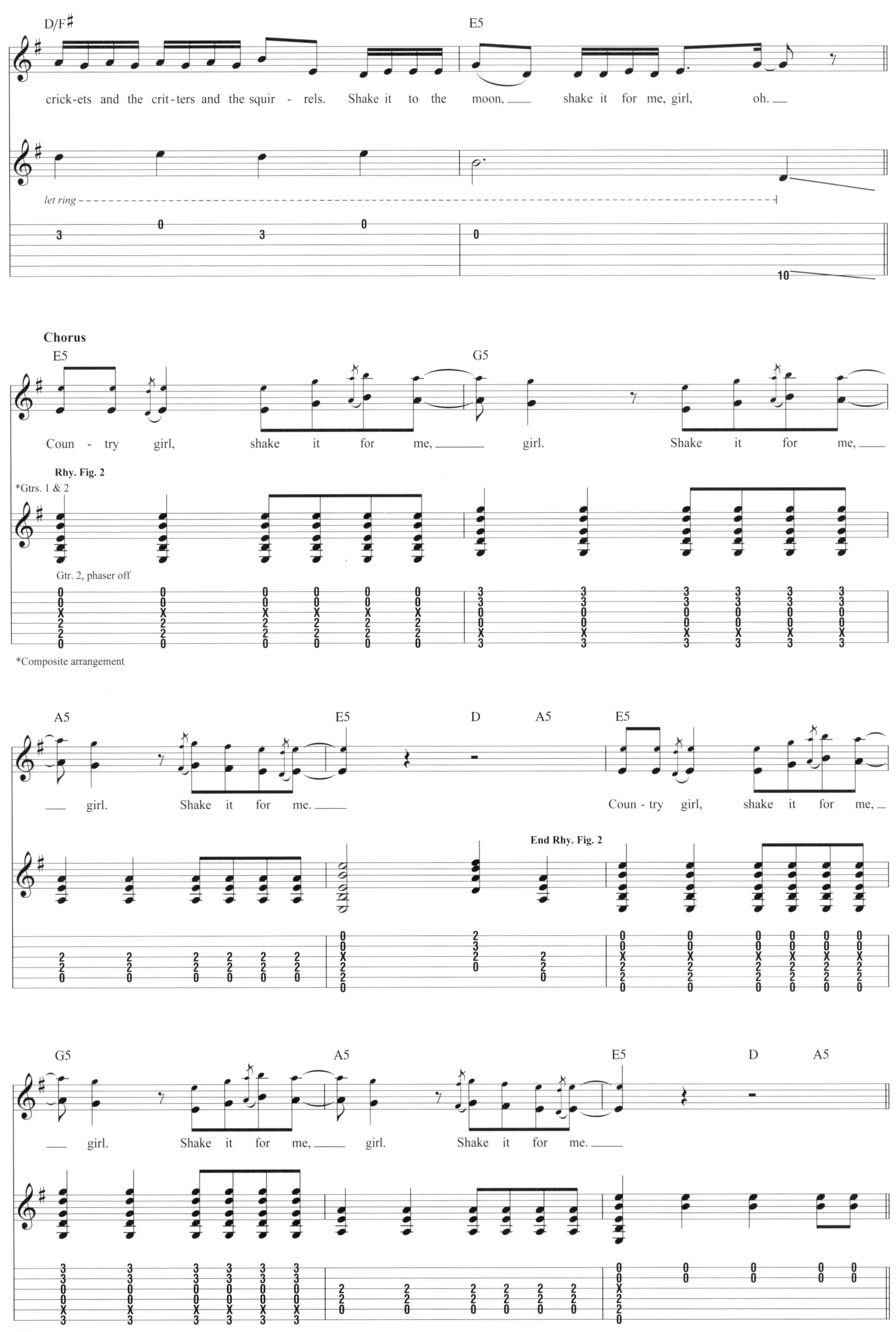
D/F#
E5
crick-ets and the crit-ters and the squir - rels. Shake it to the moon, shake it for me, girl, oh.
let ring
Chorus
E5
G5
Coun - try girl, shake it for me, girl. Shake it for me,
Rhy. Fig. 2
*Gtrs. 1 & 2
Gtr. 2, phaser off
*Composite arrangement
A5
E5
D
A5
E5
girl. Shake it for me. Coun - try girl, shake it for me,
End Rhy. Fig. 2
G5
A5
E5
D
A5
girl. Shake it for me, girl. Shake it for me.

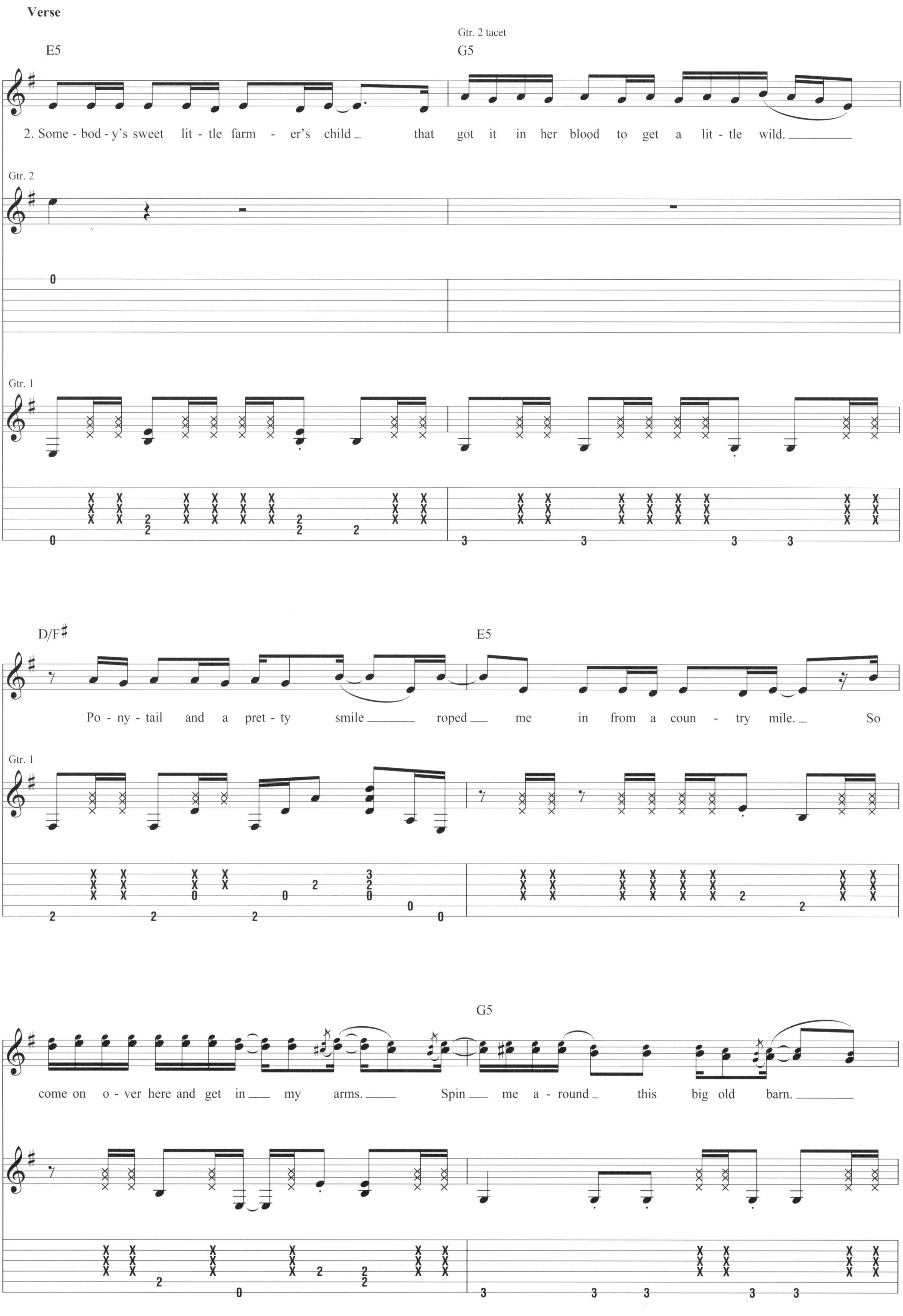

Verse
E5
Gtr. 2 tacet
G5
2. Some - bod - y's sweet lit - tle farm - er's child _ that got it in her blood to get a lit - tle wild. ___
Gtr. 2
Gtr. 1
D/F#
E5
Po - ny - tail and a pret - ty smile ___ roped _ me in from a coun - try mile. _ So
Gtr. 1
G5
come on o - ver here and get in _ my arms. ___ Spin _ me a - round _ this big old barn. ___

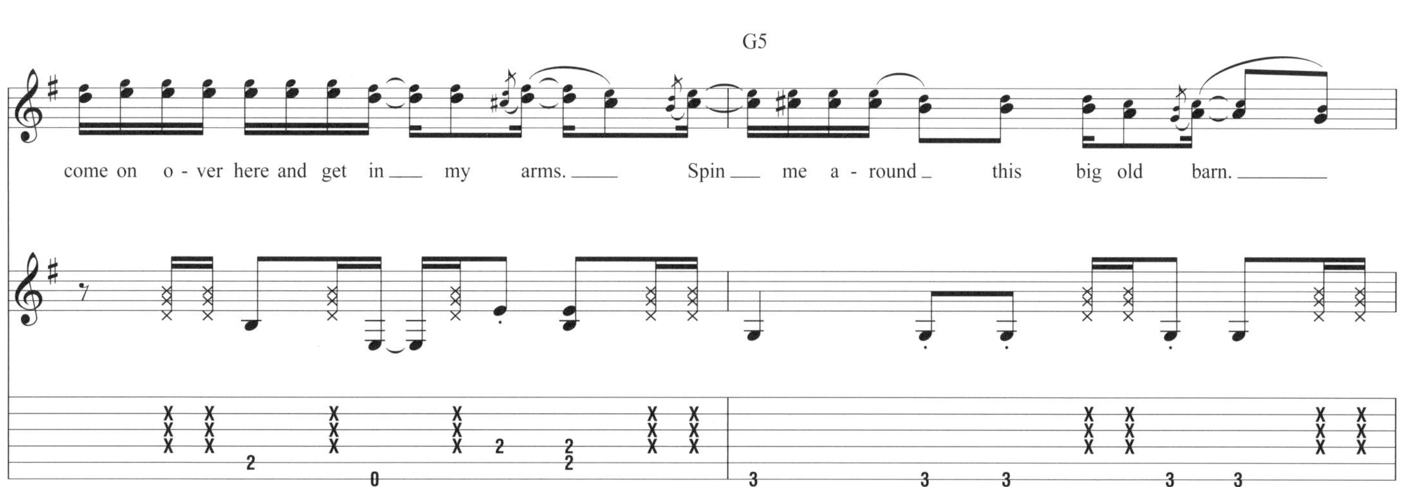

D/F♯
E5
Tan - gle me up like grand - ma's yarn.
Yeah, yeah, yeah. Shake it for the
Pre-Chorus
Gtr. 1 tacet
Gtr. 2: w/ Riff A (4 times)
E5
G6(no3rd)
young bucks sit - tin' in the honk - y - tonks, for the red - necks rock - in' 'til the break of dawn, for the
D/F♯
E5
d. j. spin - nin' that coun - try song. Come on, come on, come on. Shake it for the
G6(no3rd)
birds, shake it for the bees. Shake it for the cat - fish swim - min' down deep in the creek. For the
Gtr. 1
let ring
D/F♯
E5
crick - ets and the crit - ters and the squir - rels. Shake it to the moon, shake it for me girl.
let ring

Chorus

Gtr. 1: w/ Rhy. Fig. 2 (1 1/2 times)
E5
G5
A5
Coun - try girl, shake it for me, girl. Shake it for me, girl. Shake it for me.

To Coda
E5
D
A5
E5
G5
Coun - try girl, shake it for me, girl. Shake it for me,

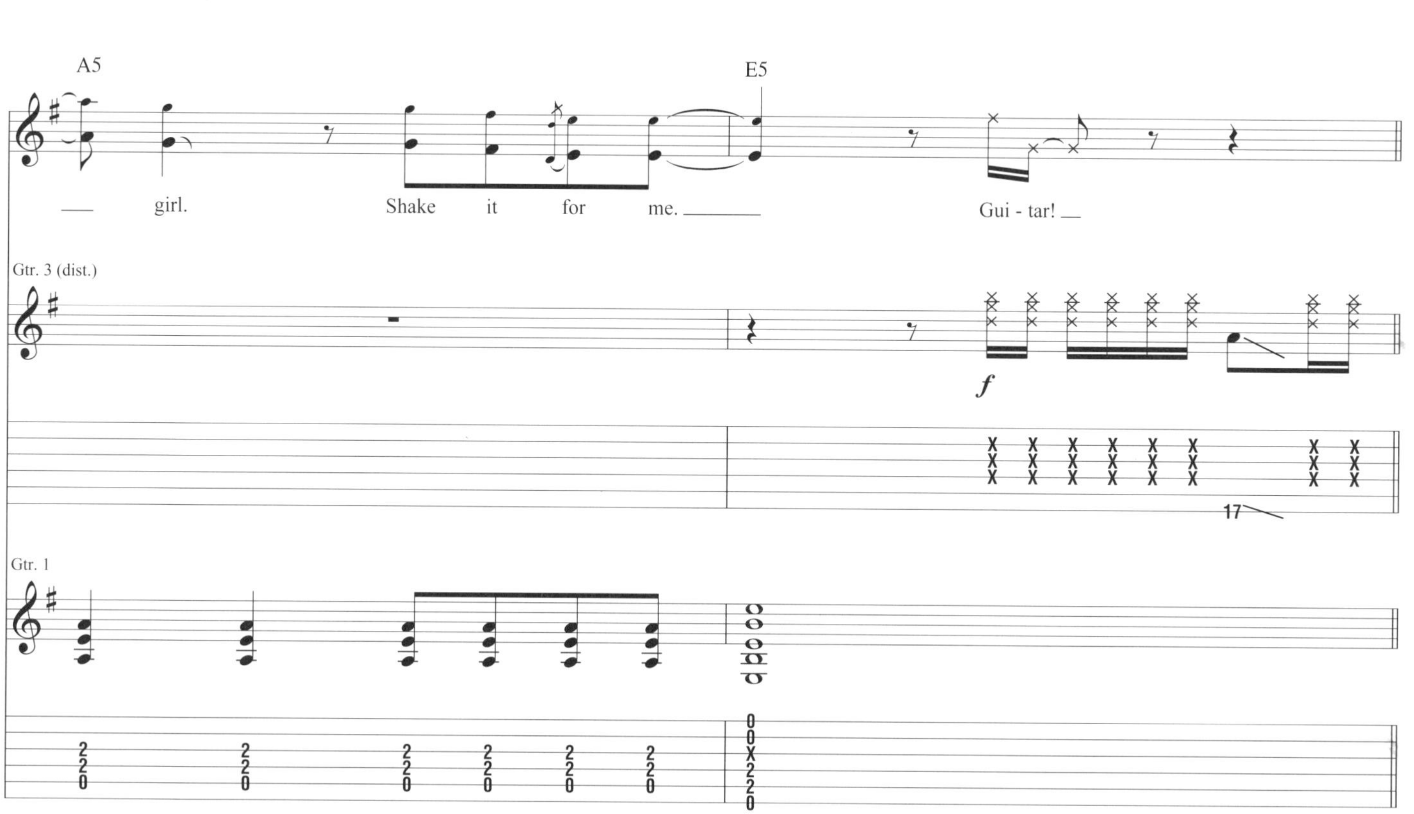
A5
E5
girl. Shake it for me. Gui - tar!
Gtr. 3 (dist.)
f
Gtr. 1

Guitar Solo
E5
G5
1/4

A5
E5
D5
A5
E5
G5
1 hold bend
A5
E5
G5
A5
B5
D5
E5
Now,

Bridge
E5
G5
dance __ like a dan - de - li - on in the wind, on the hill, un - der - neath the pines. _ Yeah,
let ring
Gtr. 3 tacet
D/F♯
E5
move like the riv - er flows. _ Feel __ the kick drum down deep in your toes. _
Gtr. 2
Harm.
w/ bar
Gtr. 1

Gtr. 2 tacet

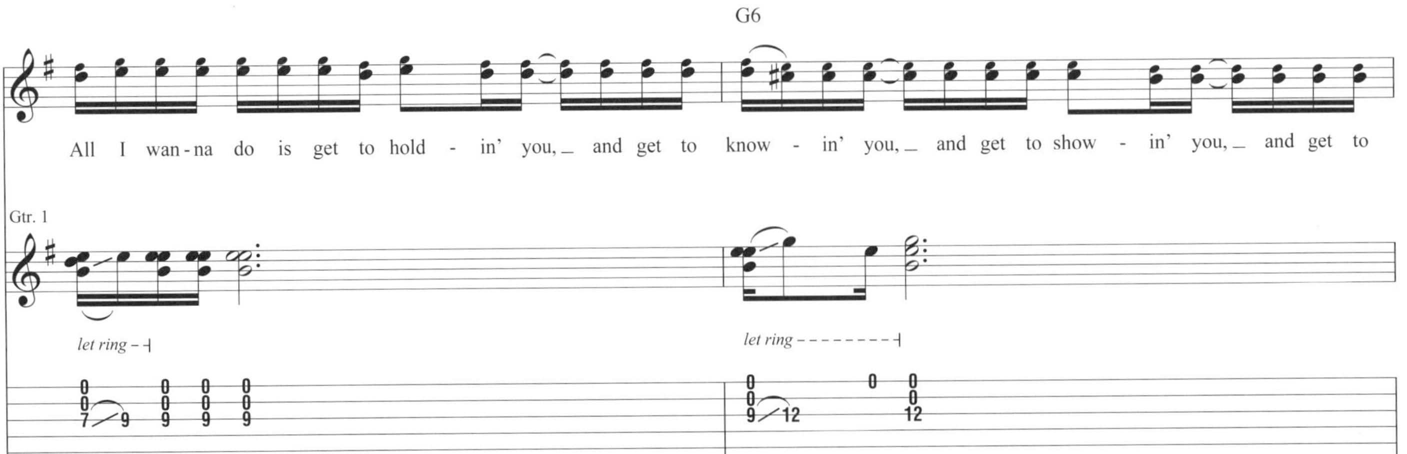
G6
All I wan-na do is get to hold - in' you, and get to know - in' you, and get to show - in' you, and get to
Gtr. 1
let ring
let ring

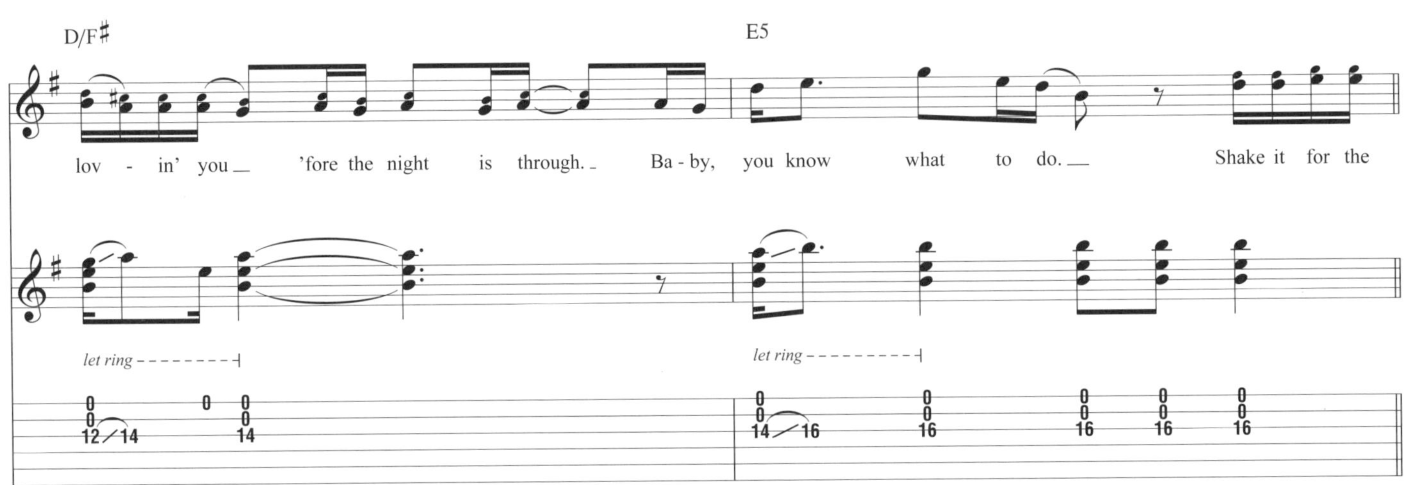
D/F♯
E5
lov - in' you 'fore the night is through. Ba-by, you know what to do. Shake it for the
let ring
let ring

Pre-Chorus
E
G5
young bucks sit-tin' in the honk - y - tonks, for the red - necks rock-in' 'til the break of dawn, for the
Riff B
Gtr. 2
End Riff B
Gtr. 1

D/F♯
E5
G5
A5
B5
d. j. spin - nin' that coun - try song. Come on, come on, come on. Shake it for the
Gtr. 2: w/ Riff B (2 times)
E5
G5
birds, shake it for the bees. Shake it for the cat - fish swim - min' down deep in the creek. For the
Gtr. 1
D.S. al Coda
D/F♯
E5
crick-ets and the crit-ters and the squir - rels. Shake it to the moon, shake it for me, girl, oh.

Coda
A5
E5
girl.
Shake it for me.
Gtr. 1
Outro-Chorus
Gtr. 1: w/ Rhy. Fig. 2 (1 1/2 times)
E5
G5
A5
Coun - try girl, shake it for me, girl. Shake it for me, girl, Shake it for me.
E5
D
A5
E5
G5
Coun - try girl, shake it for me, girl. Shake it for me,
A
E5 G5 A5 B5 D5 D♯5
E5 G A5 B5 D5 D♯5
girl. Shake it for me.
Gtr. 1
Gtrs. 1 & 2
E5 G5 A5 B5 D5 D♯5
E5
N.C.
Gtr. 2
Gtr. 1

from Florida Georgia Line - *Here's to the Good Times*

Cruise

Words and Music by Chase Rice, Tyler Hubbard, Brian Kelley, Joey Moi and Jesse Rice

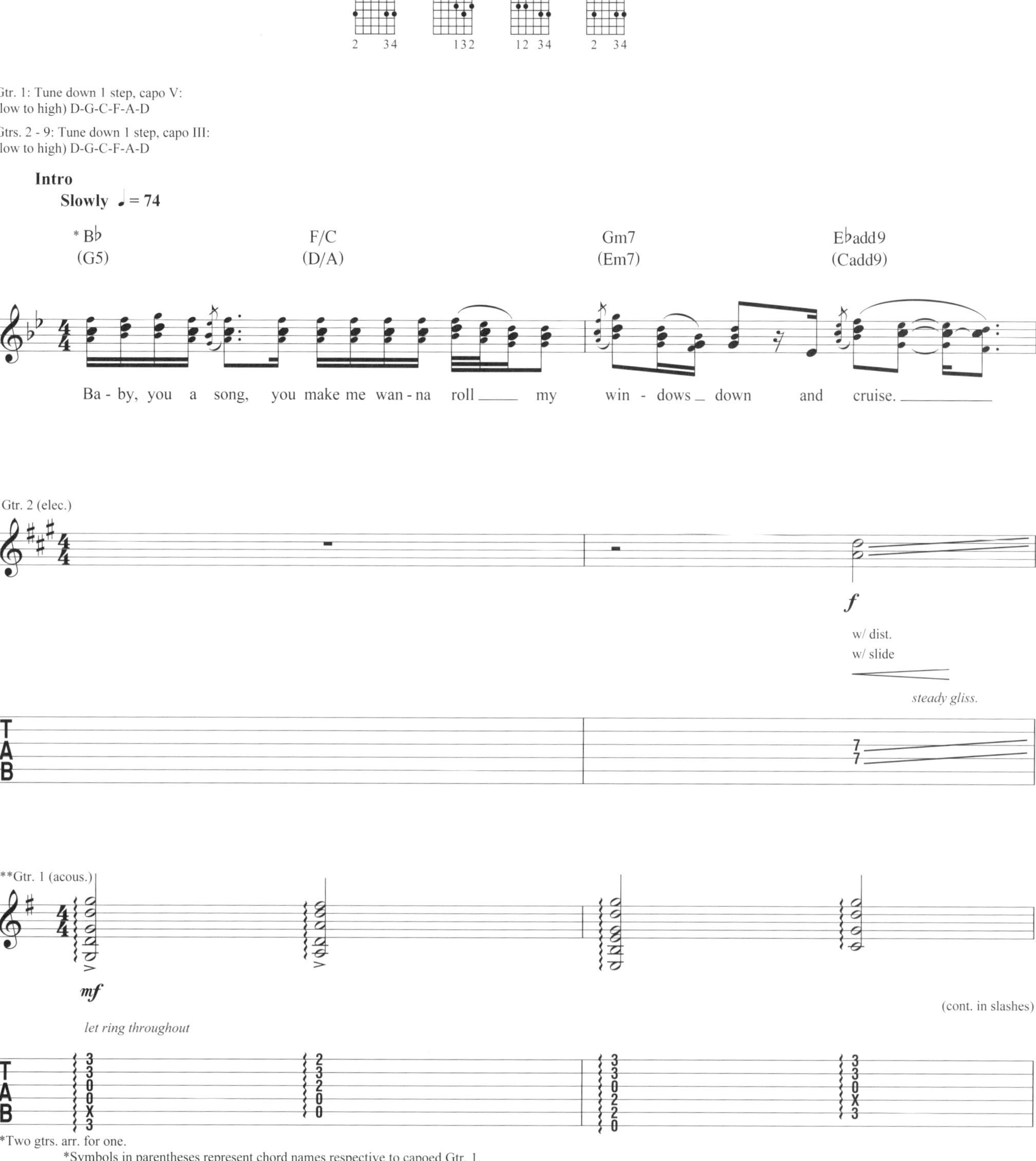

**Two gtrs. arr. for one.

*Symbols in parentheses represent chord names respective to capoed Gtr. 1.
Symbols above reflect actual sounding chords. Capoed fret is "0" in tab.

**Pedal steel arr. for gtr.

*See top of first page of song for chord diagrams pertaining to rhythm slashes.

*Symbols in double-parentheses represent chord names respective to capoed Gtrs. 2, 3, 4, 5, 6 & 7.
Capoed fret is "0" in tab.

Verse
Gtrs. 2 & 4 tacet
(G5)
(D/A)
(Em7)
(Cadd9)
Rhy. Fig. 2
Gtr. 1
I first saw that bi - ki - ni top on her, she's pop - pin' right out of the South Geor - gia wa - ter. Thought, "Oh,
Gtr. 7 (elec.)
w/ dist.
Harm.
slight P.M.
let ring
Gtr. 3
Gtr. 5
divisi
Gtrs. 3 & 5 tacet
(G5)
(D/A)
(Em7)
(Cadd9)
End Rhy. Fig. 2
Gtr. 1
good Lord, she had them long tan legs!" Could - n't help my - self so I walked up and said. Oh,
Gtr. 7
let ring
hold bend
let ring
grad. release
*Gtrs. 2 & 6
Rhy. Fill 1
End Rhy. Fill 1
*Gtr. 2 - Three gtrs. arr. for one - w/o slide.

Chorus
Gtrs. 1 & 6: w/ Rhy. Figs. 1 & 1A (4 times)
Gtr. 7 tacet
B♭
(G)
((A))
F
(D)
((E))
Gm
(Em)
((F♯m))
E♭
(C)
((D))
ba - by, you a song, you make me wan - na roll my win - dows down and cruise. Down a
Gtr. 4
let ring
Gtr. 2
back road blow - in' stop signs through the mid - dle ev - 'ry lit - tle farm town with you. And this
hold bend
slight P.H.

2nd time, Gtr. 4: w/ Fill 1
B♭
(G)
((A))
F
(D)
((E))
Gm
(Em)
((F♯m))
E♭
(C)
((D))
brand new Che-vy with a lift kit would look a hell of a lot bet-ter with you up in it. Ha. So
hold bend
To Coda
ba-by, you a song, you make me wan-na roll my win-dows down and cruise.
hold bend
hold bend
Rhy. Fill 2
End Rhy. Fill 2
slight
P.H.
Fill 1
Gtr. 4
let ring

Interlude
Gtrs. 1 & 6: w/ Rhy. Figs. 1 & 1A
Gtr. 2 tacet
B♭ (G) ((A))
F (D) ((E))
Gm (Em) ((F♯m))
E♭ (C) ((D))
2. Well, she was
Gtr. 3
Gtr. 4
let ring
Gtr. 5
Verse
Gtr. 1: w/ Rhy. Fig. 2
sip-pin' on South-ern and sing-in' Mar-shall Tuck-er. We were fall-in' in love in the sweet-heart of sum-mer. She
Gtr. 5
divisi

D.S. al Coda
Gtrs. 3 & 5 tacet
B♭
(G)
((A))
F
(D)
((E))
Gtrs. 2 & 6: w/ Rhy. Fill 1
Gm
(Em)
((F♯m))
E♭
(C)
((D))
hopped right up in - to the cab of my truck and said,
"Fire it up, let's go get this thing stuck."
Gtr. 4
let ring
hold bend
Coda
Guitar Solo
Gtr. 2: w/ Rhy. Fill 2
Gtrs. 1 & 6: w/ Rhy. Figs. 1 & 1A (2 times)
win - dows down and cruise.
Gtr. 8 (elec.)
w/ dist.
let ring
Gtr. 4
hold bend
let ring

Bridge
Gtrs. 1 & 6: w/ Rhy. Figs. 1 & 1A (1 1/2 times)
Gm
(Em)
((F♯m))
E♭
(C)
((D))
B♭
(G)
((A))
F
(D)
((E))
When that summer sun fell to his knees I
Gtr. 8
hold bend
Gtr. 4
Gtr. 2
Gtr. 8 tacet
looked at her and she looked at me. Then I turned on those K - C lights and drove

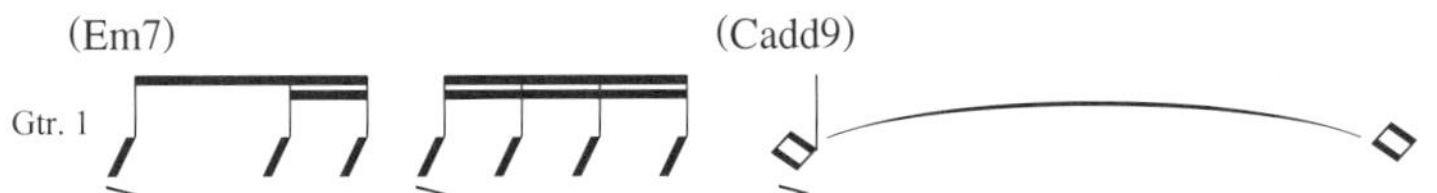

(cont. in notation)

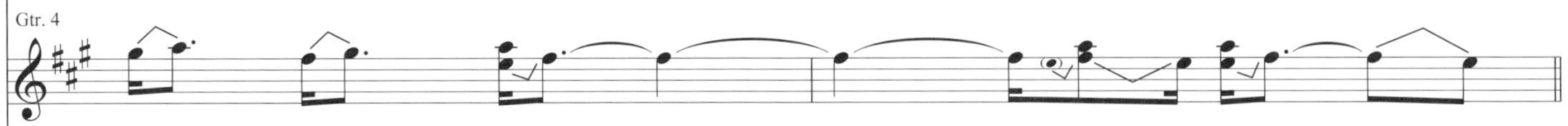

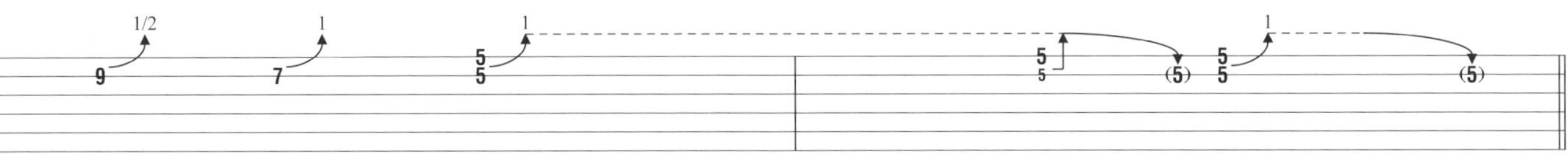

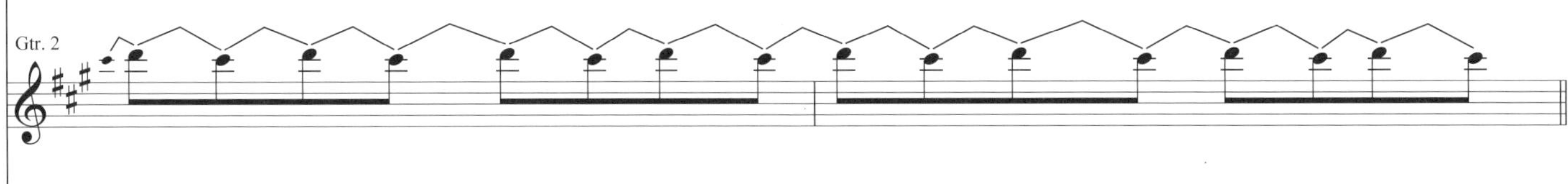

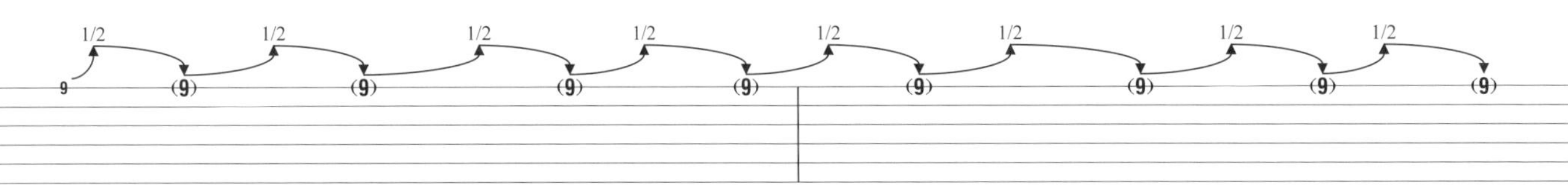

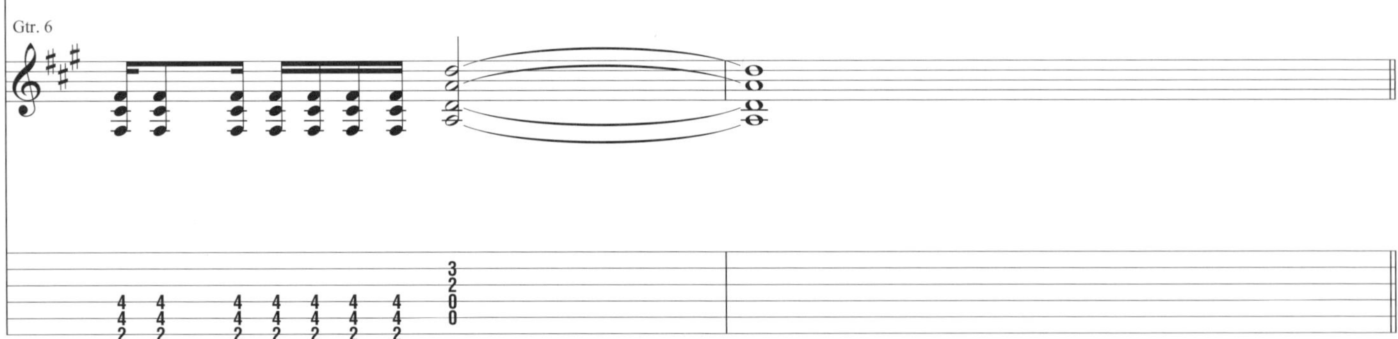

Verse
Gtrs. 2 & 6 tacet
B♭ (G) ((A))
F (D) ((E))
Gm (Em) ((F♯m))
E♭ (C) ((D))
put it in park and grab my gui - tar and strum a cou - ple chords and sang from the heart.
Gtr. 4
8va
**H.H.
**Harp harmonics produced by lightly touching string 12 frets above fretted note while picking string.
*Gtr. 9
mf
w/ clean tone
let ring
*Banjo arr. for gtr.
Gtr. 1
Girl, you sure got the beat in my chest bump - in'. Hell, I can't get you out of my head.
loco
H.H.
w/ slide
Gtr. 9
Gtr. 2
divisi
steady gliss.

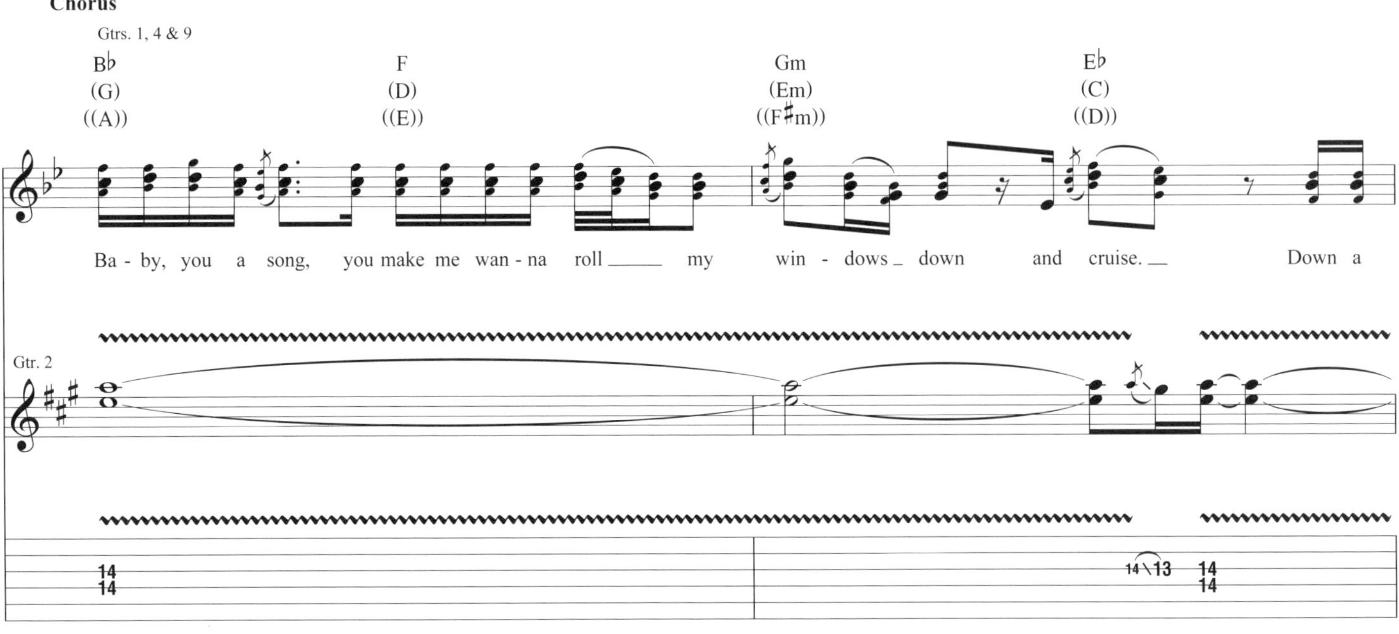

B♭ (G) ((A))
F (D) ((E))
Gm (Em) ((F♯m))
E♭ (C) ((D))

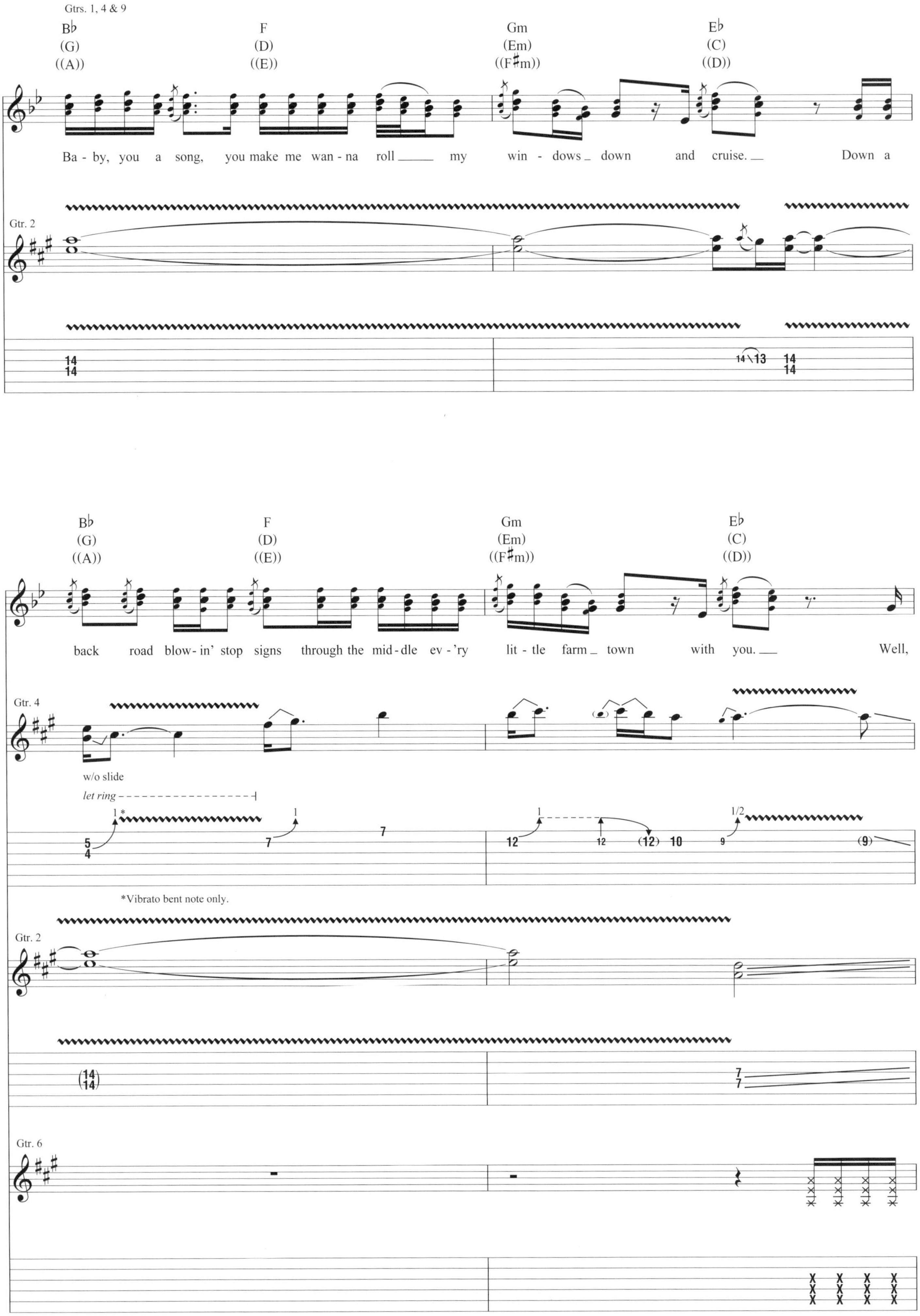

back road blow - in' stop signs through the mid - dle ev - 'ry lit - tle farm _ town with you. __ Well,

Gtr. 4

w/o slide

let ring

*Vibrato bent note only.

Gtr. 2

Gtr. 6

Gtrs. 1 & 6: w/ Rhy. Figs. 1 & 1A (2 times)

B♭ (G) ((A)) | F (D) ((E)) | Gm (Em) ((F♯m)) | E♭ (C) ((D))

Ba - by, you a song, you make me wan - na roll ___ my win - dows _ down and cruise. _ Down a

Gtr. 4

let ring

1

5
4

Gtr. 2

w/o slide

w/ slide

14
14

2 4 2

2 4 4 0

14\12 14\12 13 14

B♭ (G) ((A)) | F (D) ((E)) | Gm (Em) ((F♯m)) | E♭ (C) ((D))

back road blow - in' stop signs through the mid - dle ev - 'ry lit - tle farm _ town with you. _____ And this

let ring

1

5
4

1/2

9 (9)

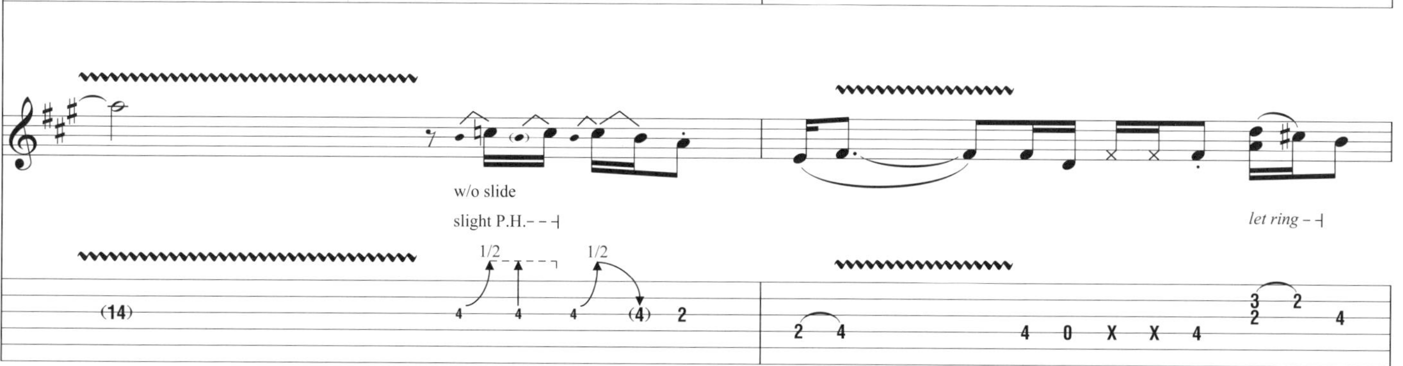

(G5)
(D/A)
(Em7)
Gtr. 1
brand new Che-vy with a lift kit would look a hell of a lot bet-ter with you up in it. C' - mon.
Gtr. 4
hold bend
Gtr. 2
Gtr. 6
Gtrs. 1 & 6: w/ Rhy. Figs. 1 & 1A
B♭
(G)
((A))
F
(D)
((E))
Gm
(Em)
((F♯m))
E♭
(C)
((D))
Ba-by, you a song, you make me wan-na roll my win - dows down and cruise.
Gtr. 4
let ring
hold bend
Gtr. 2

Outro

Gtrs. 1 & 6: w/ Rhy. Figs. 1 & 1A (2 times)
Gtrs. 3 & 5: w/ Riffs A & A1
Gtr. 2 tacet

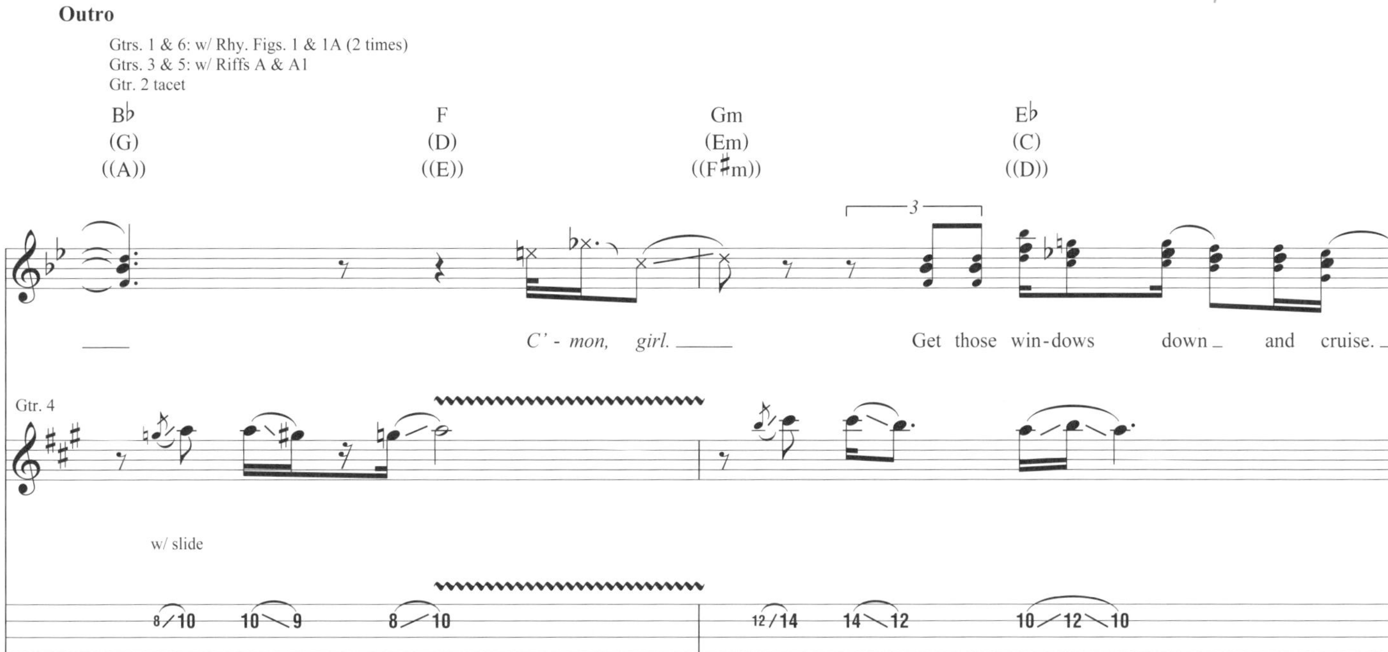

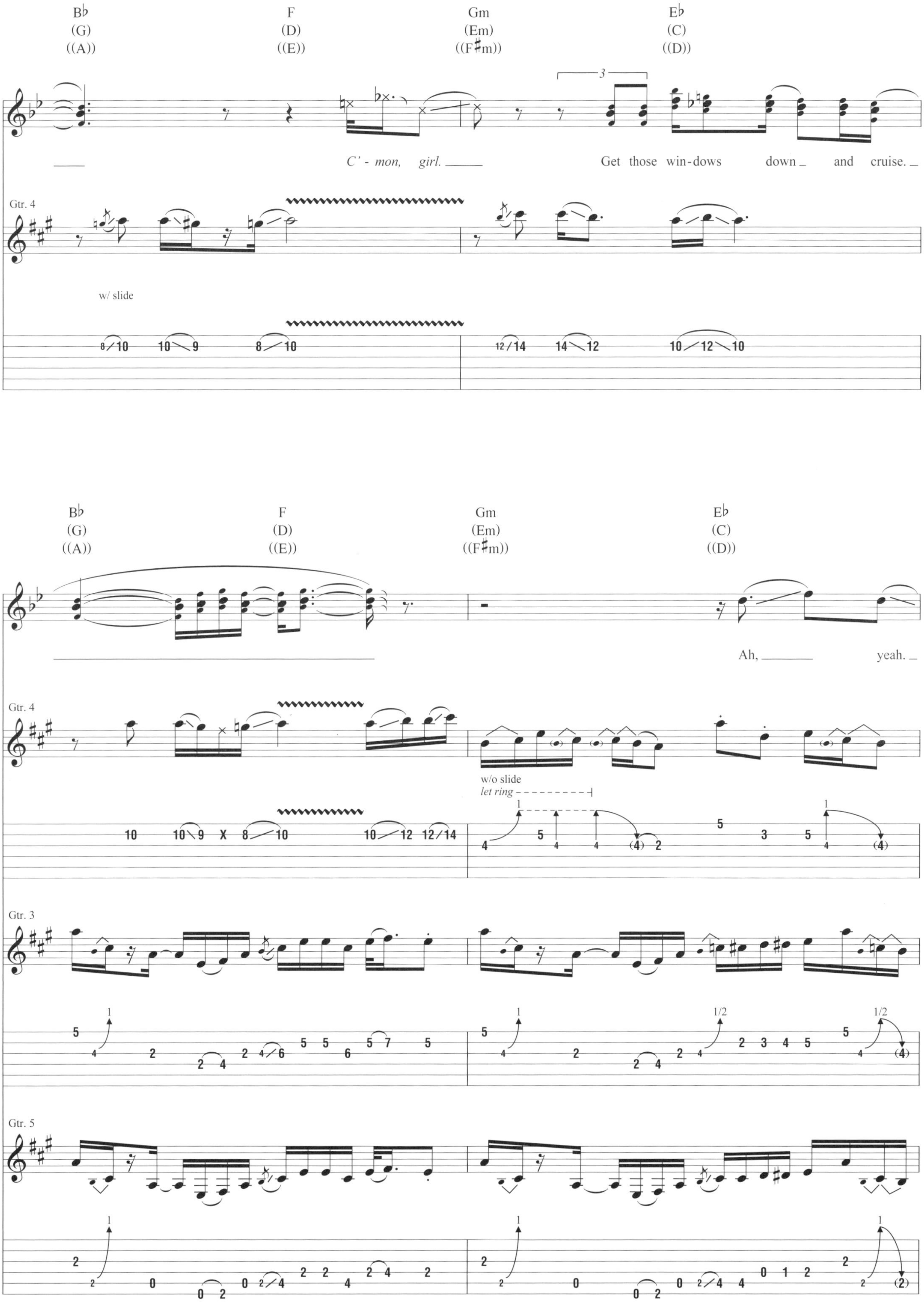

B♭ (G) ((A)) F (D) ((E)) Gm (Em) ((F♯m)) E♭ (C) ((D))

Ah, yeah.

Gtr. 4

w/o slide
let ring

Gtr. 3

Gtr. 5

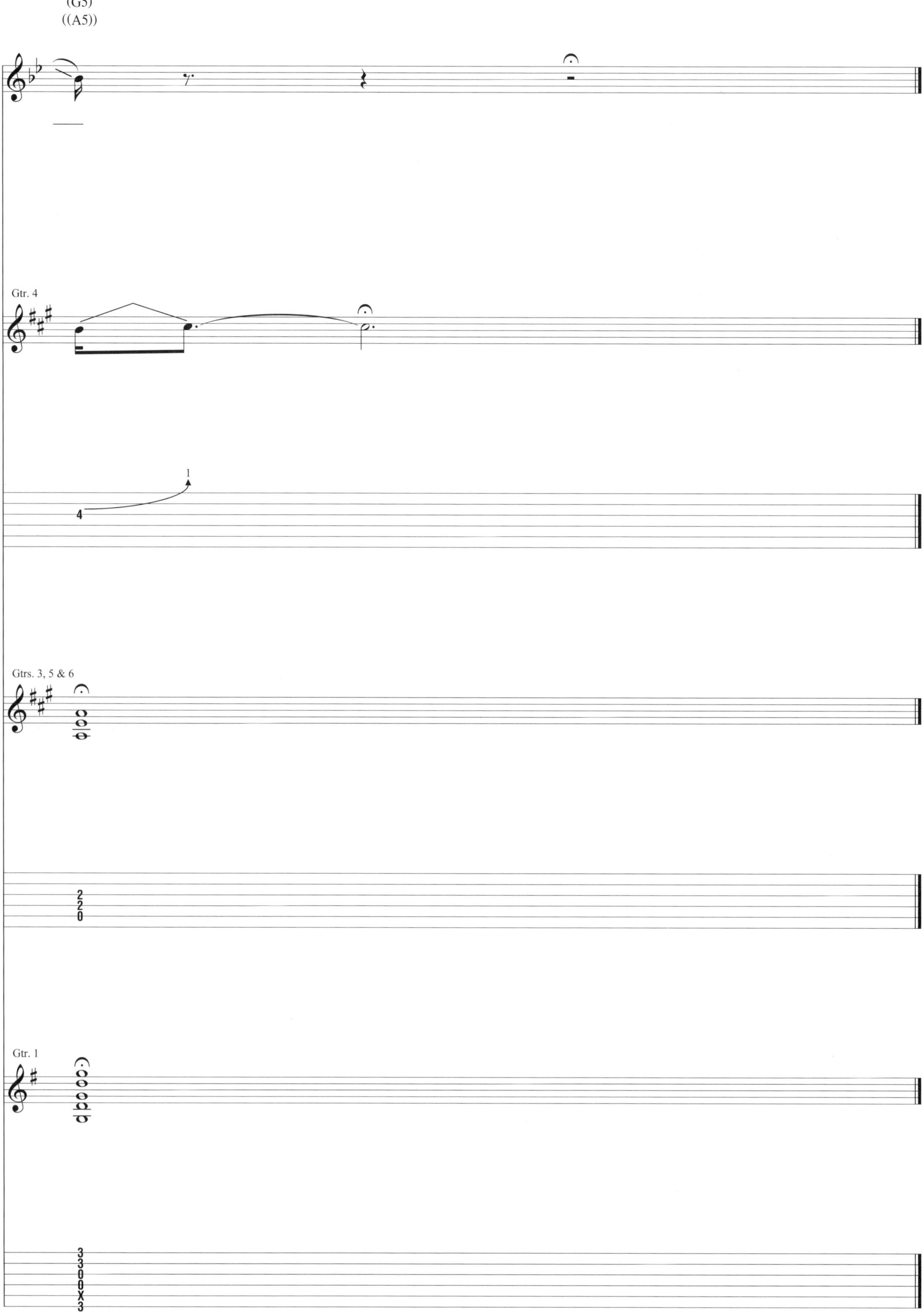
B♭5
(G5)
((A5))
Gtr. 4
1
4
Gtrs. 3, 5 & 6
2
2
0
Gtr. 1
3
3
0
0
X
3

from Luis Fonsi - *Vida*

Despacito

Words and Music by Luis Fonsi, Erika Ender, Justin Bieber, Jason Boyd, Marty James Garton and Ramón Ayala

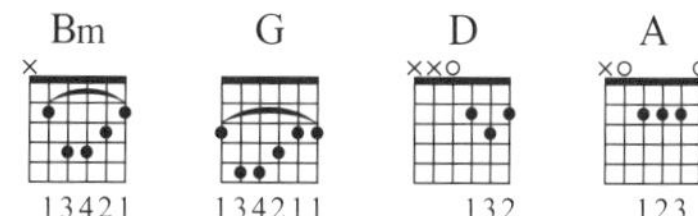

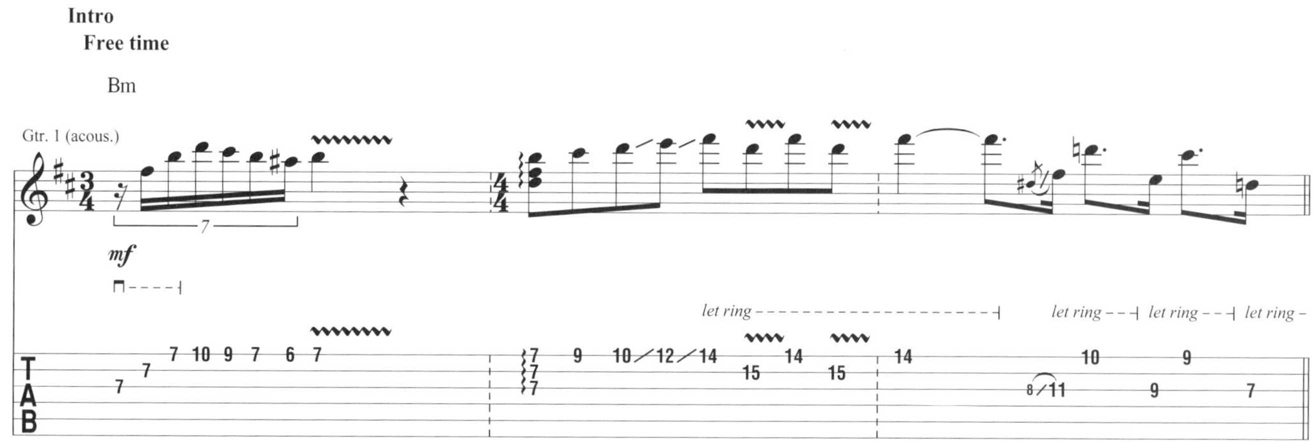

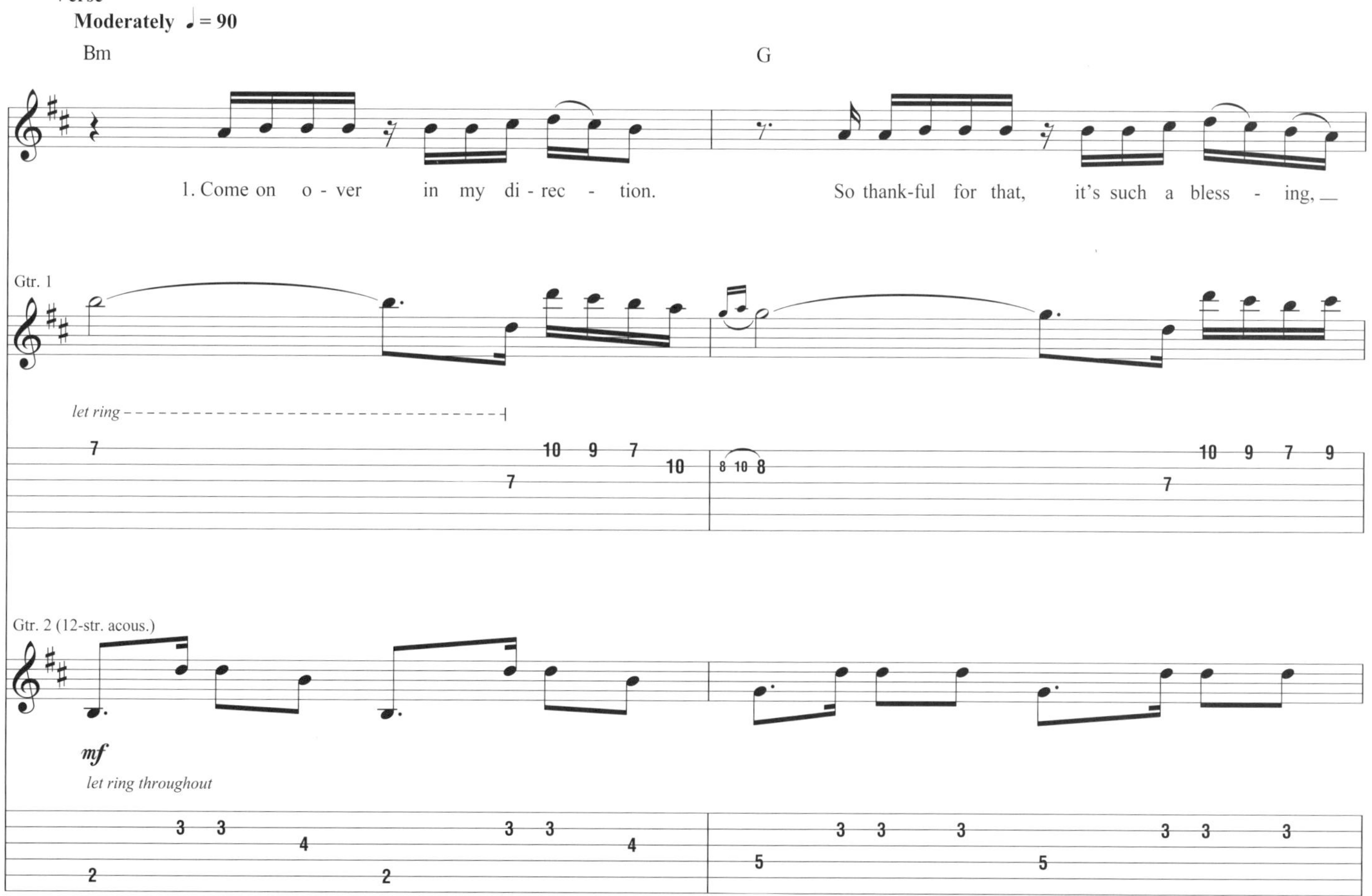

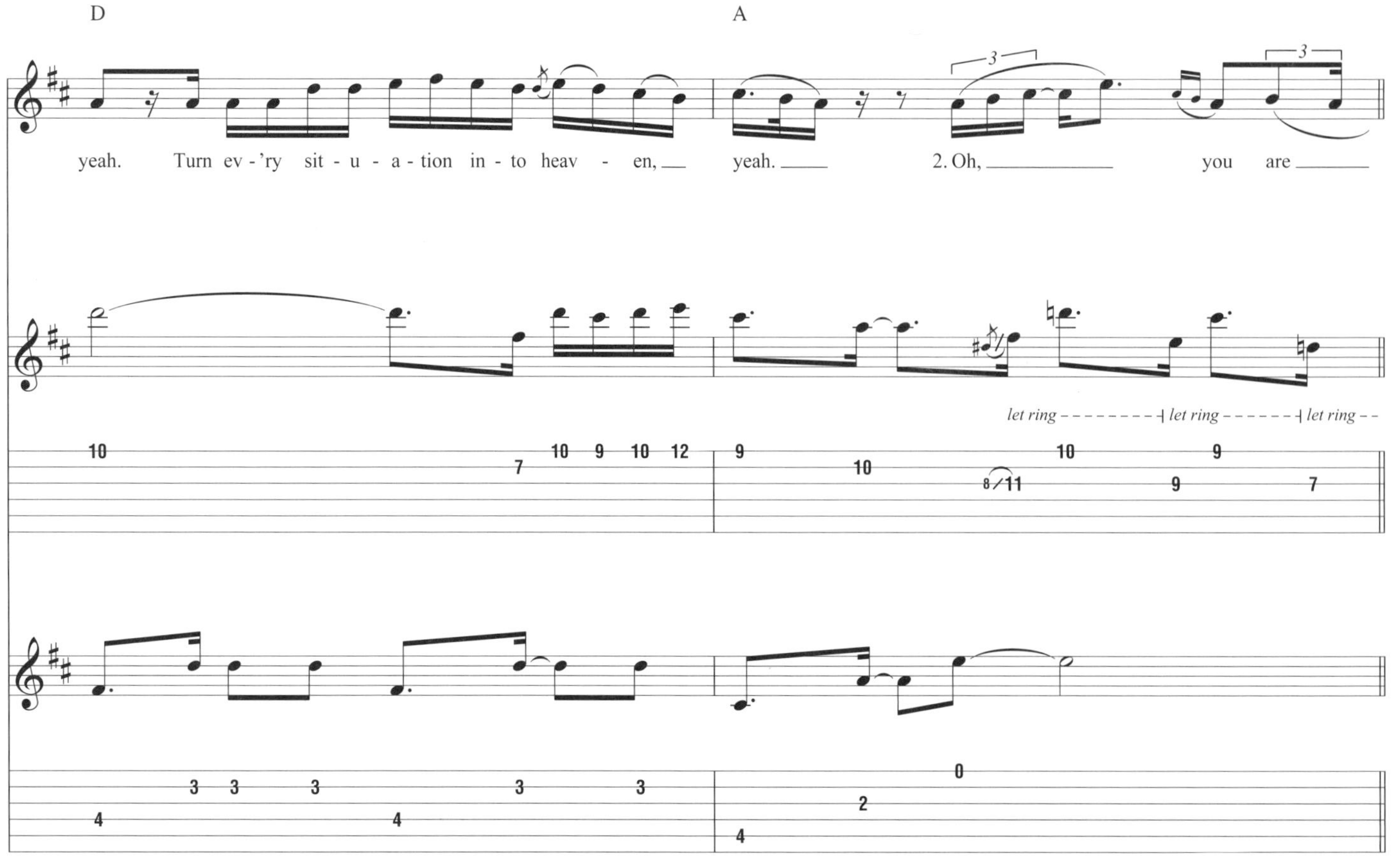

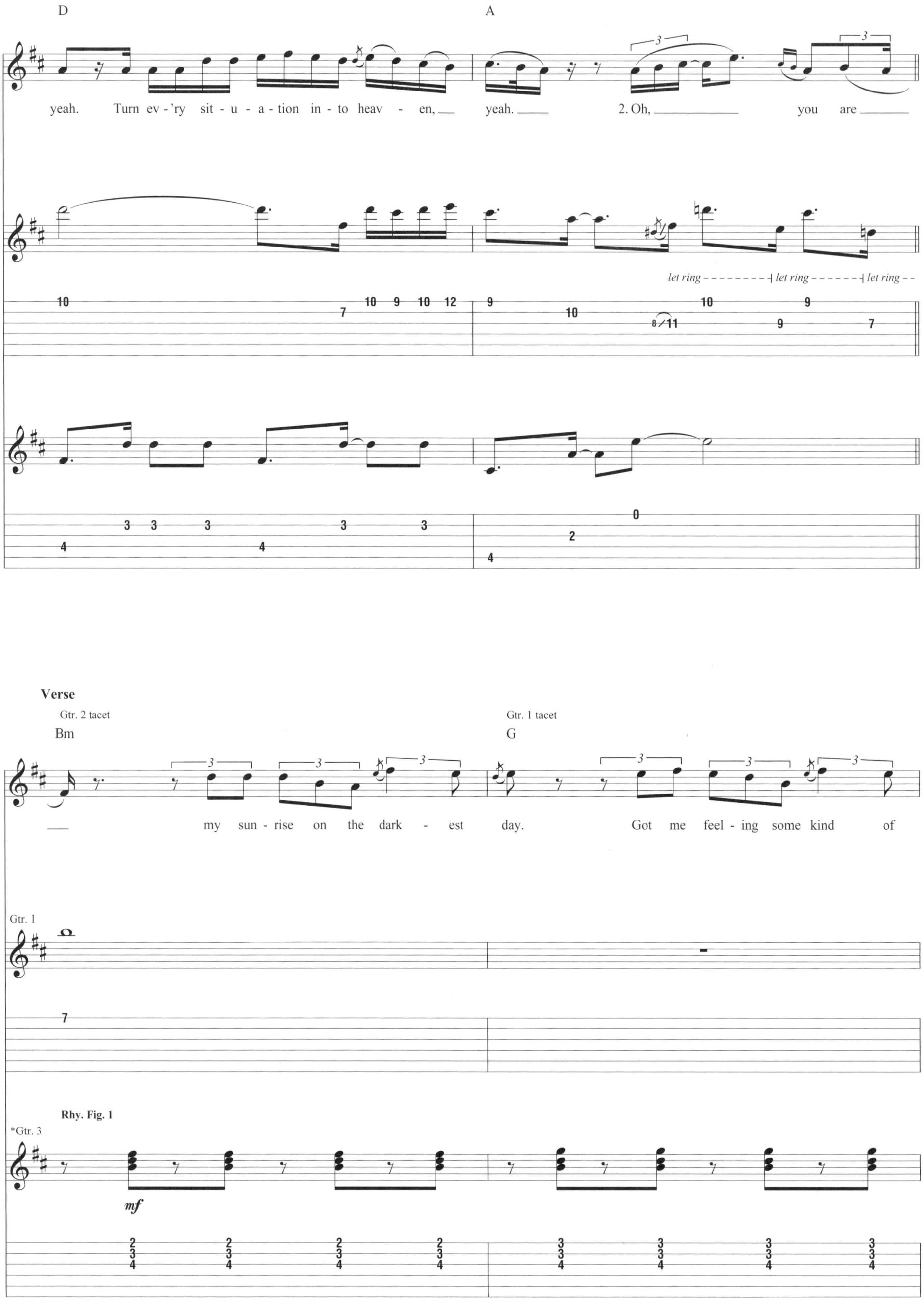

Verse

Gtr. 2 tacet

Bm

Gtr. 1 tacet

G

my sun-rise on the dark-est day. Got me feel-ing some kind of

Gtr. 1

Rhy. Fig. 1

*Gtr. 3

mf

*Kybd. arr. for gtr.

*See top of first page of song for chord diagrams pertaining to rhythm slashes.

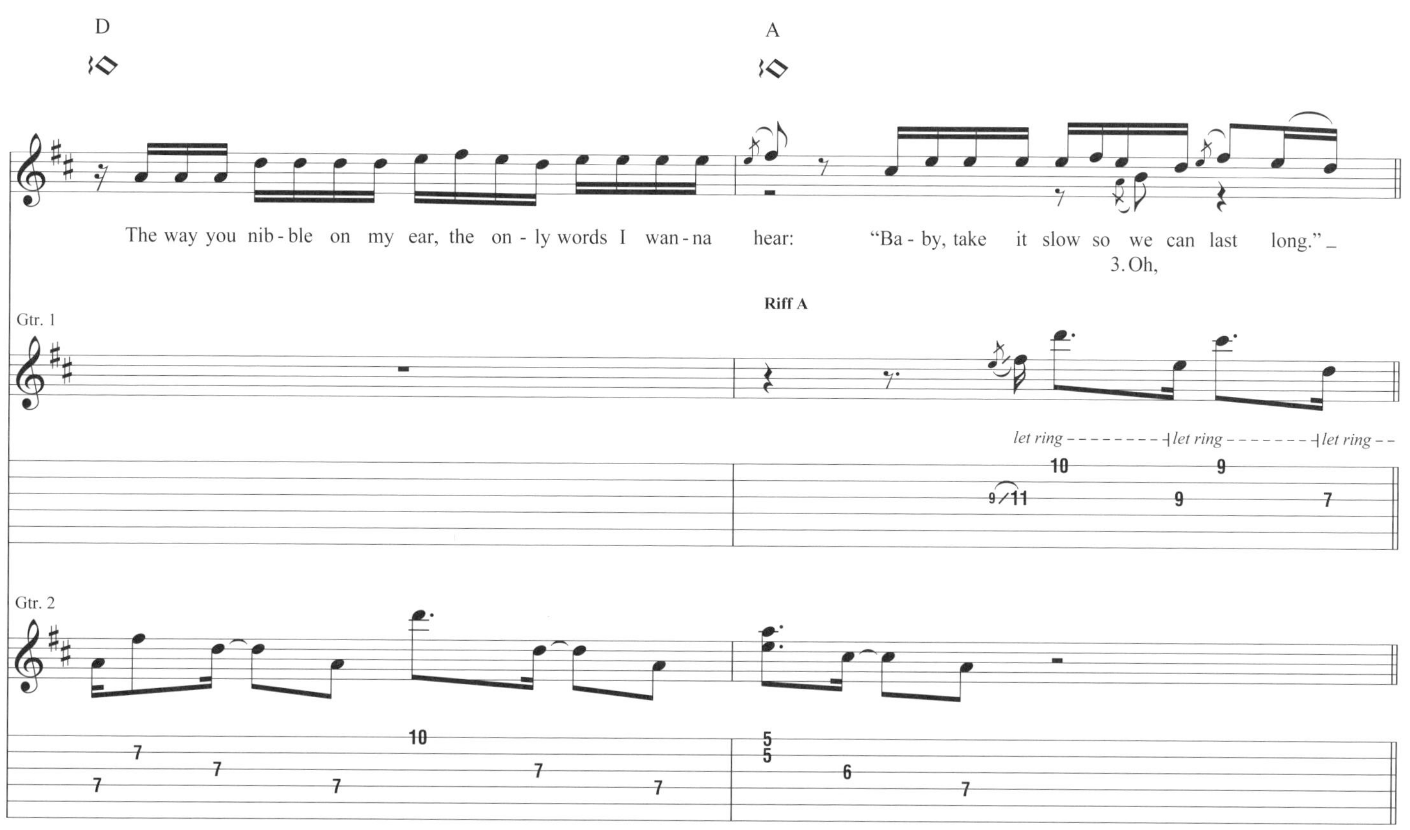

Verse
Gtr. 2 tacet
Bm
G
Rhy. Fig. 2
Gtr. 4
tú, tú er-es el i-mán y yo soy el met - al. Me voy ac-er-can-do y voy ar - man-do el
Gtr. 1
End Riff A
let ring
Rhy. Fig. 2A
Gtr. 5 (acous.)
mp
Riff B
Gtr. 6 (acous.)
mp

D
A
End Rhy. Fig. 2
plan. Só - lo con pen - sar - lo se a - ce - le - ra el pul - so. Oh, yeah.
End Rhy. Fig. 2A
End Riff B
Gtrs. 4 & 5: w/ Rhy. Figs. 2 & 2A (1st 2 meas.)
Bm
Gtr. 1 tacet
G
Ya, ya me es - tá gu - stan - do más de lo nor - mal. To - dos mis sen - ti - dos van pi - di - en - do más.
Gtr. 1

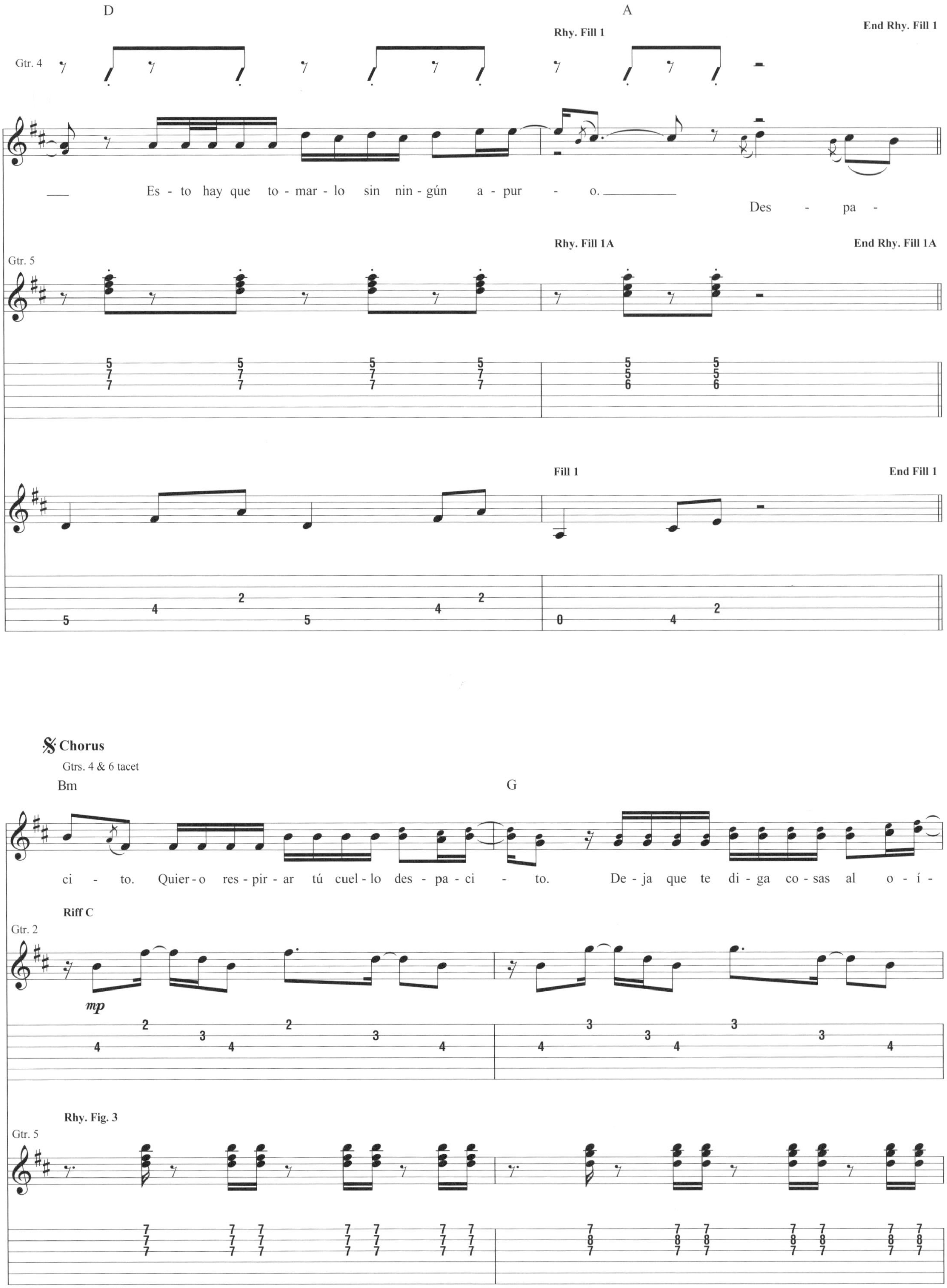

D A

Rhy. Fill 1 End Rhy. Fill 1

Gtr. 4

Es - to hay que to - mar - lo sin nin - gún a - pur - o.

Des - pa -

Rhy. Fill 1A End Rhy. Fill 1A

Gtr. 5

Fill 1 End Fill 1

D A N.C.

- do, pa-ra que te a-cuer-des si no es-tás con-mi - go. Des - pa -

End Riff C

2 2 3 2 2 3 2 | 2 0 2 2

End Rhy. Fig. 3

5 7 7 | 5 7 7 | 5 7 7 | 5 7 7 | 5 7 7 | 5 7 7 | 5 7 7 | 5 5 6 | 5 5 6 | 5 5 6

Gtr. 2: w/ Riff C
Gtr. 5: w/ Rhy. Fig. 3

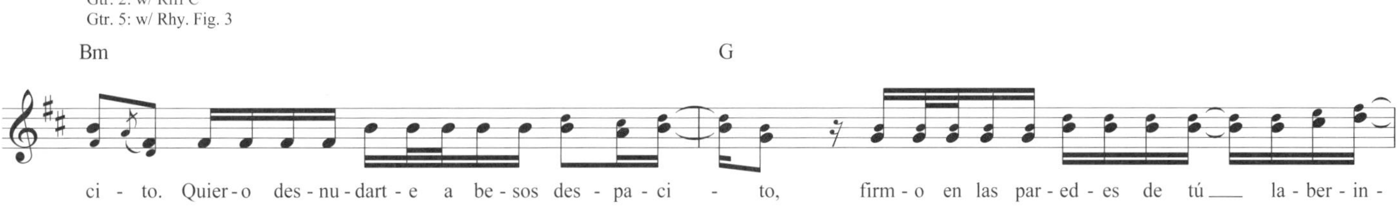

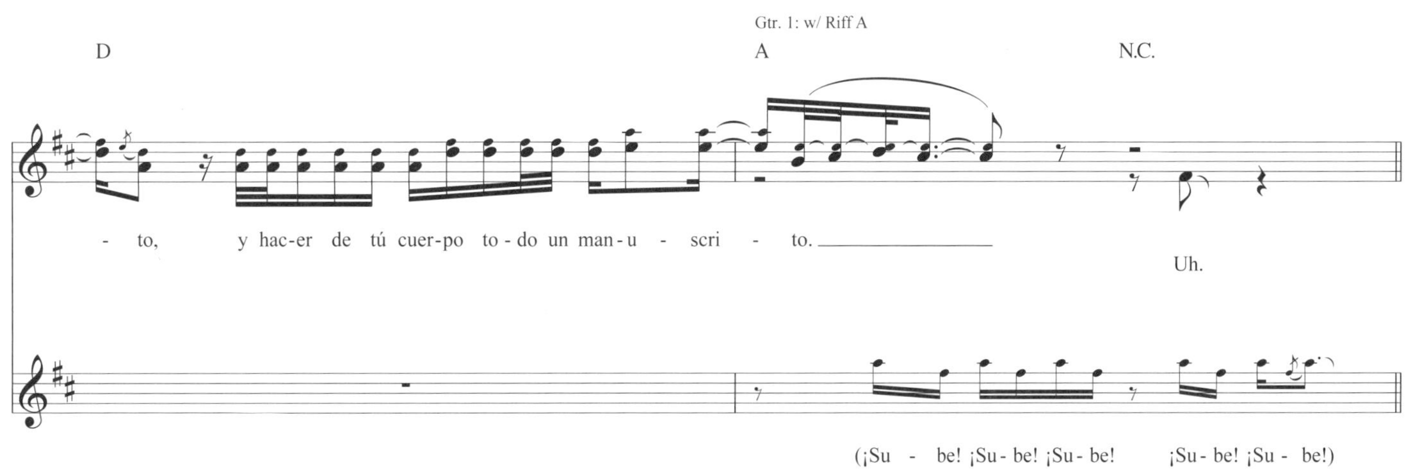

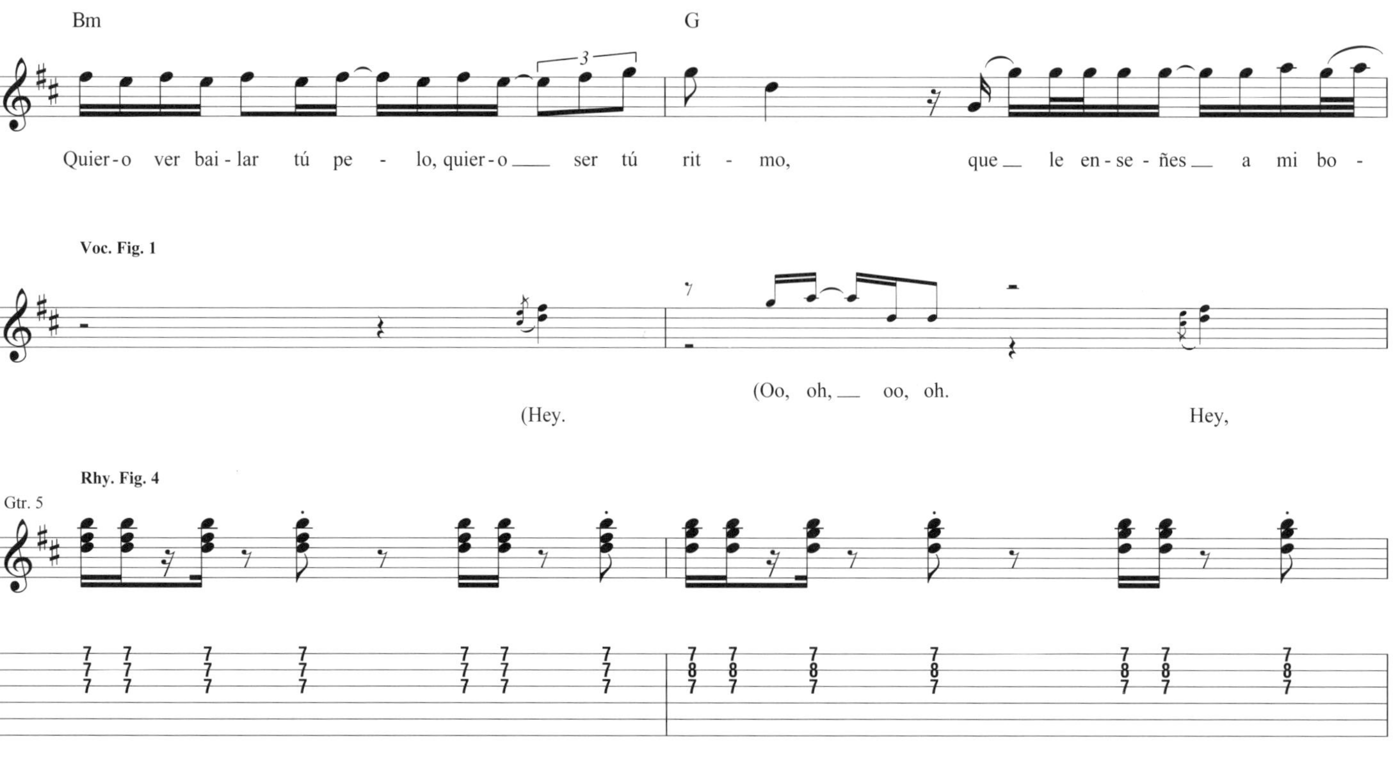

Gtr. 1: w/ Riff A

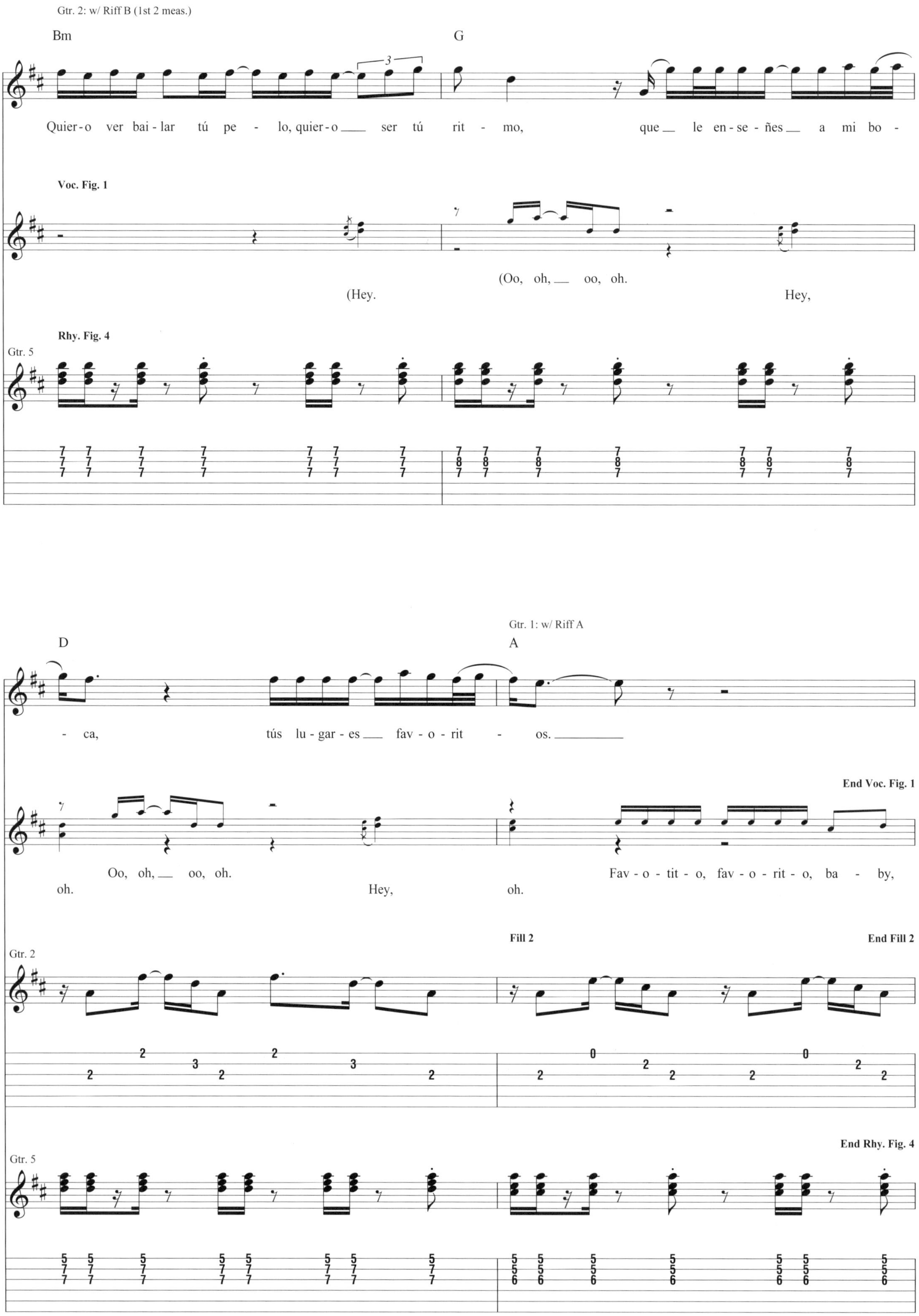

D A

- ca, tús lu-gar-es fav-o-rit - os.

End Voc. Fig. 1

Oo, oh, oo, oh. Fav - o - tit - o, fav - o - rit - o, ba - by,

oh. Hey, oh.

Fill 2 End Fill 2

Gtr. 2

End Rhy. Fig. 4

Gtr. 5

Gtr. 2: w/ Riff C
Gtr. 5: w/ Rhy. Fig. 4 (1st 2 meas.)
Bm
G
Dé - ja - me so - bre - pas - ar ___ tús zo - nas ___ de pe - li - gro, hasta pro - vo - car tús gri -
yeah. Oo, oh, ___ oo, oh.
(Hey. Hey.

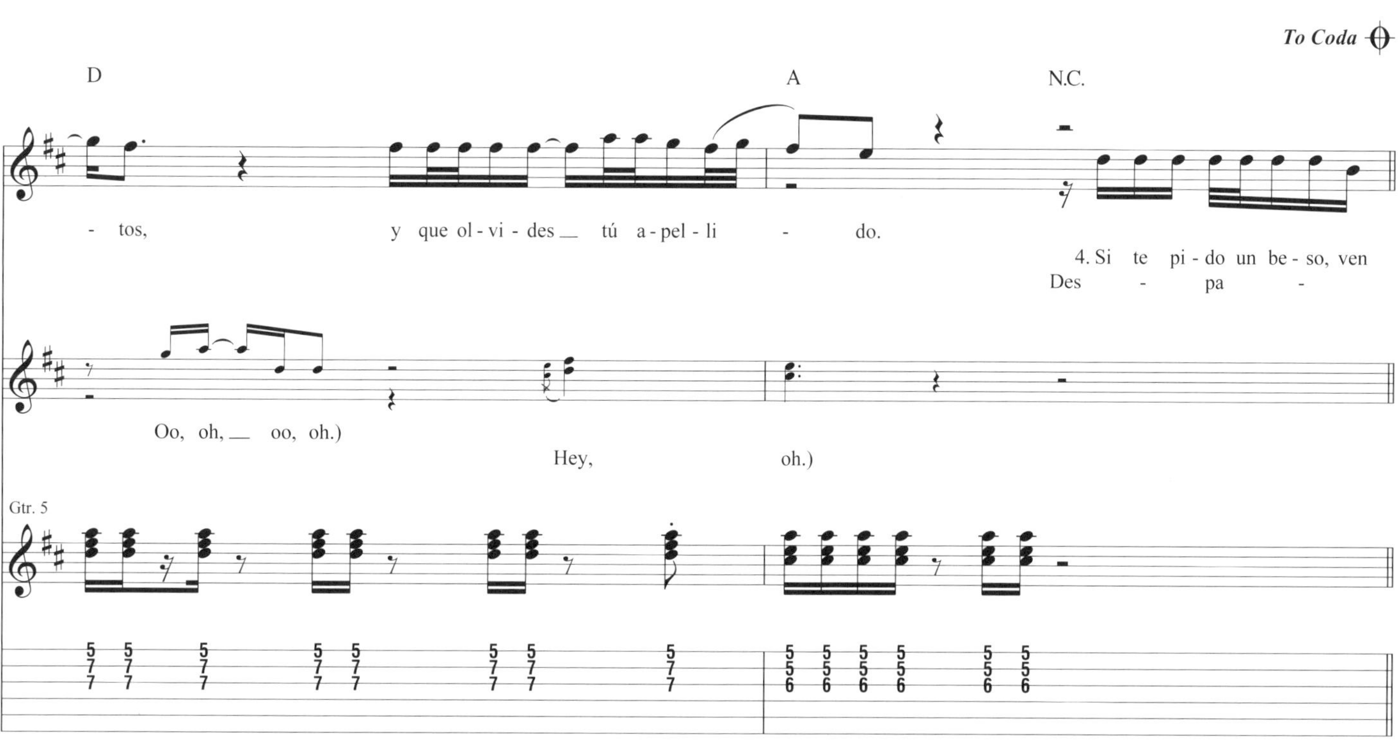
To Coda
D
A
N.C.
- tos, y que ol - vi - des ___ tú a - pel - li - do.
4. Si te pi - do un be - so, ven
Des - pa -
Oo, oh, ___ oo, oh.)
Hey, oh.)
Gtr. 5

Verse

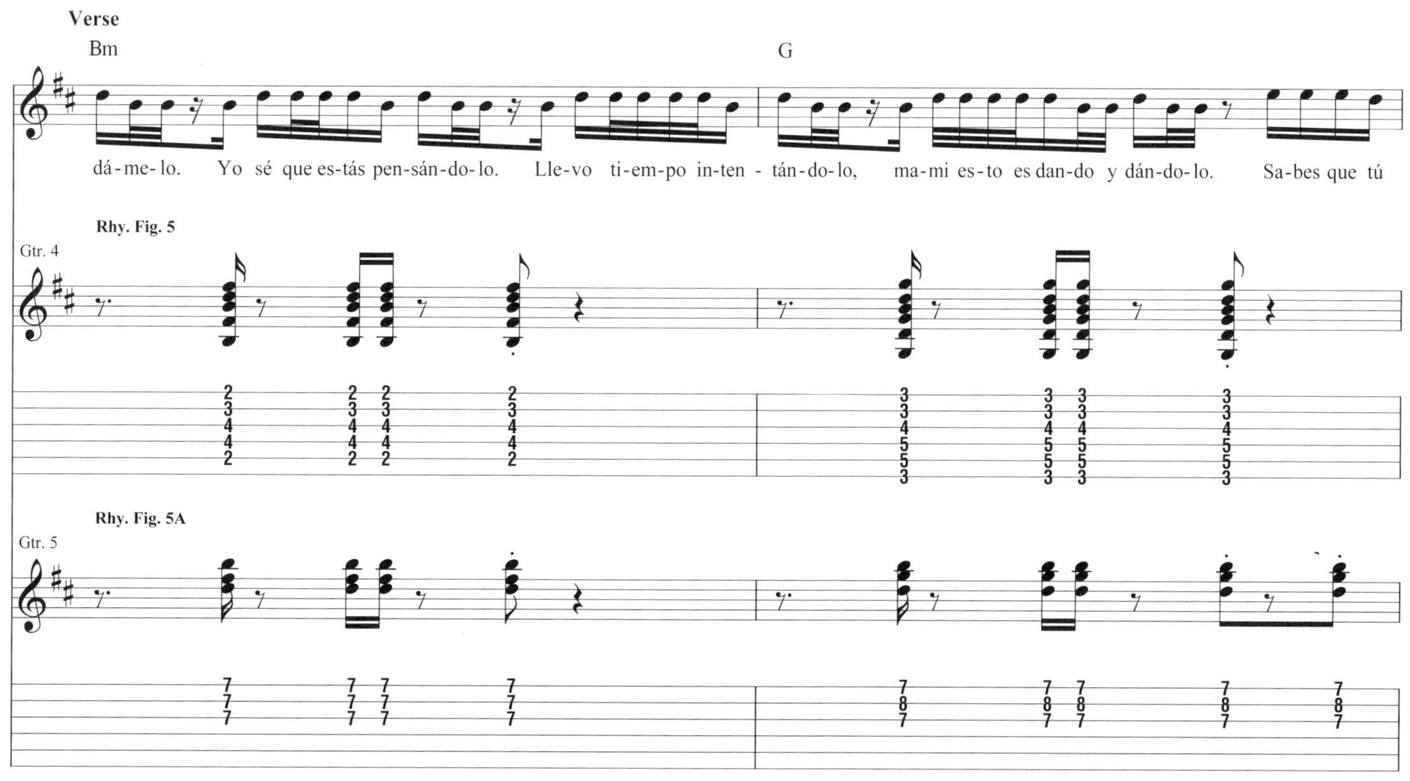
Bm
G
dá - me - lo. Yo sé que es - tás pen - sán - do - lo. Lle - vo ti - em - po in - ten - tán - do - lo, ma - mi es - to es dan - do y dán - do - lo. Sa - bes que tú
Rhy. Fig. 5
Gtr. 4
Rhy. Fig. 5A
Gtr. 5

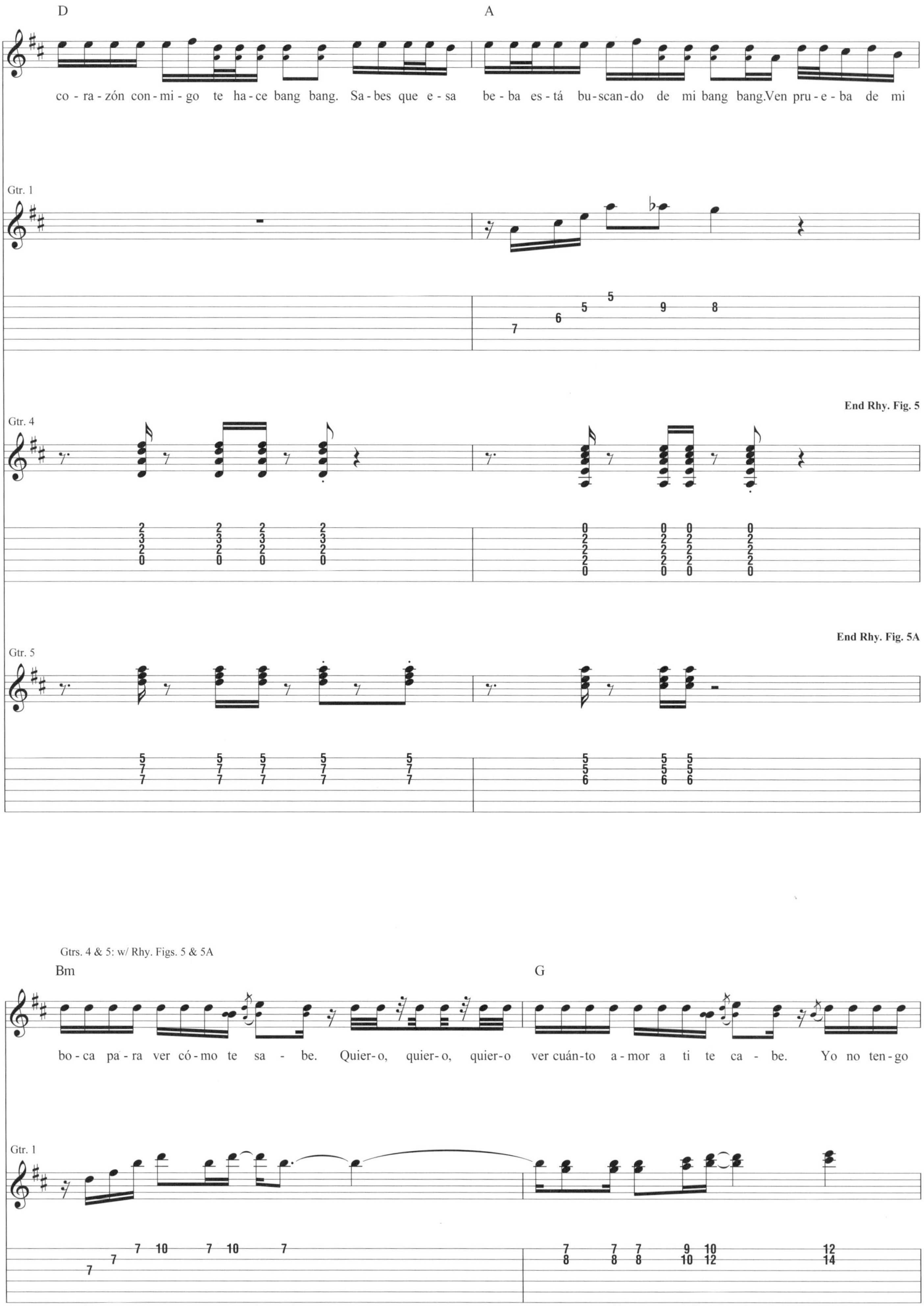

D
A
co - ra - zón con - mi - go te ha - ce bang bang. Sa - bes que e - sa be - ba es - tá bu - scan - do de mi bang bang. Ven pru - e - ba de mi
Gtr. 1
Gtr. 4
End Rhy. Fig. 5
Gtr. 5
End Rhy. Fig. 5A
Gtrs. 4 & 5: w/ Rhy. Figs. 5 & 5A
Bm
G
bo - ca pa - ra ver có - mo te sa - be. Quier - o, quier - o, quier - o ver cuán - to a - mor a ti te ca - be. Yo no ten - go
Gtr. 1

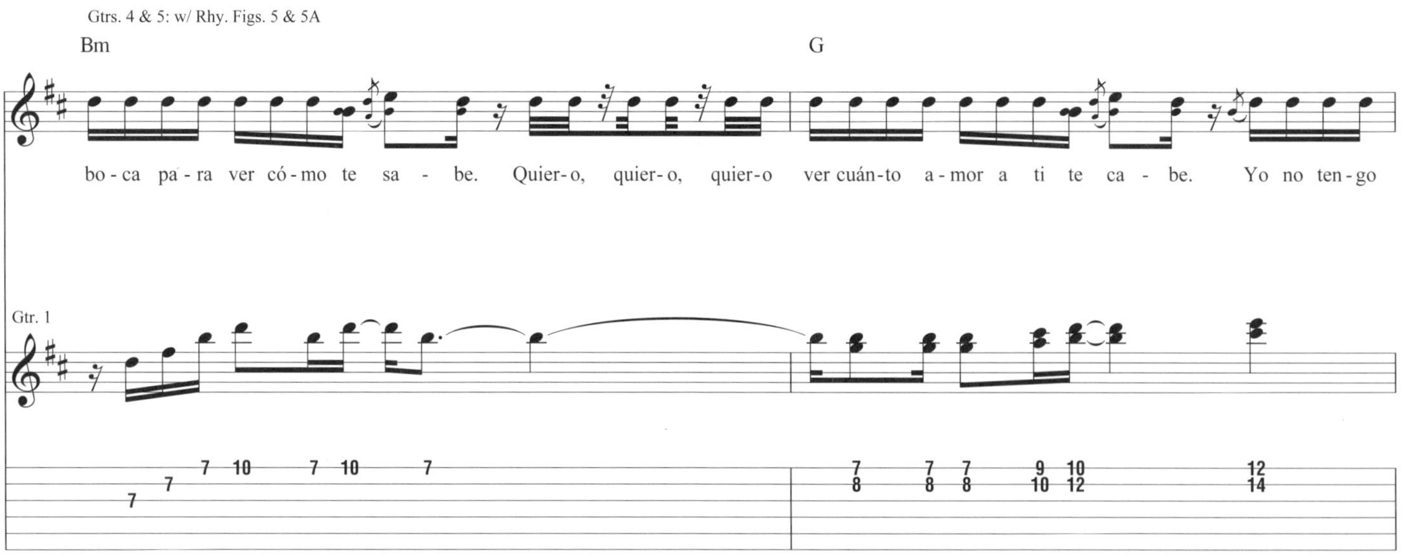

D
A
pri - sa, yo me quier-o dar el vi - a - je. Em - pe - ce - mos len - to, de - spués sal - va - je.
5. Pa - si - to a pa -
14
15
12 14
14 15
14 14 12 12
15 15 14 14
3

Verse

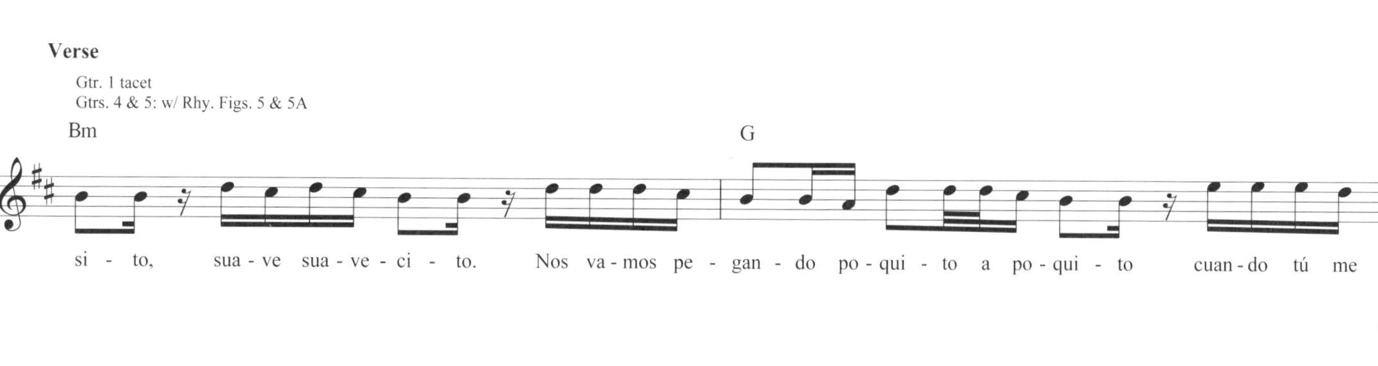
Gtr. 1 tacet
Gtrs. 4 & 5: w/ Rhy. Figs. 5 & 5A
Bm
G
si - to, sua - ve sua - ve - ci - to. Nos va - mos pe - gan - do po - qui - to a po - qui - to cuan - do tú me

D
A
be - sas con e - sa de - stre - za. Ve - o que e - res ma - lic - i - a con de - li - ca - de - za. Pa - si - to a pa -

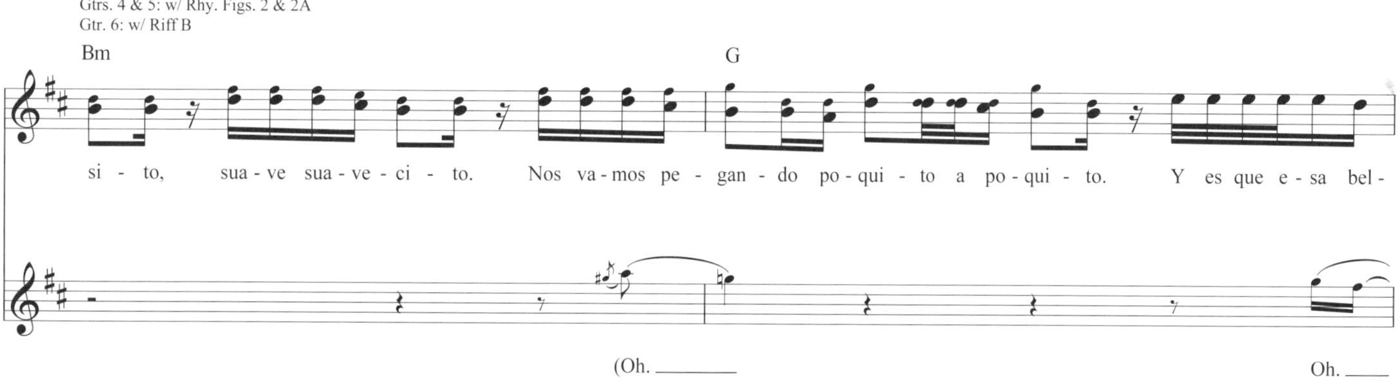
Gtrs. 4 & 5: w/ Rhy. Figs. 2 & 2A
Gtr. 6: w/ Riff B
Bm
G
si - to, sua - ve sua - ve - ci - to. Nos va - mos pe - gan - do po - qui - to a po - qui - to. Y es que e - sa bel -
(Oh.
Oh.

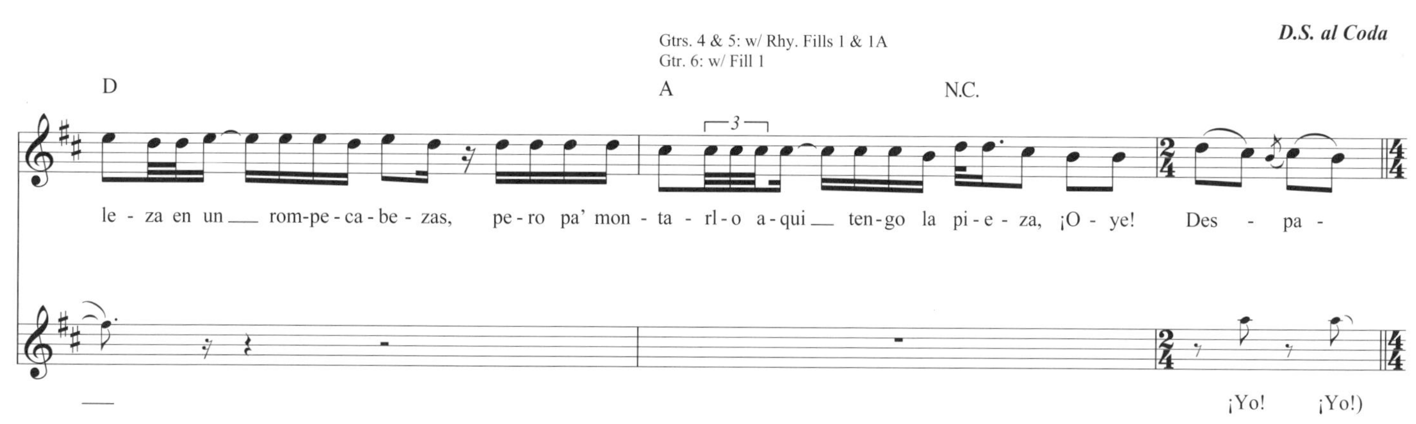
Gtrs. 4 & 5: w/ Rhy. Fills 1 & 1A
Gtr. 6: w/ Fill 1
D.S. al Coda
D
A
N.C.
3
le - za en un rom - pe - ca - be - zas, pe - ro pa' mon - ta - rl - o a - qui ten - go la pi - e - za, ¡O - ye! Des - pa -
¡Yo! ¡Yo!)

Coda

Chorus

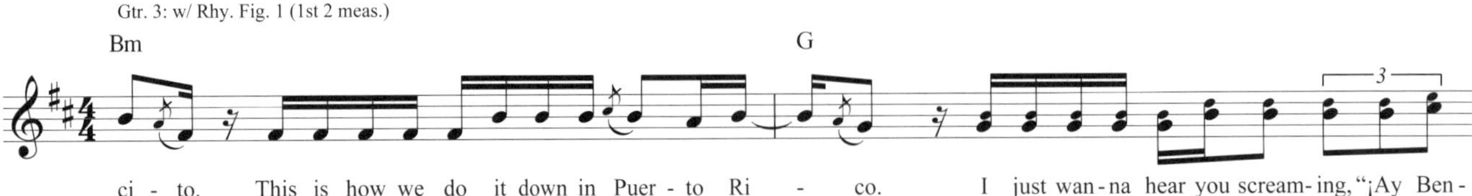
Gtr. 3: w/ Rhy. Fig. 1 (1st 2 meas.)
Bm
G
ci - to. This is how we do it down in Puer - to Ri - co. I just wan - na hear you scream - ing, "¡Ay Ben -

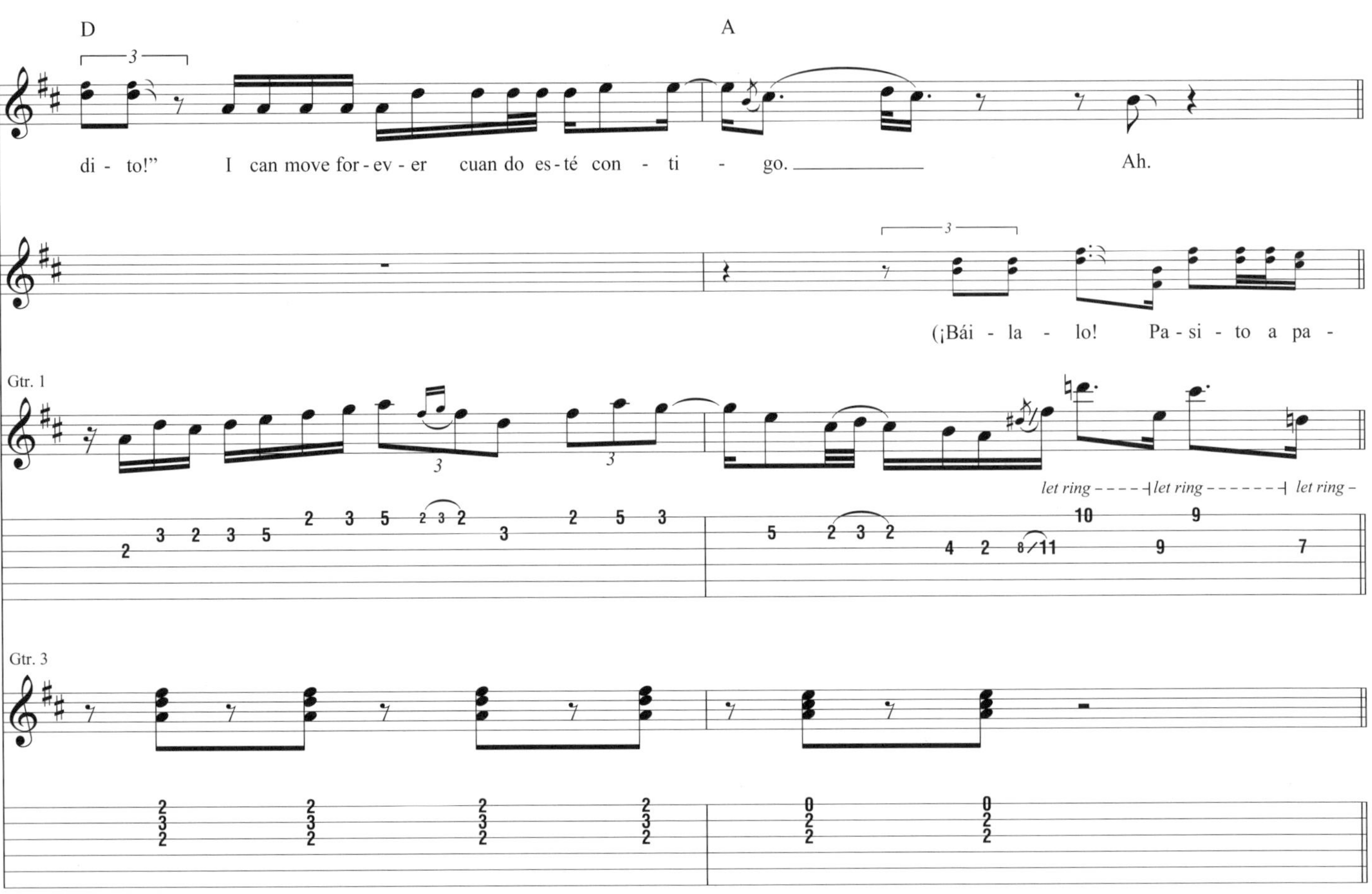
D
A
di - to!" I can move for - ev - er cuan do es - té con - ti - go.
Ah.
(¡Bái - la - lo! Pa - si - to a pa -
Gtr. 1
let ring
let ring
let ring
Gtr. 3

Chorus

Bkgd. Voc.: w/ Voc. Fig. 1
Gtr. 2: w/ Riff C (1st 3 meas.)
Gtr. 3 tacet
Gtr. 5: w/ Rhy. Fig. 4 (1 1/2 times)
Bm
G
Hey, yeah, ee, yeah. Oh, oo, oh. Oh.
Que le en - se - ñes a mi bo -
Voc. Fig. 2
End Voc. Fig. 2
si - to, sua - ve sua - ve - ci - to. Nos va - mos pe - gan - do po - qui - to a po - qui - to.
Gtr. 1
let ring

Gtr. 1 tacet
Gtr. 2: w/ Fill 2
D
A
- ca,
tús lu - gar - es fav - o - rit - os.
Ah, oo.
Pa - si - to a pa -
Bkgd. Voc.: w/ Voc. Fig. 2
Gtr. 2: w/ Riff C (1st 2 meas.)
Bm
G
Woo.
Has - ta pro - vo - car tús gri -
(Hey.
Hey,
D
A
N.C.
- tos,
y que ol - vi - des tú a - pel - li - do.
Des - pa - ci - to.
oh.)
Gtr. 1
Gtr. 2

from Arctic Monkeys - *AM*

Do I Wanna Know?

Words and Music by Alex Turner

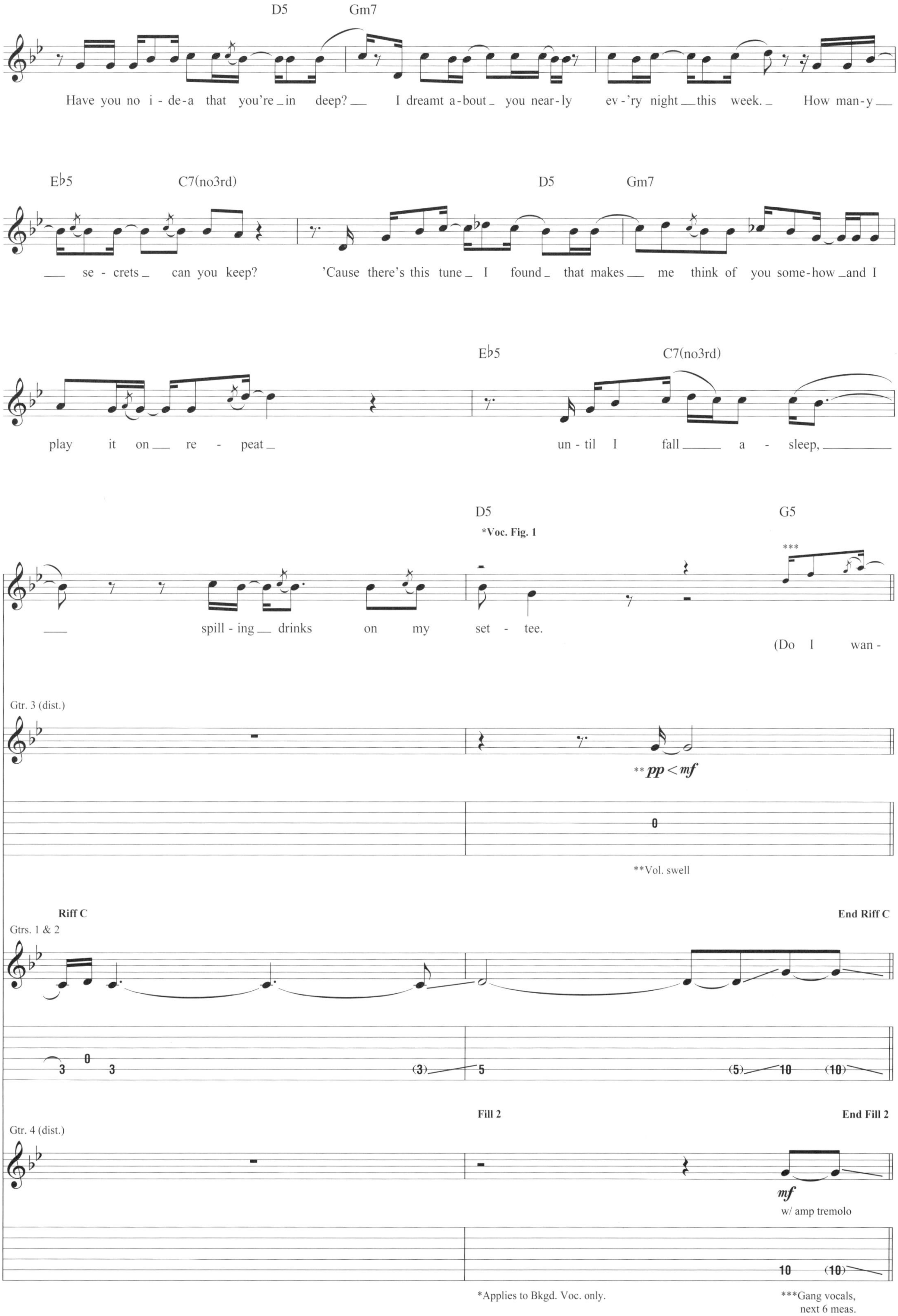

E♭5 C7(no3rd)

play it on ___ re - peat _ un - til I fall _____ a - sleep, _________

D5 G5

*Voc. Fig. 1

***

___ spill - ing ___ drinks on my set - tee.

(Do I wan -

Gtr. 3 (dist.)

** pp < mf

0

**Vol. swell

Riff C

End Riff C

Gtrs. 1 & 2

3 0 3 (3) 5 (5) 10 (10)

Fill 2

End Fill 2

Gtr. 4 (dist.)

mf

w/ amp tremolo

10 (10)

*Applies to Bkgd. Voc. only.

***Gang vocals, next 6 meas.

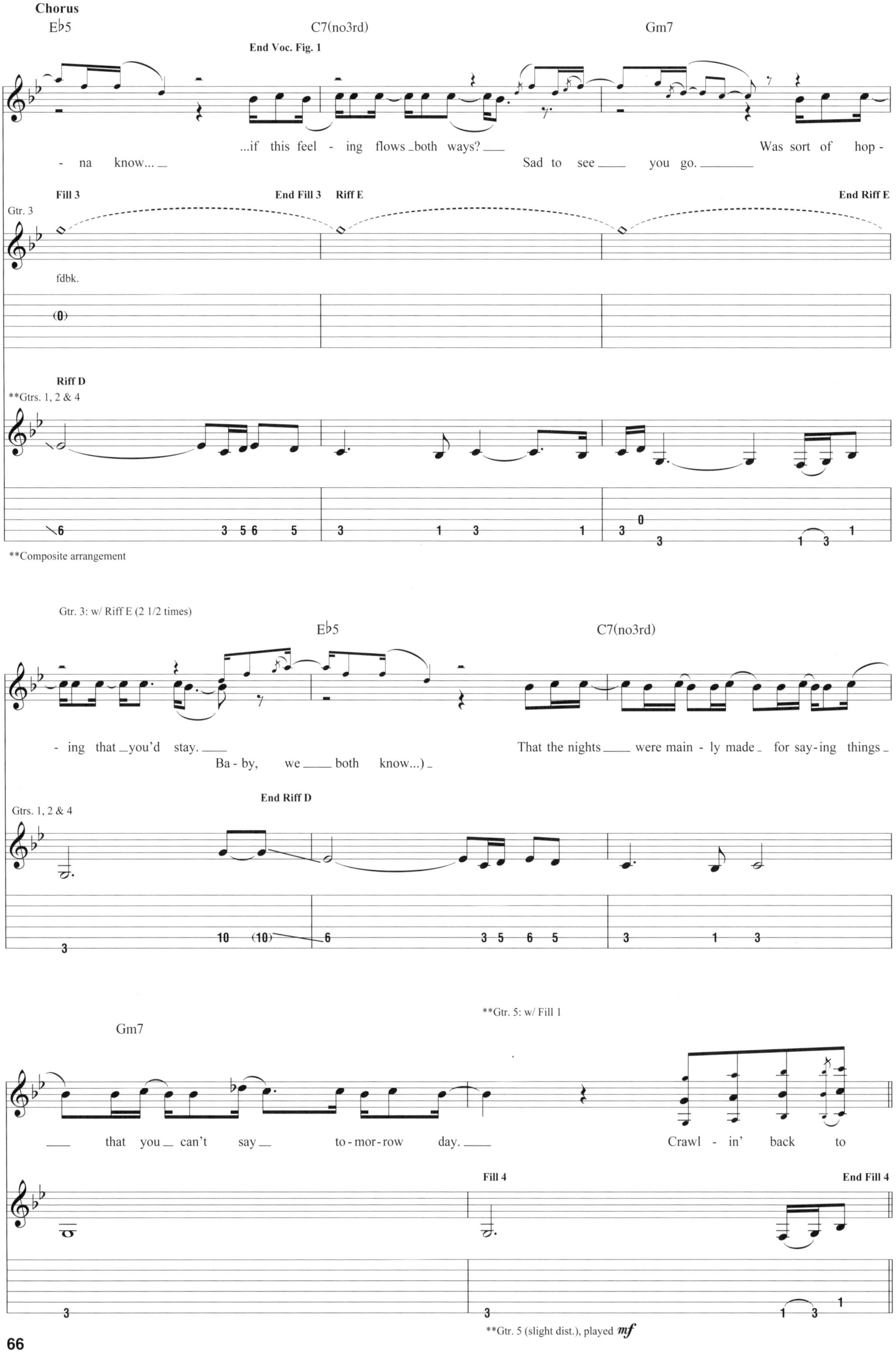

Chorus

E♭5 C7(no3rd) Gm7

End Voc. Fig. 1

...if this feel - ing flows both ways? Was sort of hop -

- na know... Sad to see you go.

Fill 3 End Fill 3 Riff E End Riff E

Gtr. 3

fdbk.

(0)

Riff D

**Gtrs. 1, 2 & 4

6 3 5 6 5 | 3 1 3 1 | 3 0 3 1 3 1

**Composite arrangement

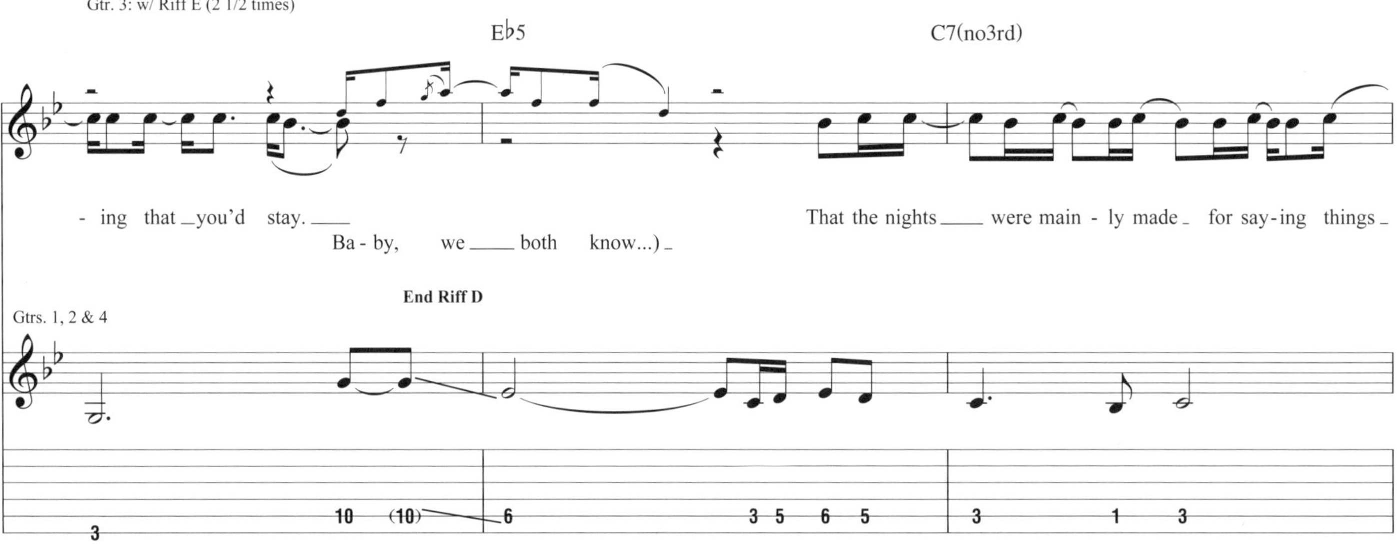

Chorus
Gtr. 1: w/ Riff A
Gtrs. 2, 4 & 5: w/ Riff B
Gtr. 3: w/ Riff E (3 times)
Gm7
E♭5
C7(no3rd)
you. Ev - er thought of call - ing when you've
D5
Gm7
had a few? 'Cause I al - ways do. May - be I'm
E♭5
C7(no3rd)
too bus - y be - ing yours to fall for some -
Riff F
*Gtrs. 1, 2, 4 & 5
End Riff F
*Composite arrangement
D5
Gm7
bod - y new. Now I've thought it through. Crawl - in' back to
Fill 5
End Fill 5
Gtr. 3
fdbk.
Gtrs. 1, 2, 4 & 5

Verse

Gtr. 3 tacet
Gm7
E♭5
C7(no3rd)
Gtrs. 1, 2, 4 & 5 tacet
D5
you. 2. So have you got the guts?
Been won-d'ring if your heart's still o-
Gtrs. 1, 2, 4 & 5
Riff G
*Gtr. 6
mf
*Bass arr. for gtr.
Gm7
E♭5
C7(no3rd)
-pen, and if so I wan-na know what time it shuts.
Simmer down and pucker up.
End Riff G
Gtr. 6
Gtr. 6: w/ Riff G (last 2 meas.)
Gtr. 1: w/ Riff A (1 1/2 times)
Gtr. 2: w/ Riff B (1 1/2 times)
Gtr. 6: w/ Riff G (1 1/2 times)
D5
Gm7
I'm sor-ry to in-ter-rupt, it's just, I'm con-stant-ly on the cusp of try - ing to kiss
E♭5
C7(no3rd)
D5
Gm7
you, I don't know if you feel the same as I do.

E♭5
C7(no3rd)
But we could be to-geth - er
Gtrs. 1 & 2: w/ Riff C
Gtr. 4: w/ Fill 2
D5
G5
if you want-ed to.
(Do I wan -
Gtr. 3
pp
mf
Gtr. 6
*Gang vocals, next 6 meas.
Chorus
Gtrs. 1, 2 & 4: w/ Riff D (1 3/4 times)
Gtr. 3: w/ Fill 3
Gtr. 6 tacet
Gtr. 3: w/ Riff E (3 1/2 times)
E♭5
C7(no3rd)
Gm7
...if this feel - ing flows both ways?
Was sort of hop -
- na know...
Sad to see you go.
E♭5
- ing that you'd stay.
that the nights
Ba - by, we both know...)
C7(no3rd)
Gm7
Gtrs. 1, 2 & 4: w/ Fill 4
Gtr. 5: w/ Fill 1
were main - ly made for say - ing things that you can't say to - mor - row day.
Crawl - in' back to
Gtr. 7 (dist.)
**pp
mf
fdbk.
don't pick
**Vol. swell

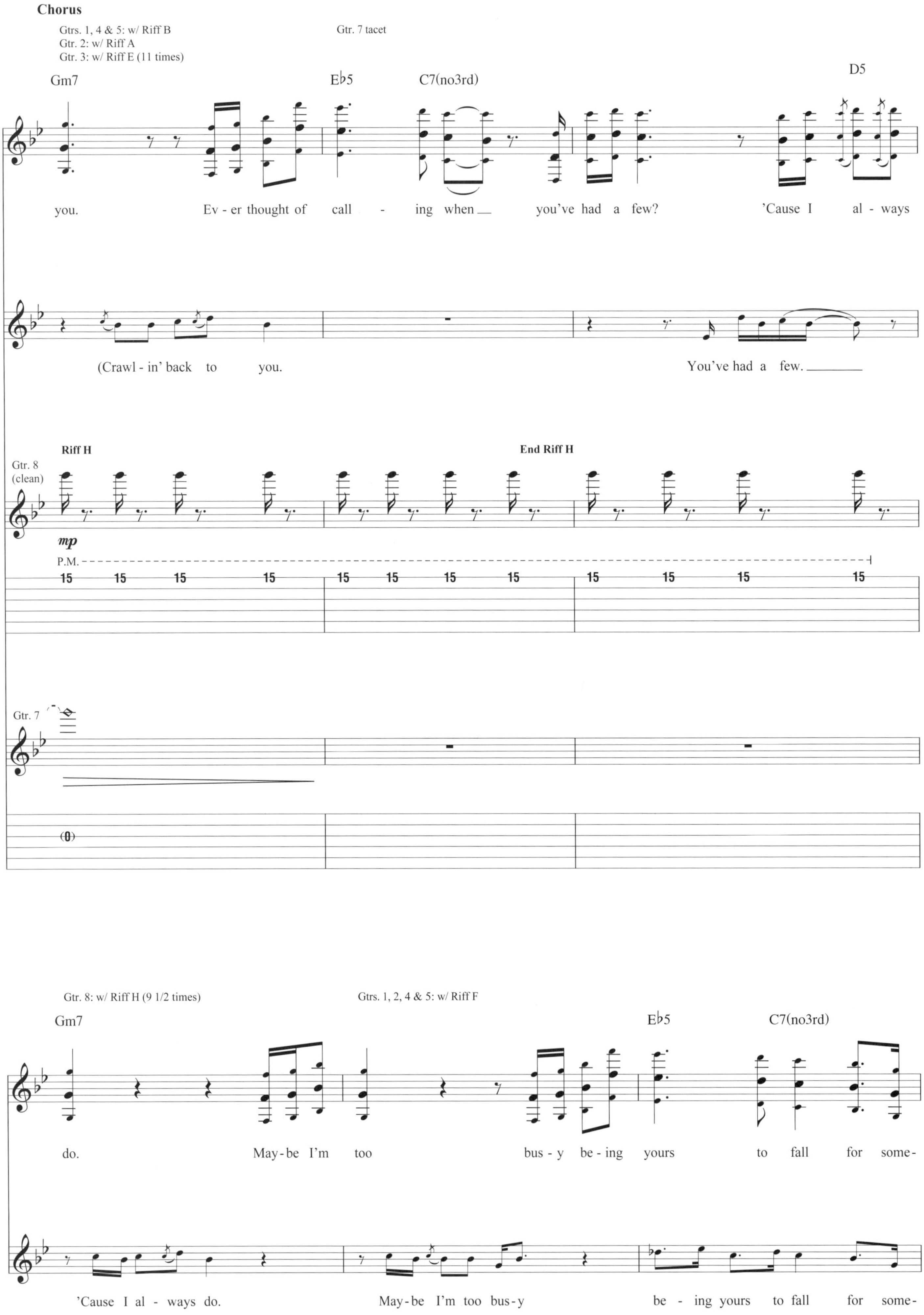

Chorus

Gtrs. 1, 4 & 5: w/ Riff B
Gtr. 2: w/ Riff A
Gtr. 3: w/ Riff E (11 times)

Gtr. 7 tacet

Gm7 E♭5 C7(no3rd) D5

you. Ev - er thought of call - ing when __ you've had a few? 'Cause I al - ways

(Crawl - in' back to you. You've had a few. ___

Riff H End Riff H

Gtr. 8 (clean)

mp

P.M.

15 15 15 15 | 15 15 15 15 | 15 15 15 15

Gtr. 7

(0)

D5
Gm7
***
bod - y new.
Now I've thought it through.
Crawl - in' back to
(Do I wa -
bod - y new.)
Gtr. 7
**w/ delay
**Set for quarter-note regeneration w/ 1 repeat.
*Gtrs. 1, 2, 4 & 5
*Composite arrangement
***Gang vocals, next 6 meas.
Gtrs. 1, 2, 4 & 5: w/ Riff D (2 3/4 times)
E♭5
C7(no3rd)
you.
...if this feel - ing flows both ways?
- na know...
Sad to see
Riff I
Gtr. 7
End Riff I
Riff I1
Gtr. 9 (slight dist.)
End Riff I1
mp
P.M.

Gtrs. 7 & 9: w/ Riffs I & II (6 times)
Gm7
Eb5
Was sort of hop - ing that you'd stay.
that the nights
you go.
Ba-by, we both know...)

C7(no3rd)
Gm7
were main - ly made for say - ing things that you can't say to-mor-row day.
(Do I wan-

Eb5
C7(no3rd)
Gm7
Too bus-y be-ing yours to fall.
Ev-er thought of
- na know?
Sad to see you go.)

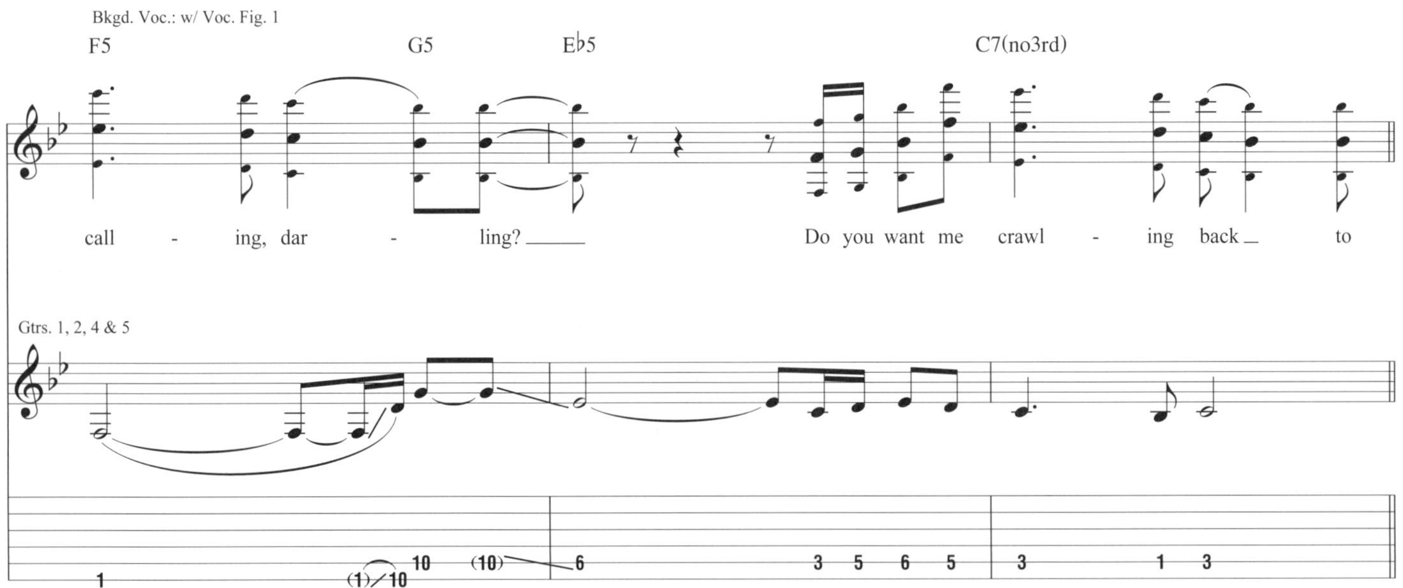
Bkgd. Voc.: w/ Voc. Fig. 1
F5
G5
Eb5
C7(no3rd)
call - ing, dar - ling?
Do you want me crawl - ing back to
Gtrs. 1, 2, 4 & 5

Outro
Gtr. 3: w/ Riff E (3 times)
Gtrs. 7 & 9: w/ Riffs I & I1 (3 times)
Gtr. 8: w/ Riff H (3 times)
Gm
you?
Riff K
End Riff K
Gtrs. 1, 2 & 5: w/ Riff K (2 times)
Gtr. 4 tacet
Gtr. 3: w/ Fill 5
N.C.
Gtr. 8
P.M.
Gtr. 7
Gtr. 9
P.M.
Gtrs. 1, 2 & 5

from Elle King - *Love Stuff*

Ex's & Oh's

Words and Music by Tanner Schneider and Dave Bassett

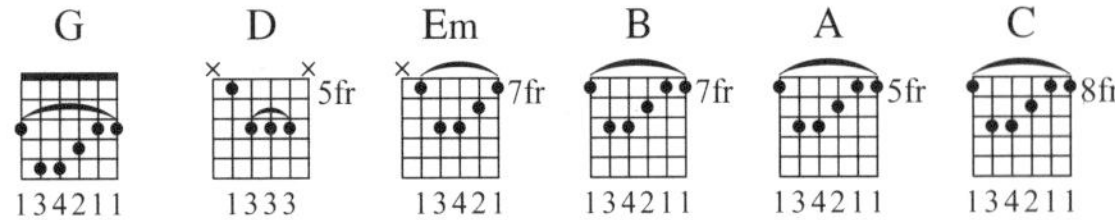

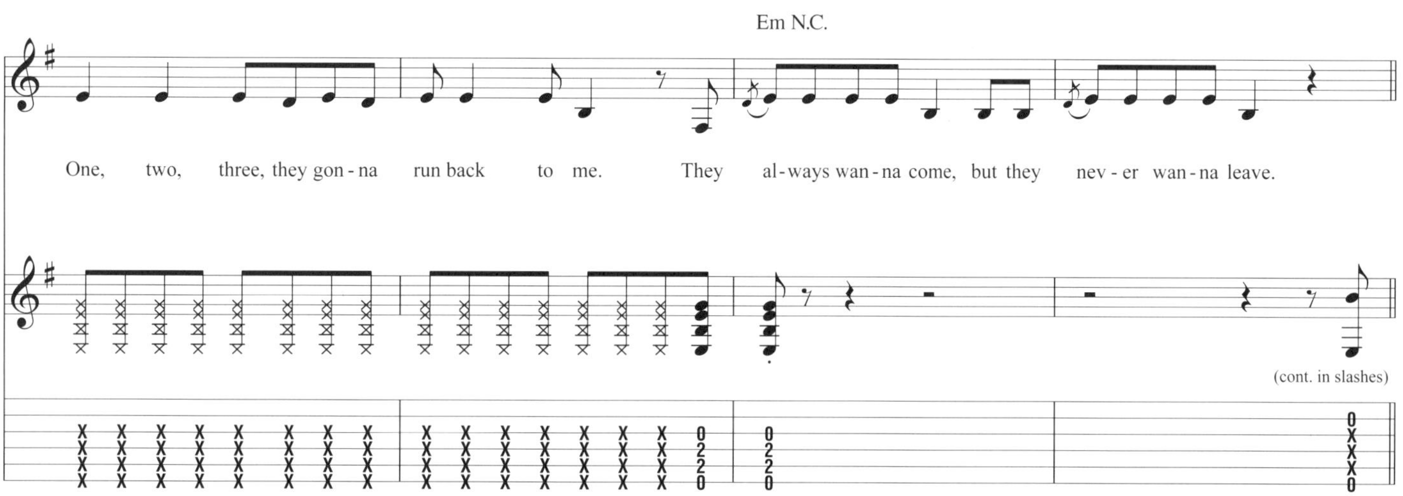

*See top of first page of song for chord diagrams pertaining to rhythm slashes.

To Coda 1
To Coda 2
G
D
A
C
End Rhy. Fig. 3
___ me to make 'em ah, ah, all. They won't let go. Ex - es and
End Riff A
Interlude
Gtr. 1: w/ Rhy. Fig. 1
Em
oh's.
Verse
Gtr. 1: w/ Rhy. Fig. 1
Em
3. Had a sum-mer lov-er down in New Or - leans. _ Kept him warm in the win-ter, left him fro-zen in the spring. My, my, _
Riff B
End Riff B

Verse

D.S. al Coda 1

Coda 1

Guitar Solo

Gtr. 1: w/ Rhy. Fig. 1
Em
oh's.
Gtr. 2

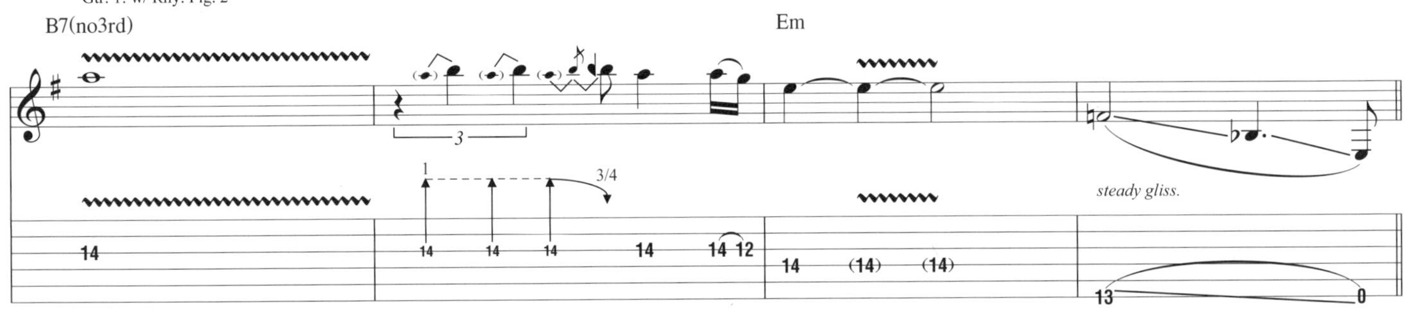
D.S. al Coda 2
Gtr. 1: w/ Rhy. Fig. 2
B7(no3rd)
Em
steady gliss.

Coda 2
Gtr. 1: w/ Rhy. Fig. 3 (last meas.)
Gtr. 2: w/ Riff A (last meas.)
Gtr. 1: w/ Rhy. Fig. 3
Gtr. 2: w/ Riff A
C G D Em B
go. Ex - es and the oh, oh, oh's, they haunt me. Like gho - o - osts, they want

G D A C
me to make 'em ah, ah, all. They won't let go. Ex - es and

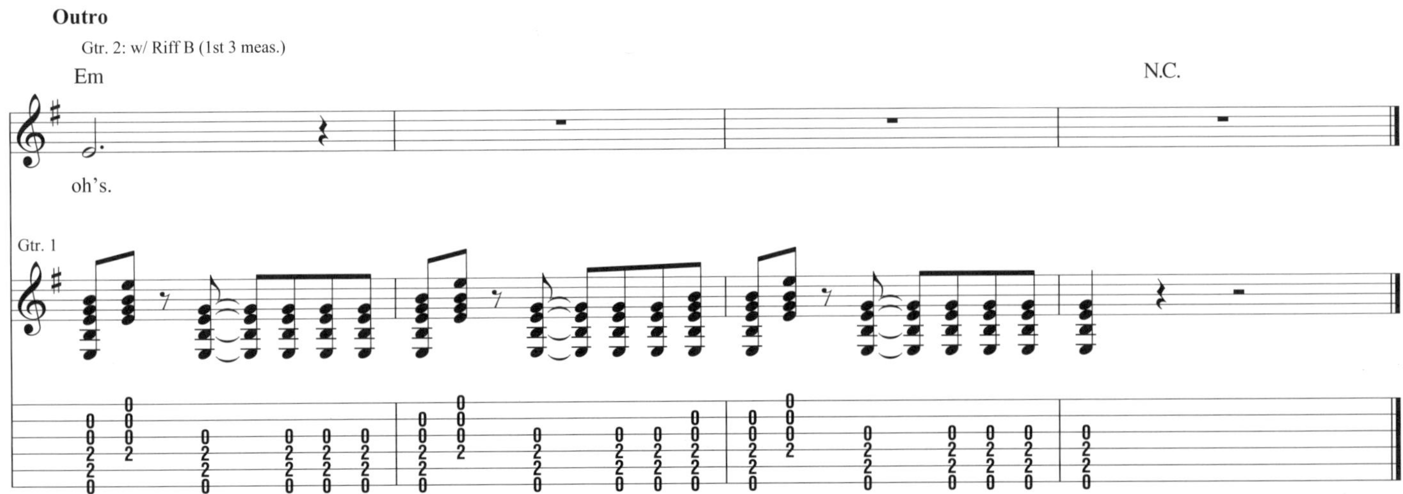
Outro
Gtr. 2: w/ Riff B (1st 3 meas.)
Em
N.C.
oh's.
Gtr. 1

from Daft Punk - *Random Access Memories*

Get Lucky

Words and Music by Thomas Bangalter, Guy Manuel Homem Christo, Nile Rodgers and Pharrell Williams

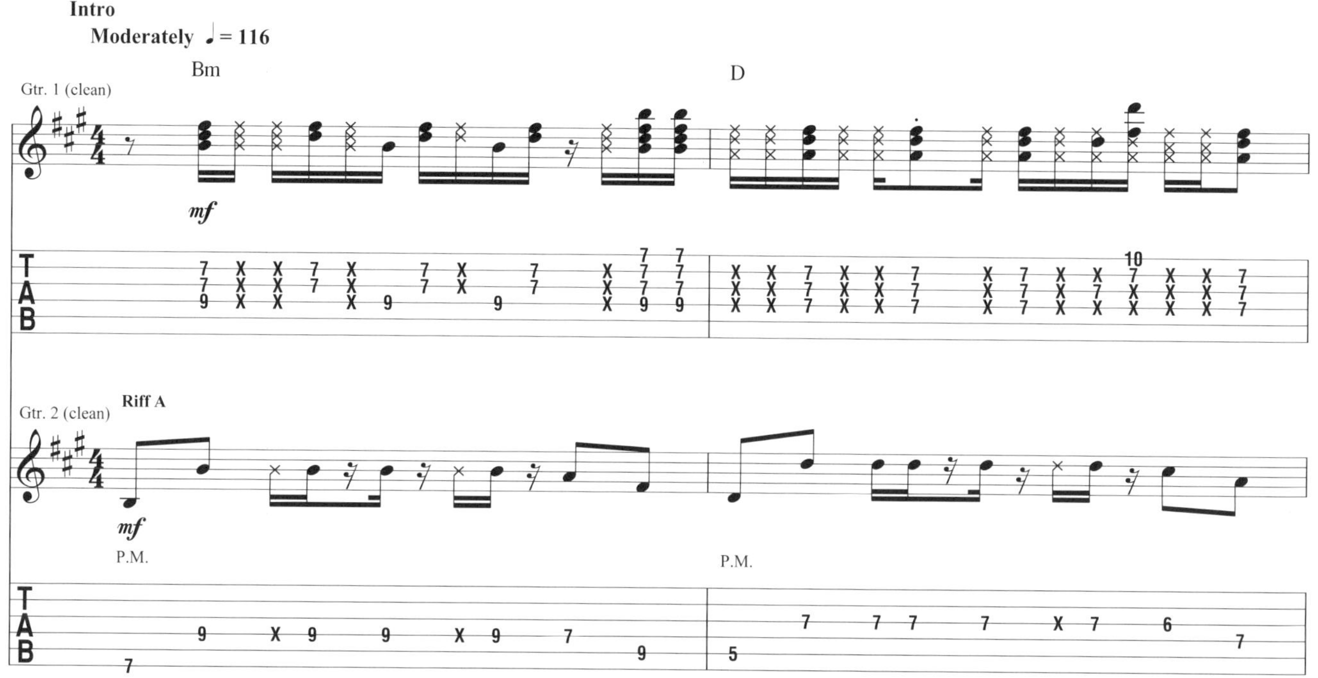

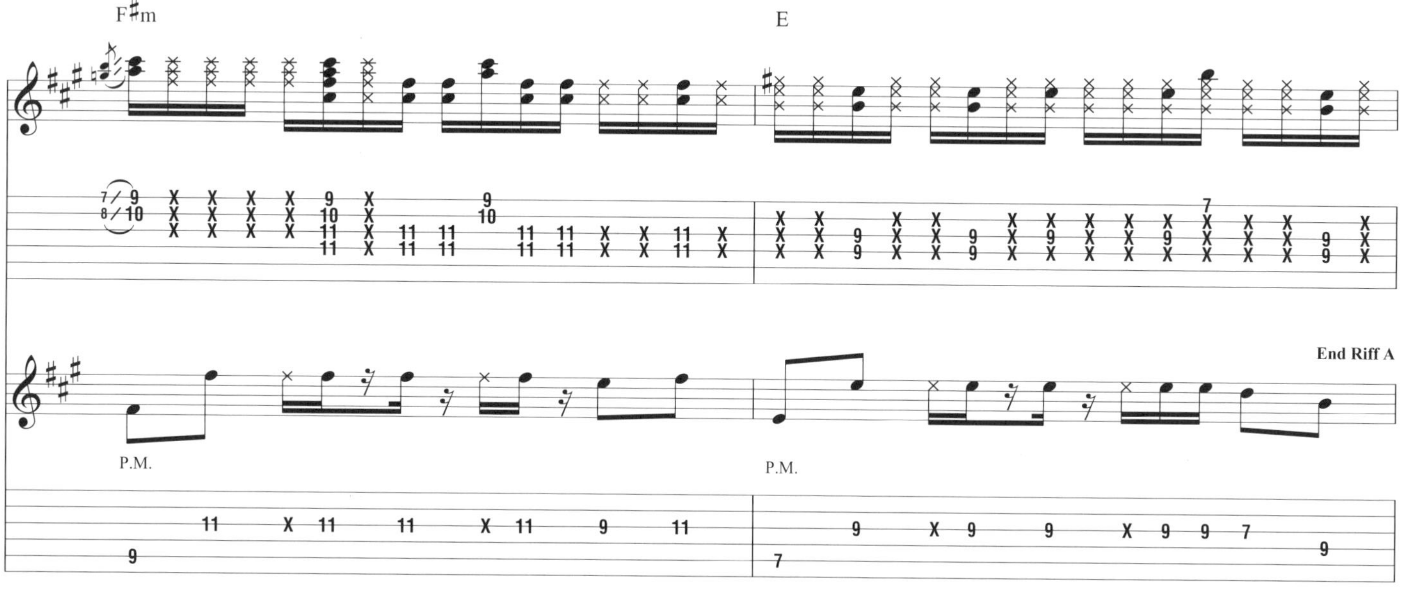

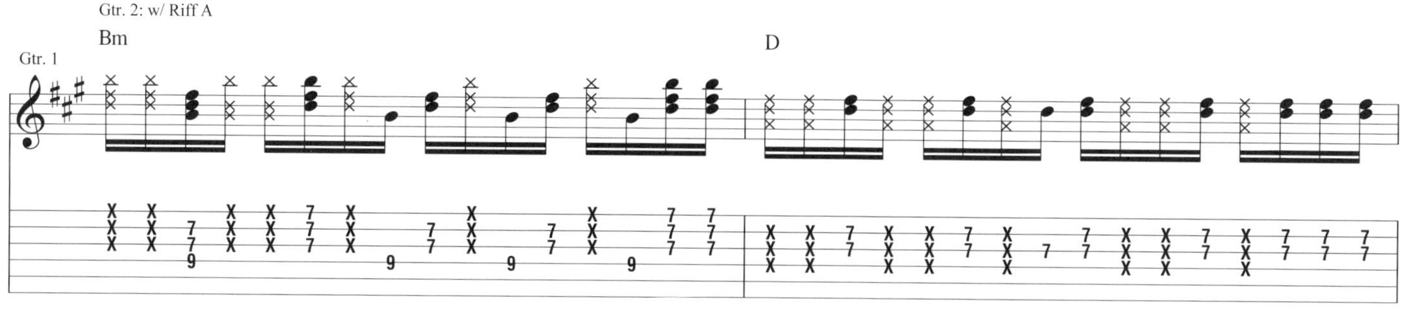

F♯m
E
1. Like the leg-end of the phoe-
Verse
Bm
D
- nix, huh, all ends with be - gin-
- bon, your gift keeps on giv-
F♯m
E
- nings. What keeps the plan - et spin-
- ing. What is this I'm feel-
Bm
D
- ning, ah, the force from the be - gin-
- ing? If you wan - na leave, I'm read-

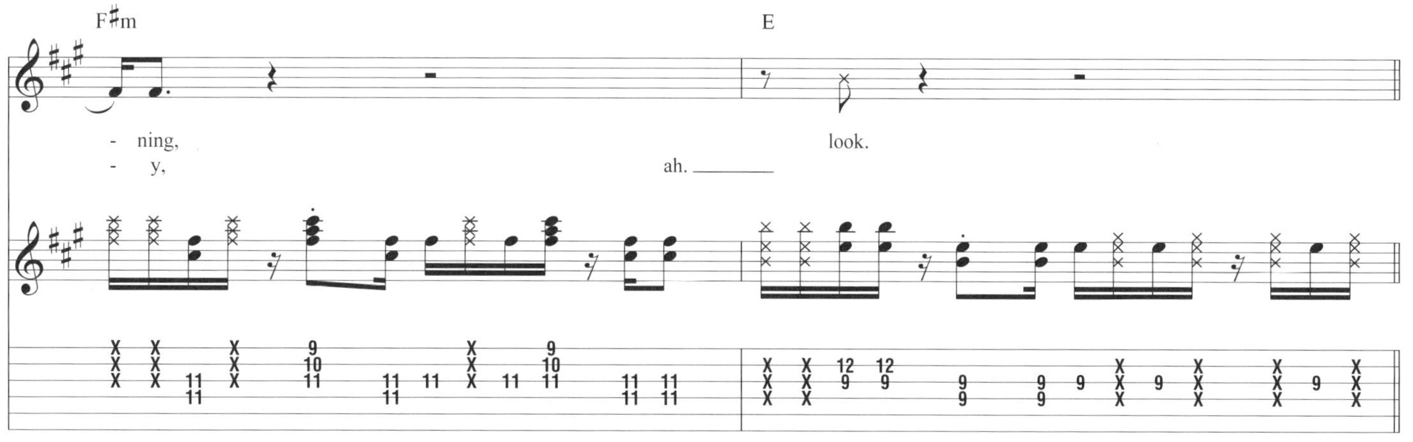

Pre-Chorus

Gtr. 2: w/ Riff A (2 times)

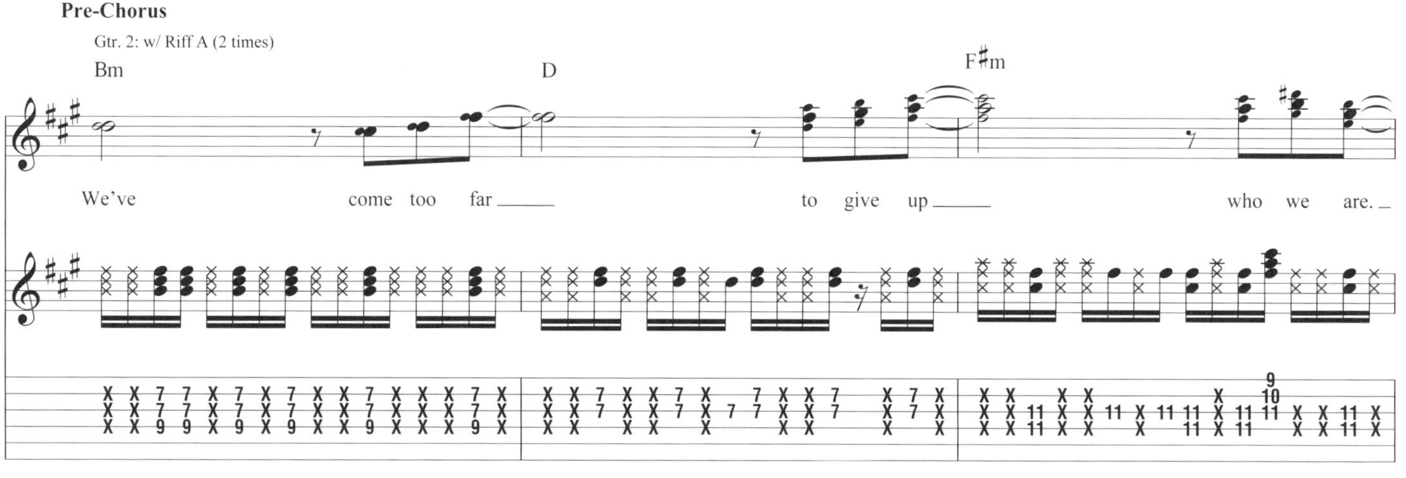

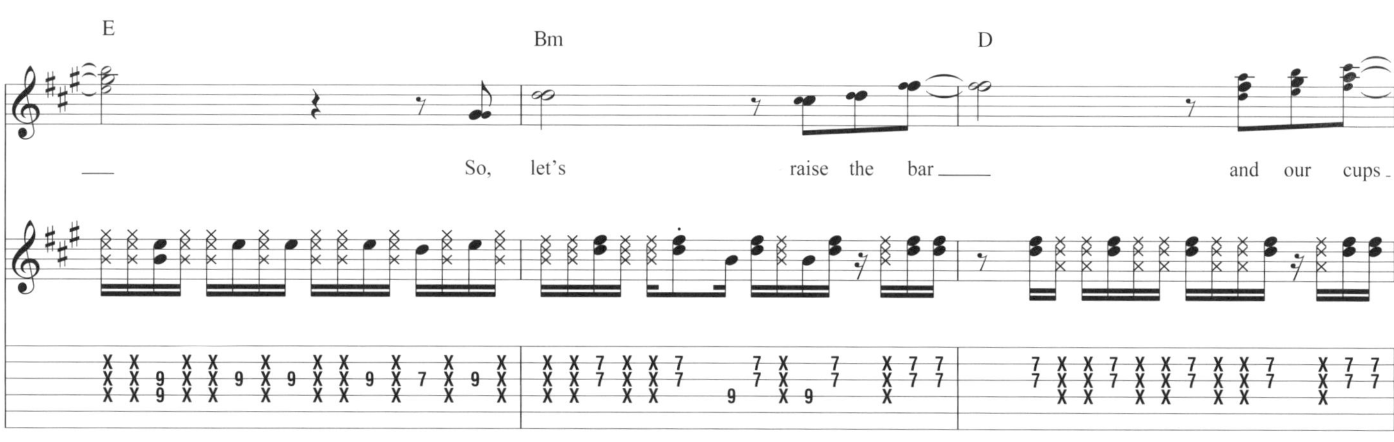

To Coda 𝄌

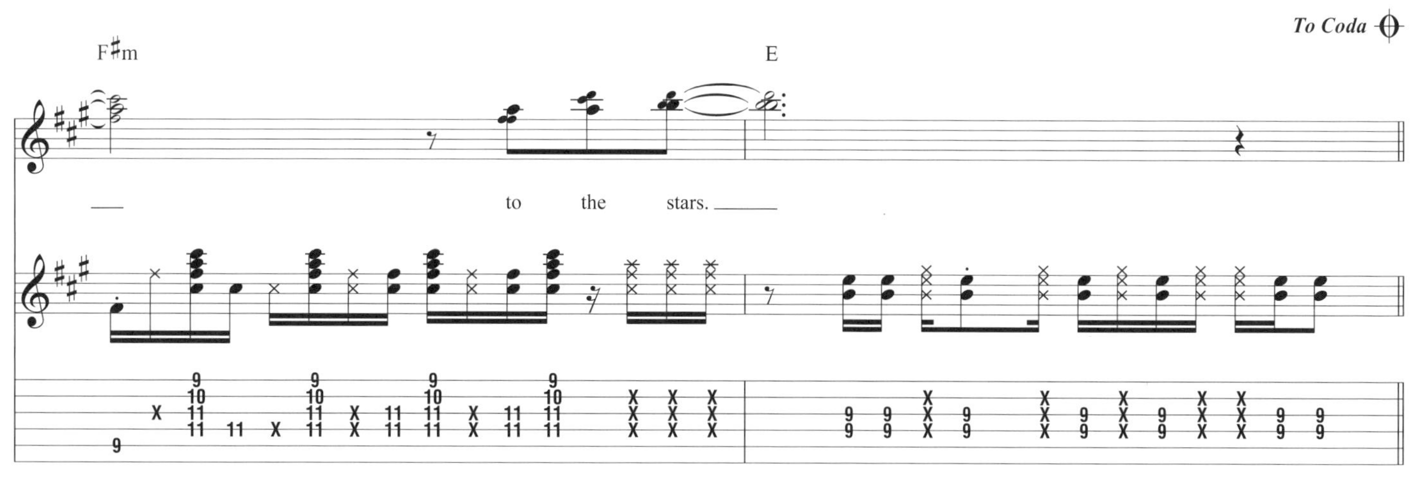

Chorus

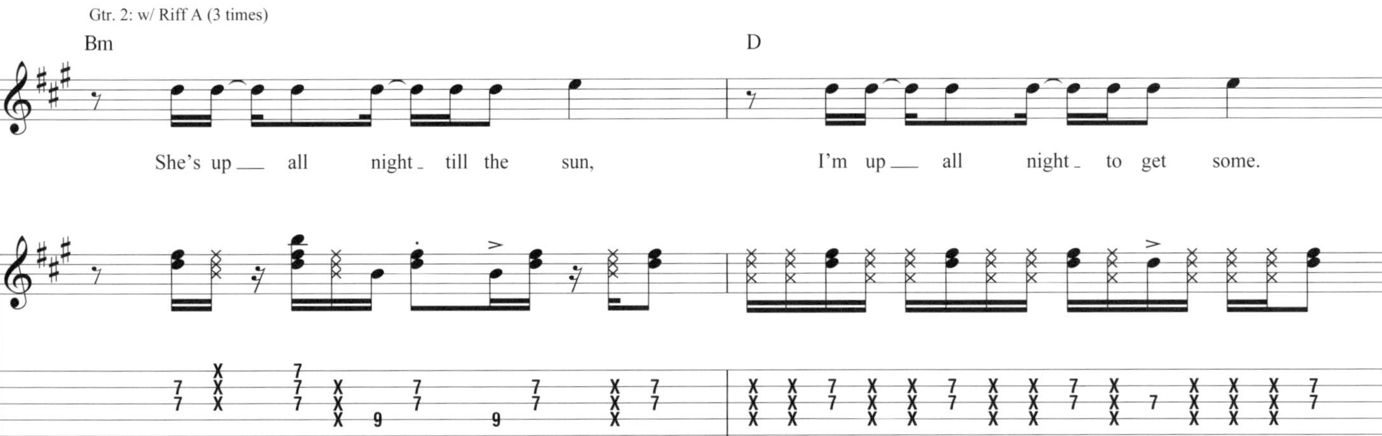
Gtr. 2: w/ Riff A (3 times)
Bm
D
She's up all night till the sun,
I'm up all night to get some.

F#m
E
She's up all night for good fun,
I'm up all night to get luck - y.

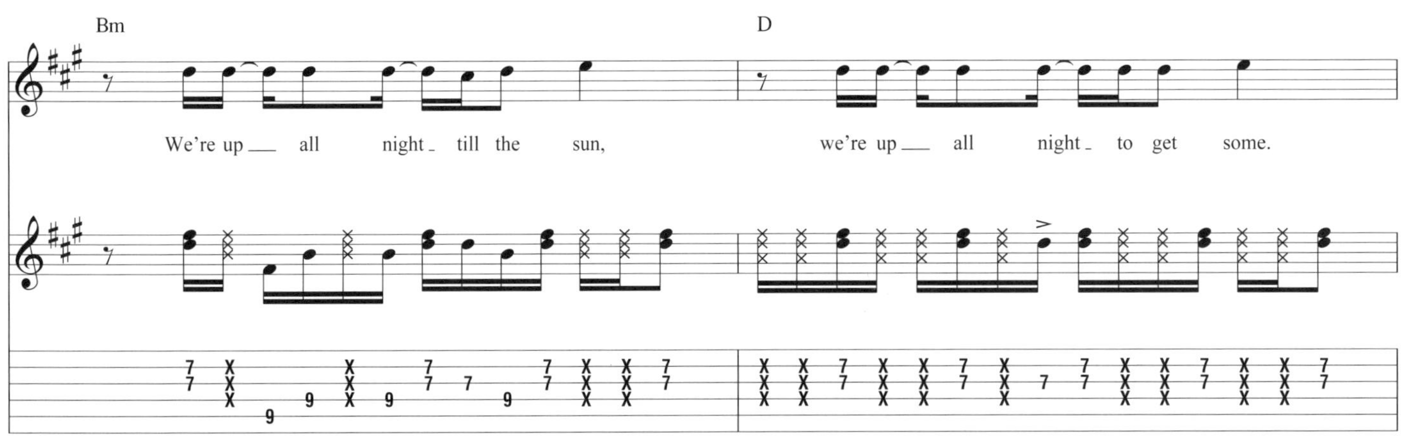
Bm
D
We're up all night till the sun,
we're up all night to get some.

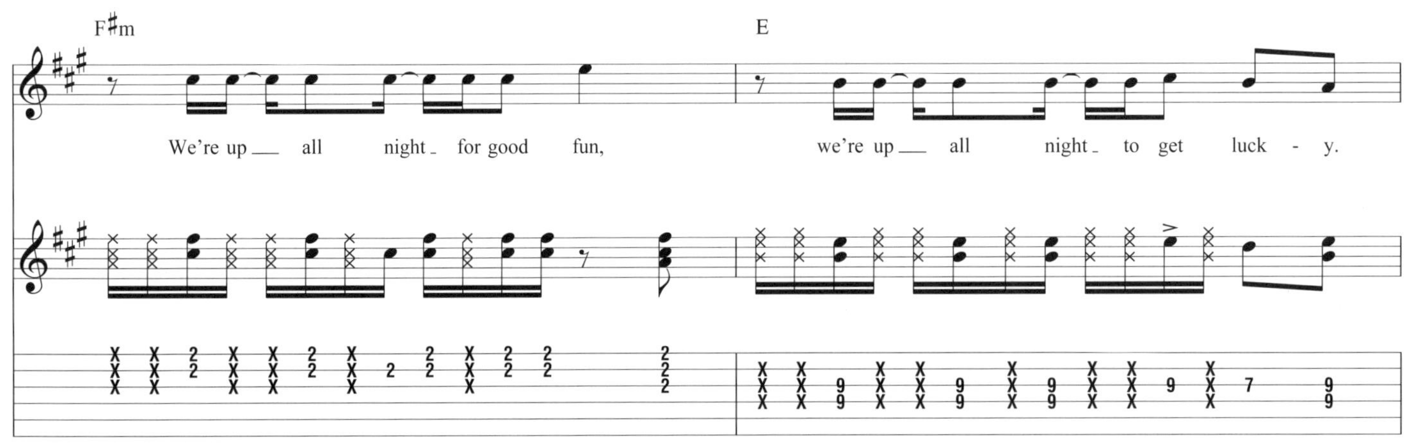
F#m
E
We're up all night for good fun,
we're up all night to get luck - y.

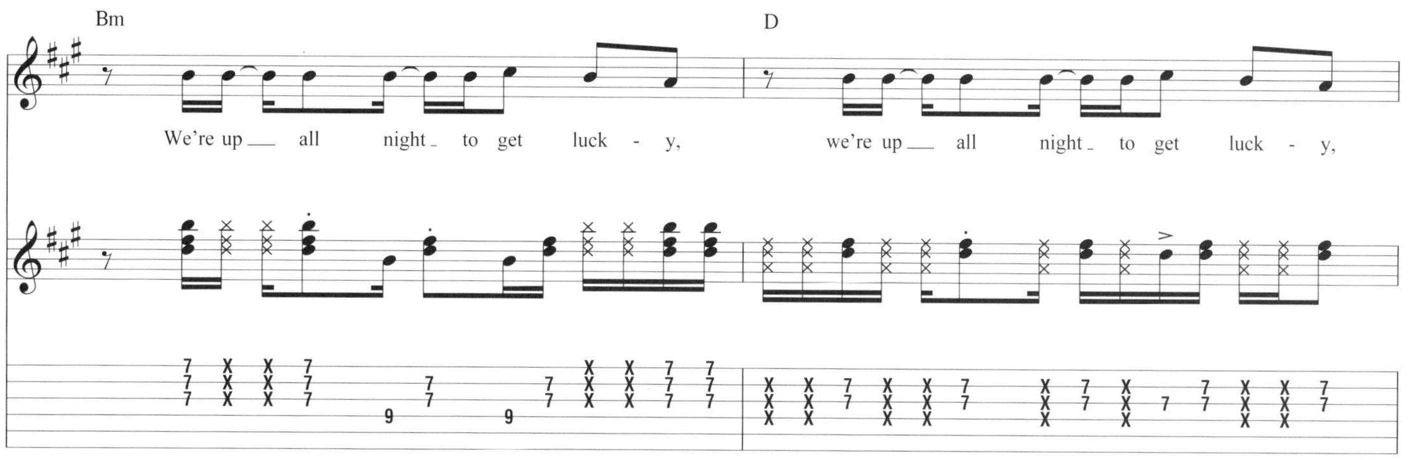
Bm
D
We're up all night to get luck - y,
we're up all night to get luck - y,

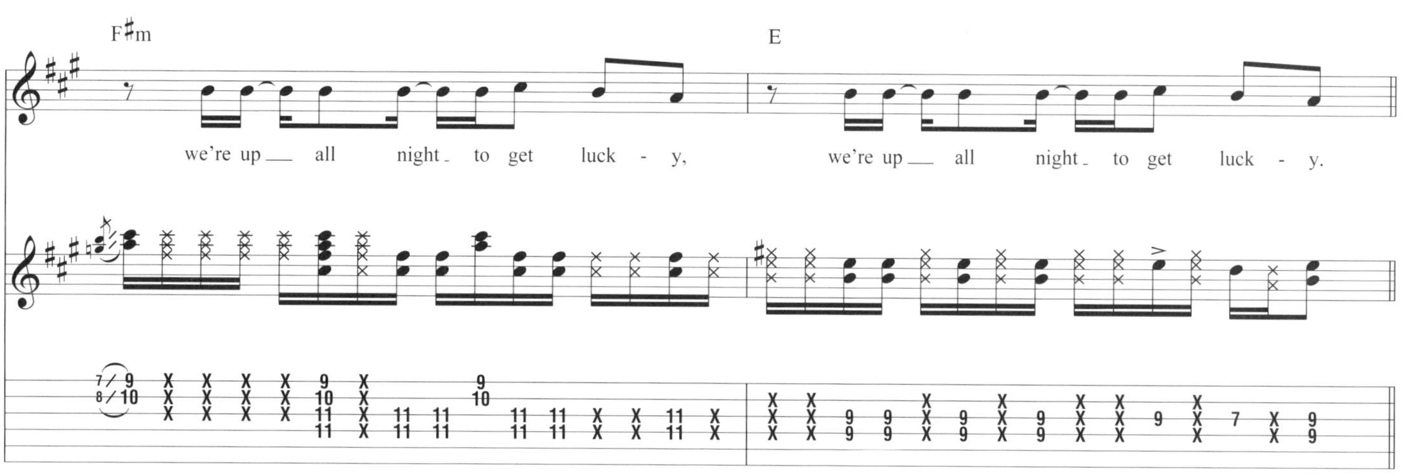
F♯m
E
we're up all night to get luck - y,
we're up all night to get luck - y.

Interlude

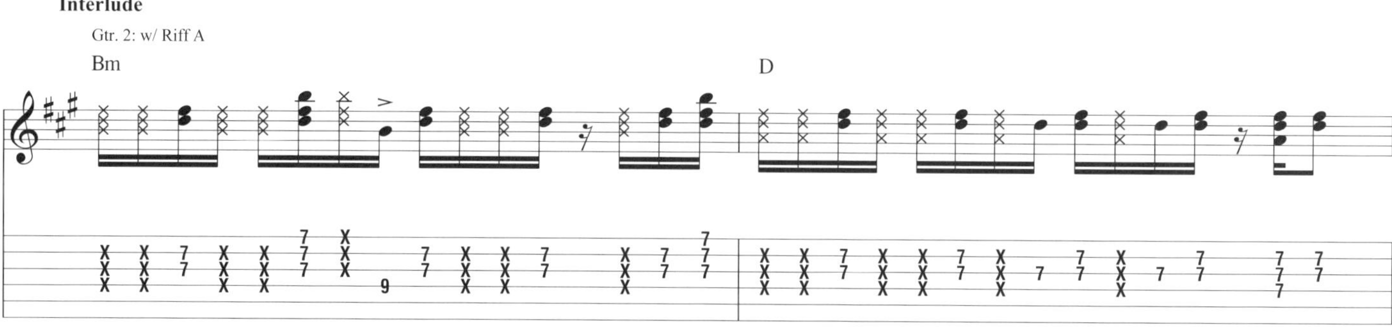
Gtr. 2: w/ Riff A
Bm
D

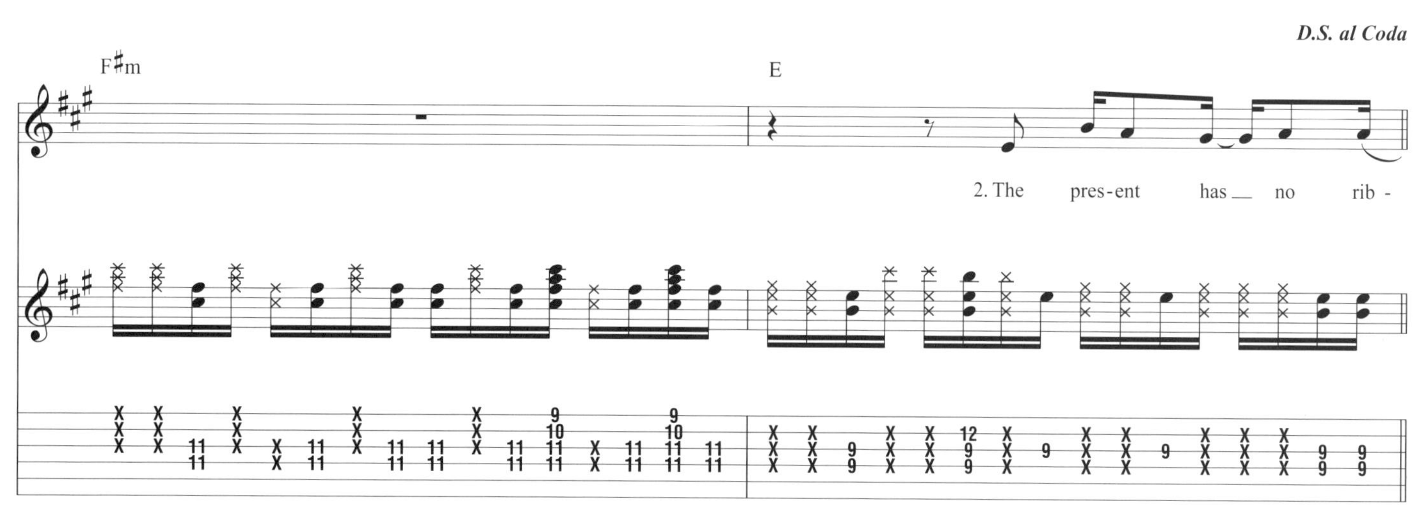
D.S. al Coda
F♯m
E
2. The pres-ent has no rib -

Coda
Chorus
Gtr. 2: w/ Riff A (2 times)
Bm
D
She's up __ all night _ till the sun,
I'm up __ all night _ to get some.
F♯m
E
She's up __ all night _ for good fun,
I'm up __ all night _ to get __ luck - y.
Bm
D
We're up __ all night _ till the sun,
we're up __ all night _ to get some.
F♯m
E
We're up __ all night _ for good fun,
we're up __ all night _ to get __ luck - y.

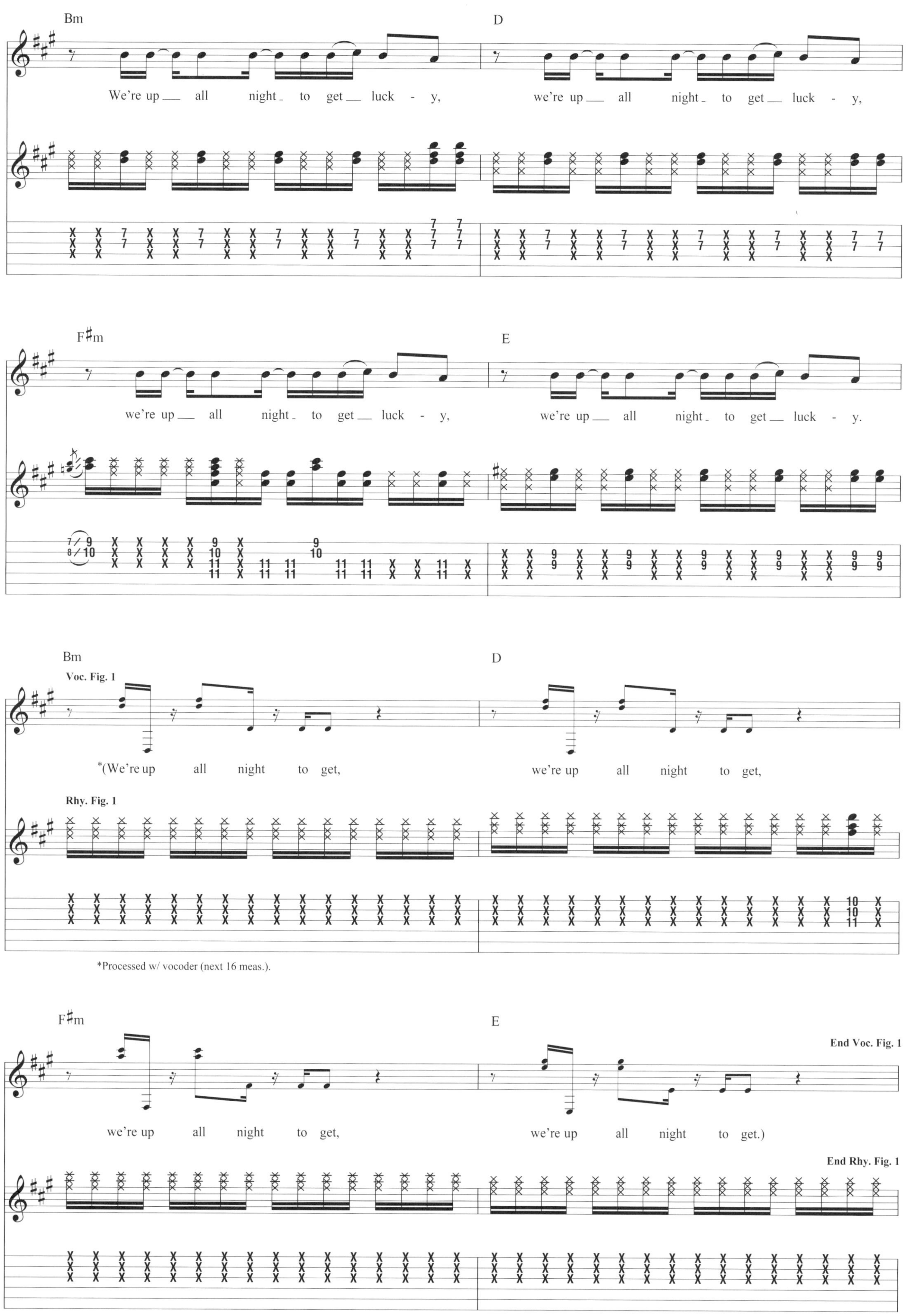
Bm
D
We're up all night to get luck - y,
we're up all night to get luck - y,
F♯m
E
we're up all night to get luck - y,
we're up all night to get luck - y.
Bm
D
Voc. Fig. 1
*(We're up all night to get,
we're up all night to get,
Rhy. Fig. 1
*Processed w/ vocoder (next 16 meas.).
F♯m
E
End Voc. Fig. 1
we're up all night to get,
we're up all night to get.)
End Rhy. Fig. 1

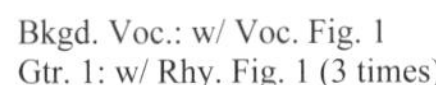
Bkgd. Voc.: w/ Voc. Fig. 1
Gtr. 1: w/ Rhy. Fig. 1 (3 times)
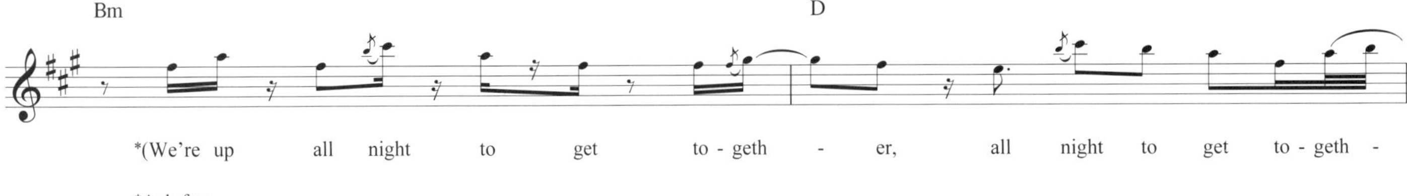
Bm
D
*(We're up all night to get to - geth - er, all night to get to - geth -
*As before
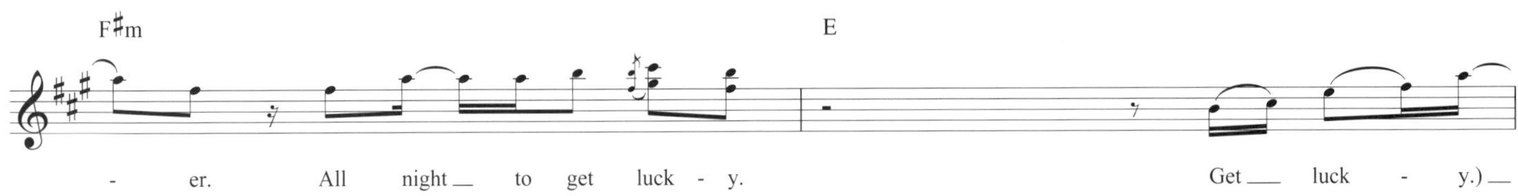
F♯m
E
- er. All night to get luck - y. Get luck - y.)
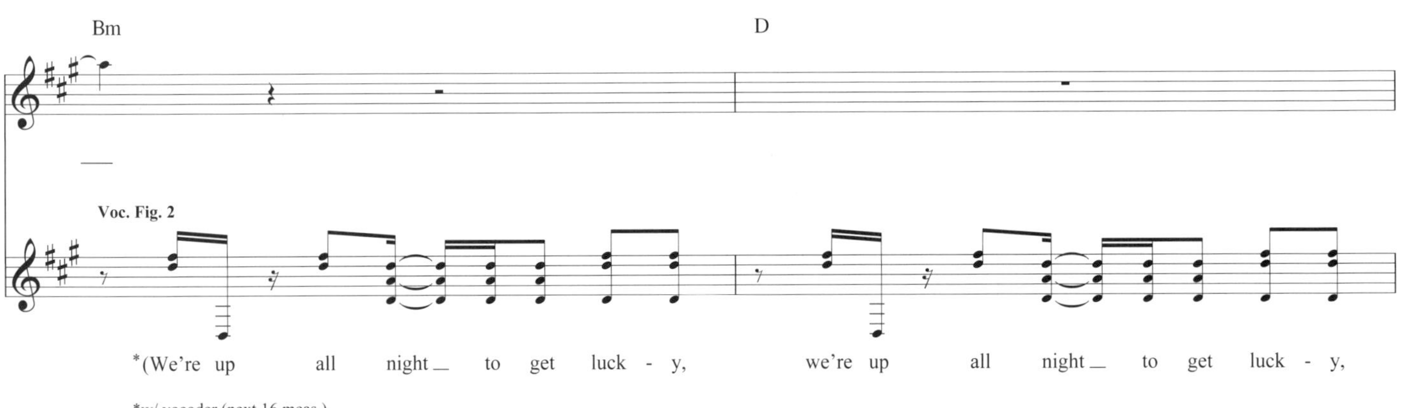
Bm
D
Voc. Fig. 2
*(We're up all night to get luck - y, we're up all night to get luck - y,
*w/ vocoder (next 16 meas.)
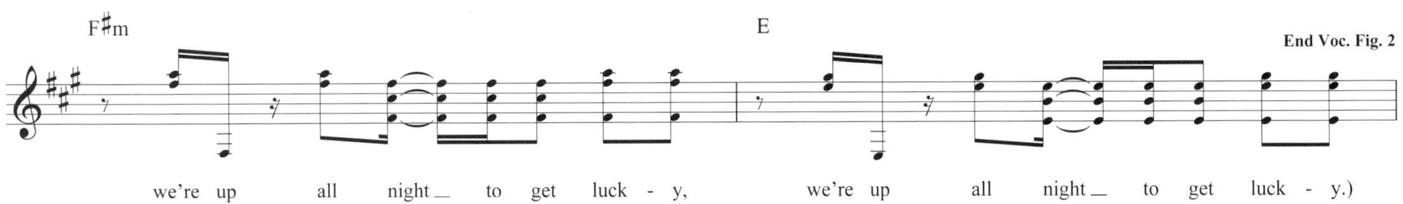
F♯m
E
End Voc. Fig. 2
we're up all night to get luck - y, we're up all night to get luck - y.)

Bkgd. Voc.: w/ Voc. Fig. 2
Bm
D
F♯m
E
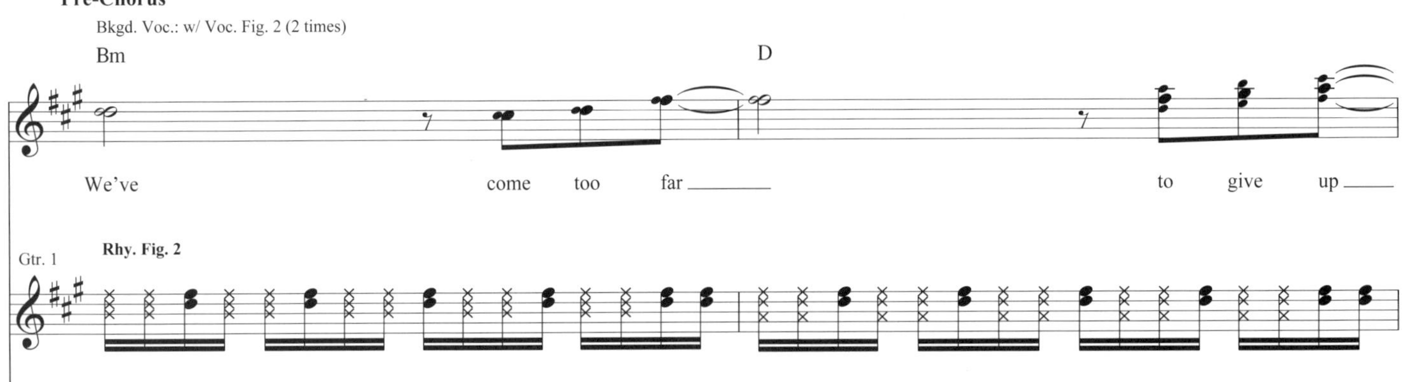
Pre-Chorus
Bkgd. Voc.: w/ Voc. Fig. 2 (2 times)
Bm
D
We've come too far to give up
Gtr. 1
Rhy. Fig. 2

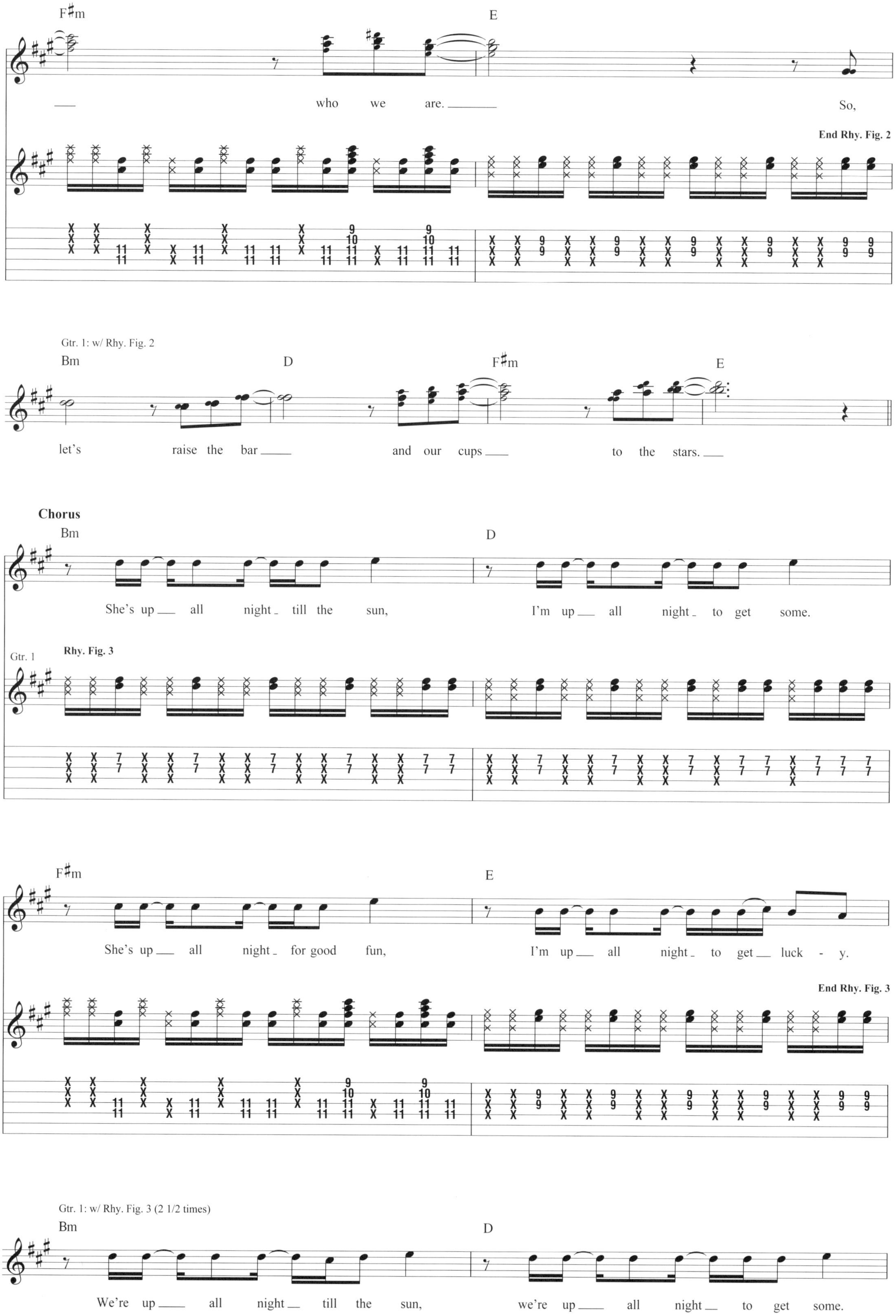

F♯m E

who we are. So,

End Rhy. Fig. 2

Gtr. 1: w/ Rhy. Fig. 2

Bm D F♯m E

let's raise the bar and our cups to the stars.

Chorus

Bm D

She's up all night till the sun, I'm up all night to get some.

Gtr. 1

Rhy. Fig. 3

F♯m E

She's up all night for good fun, I'm up all night to get luck - y.

End Rhy. Fig. 3

Gtr. 1: w/ Rhy. Fig. 3 (2 1/2 times)

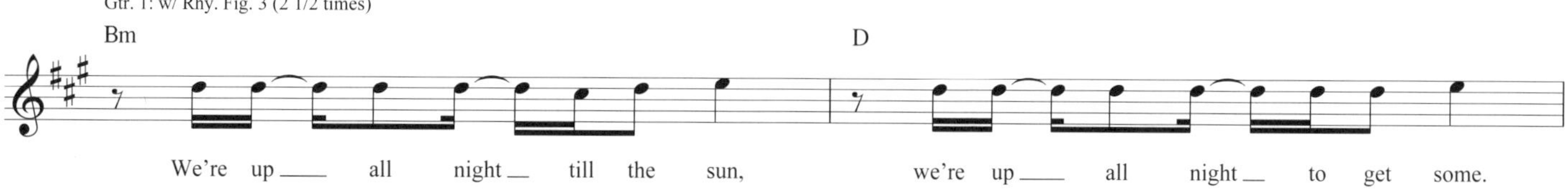

F♯m E

We're up __ all night __ for good fun, we're up __ all night __ to get __ luck - y.

Bm D

We're up __ all night __ to get __ luck - y, we're up __ all night __ to get __ luck - y,

F♯m E

we're up __ all night __ to get __ luck - y, we're up __ all night __ to get __ luck - y,

Bm D

we're up __ all night __ to get __ luck - y, we're up __ all night __ to get __ luck - y,

F♯m E

we're up __ all night __ to get __ luck - y, we're up __ all night __ to get __ luck - y.

Gtr. 1

Outro

Gtr. 2: w/ Riff A (till fade)

Bm D

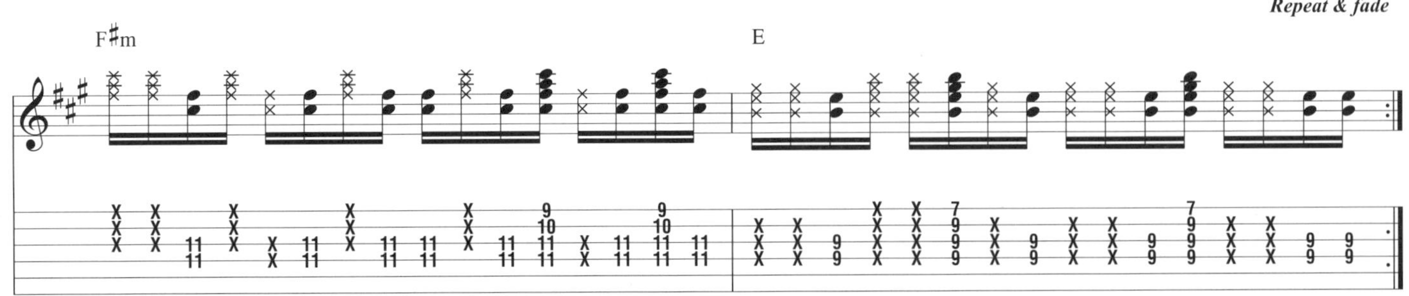

from Phillip Phillips - *The World from the Side of the Moon*

Home

Words and Music by Greg Holden and Drew Pearson

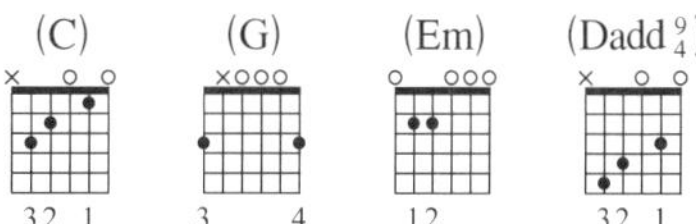

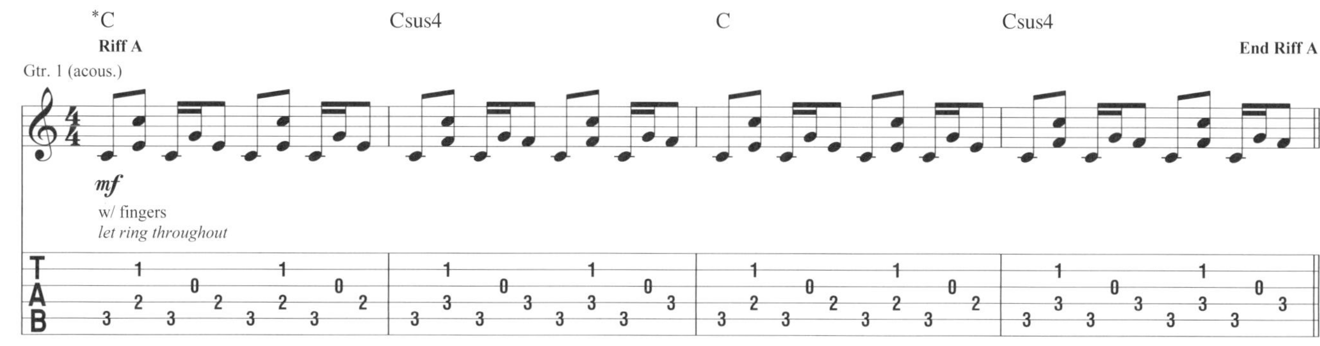

Verse

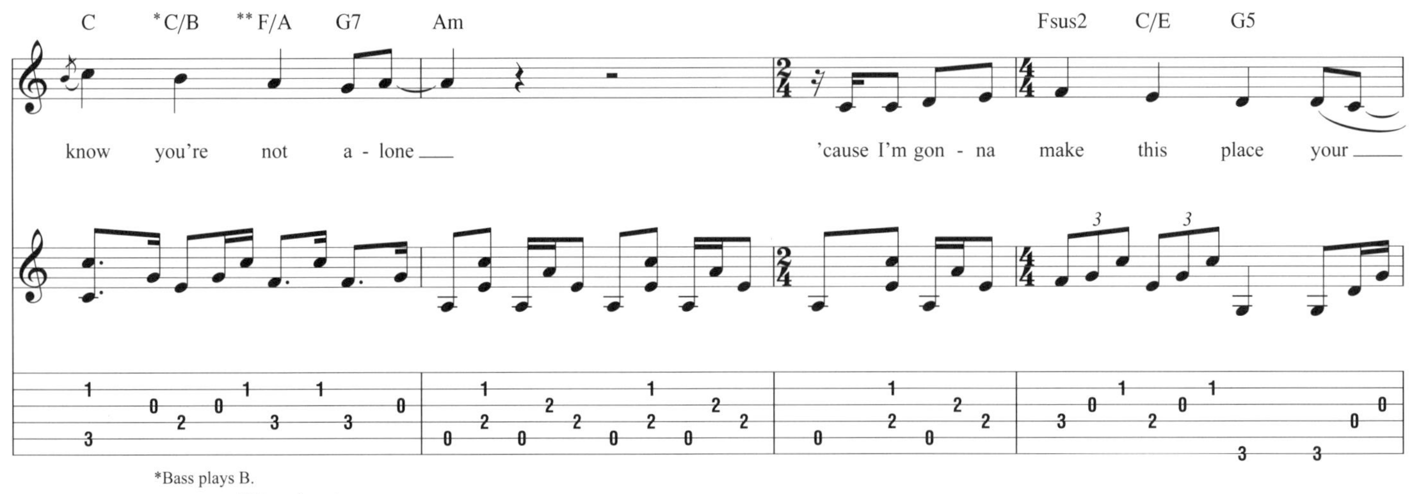
C
*C/B
**F/A
G7
Am
Fsus2
C/E
G5
know you're not a - lone
'cause I'm gon - na make this place your
*Bass plays B.
**Bass plays A.

C/G
home.
Gtr. 1
End Riff B
***Gtr. 2 (acous.)
mp
***Two gtrs. arr. for one.

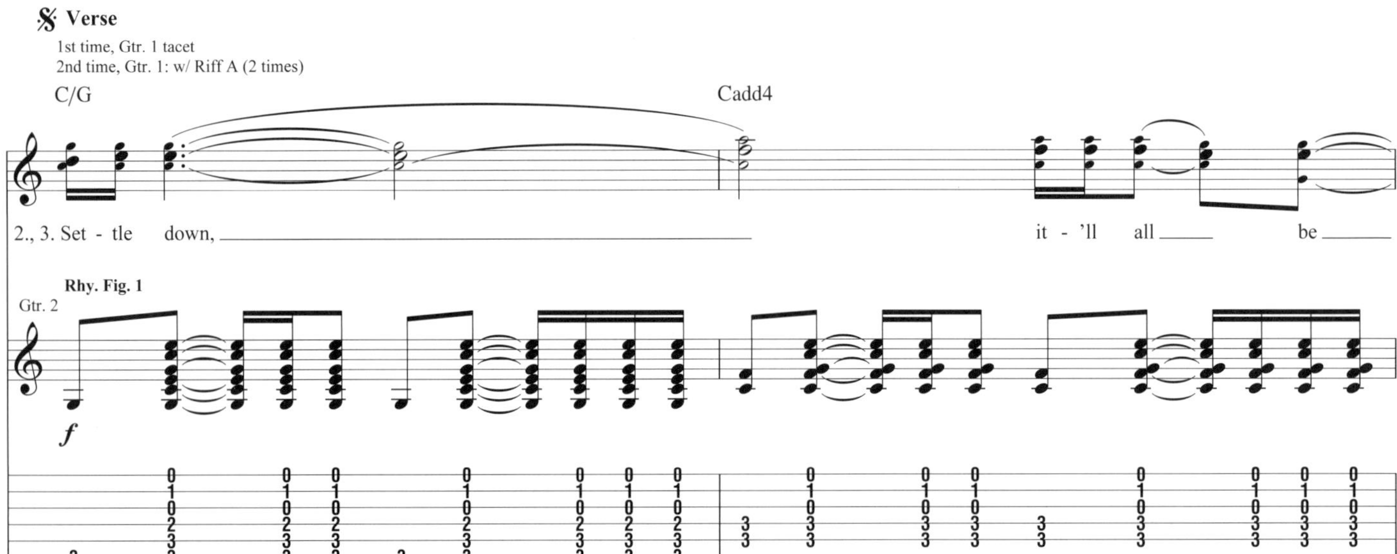
Verse
1st time, Gtr. 1 tacet
2nd time, Gtr. 1: w/ Riff A (2 times)
C/G
Cadd4
2., 3. Set - tle down,
it - 'll all be
Rhy. Fig. 1
Gtr. 2
f

C/G
Cadd4
clear.
End Rhy. Fig. 1
Gtr. 2: w/ Rhy. Fig. 1
C/G
Cadd4
C/G
Cadd4
Don't pay no mind to the de - mons, they fill you with fear. The
2nd time, Gtr. 1: w/ Riff B
Am
Cadd4
C/G
trou - ble, it might drag you down. If you get lost, you can al - ways be
(Oo.
Gtr. 2
G
C/G
C/B
Am
G
Am
found. Just know you're not a - lone
Ah.)

Chorus

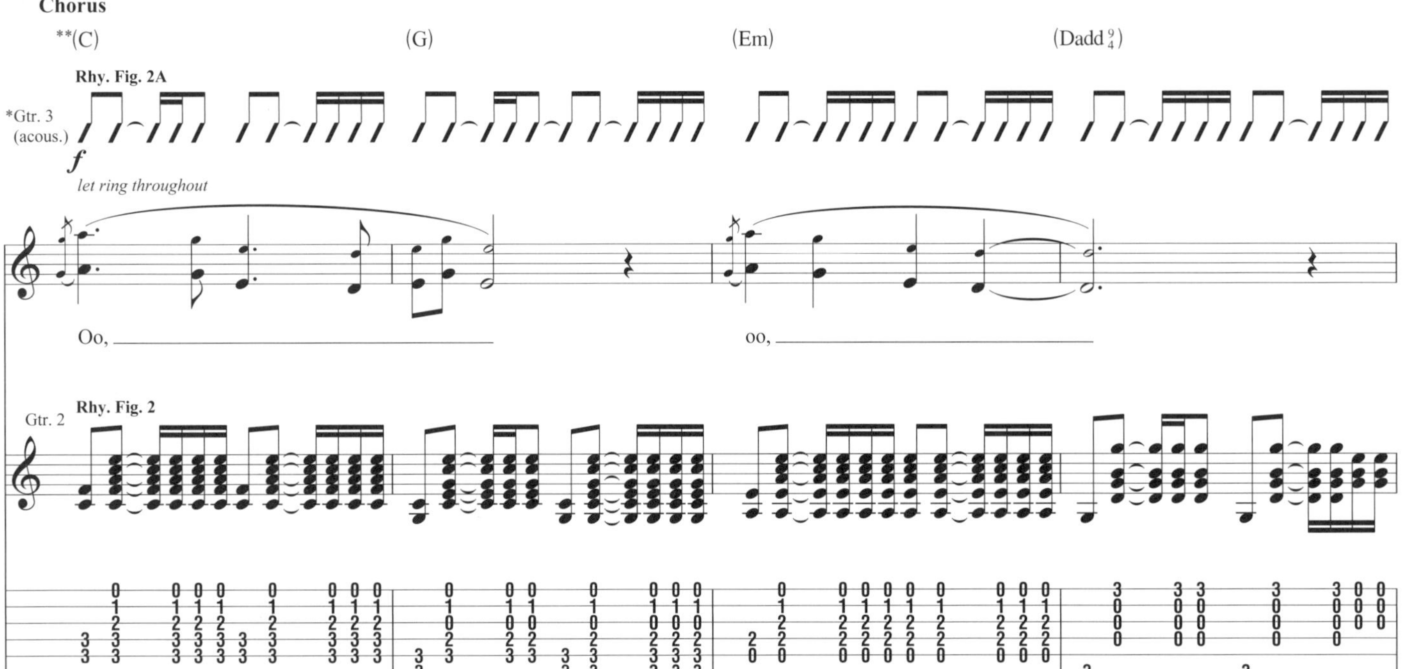

*Two gtrs. arr. for one.

**Symbols in parentheses represent chord names respective to capoed guitar. See top of first page for chord diagrams pertaining to rhythm slashes.

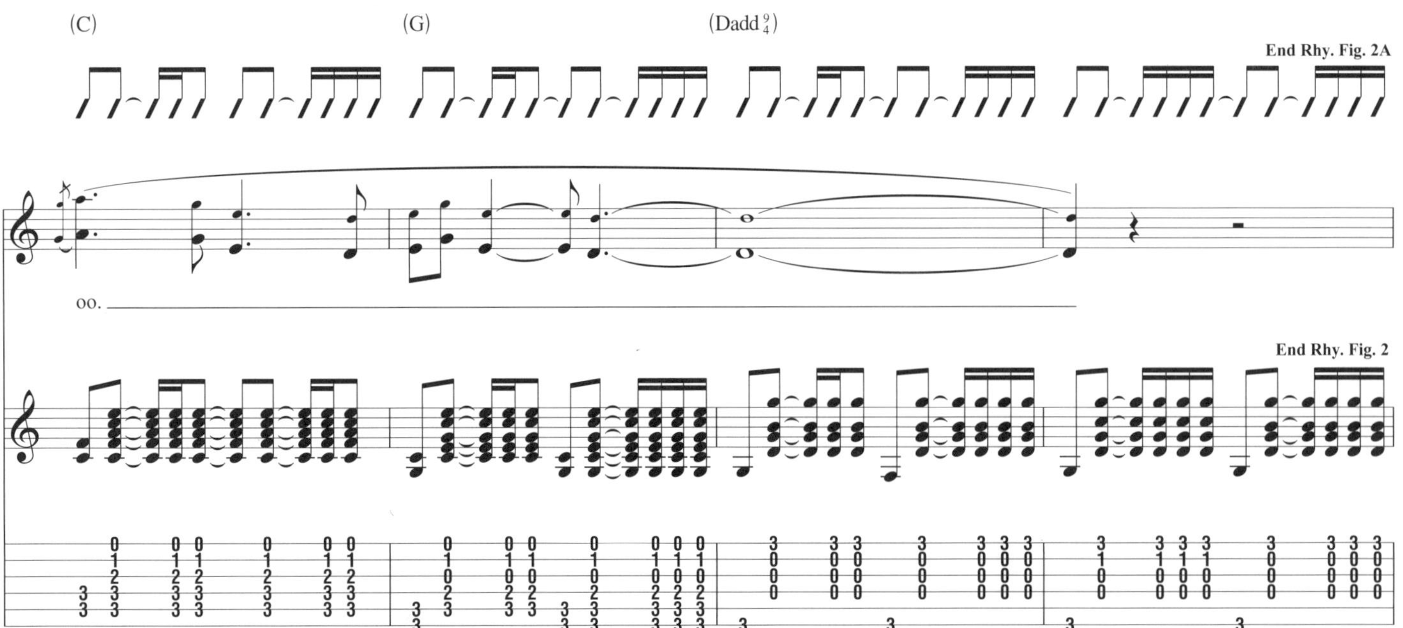

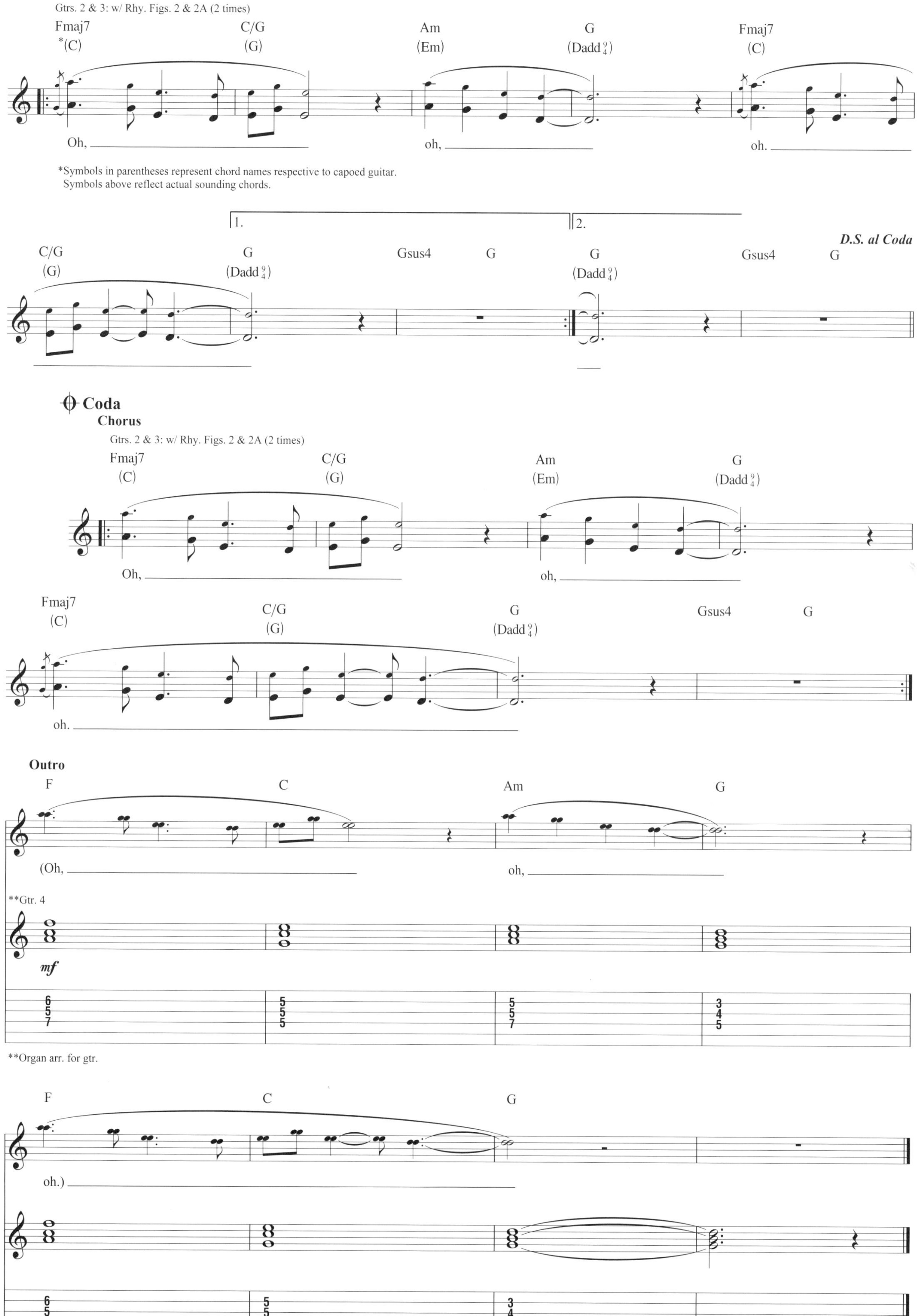
Gtrs. 2 & 3: w/ Rhy. Figs. 2 & 2A (2 times)
Fmaj7
*(C)
C/G
(G)
Am
(Em)
G
(Dadd 9/4)
Fmaj7
(C)
Oh,
oh,
oh.
*Symbols in parentheses represent chord names respective to capoed guitar. Symbols above reflect actual sounding chords.
1.
2.
D.S. al Coda
C/G
(G)
G
(Dadd 9/4)
Gsus4
G
G
(Dadd 9/4)
Gsus4
G
Coda
Chorus
Gtrs. 2 & 3: w/ Rhy. Figs. 2 & 2A (2 times)
Fmaj7
(C)
C/G
(G)
Am
(Em)
G
(Dadd 9/4)
Oh,
oh,
Fmaj7
(C)
C/G
(G)
G
(Dadd 9/4)
Gsus4
G
oh.
Outro
F
C
Am
G
(Oh,
oh,
**Gtr. 4
mf
**Organ arr. for gtr.
F
C
G
oh.)

*from Mumford & Sons - *Babel*

I Will Wait

Words and Music by Mumford & Sons

Open D tuning, down 1/2 step:
(low to high) D♭-A♭-D♭-F-A♭-D♭

Intro
Moderately fast ♩ = 132

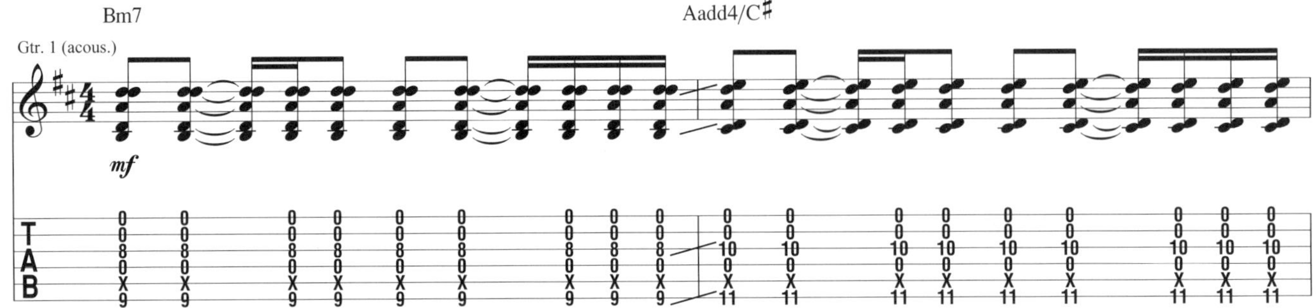

*This transcription matches the *Babel* studio recording. Live performances of this song are in a different key, different tuning, and utilize different chord voicings.

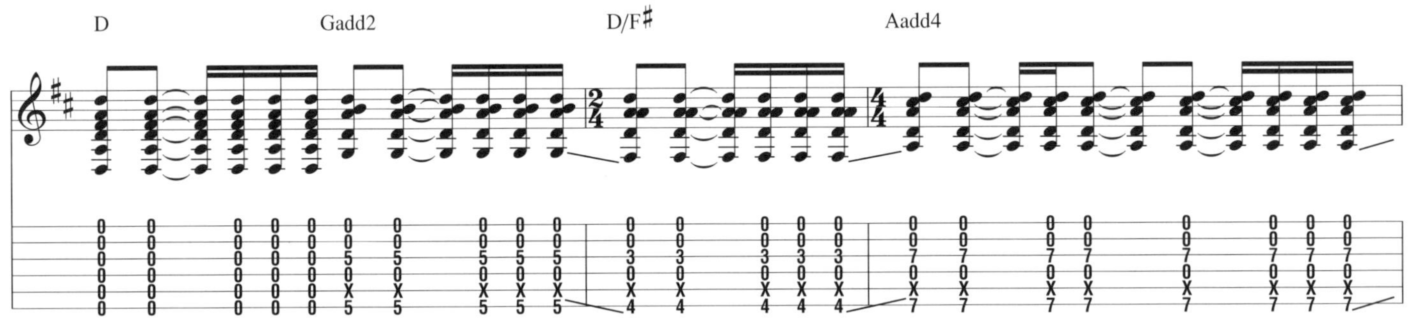

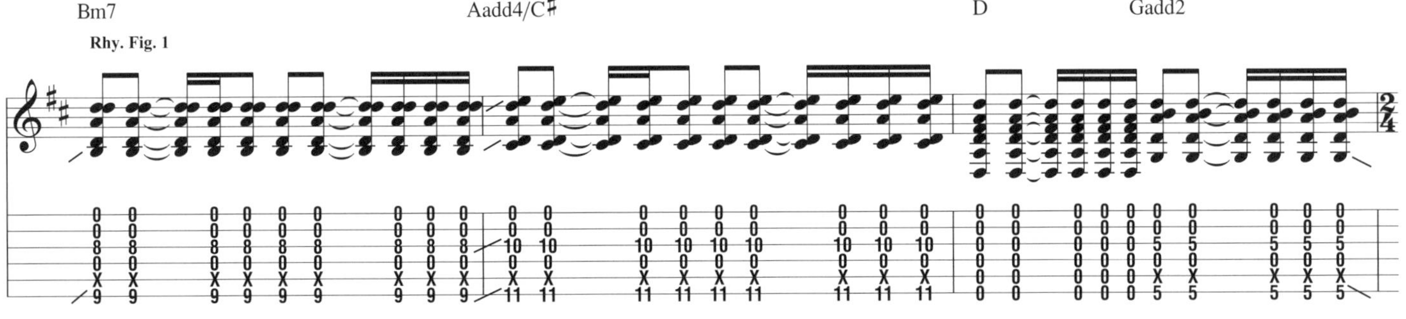

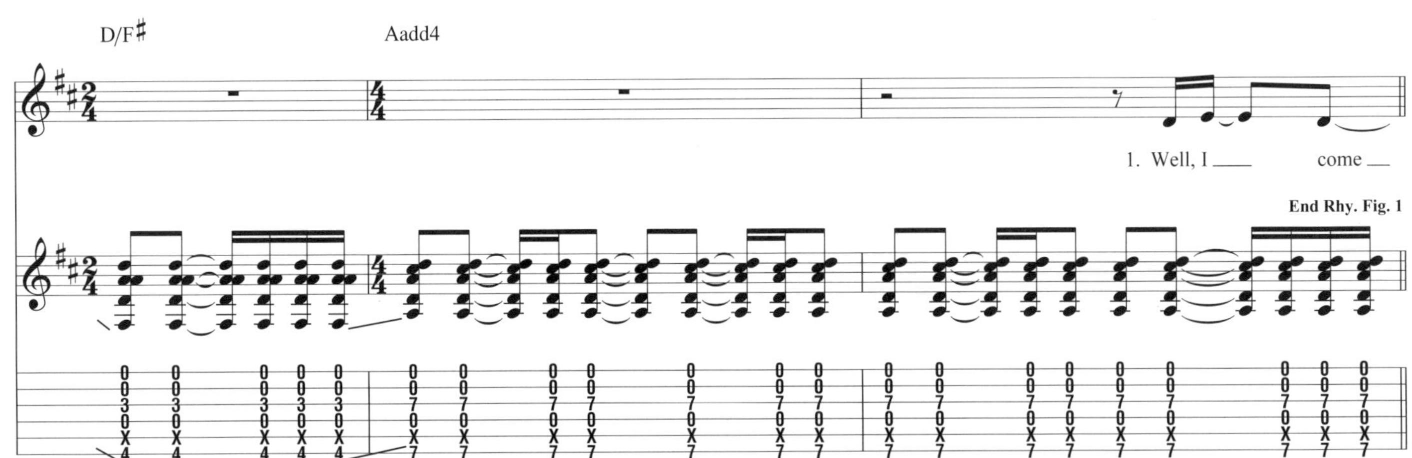

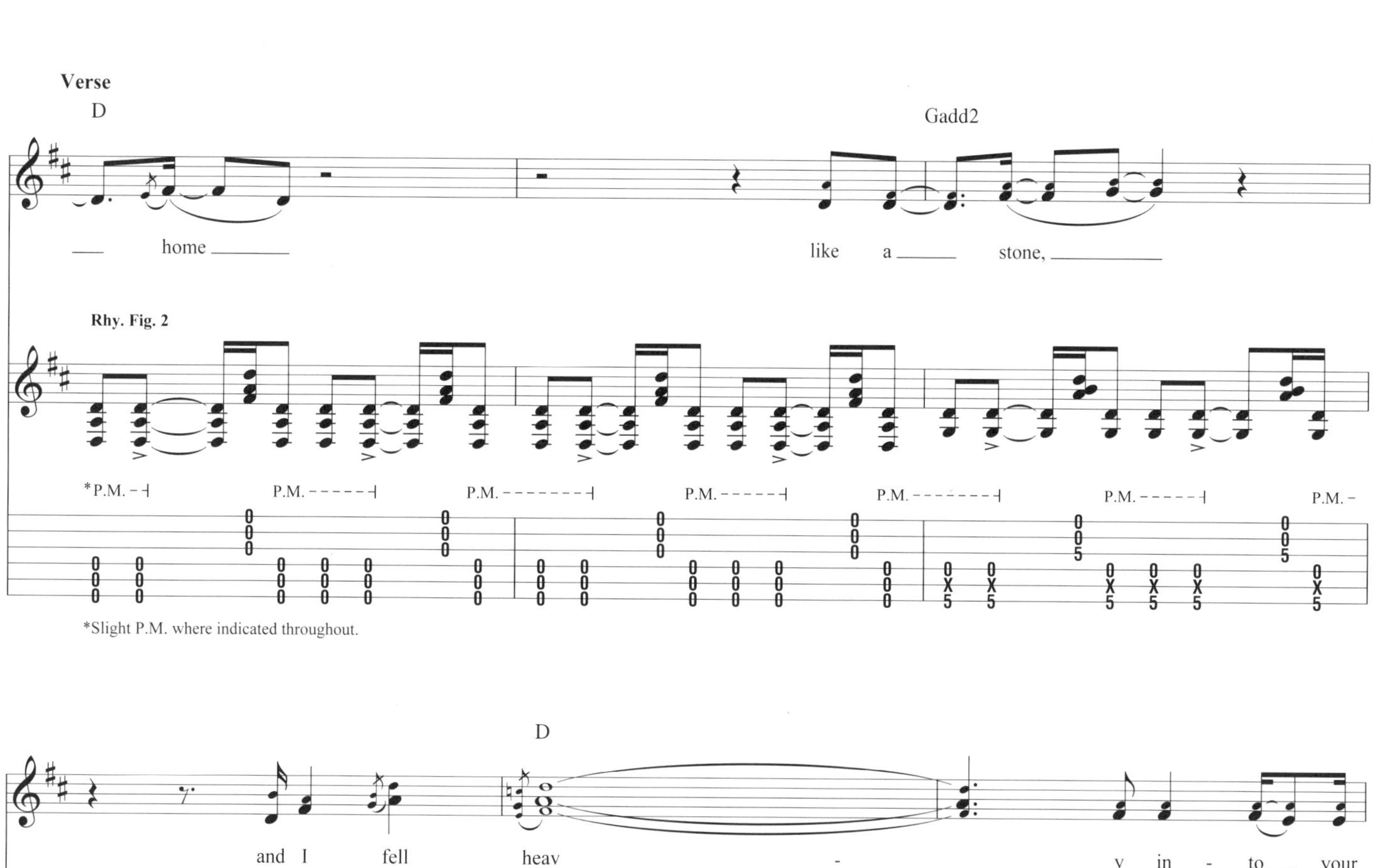
Verse
D
Gadd2
home
like a
stone,
Rhy. Fig. 2
*P.M.
P.M.
*Slight P.M. where indicated throughout.

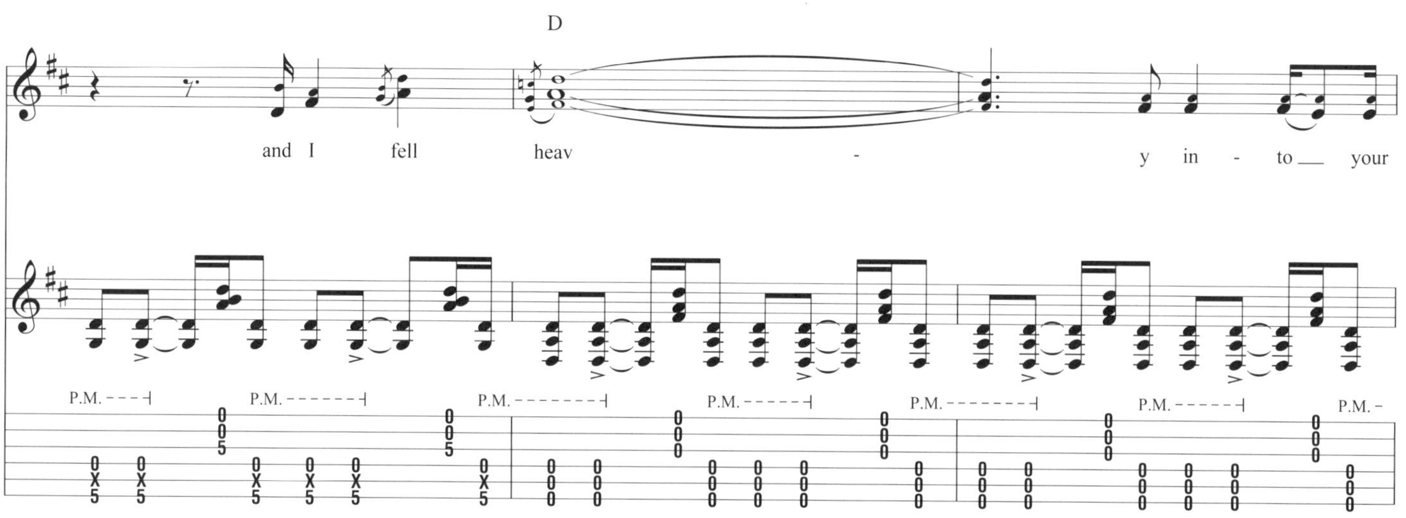
D
and I fell heav - y in - to your
P.M.

Aadd4
arms.
These days
End Rhy. Fig. 2
P.M.

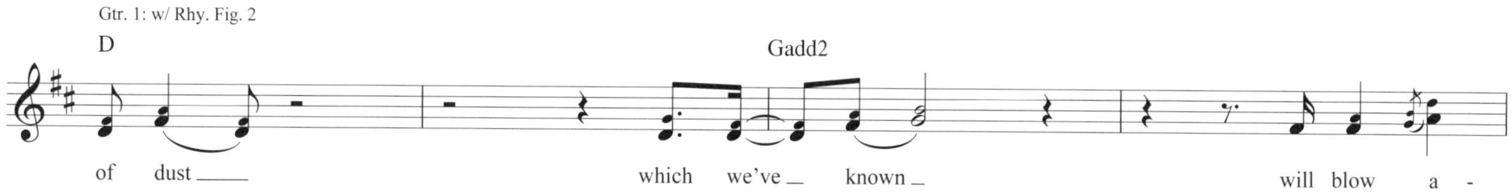
Gtr. 1: w/ Rhy. Fig. 2
D
Gadd2
of dust
which we've known
will blow a -

D
Aadd4
way with this new sun.
But

Pre-Chorus

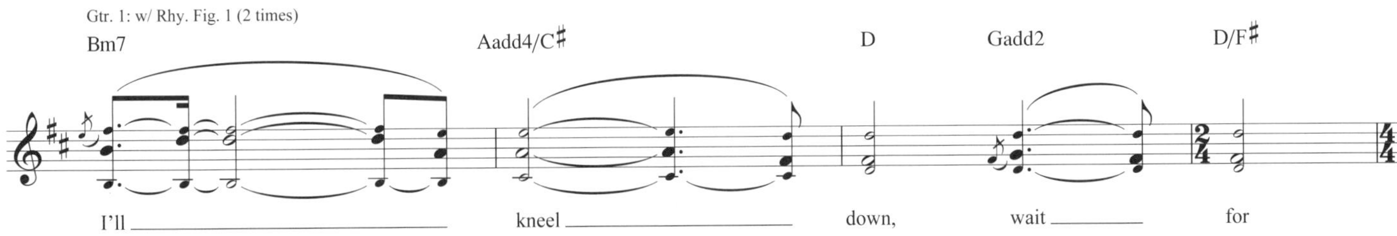
Gtr. 1: w/ Rhy. Fig. 1 (2 times)
Bm7
Aadd4/C♯
D
Gadd2
D/F♯
I'll kneel down, wait for

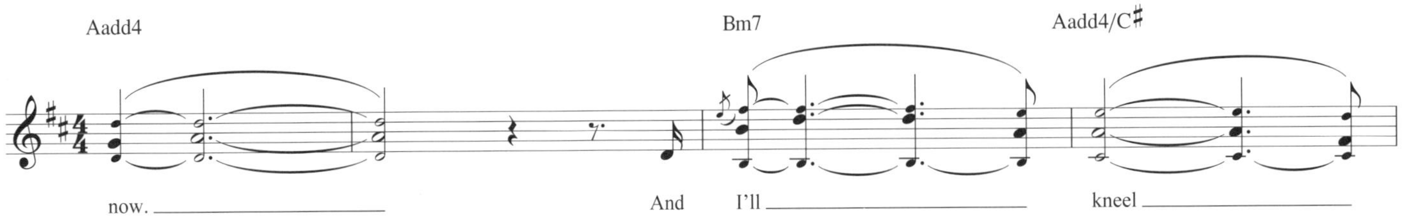
Aadd4
Bm7
Aadd4/C♯
now. And I'll kneel

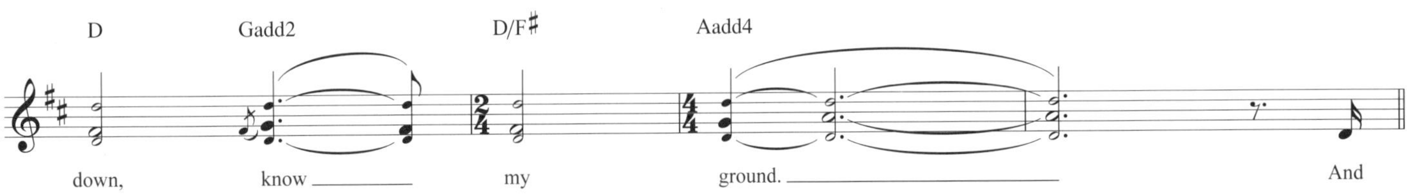
D
Gadd2
D/F♯
Aadd4
down, know my ground. And

Chorus
D
F♯m♭6
Aadd4
I will wait, I will wait for you.
And
Gtr. 1
Rhy. Fig. 3
End Rhy. Fig. 3

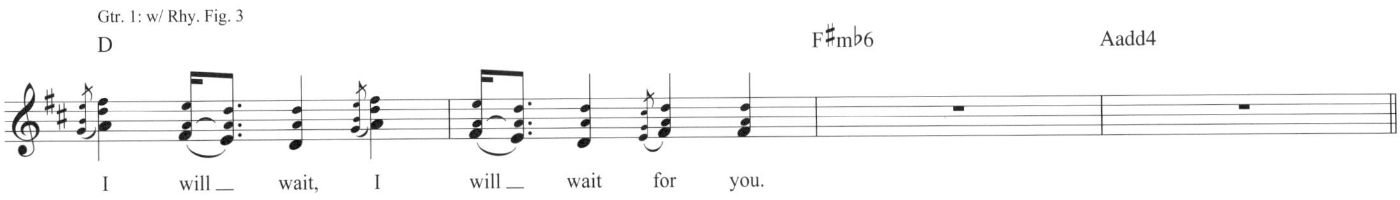
Gtr. 1: w/ Rhy. Fig. 3
D
F♯m♭6
Aadd4
I will wait, I will wait for you.

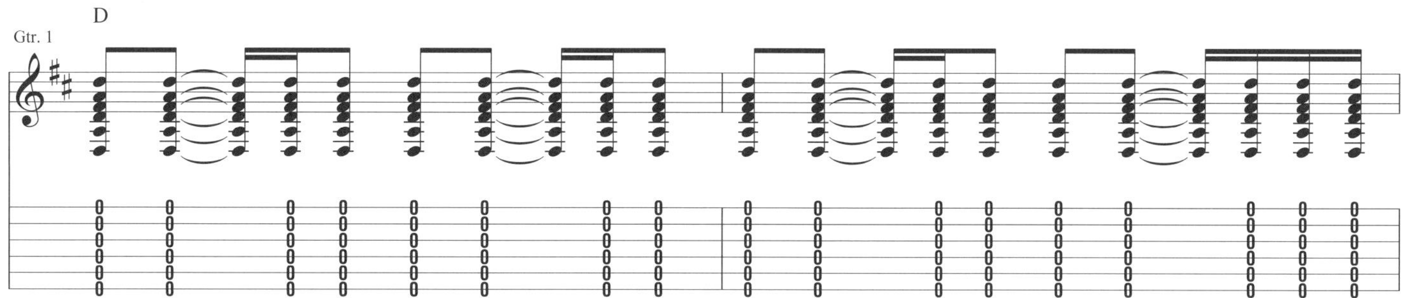

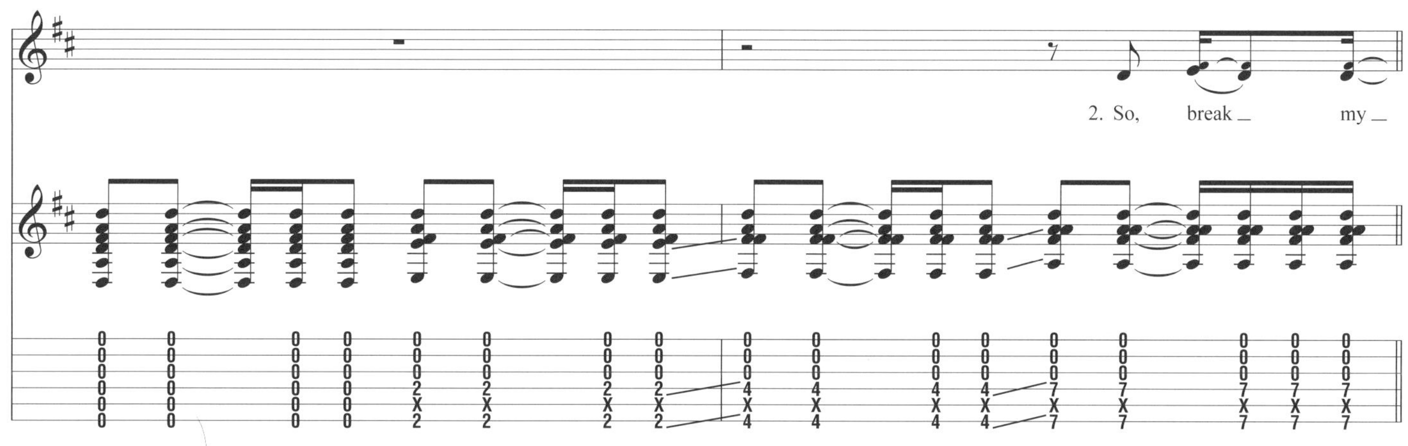

Verse

Gtr. 1: w/ Rhy. Fig. 2

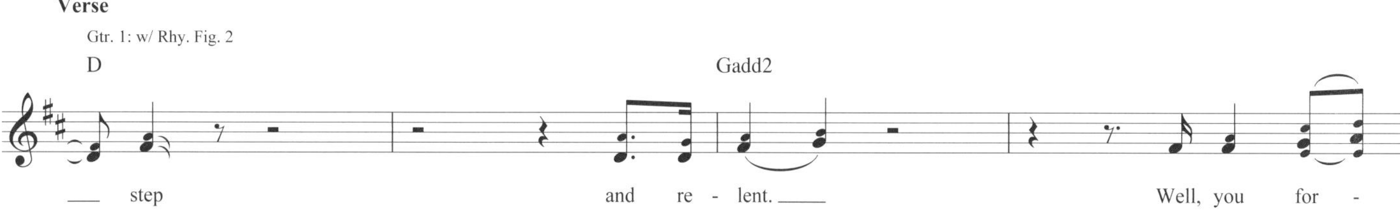

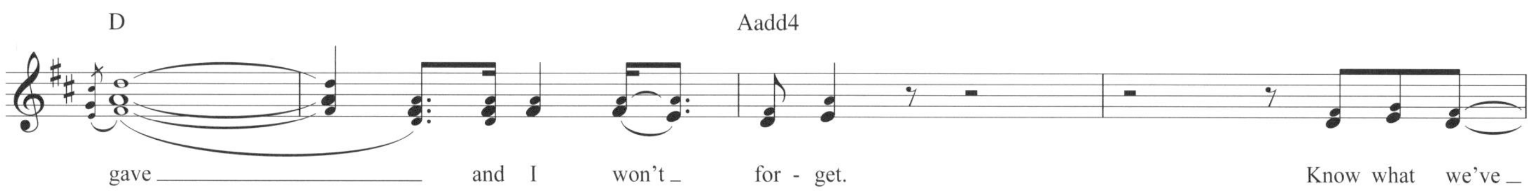

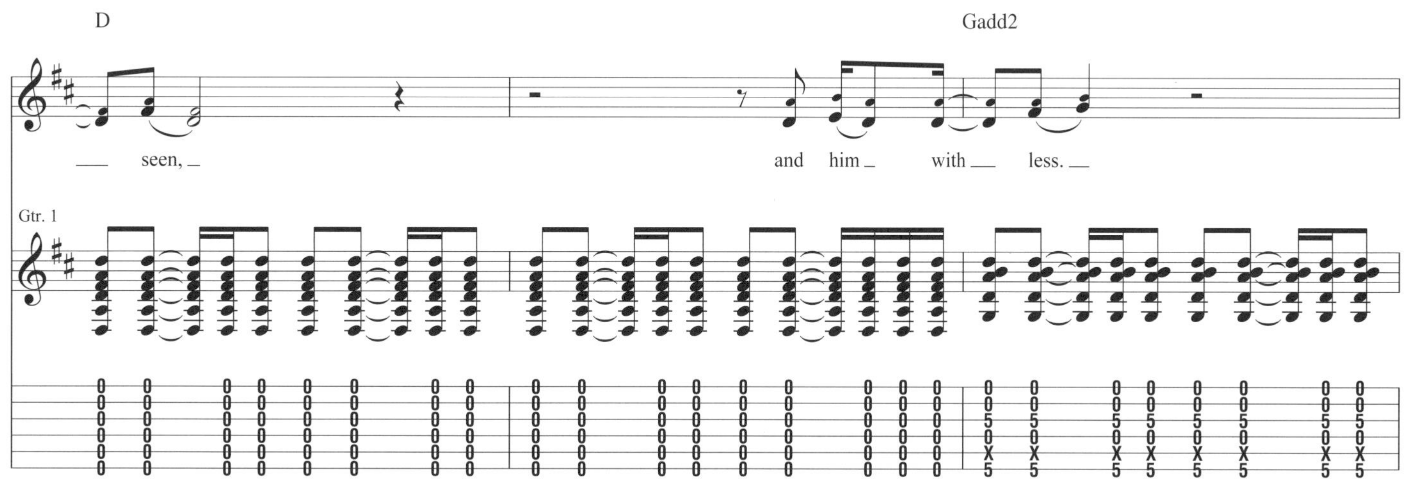

D
Now, in some way shake the ex -
Aadd4
- cess.
'Cause
Chorus
D
I will wait, I will wait for you.
Rhy. Fig. 4
f
F♯m♭6
Aadd4
And
End Rhy. Fig. 4

1st time, Gtr. 1: w/ Rhy. Fig. 4 (3 times)
2nd time, Gtr. 1: w/ Rhy. Fig. 4 (2 1/2 times)
D
F♯m♭6
Aadd4
I will wait, I will wait for you. And
D
F♯m♭6
Aadd4
I will wait, I will wait for you. And
To Coda
D
F♯m♭6
Aadd4
I will wait, I will wait for you. 3. Know I'll be
Verse
D
G
bold as well as strong, and use my
Gtr. 1
D
Aadd4
head a-long-side my heart. So take my

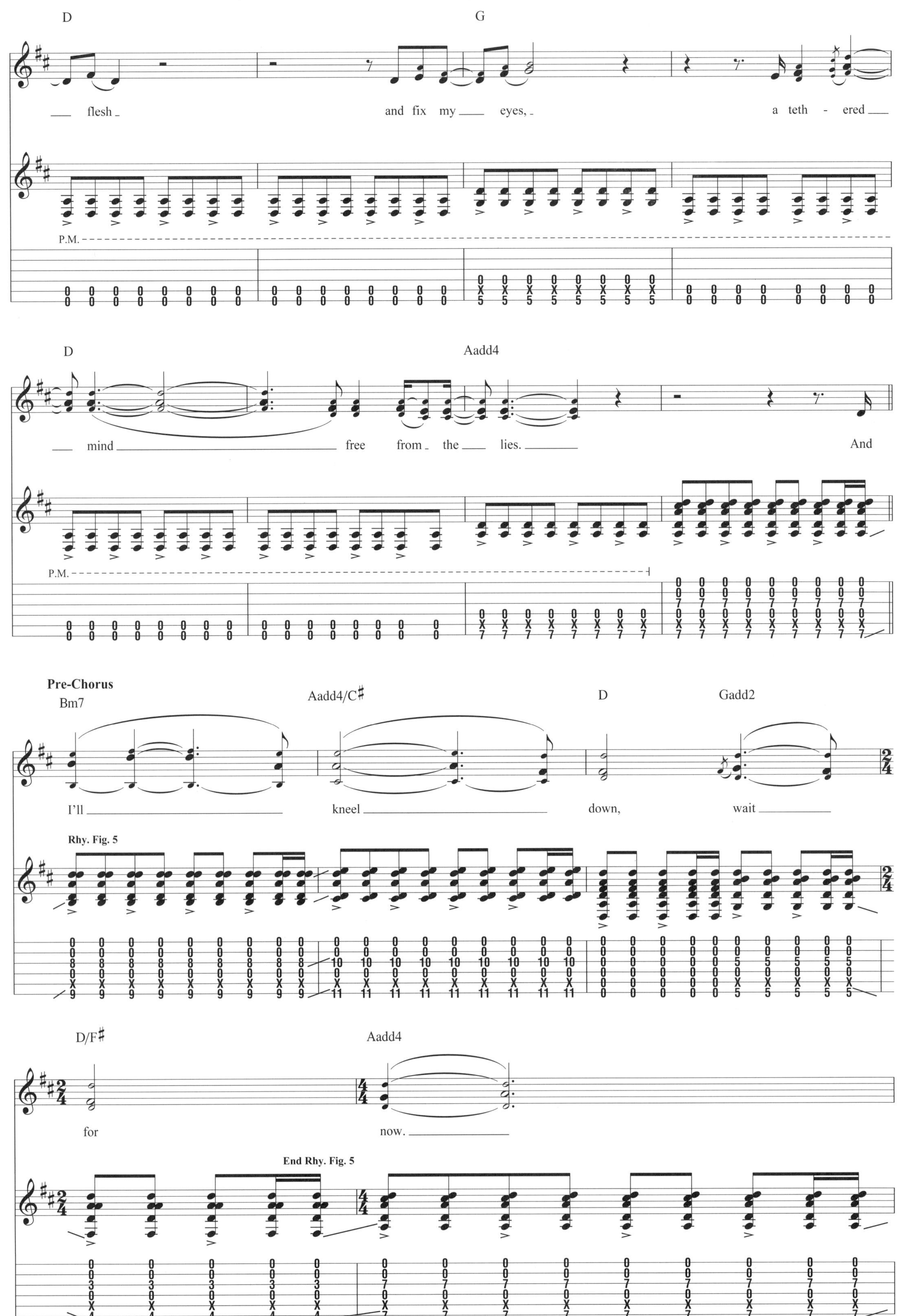
D
G
flesh
and fix my eyes,
a teth - ered
P.M.
D
Aadd4
mind
free from the lies.
And
P.M.
Pre-Chorus
Bm7
Aadd4/C♯
D
Gadd2
I'll
kneel
down,
wait
Rhy. Fig. 5
D/F♯
Aadd4
for
now.
End Rhy. Fig. 5

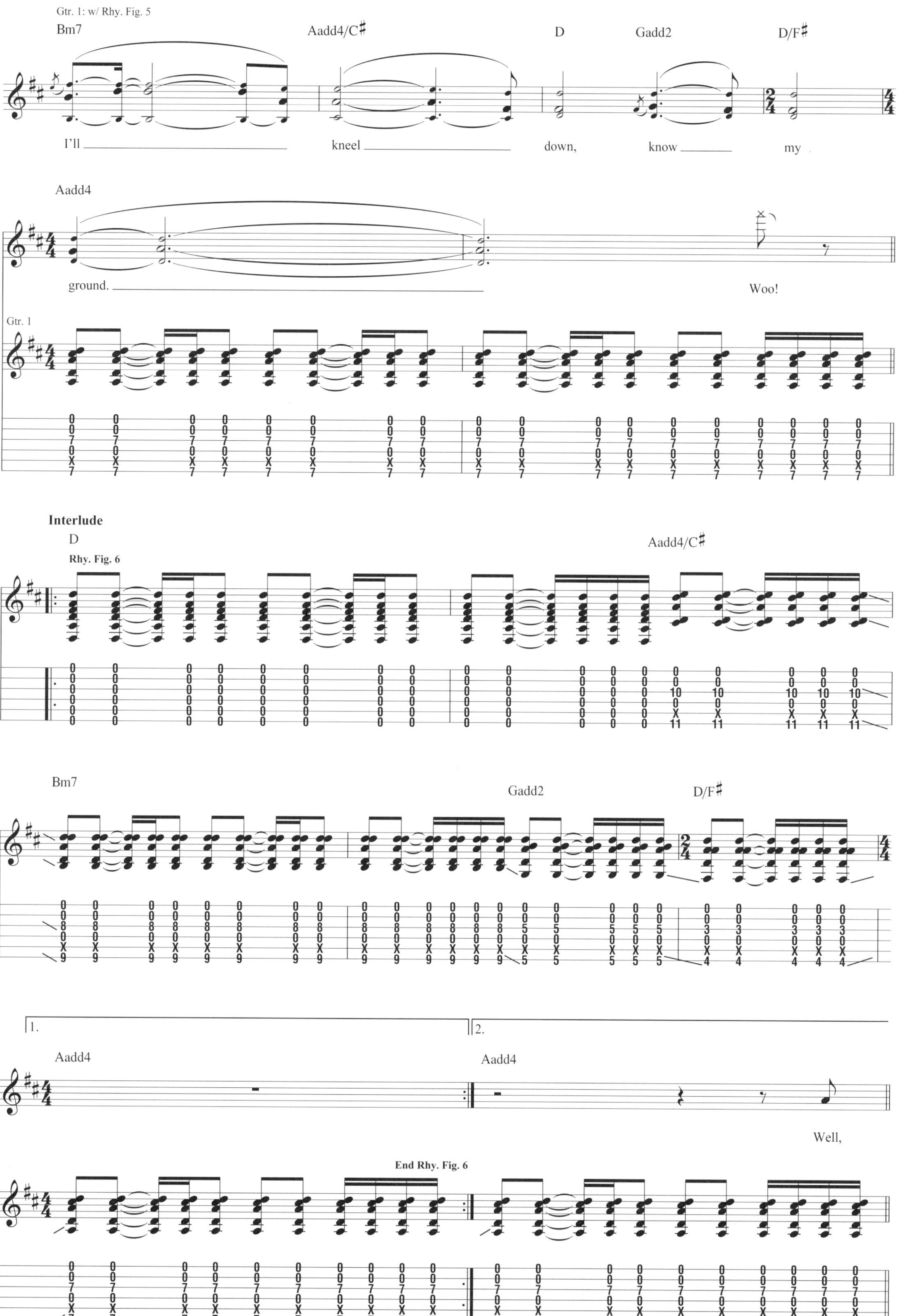
Gtr. 1: w/ Rhy. Fig. 5
Bm7
Aadd4/C♯
D
Gadd2
D/F♯
I'll kneel down, know my
Aadd4
ground.
Woo!
Gtr. 1
Interlude
D
Rhy. Fig. 6
Aadd4/C♯
Bm7
Gadd2
D/F♯
1.
2.
Aadd4
Aadd4
Well,
End Rhy. Fig. 6

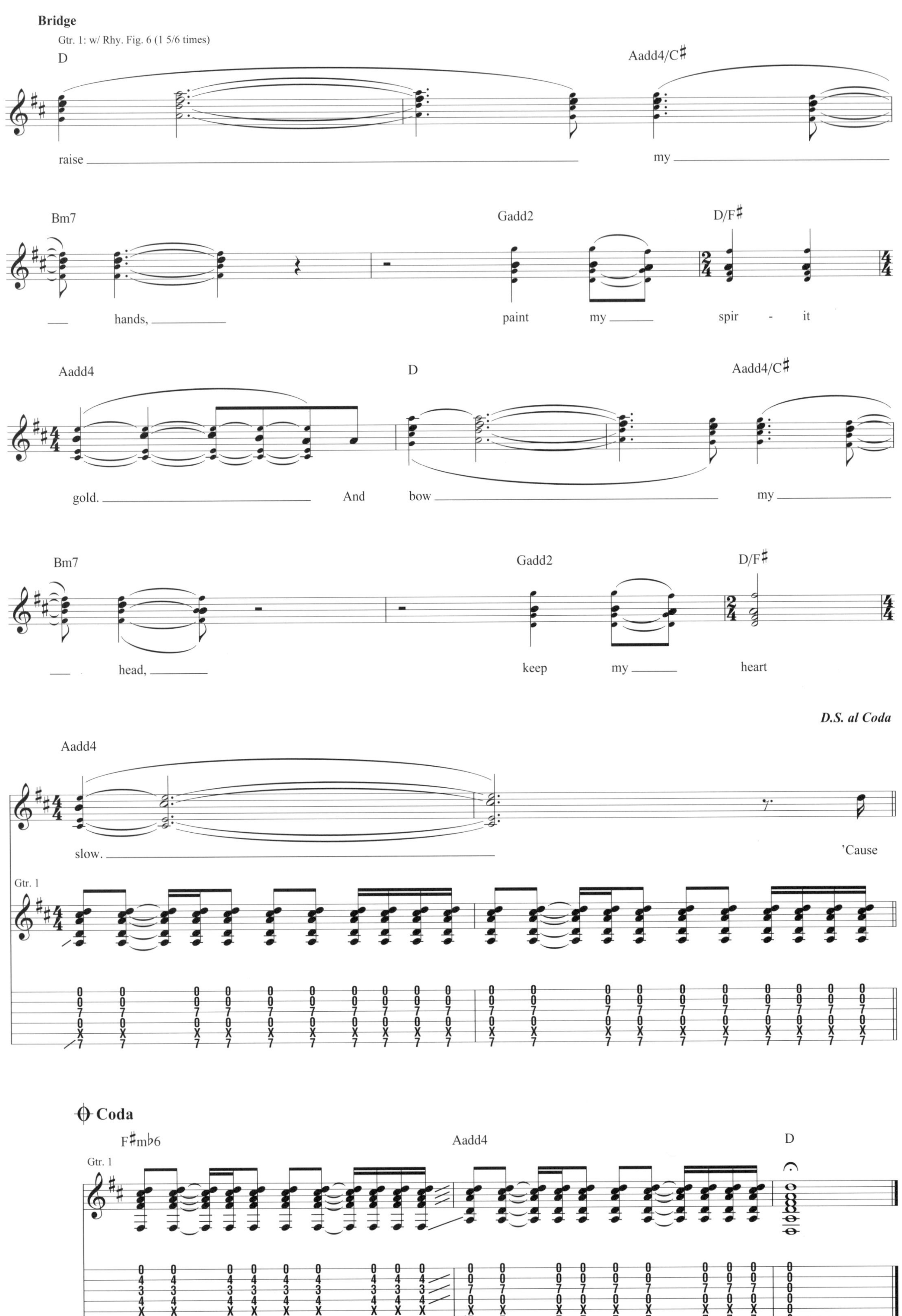

Bridge
Gtr. 1: w/ Rhy. Fig. 6 (1 5/6 times)
D
Aadd4/C♯
raise
my
Bm7
Gadd2
D/F♯
hands,
paint
my
spir - it
Aadd4
D
Aadd4/C♯
gold.
And
bow
my
Bm7
Gadd2
D/F♯
head,
keep
my
heart
D.S. al Coda
Aadd4
slow.
'Cause
Gtr. 1
Coda
F♯m♭6
Aadd4
D
Gtr. 1

from James Bay - *Chaos and the Calm*

Let It Go

Words and Music by James Bay and Paul Barry

Tune down 1 step:
(low to high) D-G-C-F-A-D

Intro
Slow ♩ = 74

N.C. | E♭ | A♭maj7 | C5 | B♭6

Riff A

Gtr. 1 (clean)
(Sound effects) 7 sec.

mf
let ring

Rhy. Fig. 1

Gtr. 2 (clean)
7 sec.

mf
w/ fingers
let ring throughout

*T

*T=Thumb on 6th string

E♭ | A♭maj7 | C5 | B♭6

End Riff A

let ring

End Rhy. Fig. 1

T

Verse

Gtr. 1 tacet
Gtr. 2: w/ Rhy. Fig. 1 (1st 2 meas., 2 times)
2nd time, Gtr. 2: w/ Rhy. Fig. 1

E♭ | A♭maj7 | C5 | B♭6 | E♭ | A♭maj7

1. From walk-ing home and talk-ing loads, see-ing shows in eve-ning clothes with you.
2. From throw-ing clothes a-cross the floor to teeth and claws and slam-ming doors at you.

Gtr. 2: w/ Rhy. Fig. 1
C5
B♭6
E♭
A♭maj7
C5
B♭6
From nerv - ous touch and get - ting drunk
If this is all we're liv - ing for
why are we
E♭
A♭maj7
C5
B♭6
to stay - ing up and wak - ing up with you.
do - ing it, do - ing it, do - ing it an - y - more?
But now we're
I used to
Pre-Chorus
Cm
Cm7/B♭
Cm6/A
A♭maj7(no3rd)
sleep - ing at the edge, hold - ing some - thing we don't need.
rec - og - nize my - self, It's fun - ny how re - flec - tions change.
All this de -
When we're be -
Gtr. 2
Cm
Cm7/B♭
Cm6/A
lu - sion in our heads is gon - na bring us to our knees.
com - ing some - thing else I think it's time to walk a - way.
So come on, let it
Chorus
A♭maj7
E♭
Cm
B♭6
go. Just let it be.
Why don't you be

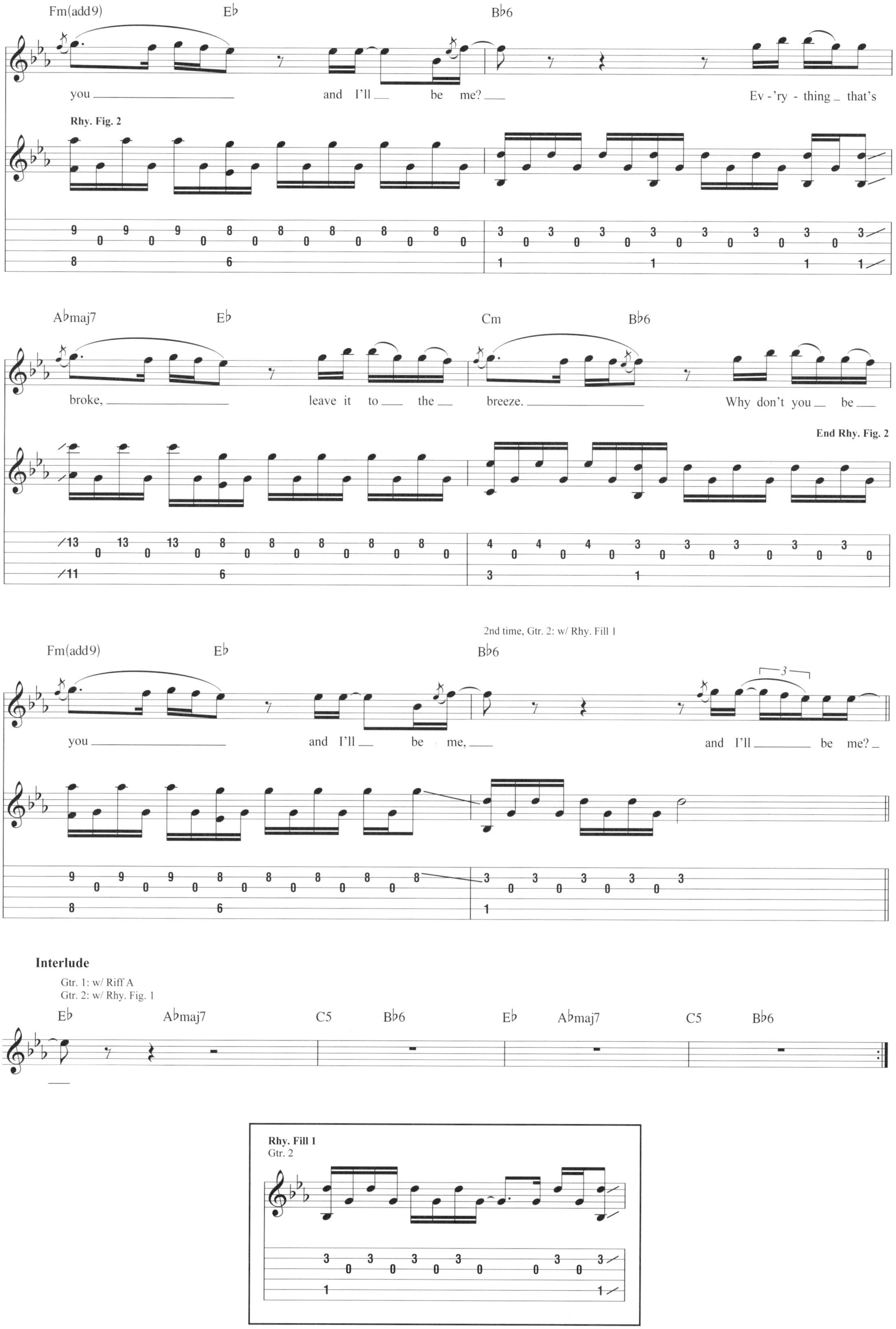

Fm(add9) E♭ B♭6

you and I'll be me? Ev - 'ry - thing that's

Rhy. Fig. 2

A♭maj7 E♭ Cm B♭6

broke, leave it to the breeze. Why don't you be

End Rhy. Fig. 2

2nd time, Gtr. 2: w/ Rhy. Fill 1

Interlude

Gtr. 1: w/ Riff A
Gtr. 2: w/ Rhy. Fig. 1

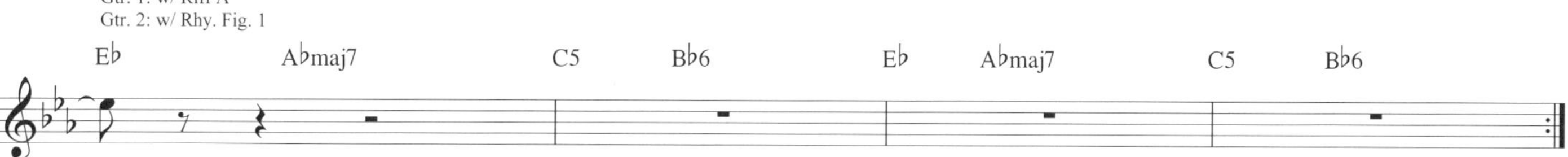

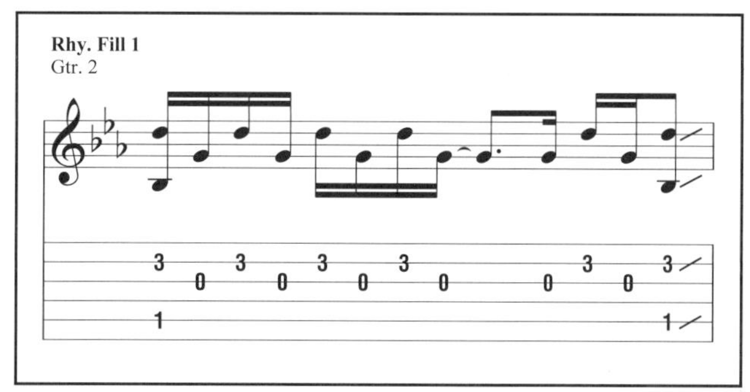

Bridge

Fm(add9)
Eb
Try to fit your hand in - side of mine when we know it just don't be - long.
Gtr. 2
Bb6
Cm
There's no force on earth could make it feel right, no. Whoa.
*Applies to 2nd string only.
Fm(add9)
Eb
Try to push this prob - lem up the hill when it's just too heav - y to hold.
Bb6
Cm
Think now's the time to let it slide. So come on, let it

Chorus

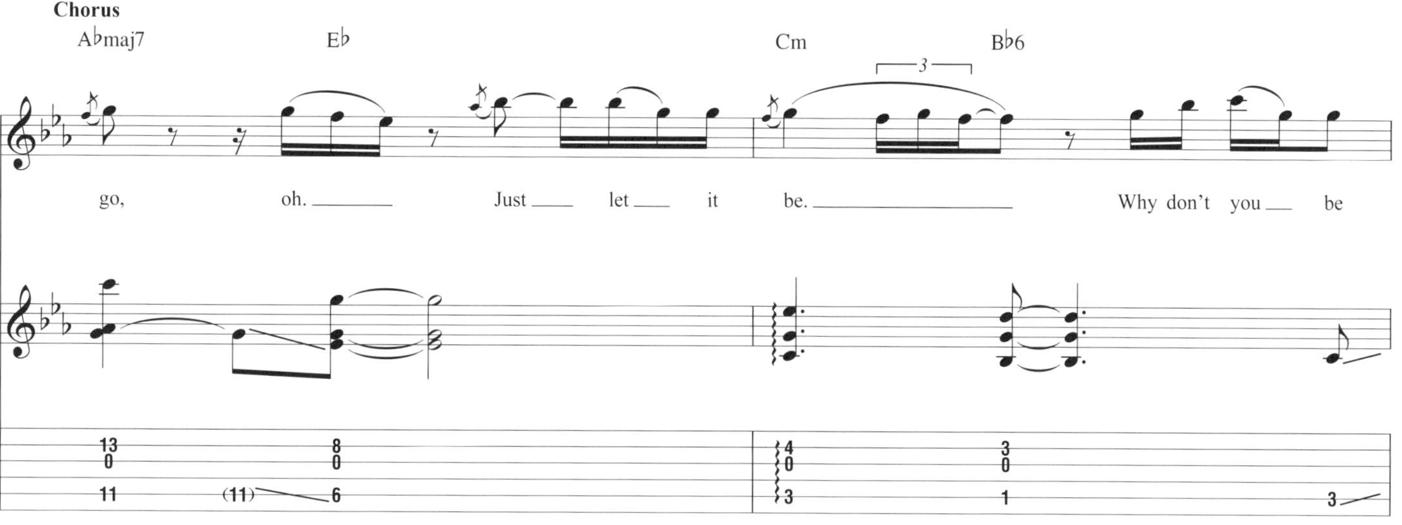
A♭maj7
E♭
Cm
B♭6
go, oh. Just let it be. Why don't you be

Fm(add9)
E♭
B♭6
you and I'll be me? Ev - 'ry - thing that's
steady gliss.

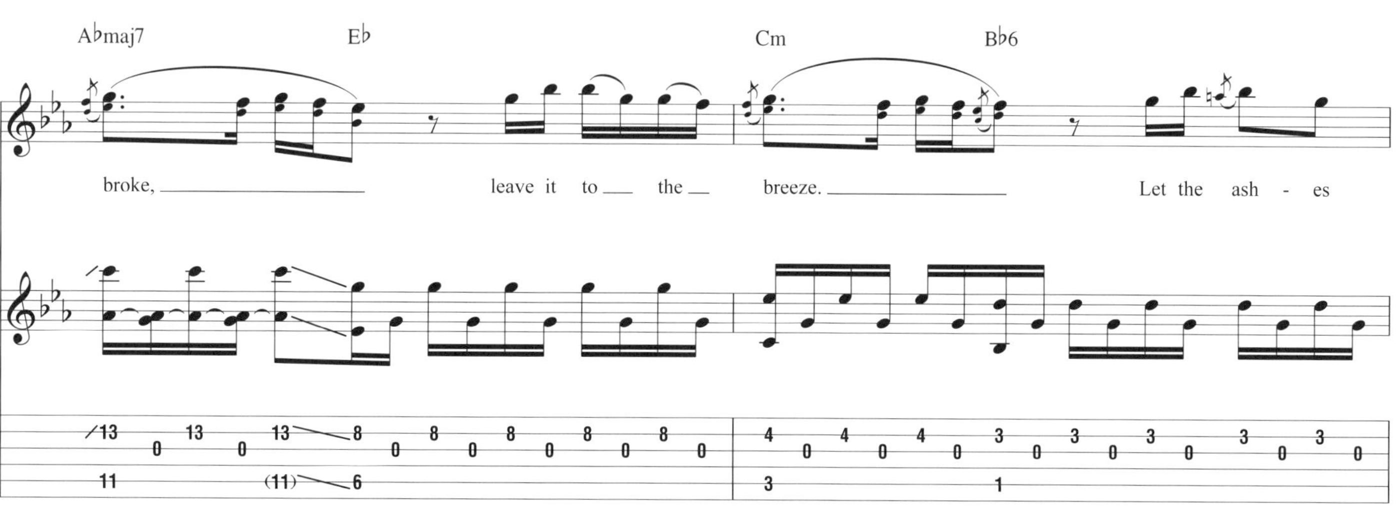
A♭maj7
E♭
Cm
B♭6
broke, leave it to the breeze. Let the ash - es

Gtr. 2: w/ Rhy. Fig. 2
Fm(add9)
E♭
B♭6
fall, for - get a - bout, mm, me. Come on, let it

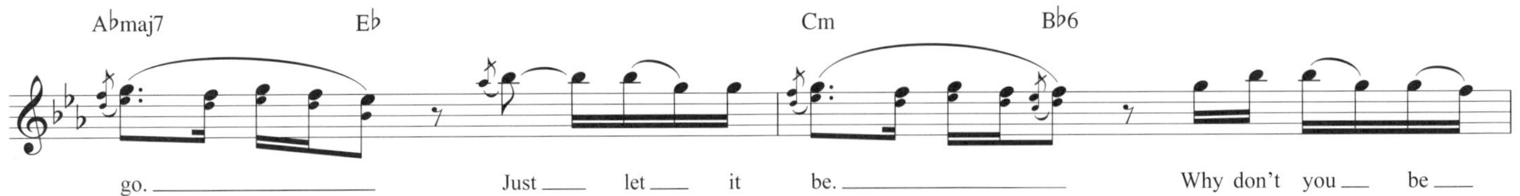
A♭maj7
E♭
Cm
B♭6
go.
Just let it be.
Why don't you be

Fm(add9)
E♭
B♭6
you
and I'll be me,
and I'll be me?
Gtr. 2

Outro

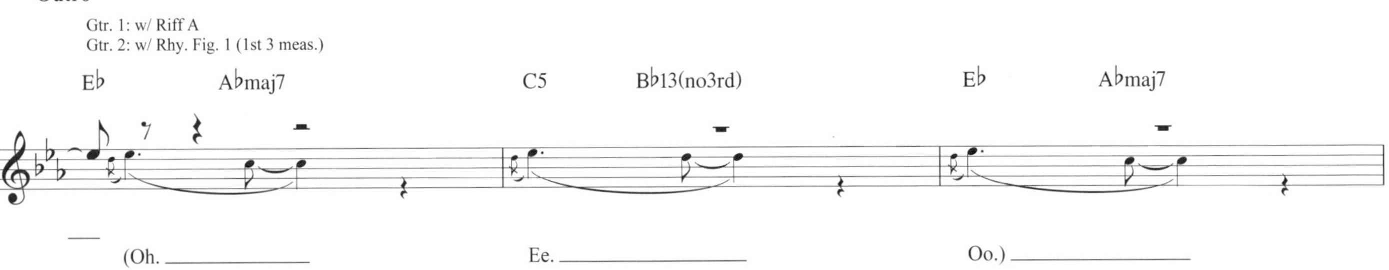
Gtr. 1: w/ Riff A
Gtr. 2: w/ Rhy. Fig. 1 (1st 3 meas.)
E♭
A♭maj7
C5
B♭13(no3rd)
E♭
A♭maj7
(Oh.
Ee.
Oo.)

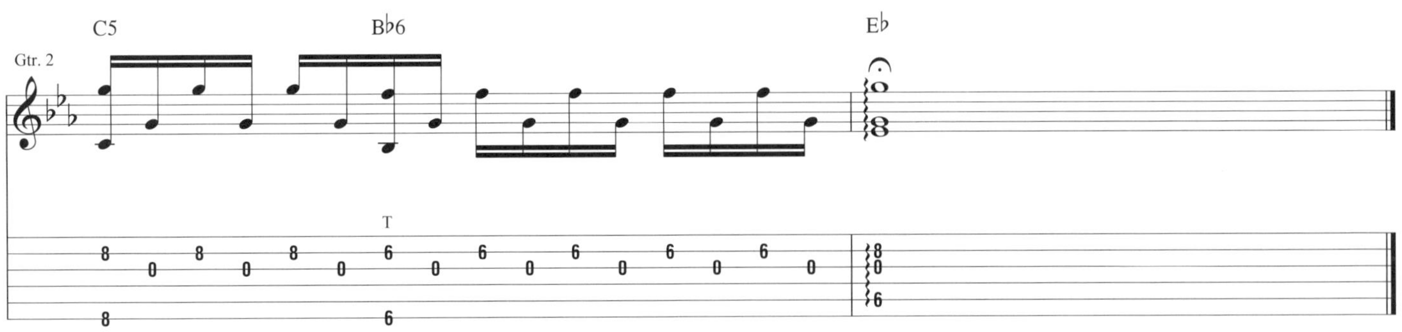
C5
B♭6
E♭
Gtr. 2
T

from Bruno Mars - *Unorthodox Jukebox*

Locked Out of Heaven

Words and Music by Bruno Mars, Ari Levine and Philip Lawrence

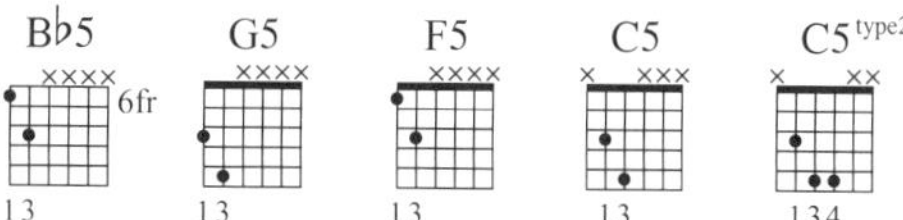

Intro

Moderately fast ♩ = 144

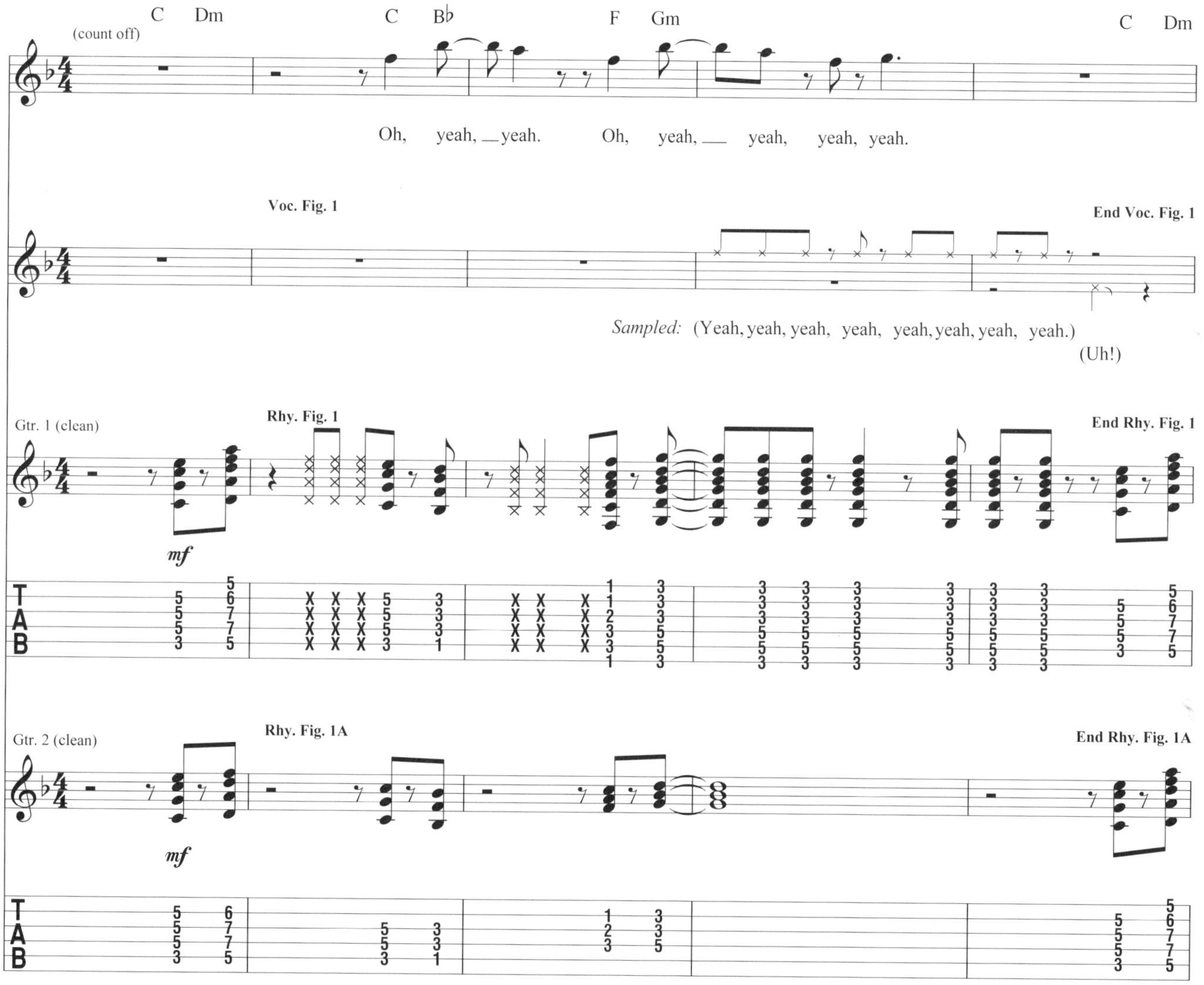

C Dm (count off) C B♭ F Gm C Dm

Oh, yeah, _ yeah. Oh, yeah, _ yeah, yeah, yeah.

Voc. Fig. 1 End Voc. Fig. 1

Sampled: (Yeah, yeah, yeah, yeah, yeah, yeah, yeah, yeah.) (Uh!)

Gtr. 1 (clean) Rhy. Fig. 1 End Rhy. Fig. 1

mf

T A B

Gtr. 2 (clean) Rhy. Fig. 1A End Rhy. Fig. 1A

mf

T A B

Bkgd. Voc.: w/ Voc. Fig. 1
Gtrs. 1 & 2: w/ Rhy. Figs. 1 & 1A

Verse

Bkgd. Voc.: w/ Voc. Fig. 1 (4 times)
Gtrs. 1 & 2: w/ Rhy. Figs. 1 & 1A (4 times)

Pre-Chorus

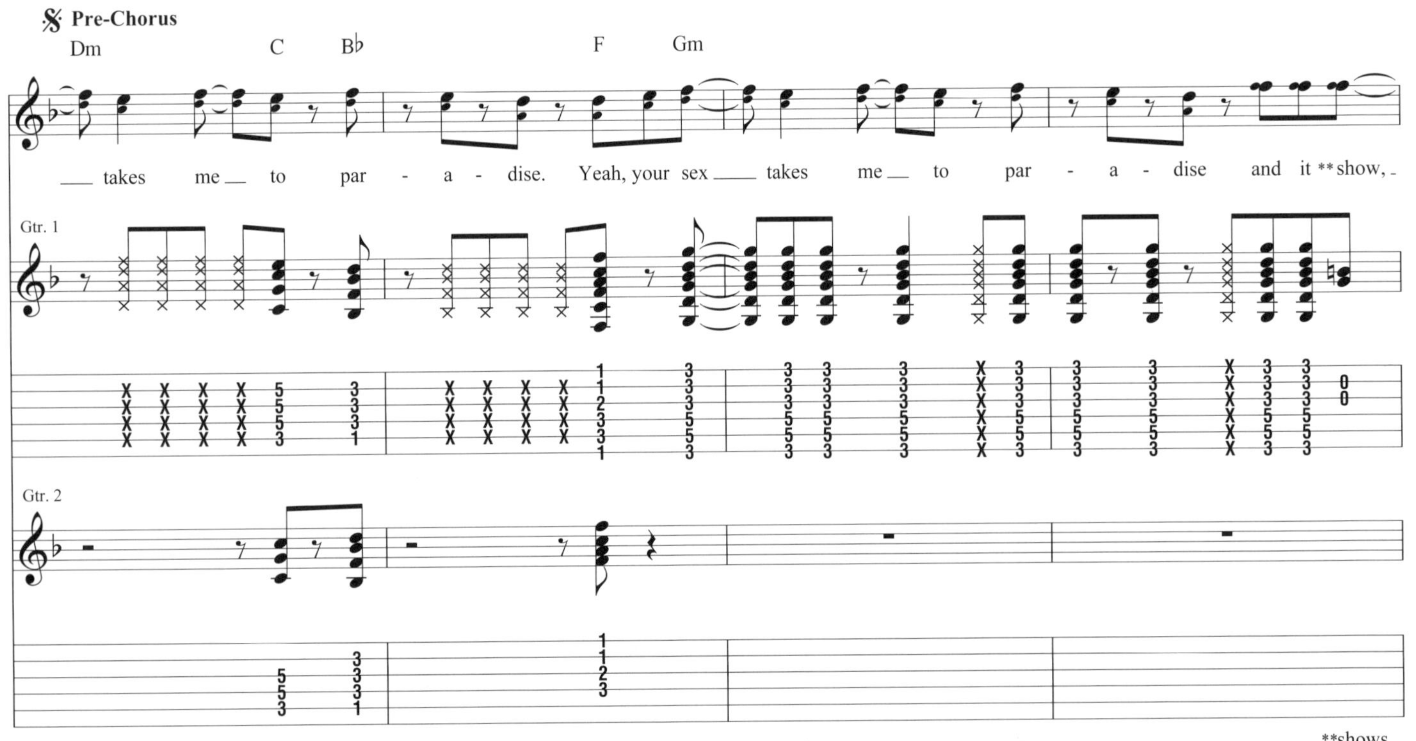

Chorus

*See top of first page of song for chord diagrams pertaining to rhythm slashes.
**w/ echo set for half-note regeneration w/ 1 repeat where indicated, next 16 meas.
***Set for quarter-note regeneration w/ 2 repeats.

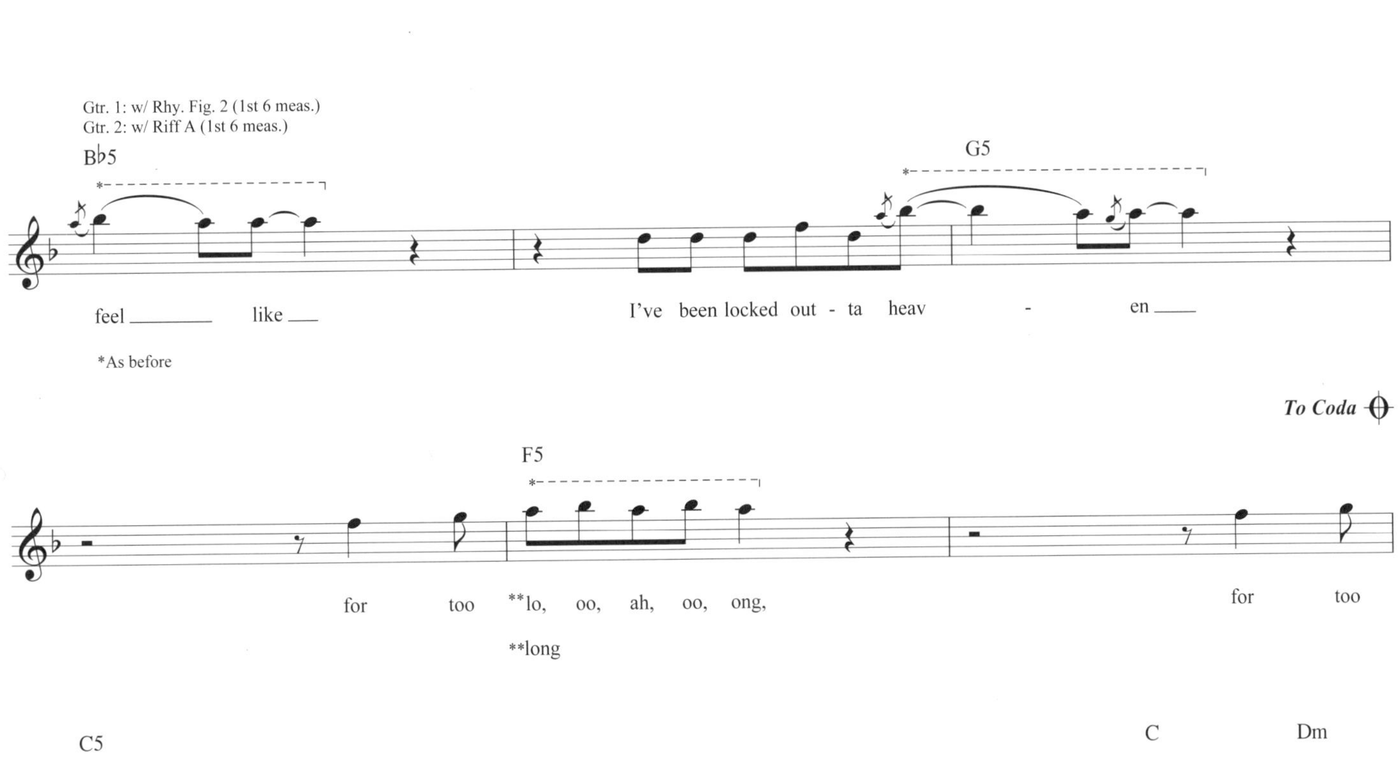
Gtr. 1: w/ Rhy. Fig. 2 (1st 6 meas.)
Gtr. 2: w/ Riff A (1st 6 meas.)
B♭5
G5
feel like
I've been locked out - ta heav - en
*As before
To Coda
F5
for too **lo, oo, ah, oo, ong,
for too
**long

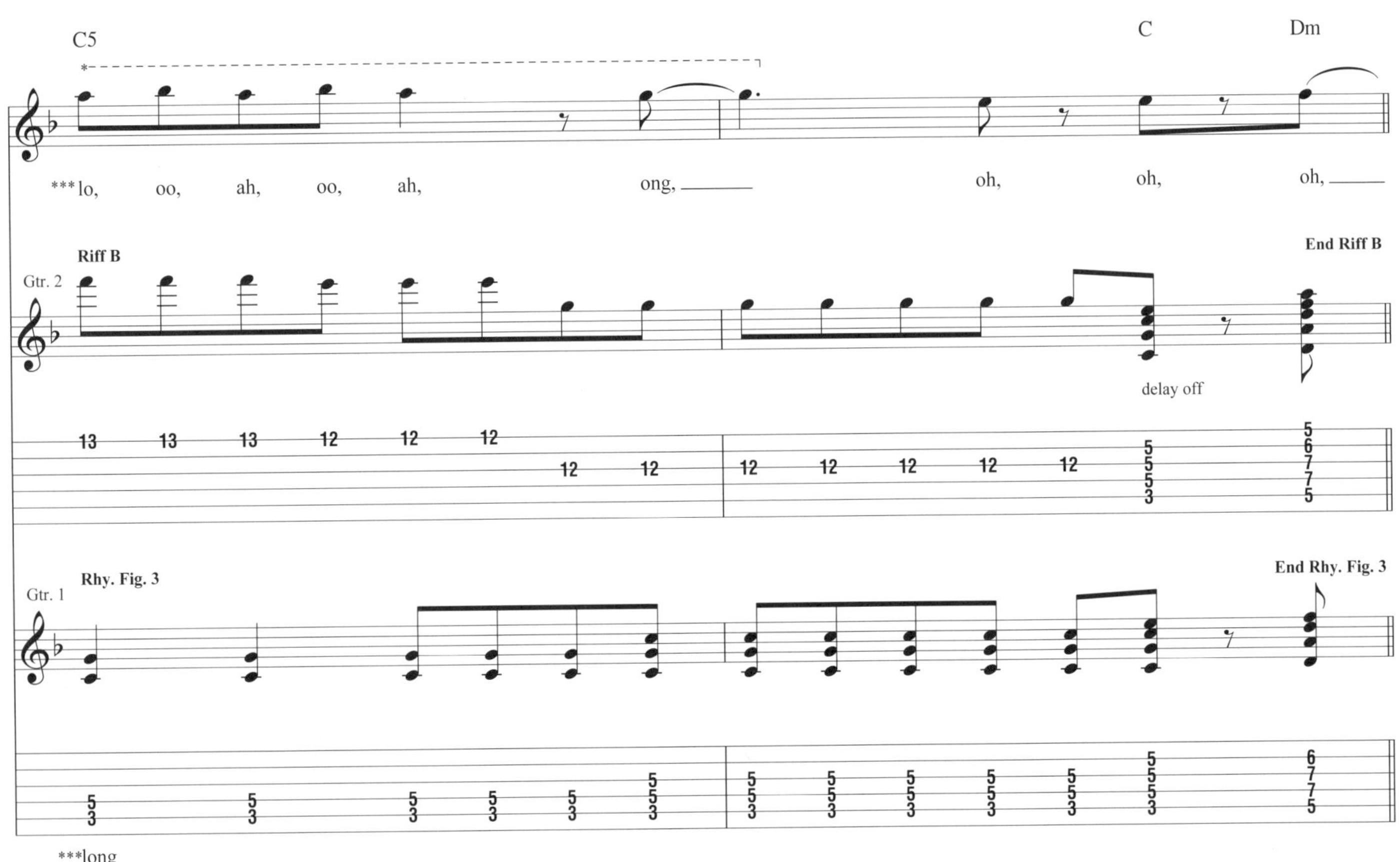
C5
C
Dm
***lo, oo, ah, oo, ah, ong,
oh, oh, oh,
Riff B
Gtr. 2
End Riff B
delay off
Rhy. Fig. 3
Gtr. 1
End Rhy. Fig. 3
***long

Interlude
Bkgd. Voc.: w/ Voc. Fig. 1 (2 times)
Gtrs. 1 & 2: w/ Rhy. Figs. 1 & 1A (2 times)
Dm
C
B♭
F
Gm
C
Dm
oh.
Oh, yeah, yeah, yeah, yeah.

C
B♭
F
Gm
C
Dm
Oh, yeah, yeah.
Oh, yeah, yeah, yeah, yeah.

Verse

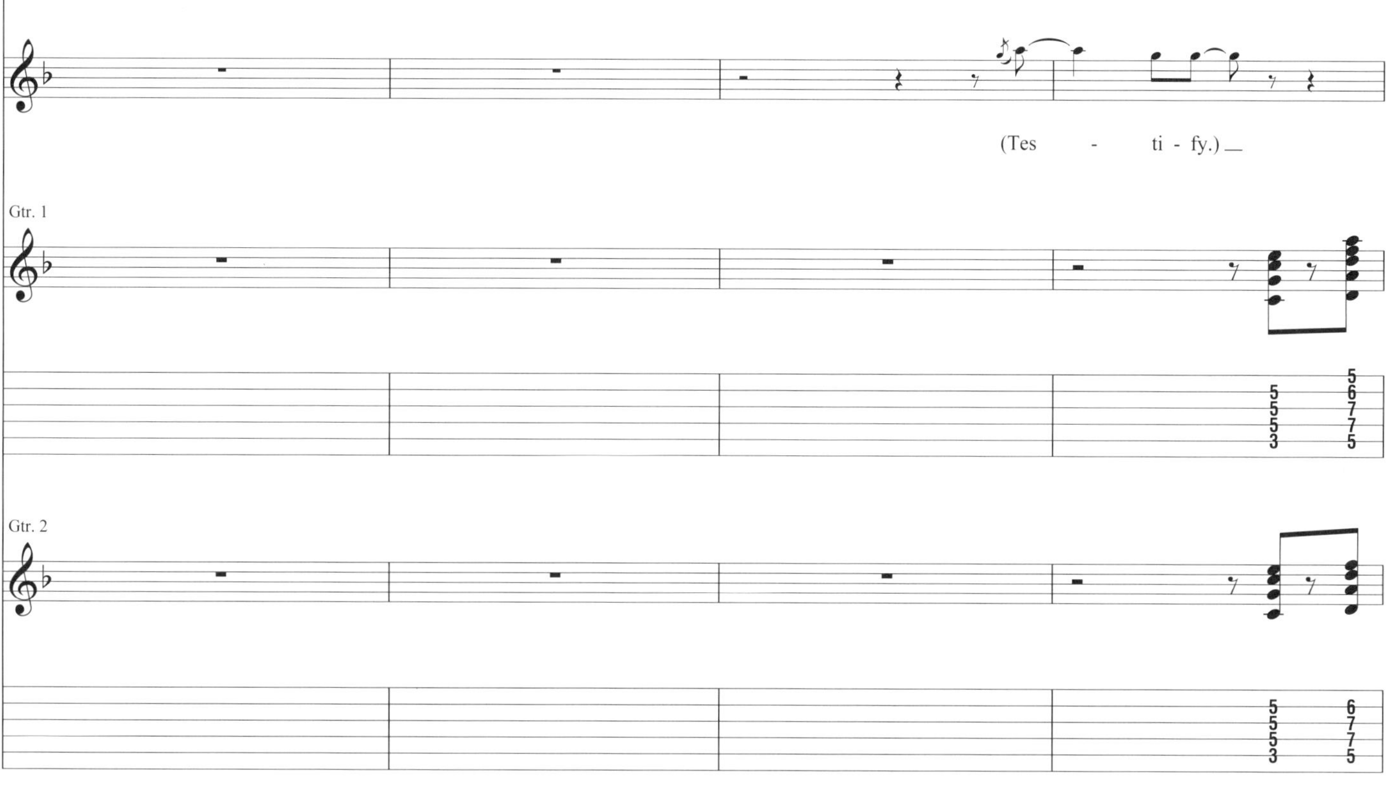
Bkgd. Voc.: w/ Voc. Fig. 1 (4 times)
N.C.(Dm) (C) (B♭) (F) (Gm) C Dm
2. You bring me to my knees, you make me tes - ti - fy.
(Tes - ti - fy.)
Gtr. 1
5 5 5 5 3
5 6 7 7 5
Gtr. 2
5 5 5 5 3
6 7 7 5

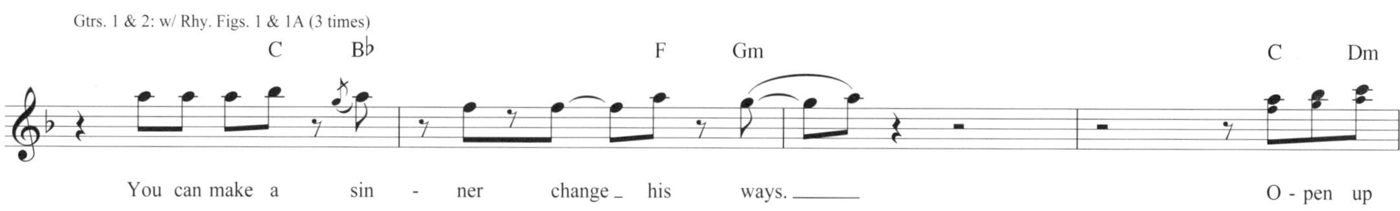
Gtrs. 1 & 2: w/ Rhy. Figs. 1 & 1A (3 times)
C B♭ F Gm C Dm
You can make a sin - ner change his ways. O - pen up

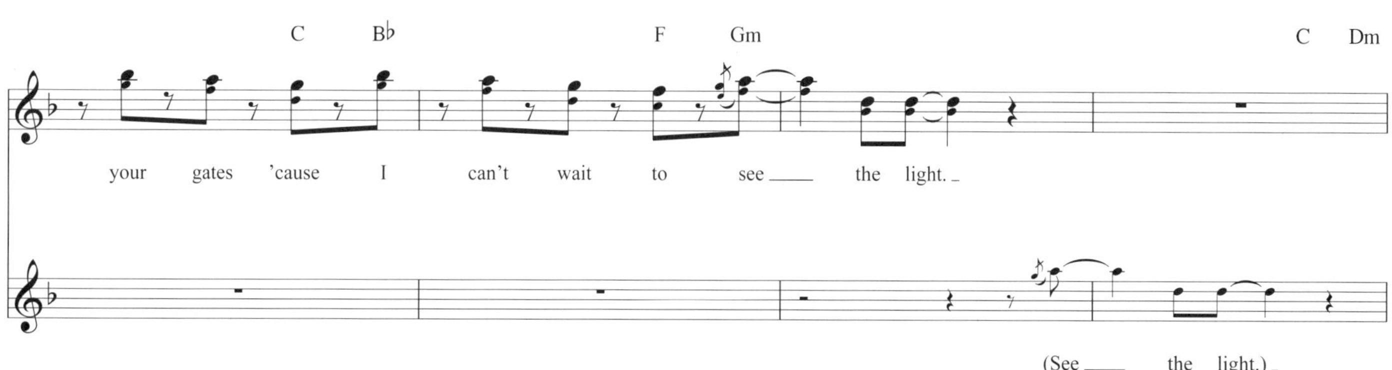
C B♭ F Gm C Dm
your gates 'cause I can't wait to see the light.
(See the light.)

D.S. al Coda
C B♭ F Gm C Dm
And right there is where I wan - na stay, ee, ay, ee, ay, ee, ay, ee, ay. 'Cause your sex

Coda
C5
N.C.
*lo, oo, ah, oo, ooh, ah, ong.
Gtr. 2
13 13 13 12 12 12 12 12 12
Gtr. 1
*long
Bridge
Gtr. 1: w/ Rhy. Fig. 2 (2 times)
Gtr. 2: w/ Riff A (2 times)
B♭5
G5
Oh, oo, whoa, oo, whoa, oo, whoa. Yeah, ee, yeah, ee, yeah. Can I just
F5
C5
1.
2.
stay here, spend the rest of my days here? 'Cause you make me
Chorus
Gtr. 2: w/ Riff A (1 3/4 times)
B♭5
G5
feel like I've been locked out - ta heav - en for too
**w/ echo as before
F5
C5
***lo, oo, ah, oo, ong, for too †lo, oo, ah, oo, ah, ong. Yeah, you make me
***long
†long

Half-time feel
B♭5
G5
feel like
I've been locked out - ta heav - en
for too
*w/ echo as before
End half-time feel
Gtr. 1: w/ Rhy. Fig. 3
Gtr. 2: w/ Riff B
F5
C5
C
Dm
**lo, oo, ah, oo, ong,
for too ***lo, oo, ah, oo, ah, ong oh, oh, oh,
**long
***long
Outro
Bkgd. Voc.: w/ Voc. Fig. 1 (2 times)
Gtrs. 1 & 2: w/ Rhy. Figs. 1 & 1A (1 1/2 times)
Dm
C
B♭
F
Gm
oh.
Oh, yeah, yeah, yeah, yeah.
C
Dm
C
B♭
F
Gm
Oh, yeah, yeah.
Oh, yeah,
C
Dm
yeah, yeah, yeah.
Gtr. 1
Gtr. 2

from The Black Keys - *El Camino*

Lonely Boy

Words and Music by Dan Auerbach, Patrick Carney and Brian Burton

Verse
E5
G
A
so a - bove you, and it's plain to see, but I
ma - ma kept you, and your dad - dy left you, and I
Rhy. Fig. 1
End Rhy. Fig. 1
P.M.
*T
T
let ring
T
*T = Thumb on 6th string.
Gtr. 1: w/ Rhy. Fig. 1 (3 times)
came to love you an - y - way. So you
should have done you just the same. But I
pulled my heart out, and I don't mind bleed - ing
came to love you. Am I born to bleed
an - y old time you keep me wait - ing, wait - ing, wait - ing.
an - y old time you keep me wait - ing, wait - ing, wait - ing?
Chorus
E5
G5
A5
Oh, oh, oh,
I got a love that keeps me wait - ing.
Rhy. Fig. 2
**Gtrs. 1 & 2
End Rhy. Fig. 2
**Composite arrangement
Gtrs. 1 & 2: w/ Rhy. Fig. 2 (3 times)
Oh, oh,
I got a love that keeps me wait - ing.

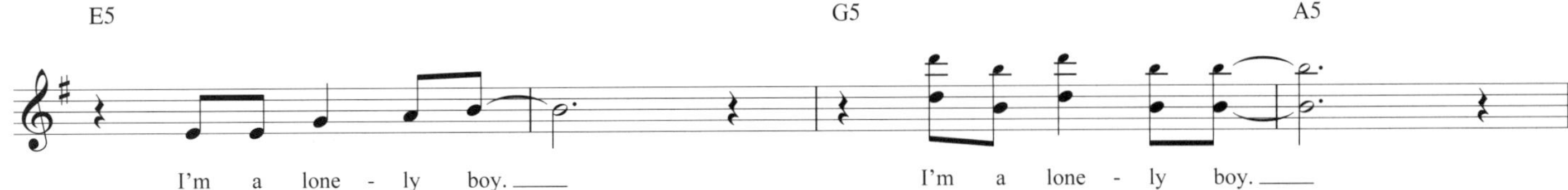

Interlude

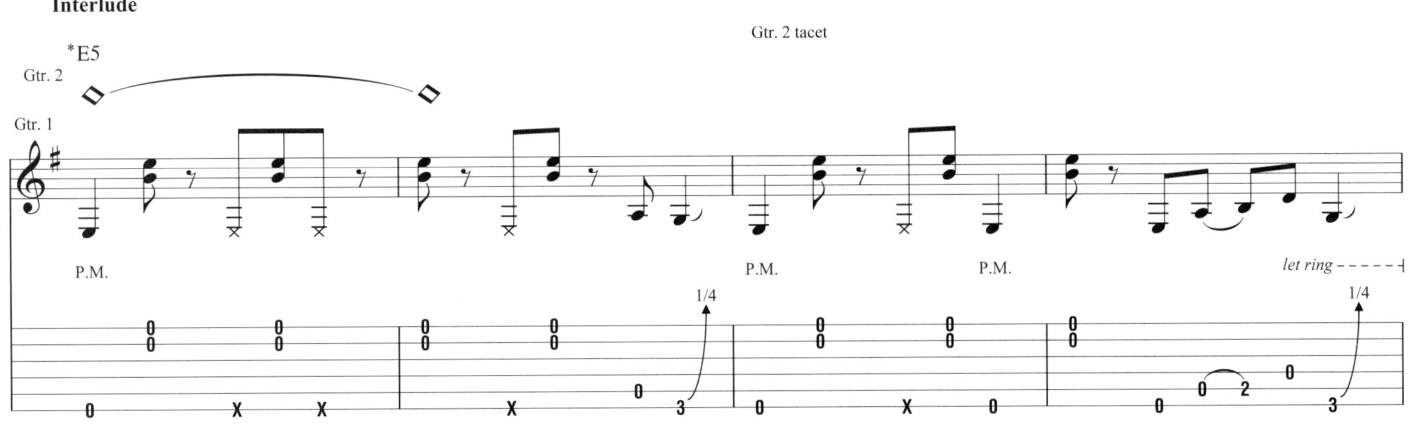

*See top of first page of song for chord diagram pertaining to rhythm slashes.

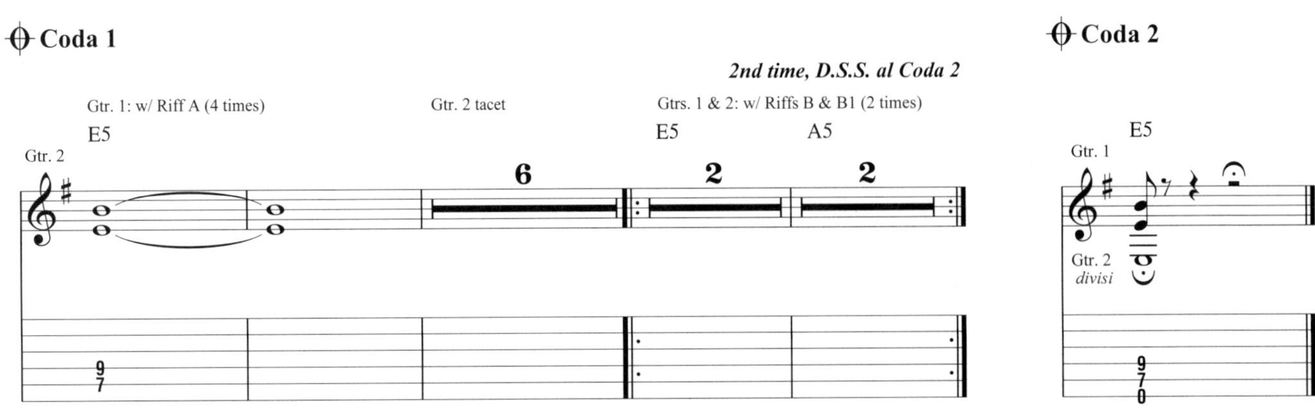

from Maroon5 - *Hands All Over*

Moves Like Jagger

Words and Music by Adam Levine, Benjamin Levin, Ammar Malik and Shellback

*○ = open (toe up); + = closed (toe down).

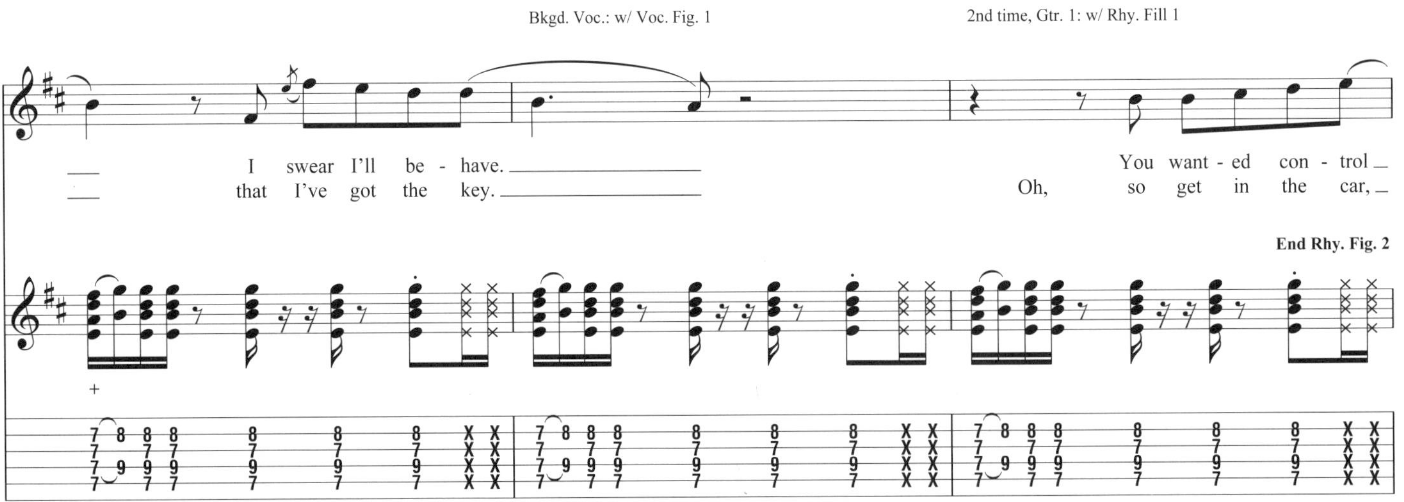

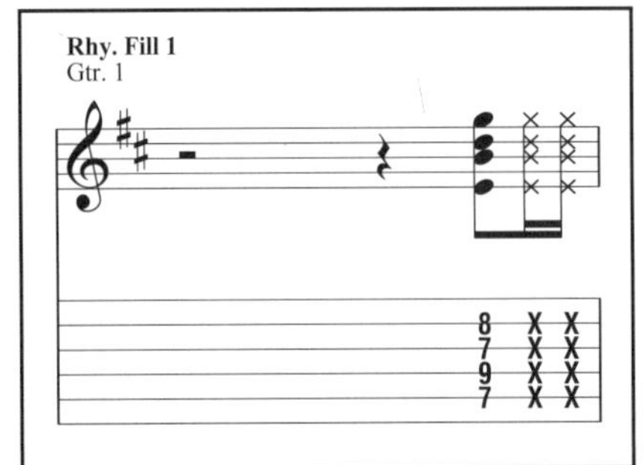

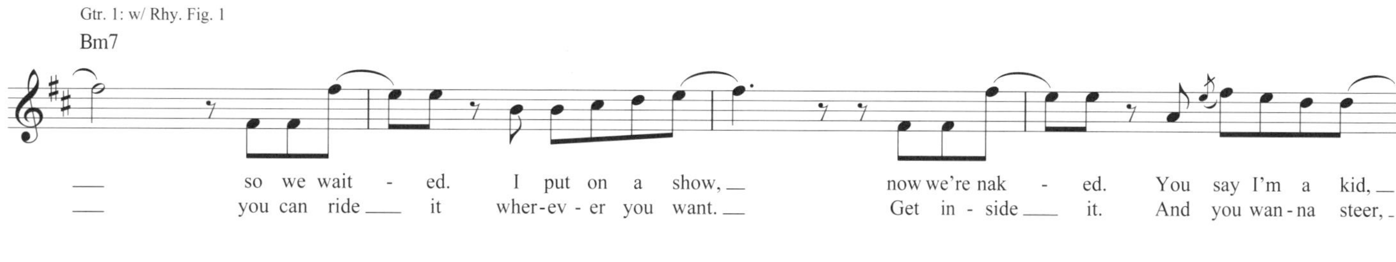

*Bkgd. Vocal is female.

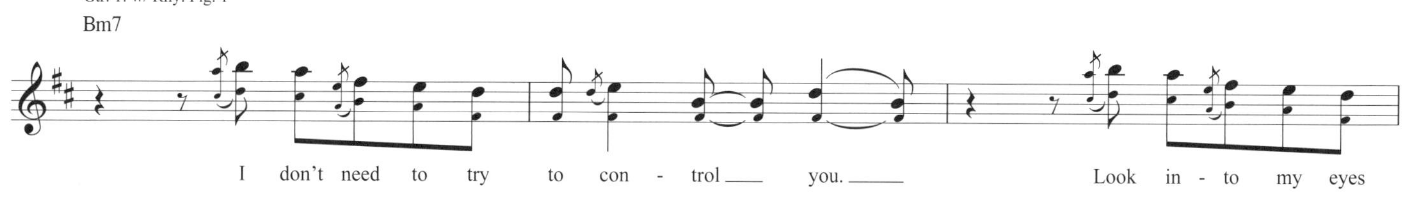

Em7
and I'll own you with the moves like Jag - ger. I've got the moves like Jag - ger. I've got the

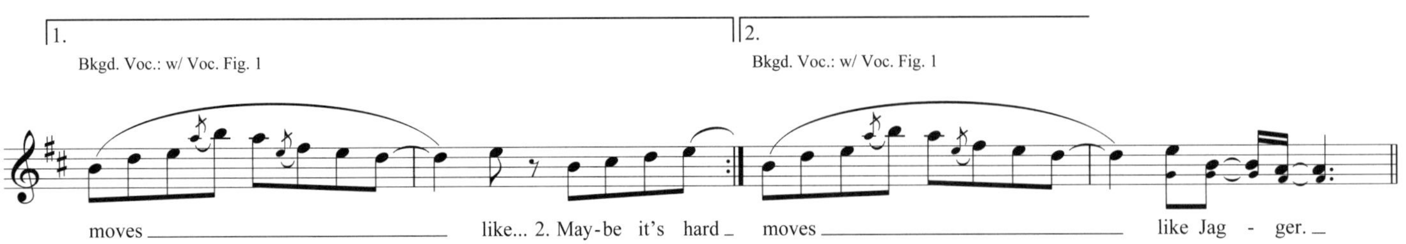
1.
Bkgd. Voc.: w/ Voc. Fig. 1
2.
Bkgd. Voc.: w/ Voc. Fig. 1
moves like... 2. May-be it's hard moves like Jag - ger.

Verse
Gtr. 1: w/ Rhy. Fig. 2
Bm7
*Female: 3. Uh, you wan - na know how to make me smile? Take con - trol,
Voc. Fig. 2
Female: (Oo. Ah.
*Christina Aguilera

Em7
own me just for the night. But if I share my se - cret, you're gon-na have to keep it.
Oo.

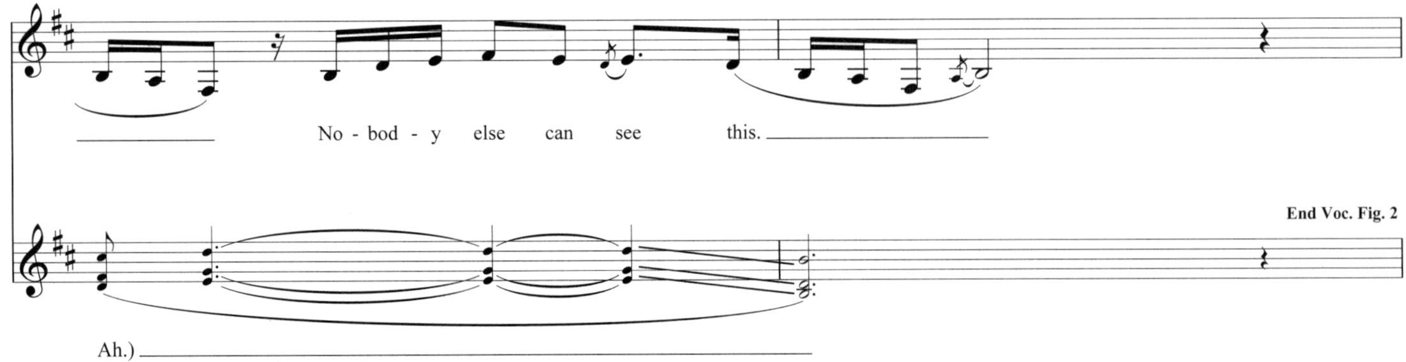
Bkgd. Voc.: w/ Voc. Fig. 1
No - bod - y else can see this.
End Voc. Fig. 2
Ah.)

Bkgd. Voc.: w/ Voc. Fig. 2
Gtr. 1: w/ Rhy. Fig. 1

Bkgd. Voc.: w/ Voc. Fig. 1

Chorus
Gtr. 1: w/ Rhy. Fig. 1 (2 times)

*As before

Bkgd. Voc.: w/ Voc. Fig. 1
Bm7
moves like Jag - ger. I don't need to try
Ah, yeah.
to con - trol you. Look in - to my eyes
Yeah.)
(Oo.)
Em7
and I'll own you with the moves like Jag - ger. I've got the
Ah, oh.)
Bkgd. Voc.: w/ Voc. Fig. 1
moves like Jag - ger. I've got the moves like Jag - ger.
Outro
Bm7
N.C.
Whistle
Gtr. 1

from Fall Out Boy - *Save Rock and Roll*

My Songs Know What You Did in the Dark (Light Em Up)

Words and Music by Andrew Hurley, Joseph Trohman, Patrick Stump, Peter Wentz, Butch Walker and John Hill

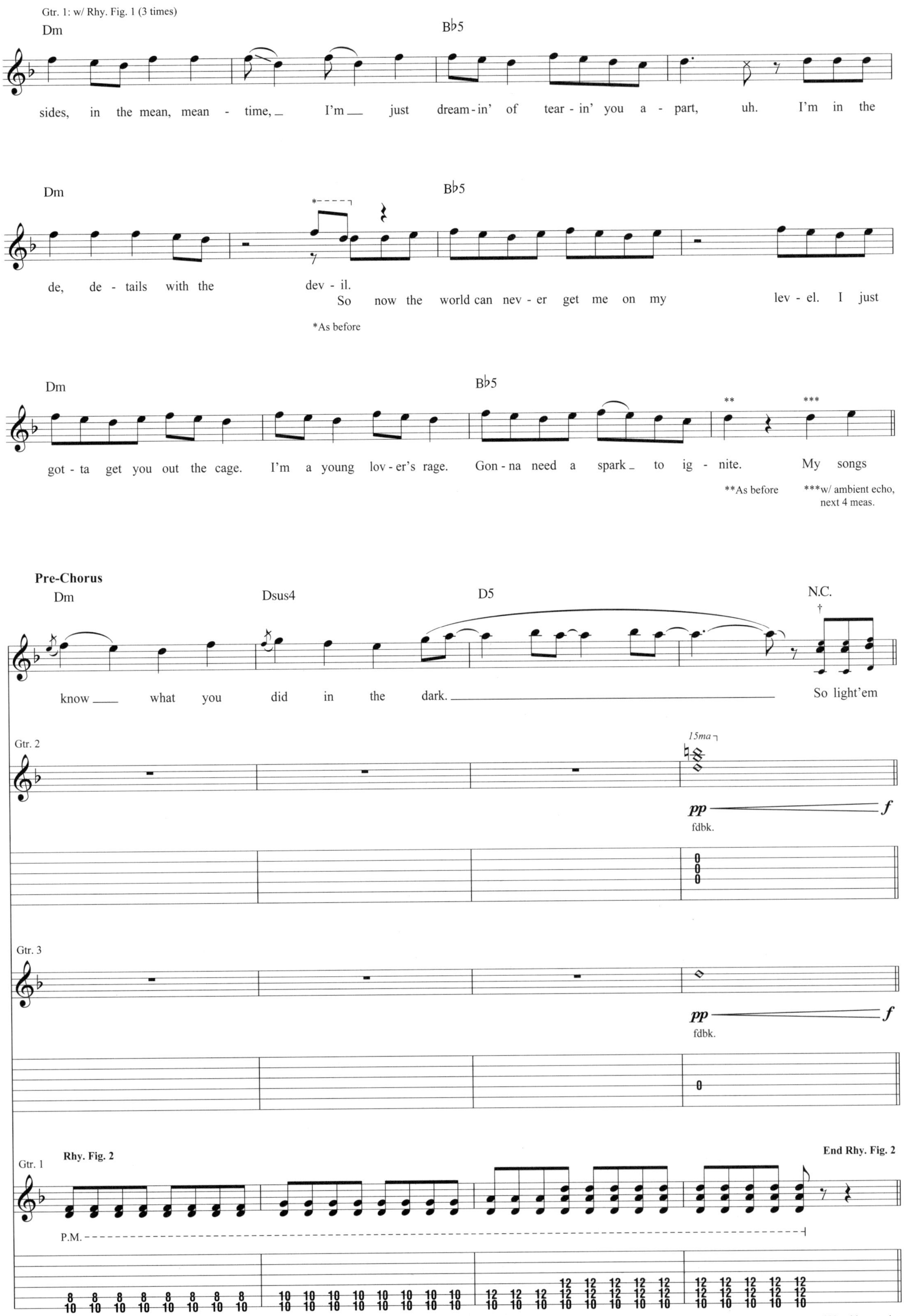

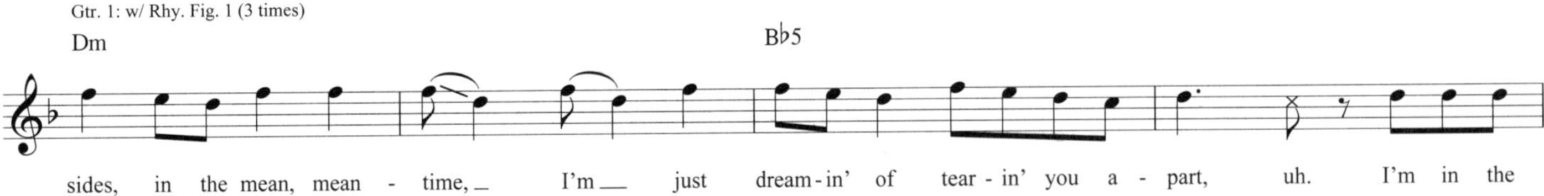

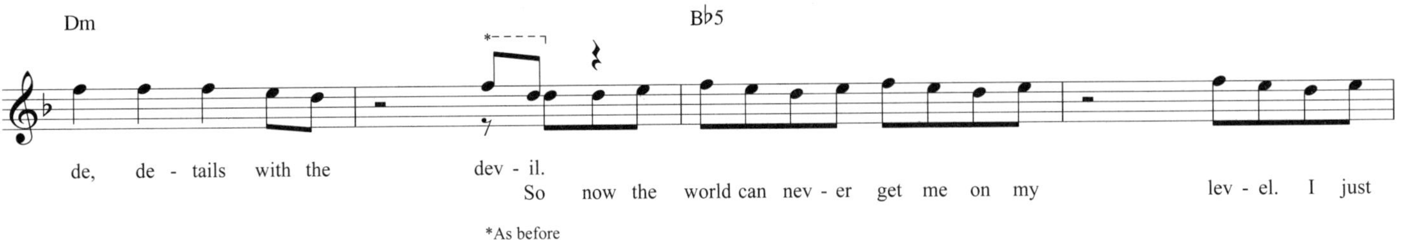

Gtr. 1: w/ Rhy. Fig. 1 (3 times)
Dm
B♭5
sides, in the mean, mean - time, I'm just dream-in' of tear-in' you a - part, uh. I'm in the
Dm
B♭5
de, de - tails with the dev - il.
So now the world can nev - er get me on my lev - el. I just
*As before
Dm
B♭5
got - ta get you out the cage. I'm a young lov - er's rage. Gon - na need a spark to ig - nite. My songs
**As before
***w/ ambient echo, next 4 meas.
Pre-Chorus
Dm
Dsus4
D5
N.C.
know what you did in the dark. So light'em
Gtr. 2
15ma
pp
f
fdbk.
Gtr. 3
pp
f
fdbk.
Gtr. 1
Rhy. Fig. 2
End Rhy. Fig. 2
P.M.

†Vocal harmonies sung *pp*.

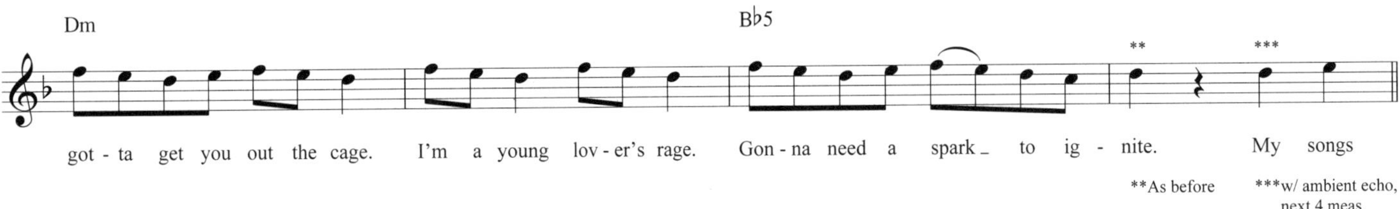

Chorus
Half-time feel
Gtrs. 2 & 3 tacet
D5
B♭5
*Dm/F
C5
up, up, up. Light 'em up, up, up. Light 'em up, up, up. So light 'em
I'm on fi - re.
Gtr. 1
Riff A
End Riff A
P.M.
*Bass plays F.
Gtr. 1: w/ Riff A (3 times)
D5
B♭5
Dm/F
C5
up, up, up. Light'em up, up, up. Light 'em up, up, up.
I'm on fi - re.
D5
B♭5
Dm/F
C5
Oh, oh, oh, oh.
(In the dark, dark.
Gtr. 4 (dist.)
f

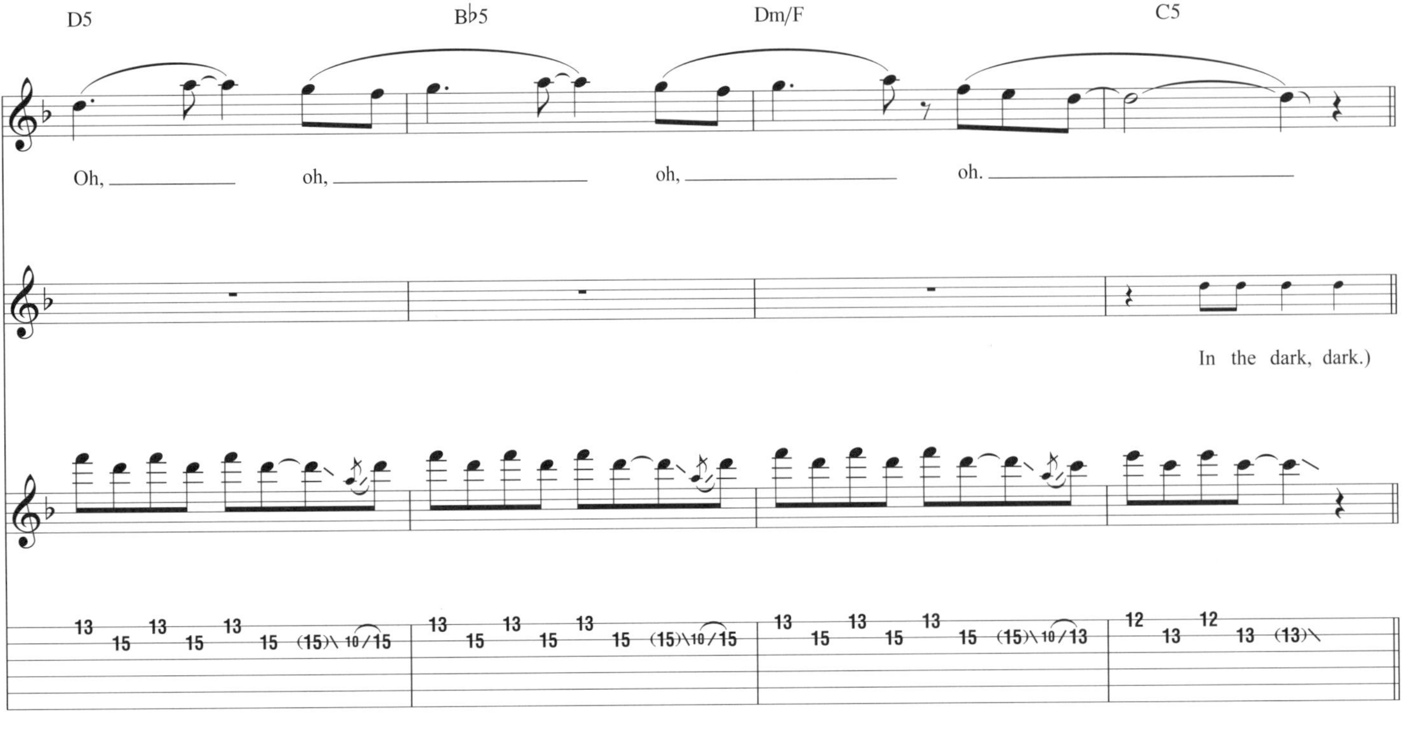

Verse

Gtr. 1: w/ Rhy. Fig. 1 (2 times)
Gtr. 4 tacet

Gtr. 1: w/ Rhy. Fig. 1
Dm
B♭5
*
In the end ev - 'ry - thing col - lides. My child - hood spat back out the mon - ster that you see. My songs
*w/ ambient echo, next 4 meas.
Pre-Chorus
Gtr. 1: w/ Rhy. Fig. 2
Dm
Dsus4
D5
N.C.
**
know what you did in the dark. So light 'em
Gtr. 2
15ma
pp
f
fdbk.
0
0
0
Gtr. 3
pp
f
fdbk.
0
**Vocal harmonies sung pp.
Chorus
***
Gtr. 1: w/ Riff A (4 times)
Gtrs. 2 & 3 tacet
D5
B♭5
Dm/F
up, up, up. Light 'em up, up, up. Light 'em up, up, up.
I'm on fi -
Gtr. 4
sim.
9 10 10 10 10 10 10 10
10 12 12 12 12 12 12 12
***2nd time, resume Half-time feel.

C5
D5
B♭5
So light 'em up, up, up. Light 'em up, up, up. Light 'em
- re.
Dm/F
C5
D5
up, up, up.
Oh, oh,
I'm on fi - re.
B♭5
Dm/F
C5
oh, oh.
(In the dark, dark.

To Coda
End half-time feel
D5
B♭5
Dm/F
C5
Oh,
oh,
oh,
oh.
In the dark, dark.)
13 15 13 15 13 15 (15) 10 15
13 15 13 15 13 15 (15) 10 15
13 15 13 15 13 13 (13) 10 13
12 13 12 13 (13)
Interlude
Gtr. 4 tacet
N.C.
(Sampled vocals & percussion)
My songs
Pre-Chorus
Bkgd. Voc.: w/ Voc. Fig. 1 (2 times)
N.C.
know what you did in the dark.
(My songs
*w/ tone filter, next 5 meas.
**D5
C5
N.C.
D.S. al Coda
So light'em
know what you did in the dark.)
**Chords implied by bass.
***Vocal harmonies sung pp.
Coda
Outro
Gtr. 4 tacet
N.C.
(Oh,
oh,
oh,
oh.)
†w/ ambient echo, till end.

from Alice Merton - *Mint*

No Roots

Words and Music by Nicolas Rebscher and Alice Merton

Intro
Moderately ♩ = 116

Em
I won't for - get to find them 'cause
I'll say a dif - f'rent land. But
I've got mem - o - ries and
P.M.
G
A
Bm
trav - el like gyp - sies in the night.
Gr. 2 (slight dist.)
Fill 1
End Fill 1
mf
Gtr. 1
End Riff A
P.M.
Gtr. 2 tacet
I build a home and wait for some - one to tear it down,
I count gates and num - bers, then play the guess - ing game.
Gtr. 1
P.M.

Gtr. 2: w/ Fill 1
Em
then pack it up in box - es, head for the next town run-ning. 'Cause
It's just the place that chang - es, the rest is still the same. But
I've got mem-o-ries and
P.M.

G
A
Bm
trav - el like gyp - sies in the night.
And a
P.M.

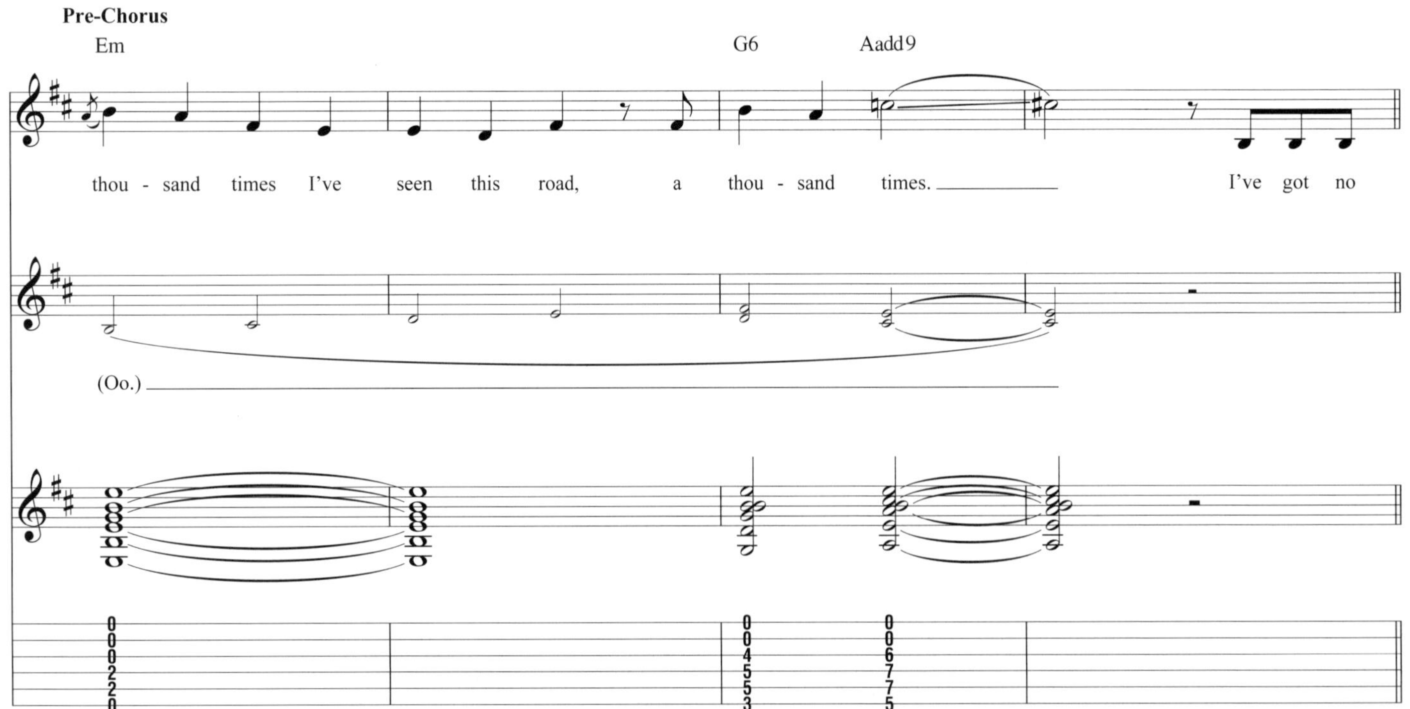
Pre-Chorus
Em
G6
Aadd9
thou - sand times I've seen this road, a thou - sand times.
I've got no
(Oo.)

Chorus

Gtr. 1: w/ Riff A (2 times)

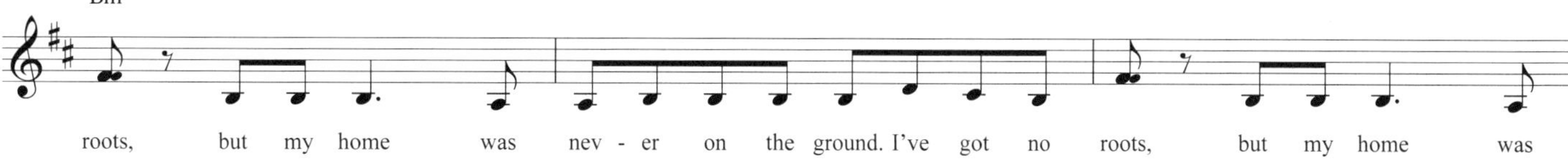
Bm
roots, but my home was nev - er on the ground. I've got no roots, but my home was

Gtr. 2: w/ Fill 1
Em
G
A
nev - er on the ground. I've got no roo - oo - oo - oots. I've got no

To Coda

Gtr. 2: w/ Fill 1
Bm
roo - oo - oo - oots. I've got no roots, but my home was

Gtr. 2: w/ Fill 1
nev - er on the ground. I've got no roots, but my home was nev - er on the ground. I've got no

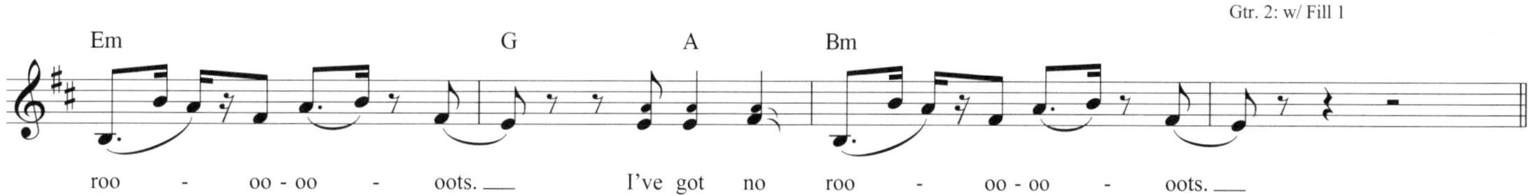
D.S. al Coda
Gtr. 2: w/ Fill 1
Em
G
A
Bm
roo - oo - oo - oots. I've got no roo - oo - oo - oots.

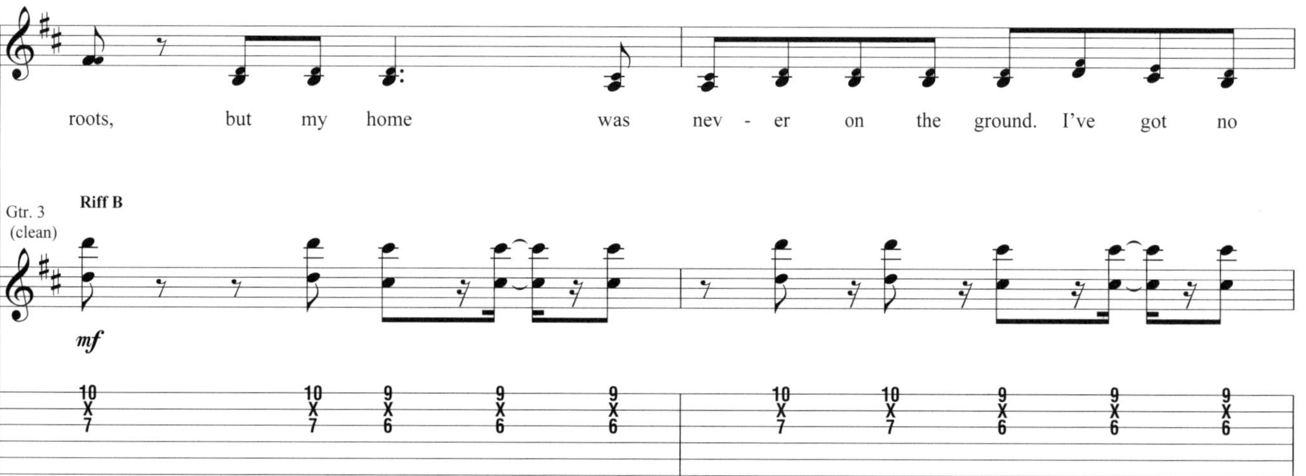
Coda
roots, but my home was nev - er on the ground. I've got no
Gtr. 3
(clean)
Riff B
mf

Gtr. 2: w/ Fill 1
Em
roots, but my home was nev - er on the ground. I've got no roo - oo - oo - oots.
10 X 7 10 X 7 9 X 6 9 X 6 9 X 6
10 X 7 10 X 7 9 X 6 9 X 6 9 X 6
8 X 5 8 X 5 7 X 4 7 X 4 7 X 4

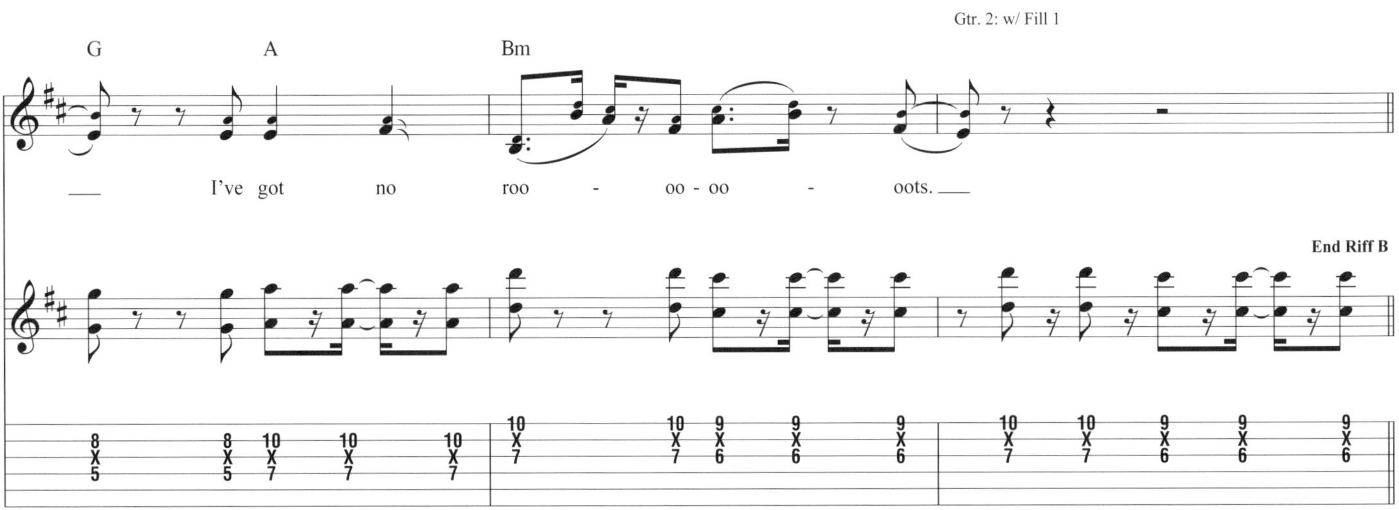
Gtr. 2: w/ Fill 1
G A Bm
I've got no roo - oo - oo - oots.
End Riff B
8 X 5 8 X 5 10 X 7 10 X 7 10 X 7
10 X 7 10 X 7 9 X 6 9 X 6 9 X 6
10 X 7 10 X 7 9 X 6 9 X 6 9 X 6

Bridge
N.C.
I like dig-ging holes, hid - ing things in - side them.
Riff C
Gtr. 3
End Riff C
9 9 X 9 X 9 X 9 X 9 X 9 X 9 7 7
9 9 X 9 X 9 X 9 X 9 X 9 X 9 7 7

Gtr. 3: w/ Riff C (2 1/2 times)
When I grow old I won't for - get to find them. I like dig-ging holes,

hid - ing things in - side them. When I grow old I won't for - get to find them.
(I've got no
Interlude
Gtr. 3: w/ Riff C
Bm
roots!
*Gtr. 4
mf
*Synth arr. for gtr.
Gtr. 1
P.M.
Em
G
A
No roots!)
Fill 2
End Fill 2
P.M.

Outro-Chorus

Gtr. 1: w/ Riff A (1st 5 meas.)
Gtr. 3: w/ Riff B (2 times)

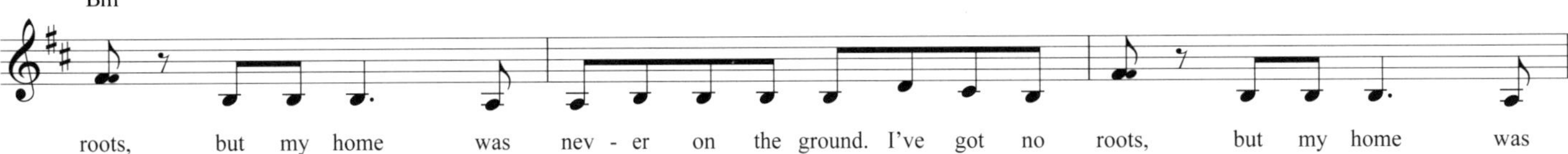

from Vance Joy - *Dream Your Life Away*

Riptide

Words and Music by Vance Joy

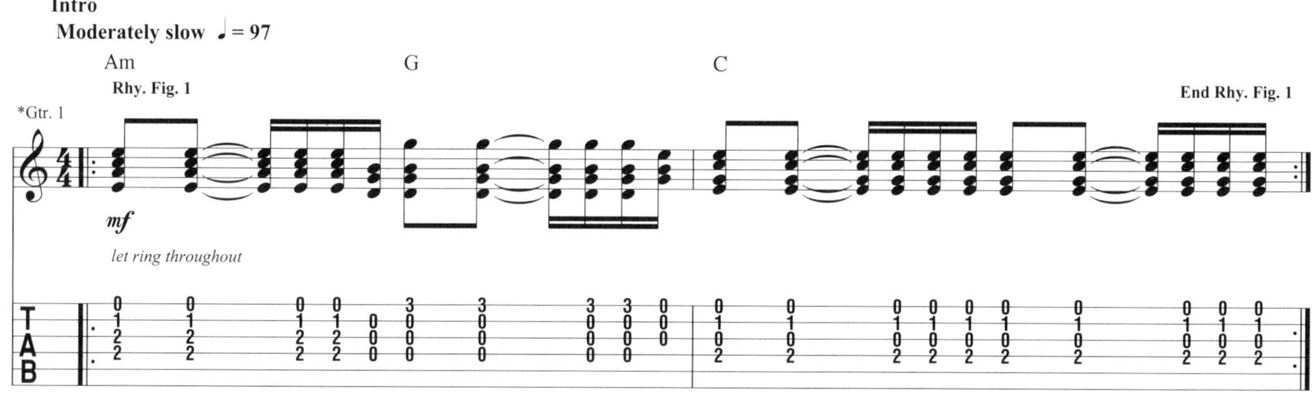

*Baritone ukulele arr. for gtr.
To match recording, tune up 1/2 step.

Verse

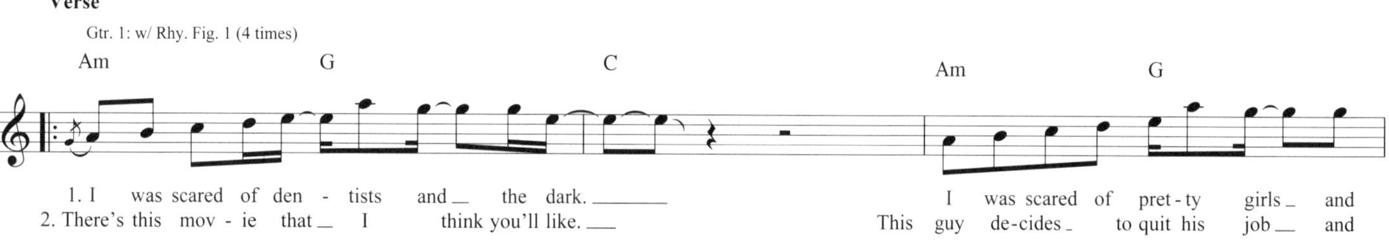

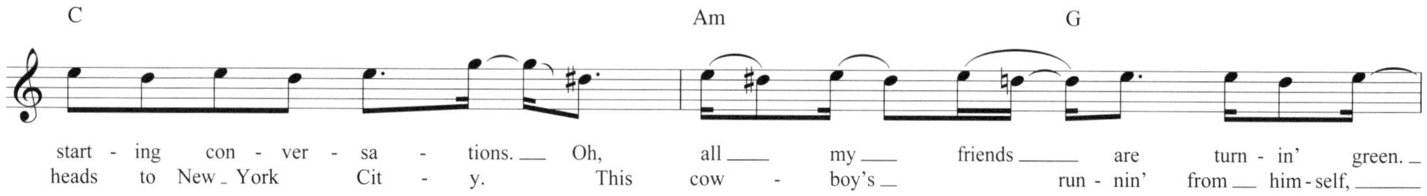

Pre-Chorus

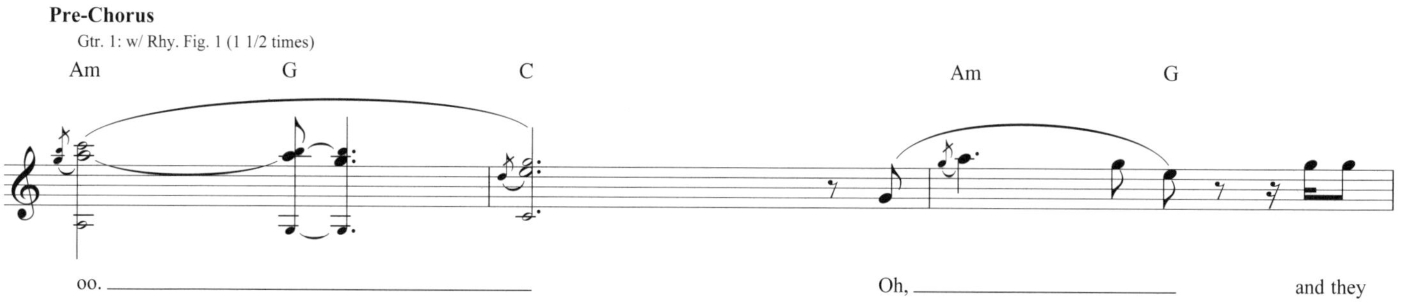

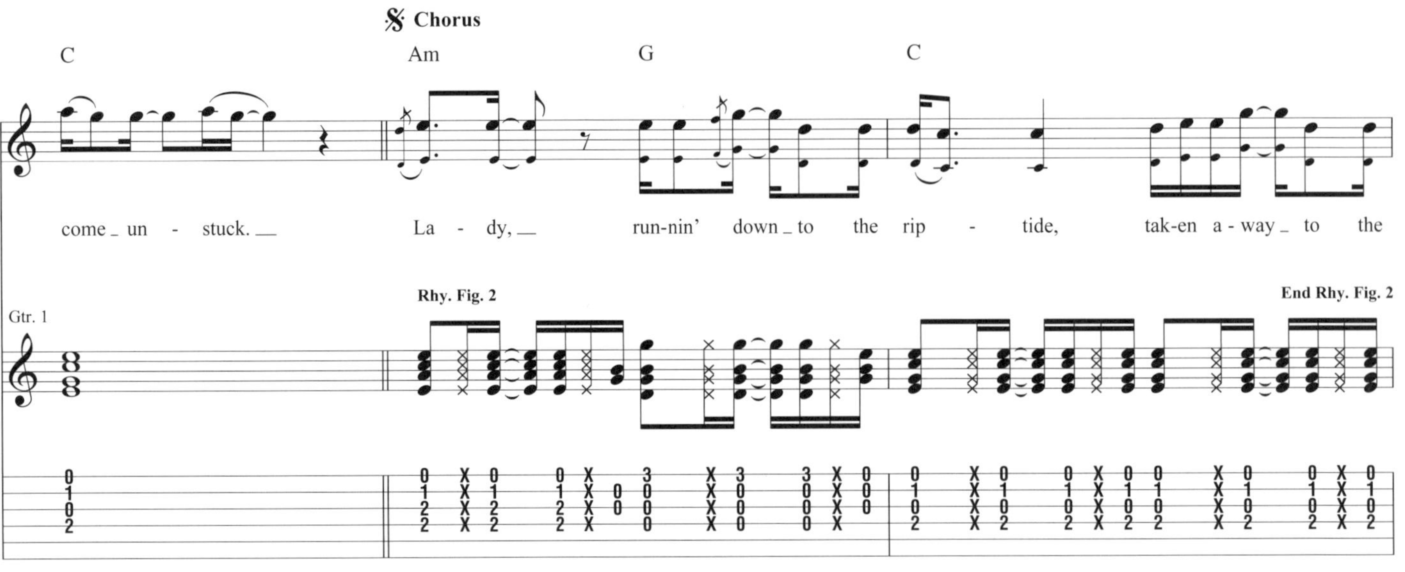

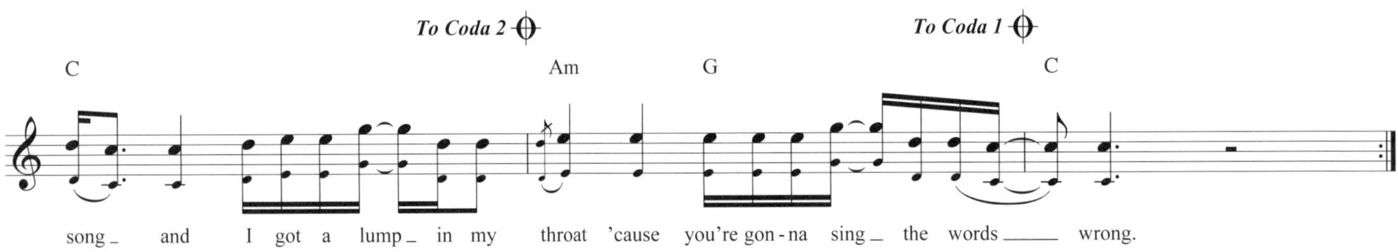

*Chord symbols reflect overall harmony.

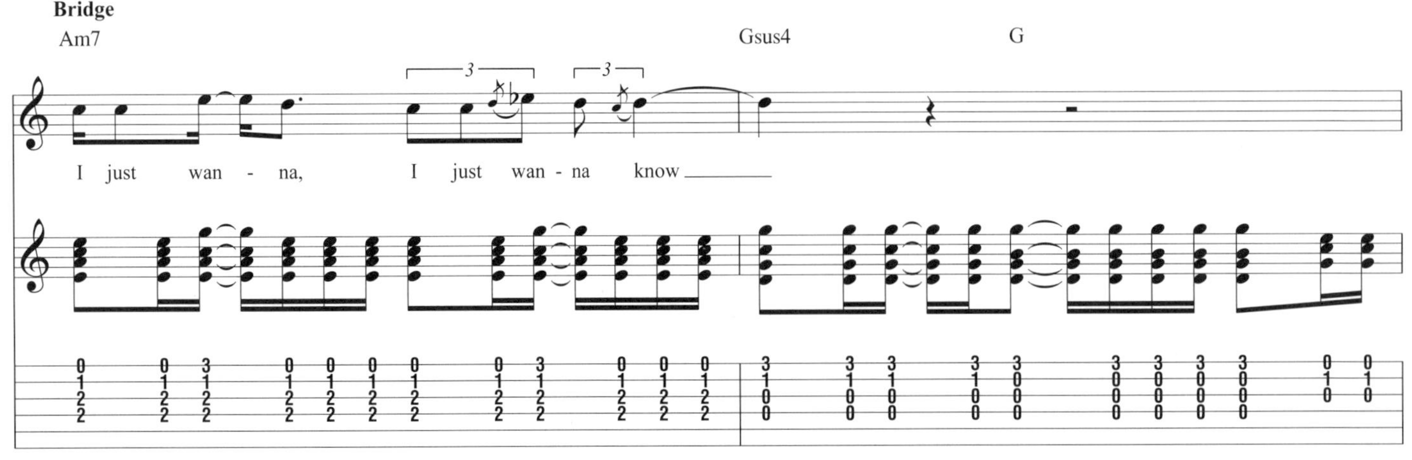

C
Fmaj7
if you're gon - na, if you're gon - na stay.
Am7
Gsus4
G
I just got - ta, I just got - ta know
C
Fmaj7
Am
G
I can't have it, I can't have it an - y oth - er way. I swear she's des - tined for the
C
Am
G
C
screen. Clos - est thing to Mi - chelle Pfeif - fer that you've ev - er seen, oh.

Chorus
Gtr. 1: w/ Rhy. Fig. 2 (3 times)
Am G C Am G
La - dy, run-nin' down to the rip - tide, tak-en a - way to the dark side. I wan-na be your
C Am G C
left hand man. I love you when you're sing - ing that song and I got a lump in my
D.S. al Coda 1
Am G C
throat 'cause you're gon - na sing the words wrong. Oh,
Gtr. 1
Rhy. Fill 1
End Rhy. Fill 1
Coda 1
Coda 2
D.S. al Coda 2
Gtr. 1: w/ Rhy. Fill 1
C
wrong. Oh,
Am G C
throat 'cause you're gon-na sing the words wrong, yeah. I got a lump in my
Am G C
slight rit.
throat 'cause you're gon - na sing the words wrong.
Gtr. 1
slight rit.

from Adele - *21*

Rolling in the Deep

Words and Music by Adele Adkins and Paul Epworth

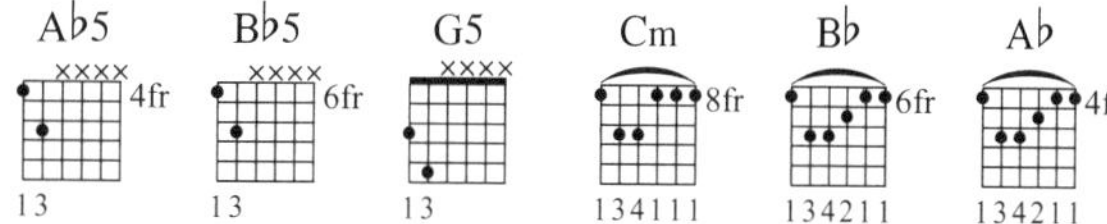

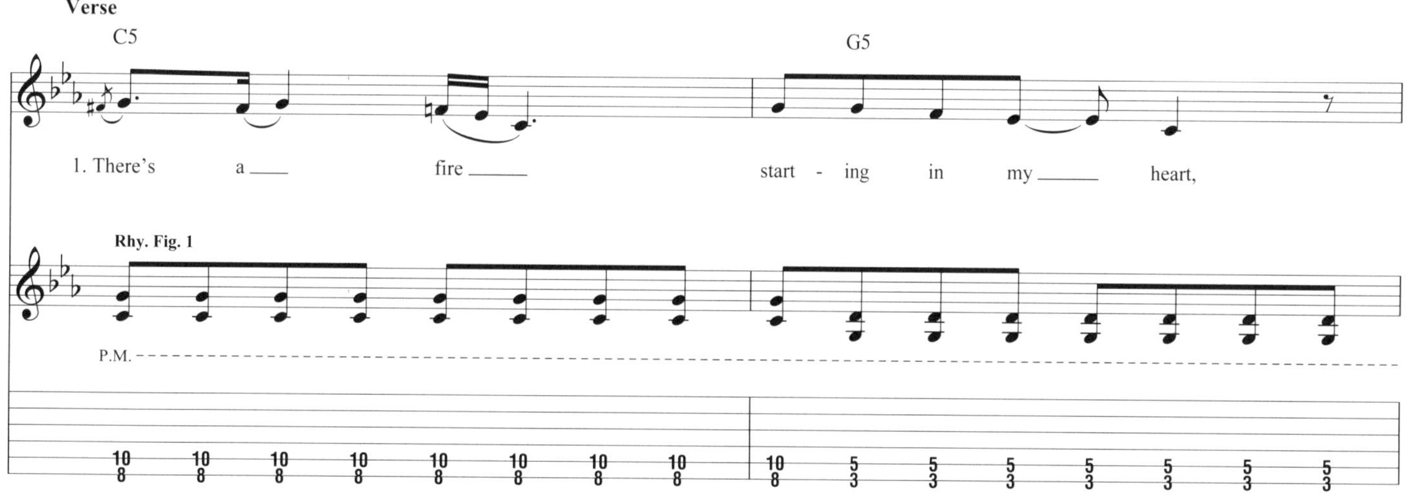

Verse

Pre-Chorus

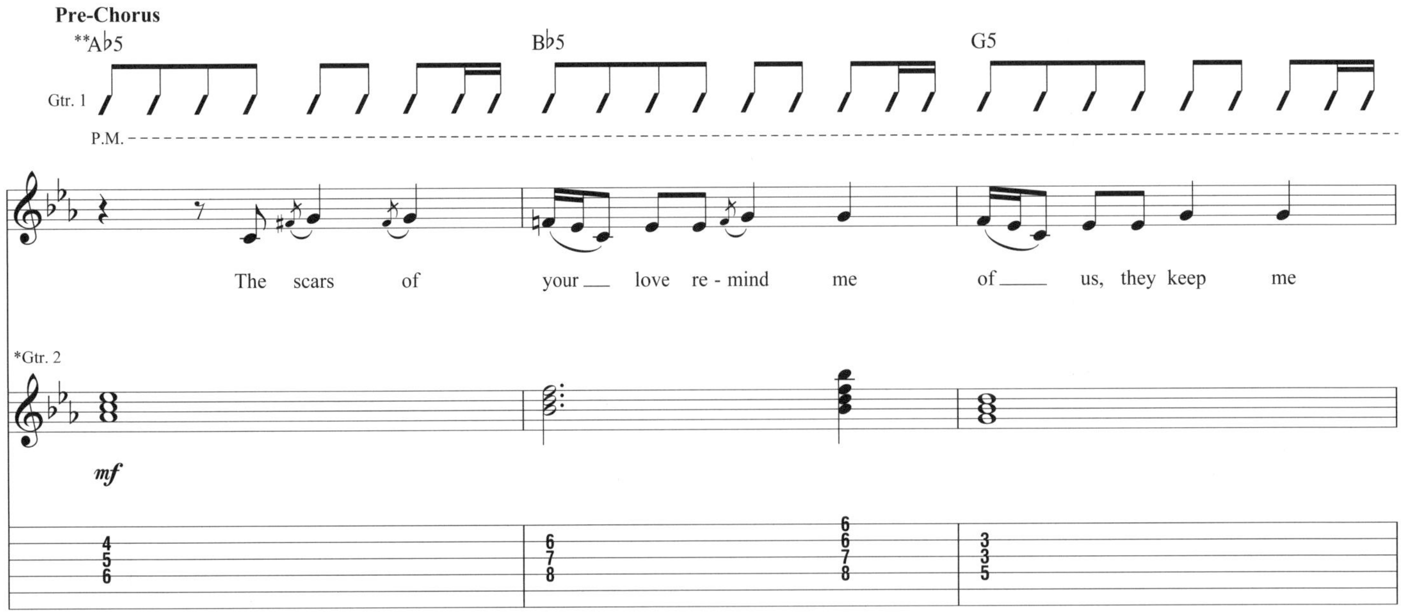

*Piano arr. for gtr.

**See top of first page of song for chord diagrams pertaining to rhythm slashes.

Ab5
Bb5
P.M.
thinking that we almost had it all. The scars of your love, they leave me
let ring
G5
P.M.
breath - less. I can't help feel - ing we could have had it
Chorus
Cm
Bb
Ab
Bb
Rhy. Fig. 2
End Rhy. Fig. 2
all, rolling in the deep. You had my heart in-
Voc. Fig. 1
End Voc. Fig. 1
(You're gon-na wish you nev-er had met me. Tears are gon-na fall, roll-ing in the deep.)
Rhy. Fig. 2A
End Rhy. Fig. 2A

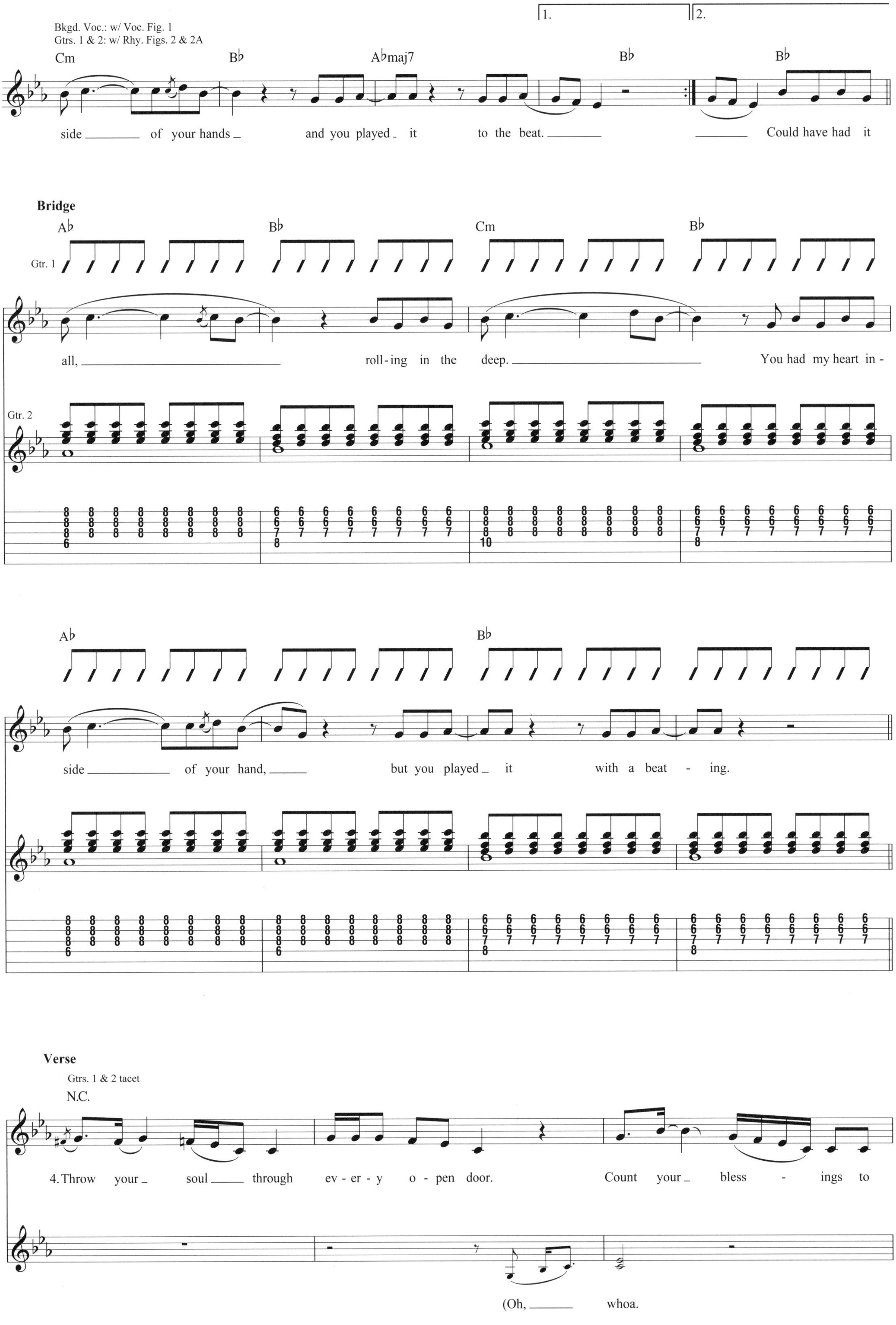

1. 2.

Bkgd. Voc.: w/ Voc. Fig. 1
Gtrs. 1 & 2: w/ Rhy. Figs. 2 & 2A

Cm Bb Abmaj7 Bb Bb

side ___ of your hands _ and you played _ it to the beat. ___ ___ Could have had it

Bridge

Ab Bb Cm Bb

Gtr. 1

all, ___ roll-ing in the deep. ___ You had my heart in-

Gtr. 2

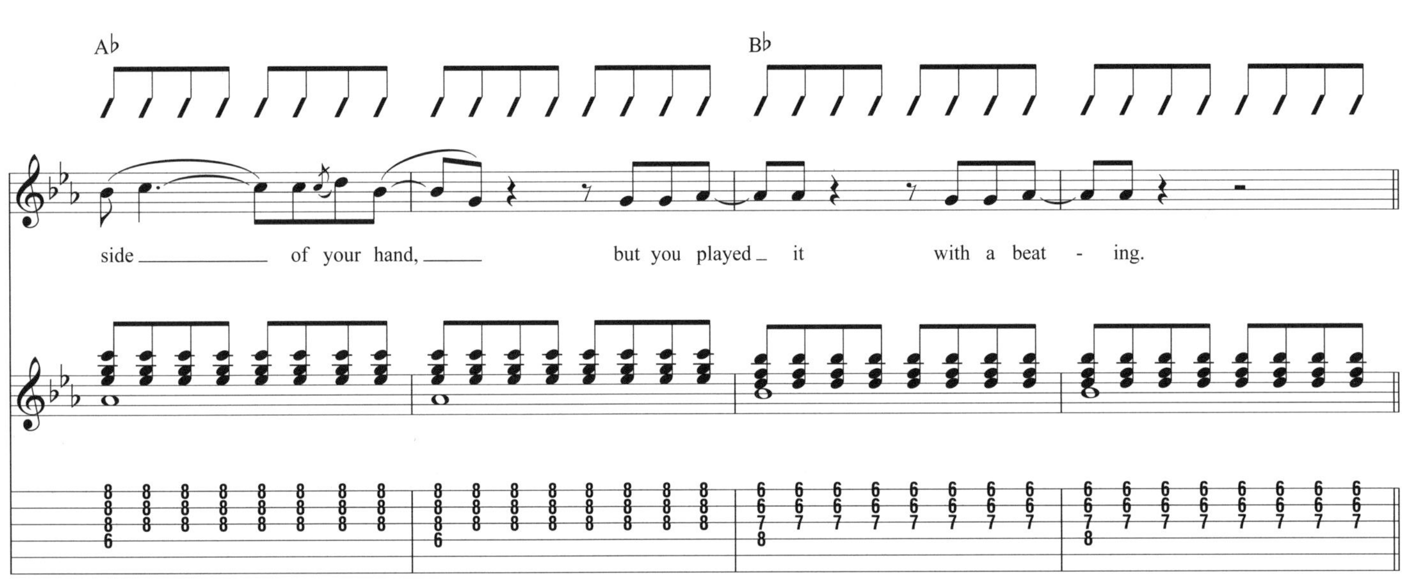

find what you look for.
Turned my sorrow into treasured gold. You
Whoa.
Oh,
Gtr. 3 (elec.)
mf
w/ clean tone

pay me back in kind and reap just what you sow.
whoa.)

Interlude

Bkgd. Voc.: w/ Voc. Fig. 1 (2 times)
Gtr. 2: w/ Rhy. Fig. 2A (2 times)
Gtr. 3 tacet
Cm
B♭
A♭maj7
B♭
We could have had it all.
We could have had it

Cm
B♭
A♭maj7
B♭
all, it all, it all, it all. We could have had it
Outro-Chorus
Bkgd. Voc.: w/ Voc. Fig. 1 (3 1/2 times)
Gtrs. 1 & 2: w/ Rhy. Figs. 2 & 2A (3 1/2 times)
all, roll - ing in the deep. You had my heart in -
side of your hand, and you played it to the beat. Could have had it
all, roll - ing in the deep.
(You're gon - na wish you nev - er had
You had my heart in - side of your hand, but you played
met me. You're gon - na wish.)
A♭
Cm
Gtr. 1
it, you played it, you played it, you played it to the beat.
Gtr. 2

from Shawn Mendes - *Shawn Mendes*

Señorita

Words and Music by Camila Cabello, Charlotte Aitchison, Jack Patterson, Shawn Mendes, Magnus Hoiberg, Benjamin Levin, Ali Tamposi and Andrew Wotman

Chorus

Gtr. 2: w/ Rhy. Fig. 1
Gtr. 1 tacet
Am
Cmaj7
call me se - ño - ri - ta. I wish I could pre - tend I ___ did - n't need ___ you, but ev - 'ry touch is
Gtr. 1
5

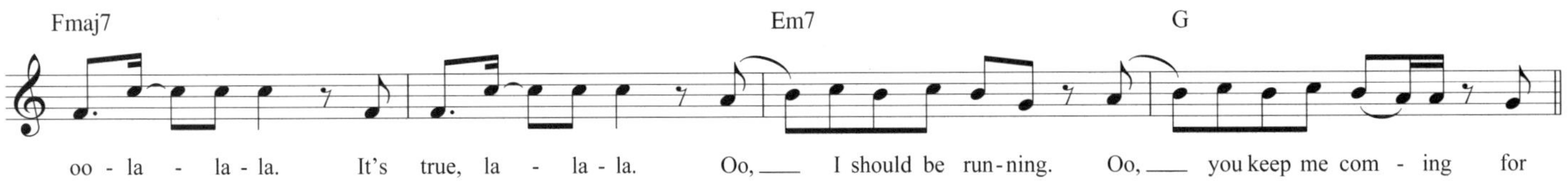
Fmaj7
Em7
G
oo - la - la - la. It's true, la - la - la. Oo, ___ I should be run - ning. Oo, ___ you keep me com - ing for

Verse

Gtr. 2: w/ Rhy. Fig. 1 (1 1/2 times)
Am
Cmaj7
you.
Male: 1. Land in Mi - a - mi, the air was hot from sum - mer rain. Sweat drip - ping off me ___ be - fore I e - ven knew her

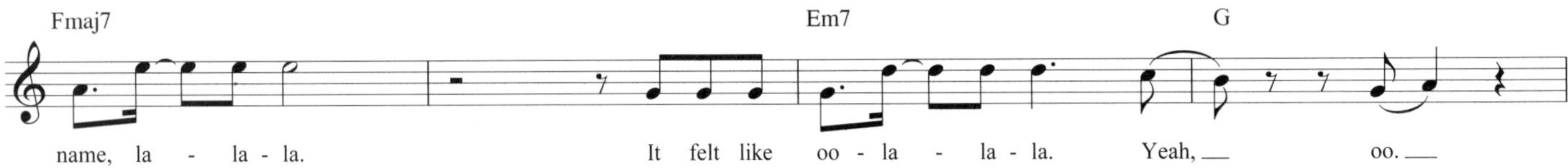
Fmaj7
Em7
G
name, la - la - la. It felt like oo - la - la - la. Yeah, ___ oo. ___

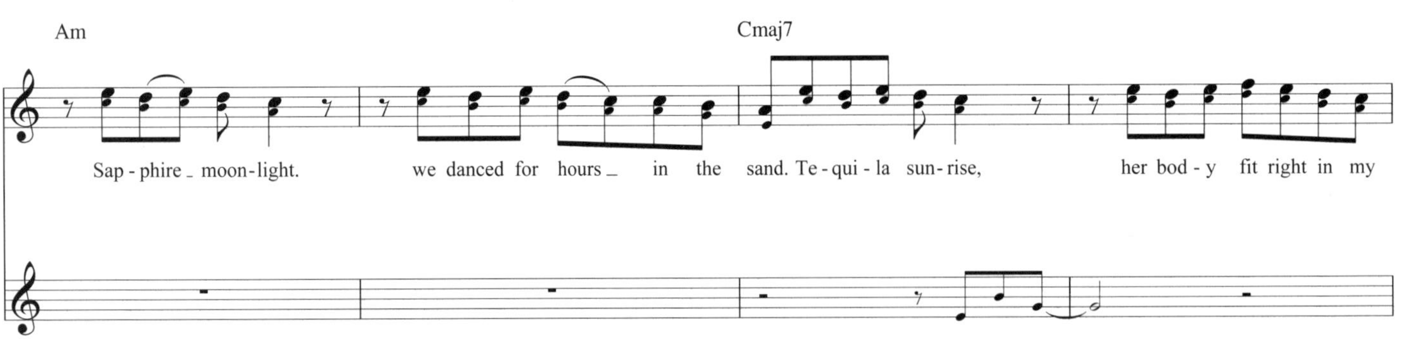
Am
Cmaj7
Sap - phire _ moon - light. we danced for hours _ in the sand. Te - qui - la sun - rise, her bod - y fit right in my
Female: (Te - qui - la.) ___

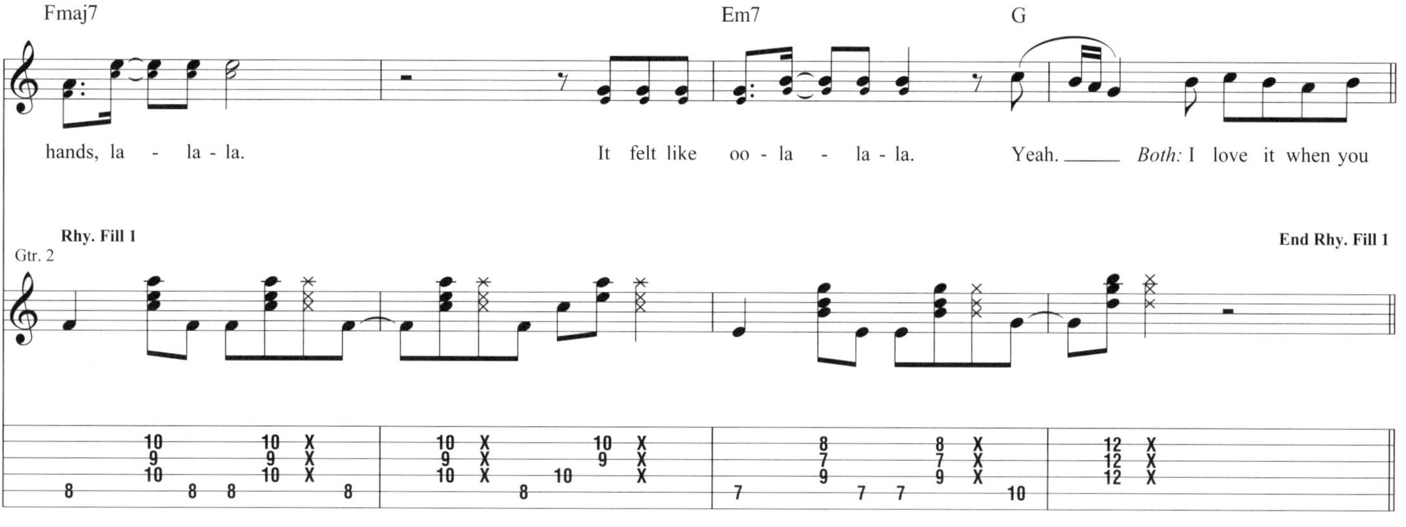

Gtr. 2: w/ Rhy. Fig. 1 (2 times)

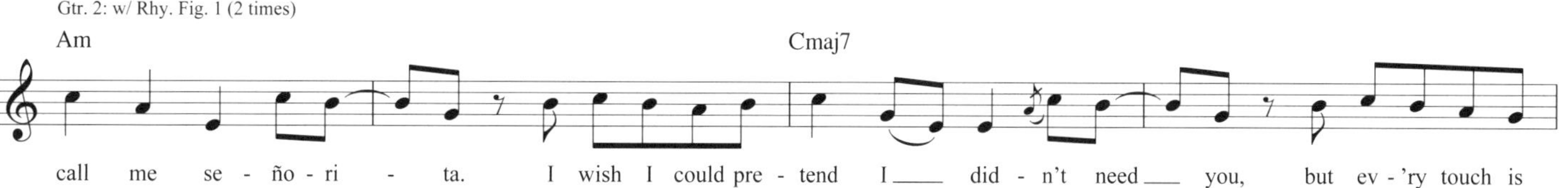

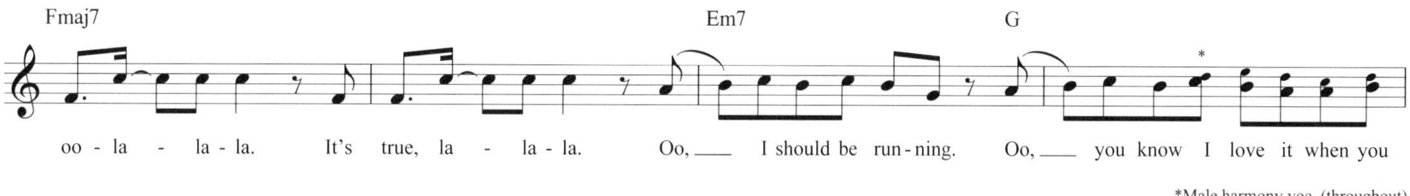

*Male harmony voc. (throughout)

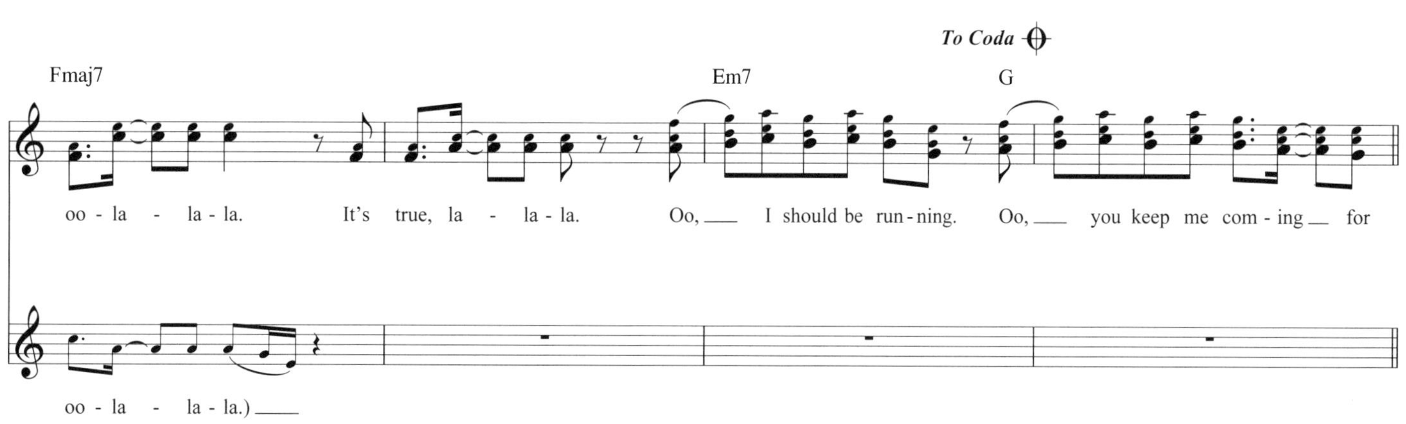

Verse

Gtr. 2: w/ Rhy. Fig. 1 (1st 4 meas.)
Am
Cmaj7
you.
Female: 2. Locked in the ho - tel, there's just some things that nev - er change. You say we're just friends,

Gtr. 2: w/ Rhy. Fill 1 (1st 2 meas.)
Fmaj7
but friends don't know the way you taste, la - la - la. 'Cause you
Male: (La - la - la - la - la.)

Em7
G
Am
know it's been a long time com-ing. Don't you let me fall. Oh. Oh, when your lips un - dress me,
Gtr. 2

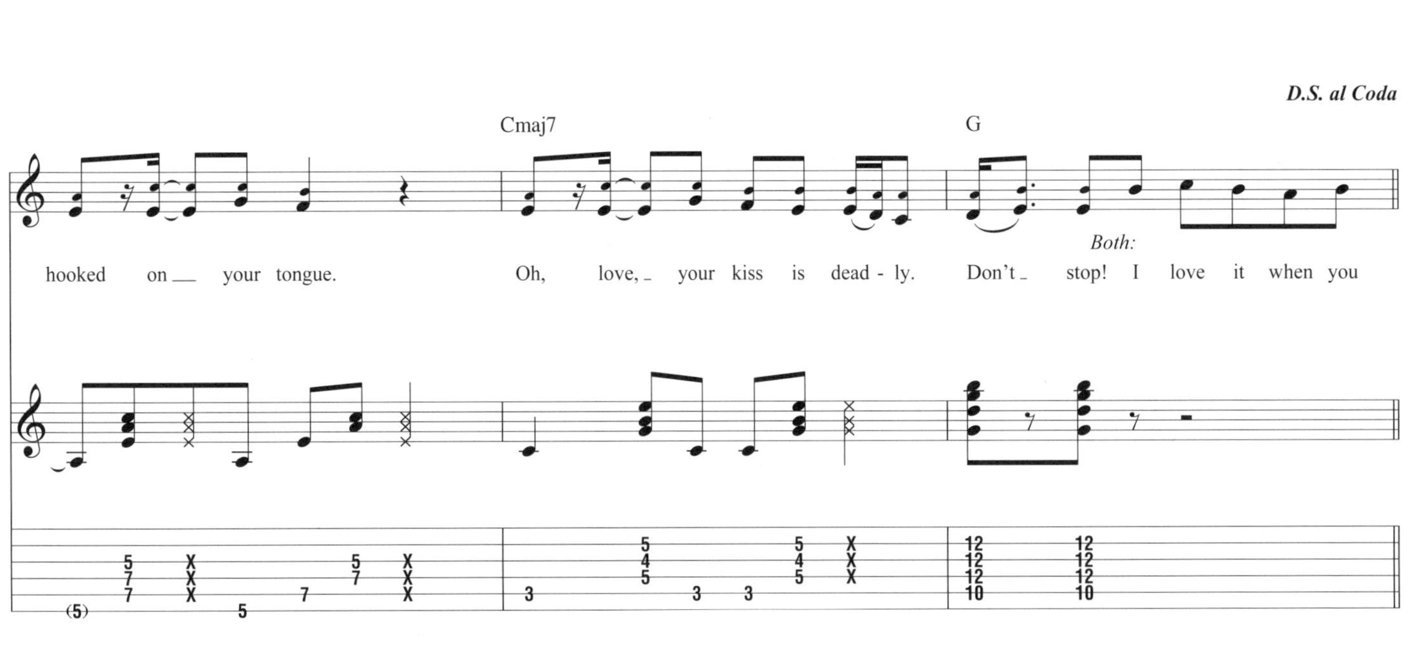
D.S. al Coda
Cmaj7
G
hooked on your tongue. Oh, love, your kiss is dead - ly. Don't stop! I love it when you
Both:

Coda

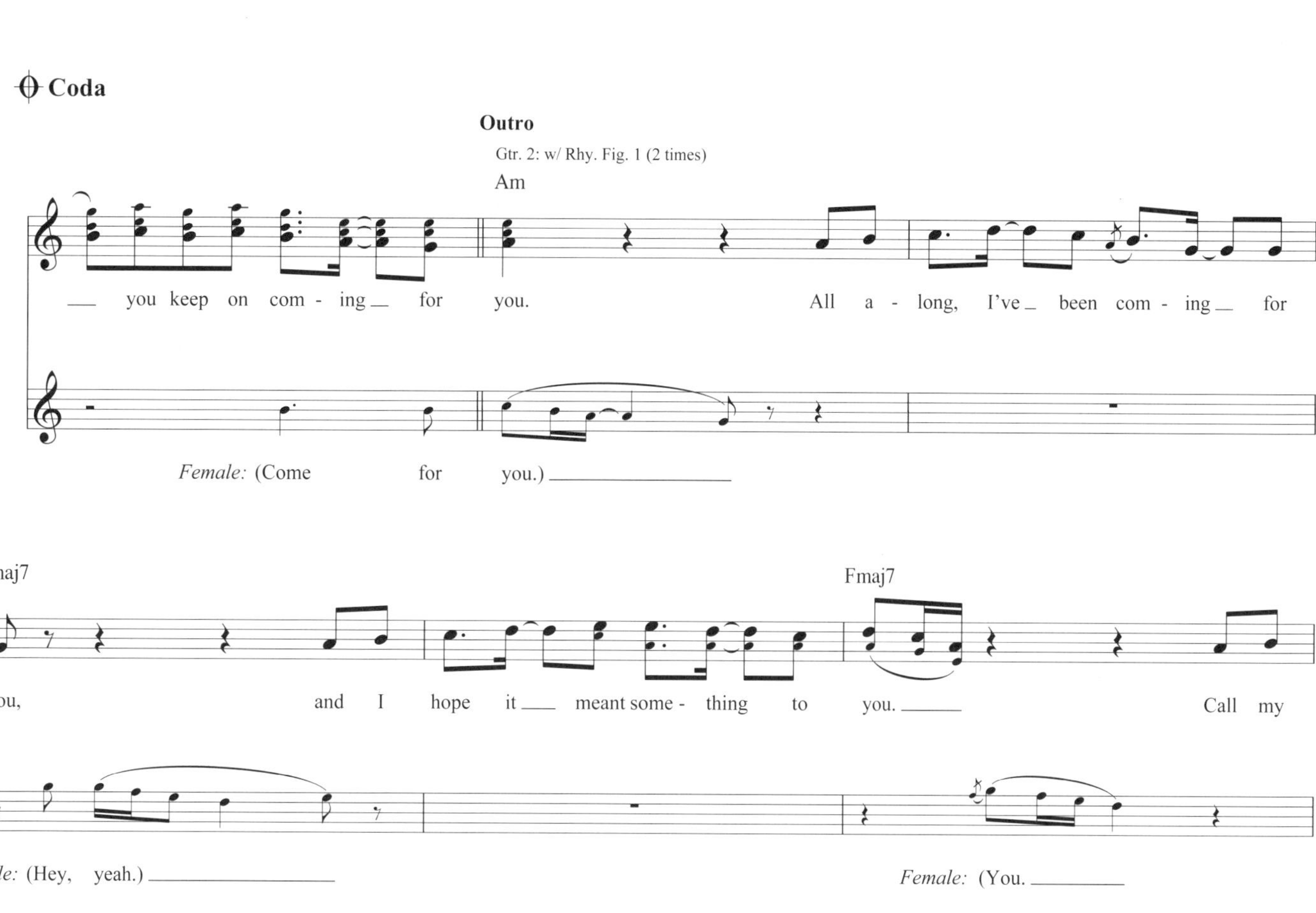

Outro
Gtr. 2: w/ Rhy. Fig. 1 (2 times)
Am
you keep on com - ing for you. All a - long, I've been com - ing for
Female: (Come for you.)
Cmaj7
Fmaj7
you, and I hope it meant some - thing to you. Call my
Male: (Hey, yeah.)
Female: (You.

Em7
G
Gtr. 1: w/ Riff A
Am
name, I'll be com - ing for you, com - ing for you.
Male: (Oh, yeah.
Com - ing for you, com - ing for you.)

Cmaj7
Fmaj7
For you, for you.
Oo, she loves it when I come.)

Em7
G
N.C.
Oo, I should be run-ning. Oo, you keep me com - ing for you.

from Lady Gaga & Bradley Cooper - *A Star is Born Soundtrack*

Shallow

from A STAR IS BORN

Words and Music by Stefani Germanotta, Mark Ronson, Andrew Wyatt and Anthony Rossomando

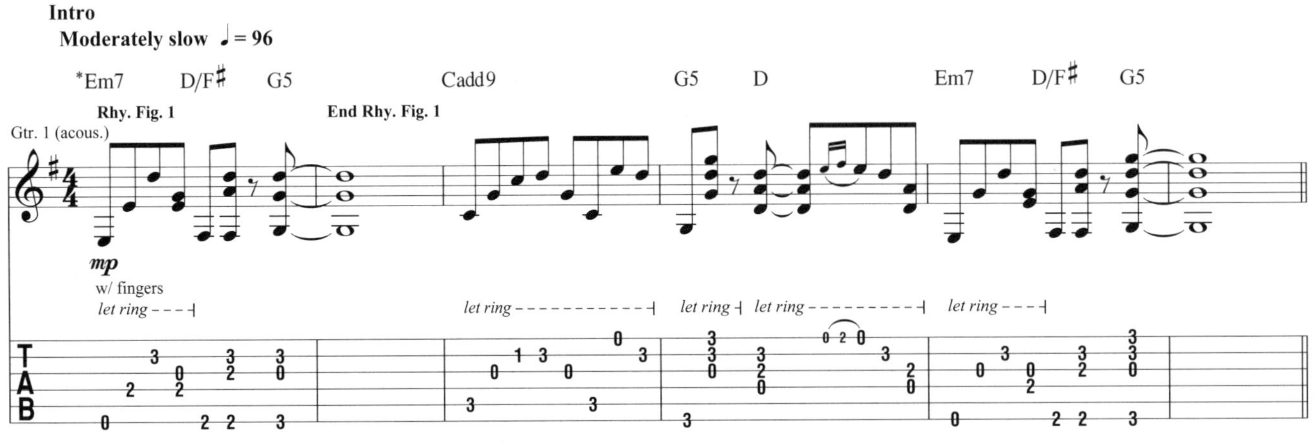

*Chord symbols reflect implied harmony.

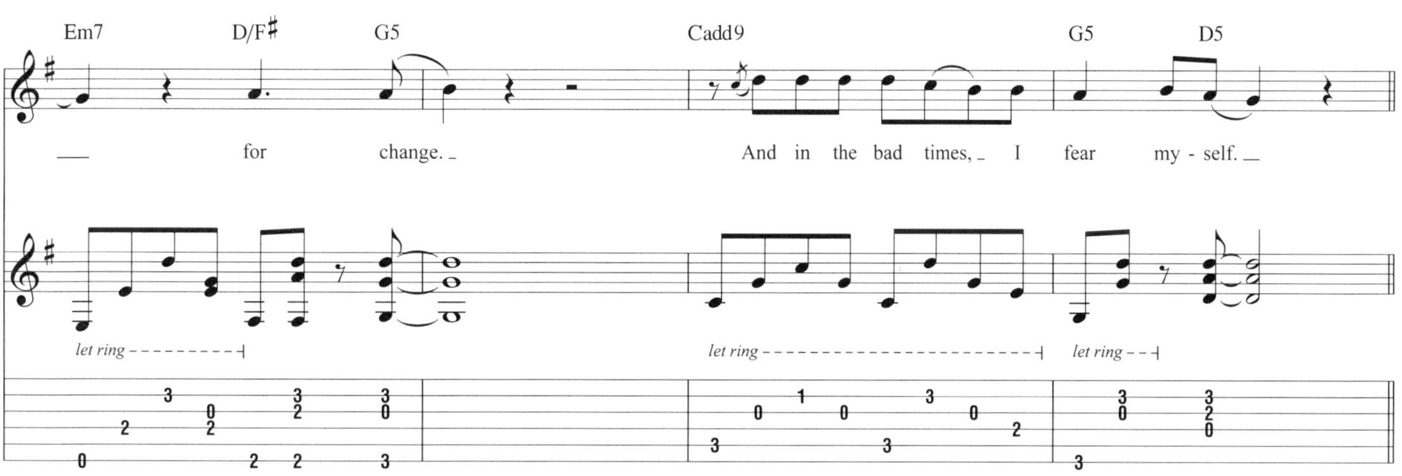

Interlude

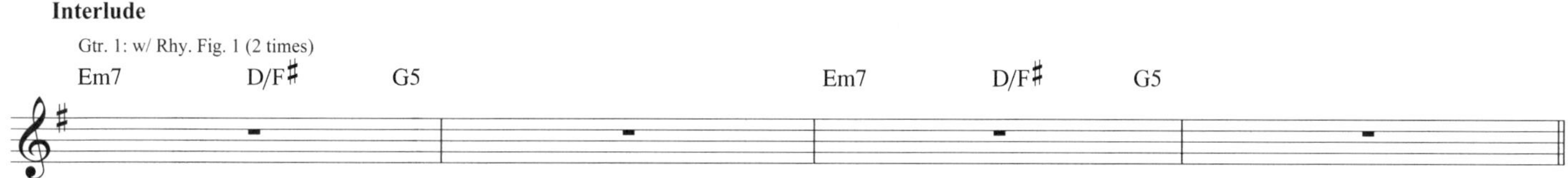

Verse

*Pedal steel arr. for gtr.

**Vol. swells (throughout)

Gtr. 1: w/ Rhy. Fill 1
Em7 D/F♯ G5 C G5 D
Or do you need more?
Ain't it hard keep-ing it so hard - core?
mp
I'm fall - ing.
In all the good times, I find my-self long-ing
Gtr. 2
Gtr. 1
let ring
for change.
And in the bad times, I fear my-self.

Pre-Chorus
Am
Dadd9/F♯
G5
D5
Em7
I'm off the deep - end; watch as I dive - in. I'll nev - er meet - the ground.
Riff A
End Riff A
w/ pick
let ring
Gtr. 1: w/ Riff A
Crash through the sur - face, where they can't hurt - us. We're far from the shal - low now.
Gtr. 2
Chorus
Am/G
*Both: In the sha - ha - sha - al - low.
In the sha - ha - sha - la - la - la - low.
steady gliss.
Gtr. 1
Riff B
End Riff B
*Female voice sings melody.

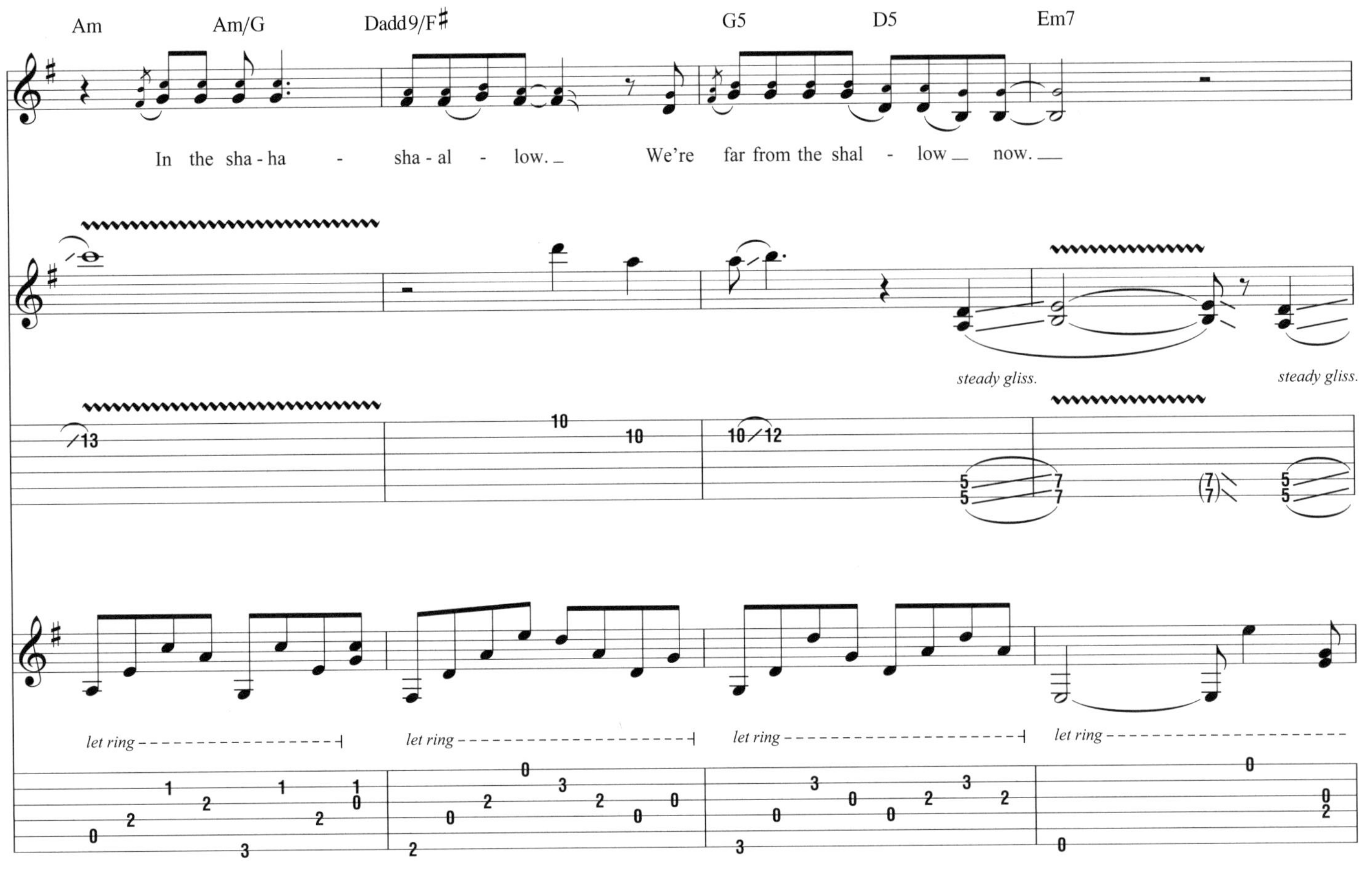

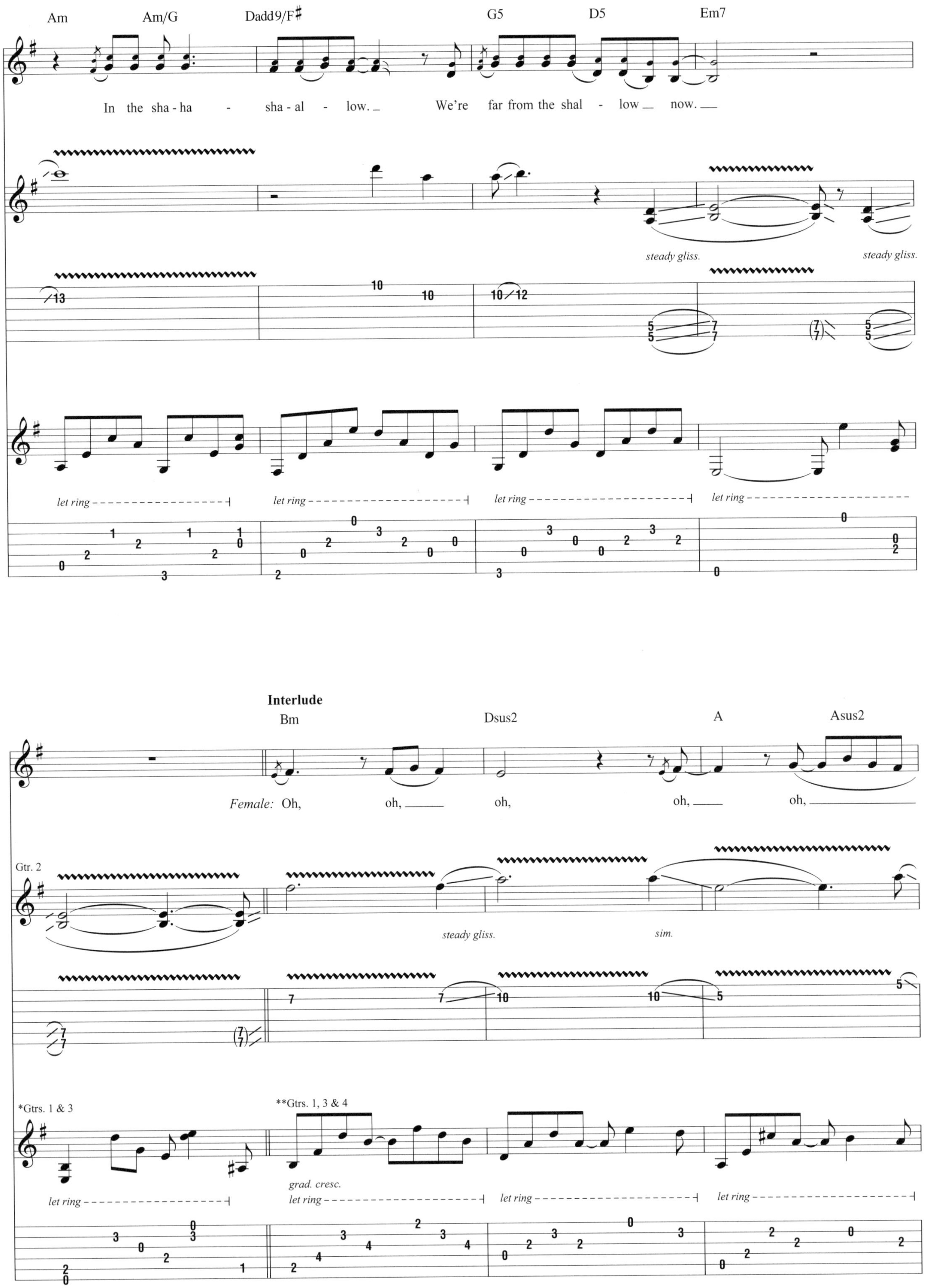

Interlude

Bm Dsus2 A Asus2

Female: Oh, oh, oh, oh, oh,

Gtr. 2

steady gliss. *sim.*

*Gtrs. 1 & 3

**Gtrs. 1, 3 & 4

grad. cresc.

let ring *let ring* *let ring* *let ring*

*Gtr. 3 (acous.), played ***mp***.

Gtr. 4 (elec.) w/ dist., played ***p*.
Composite arrangement

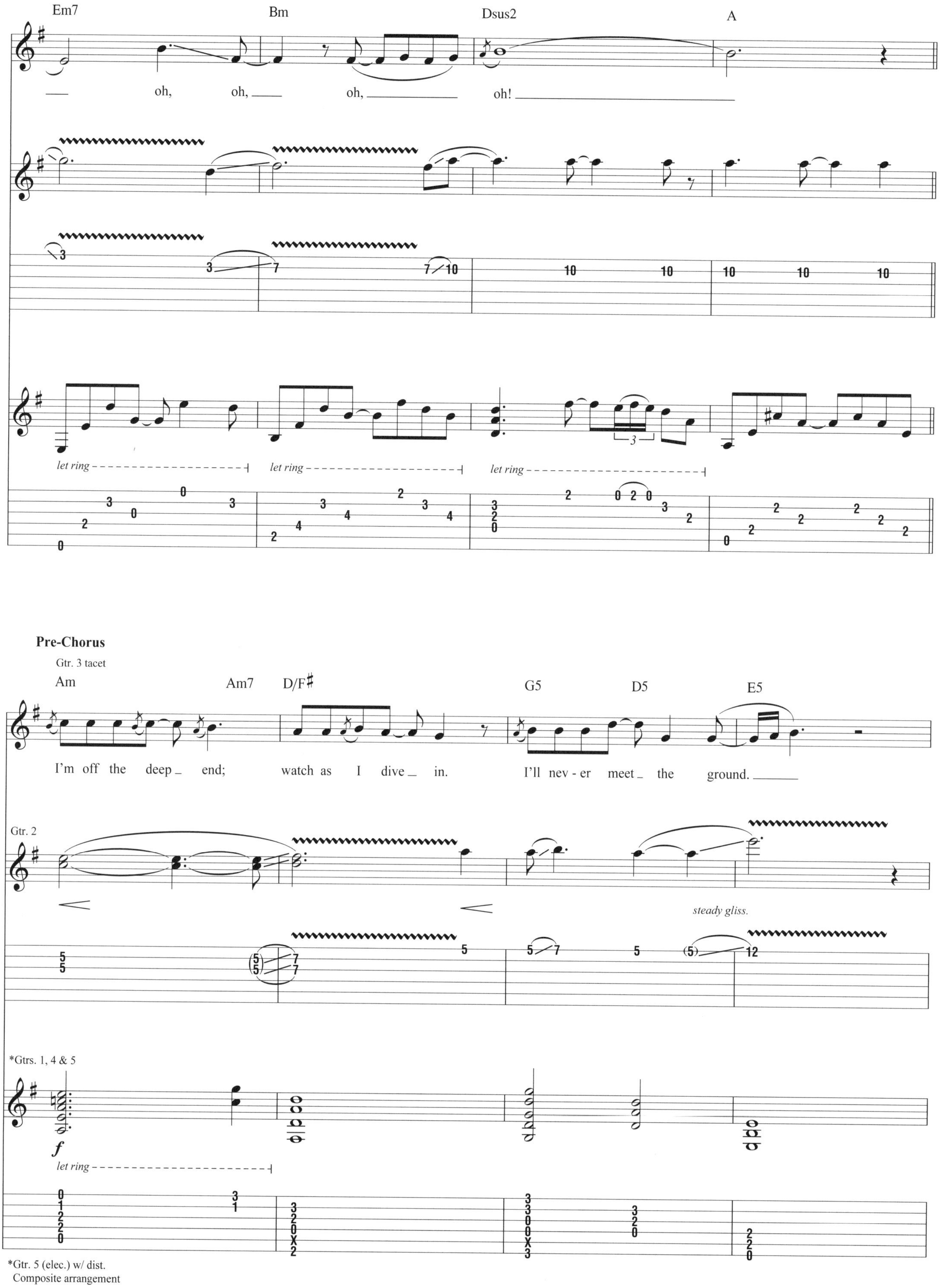

Pre-Chorus

Gtr. 3 tacet

Am Am7 D/F♯ G5 D5 E5

I'm off the deep _ end; watch as I dive _ in. I'll nev - er meet _ the ground. ____

Gtr. 2

steady gliss.

*Gtrs. 1, 4 & 5

f

let ring

*Gtr. 5 (elec.) w/ dist.
Composite arrangement

Gtrs. 1, 4 & 5: w/ Riff A
Am
Dadd9/F♯
G5
D5
Em7
Crash through the sur - face, where they can't hurt _ us. We're far from the shal - low _ now. ___
Gtr. 2

Chorus

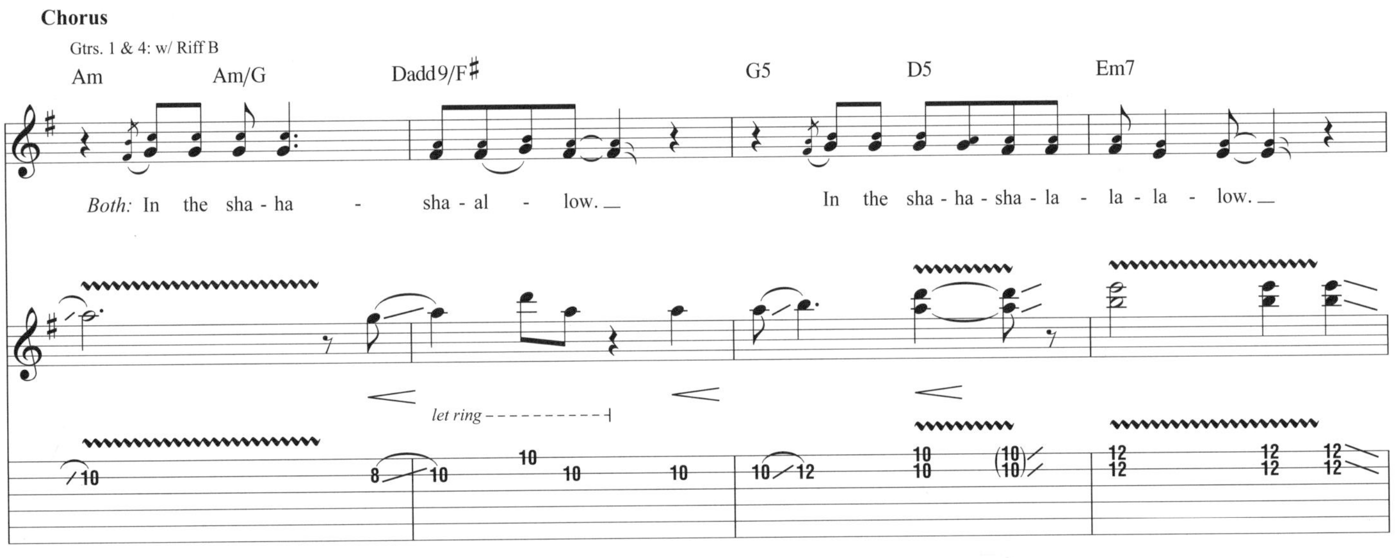
Gtrs. 1 & 4: w/ Riff B
Am
Am/G
Dadd9/F♯
G5
D5
Em7
Both: In the sha - ha - sha - al - low. _ In the sha - ha - sha - la - la - la - low. _
let ring

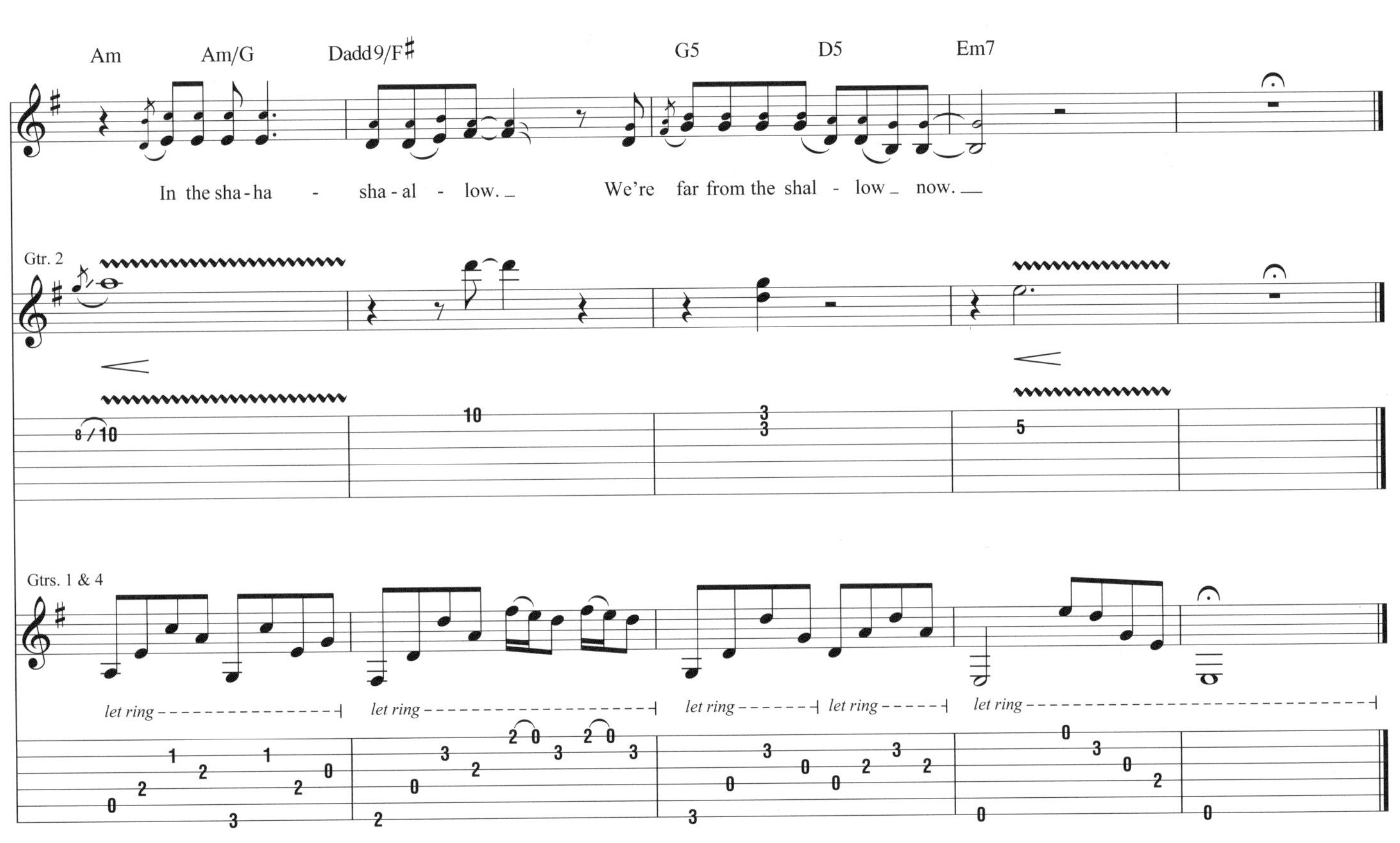
Am
Am/G
Dadd9/F♯
G5
D5
Em7
In the sha - ha - sha - al - low. _ We're far from the shal - low _ now. ___
Gtr. 2
Gtrs. 1 & 4
let ring
let ring
let ring
let ring
let ring

from Walk the Moon - *Talking Is Hard*

Shut Up and Dance

Words and Music by Ryan McMahon, Ben Berger, Sean Waugaman, Eli Maiman, Nicholas Petricca and Kevin Ray

Interlude

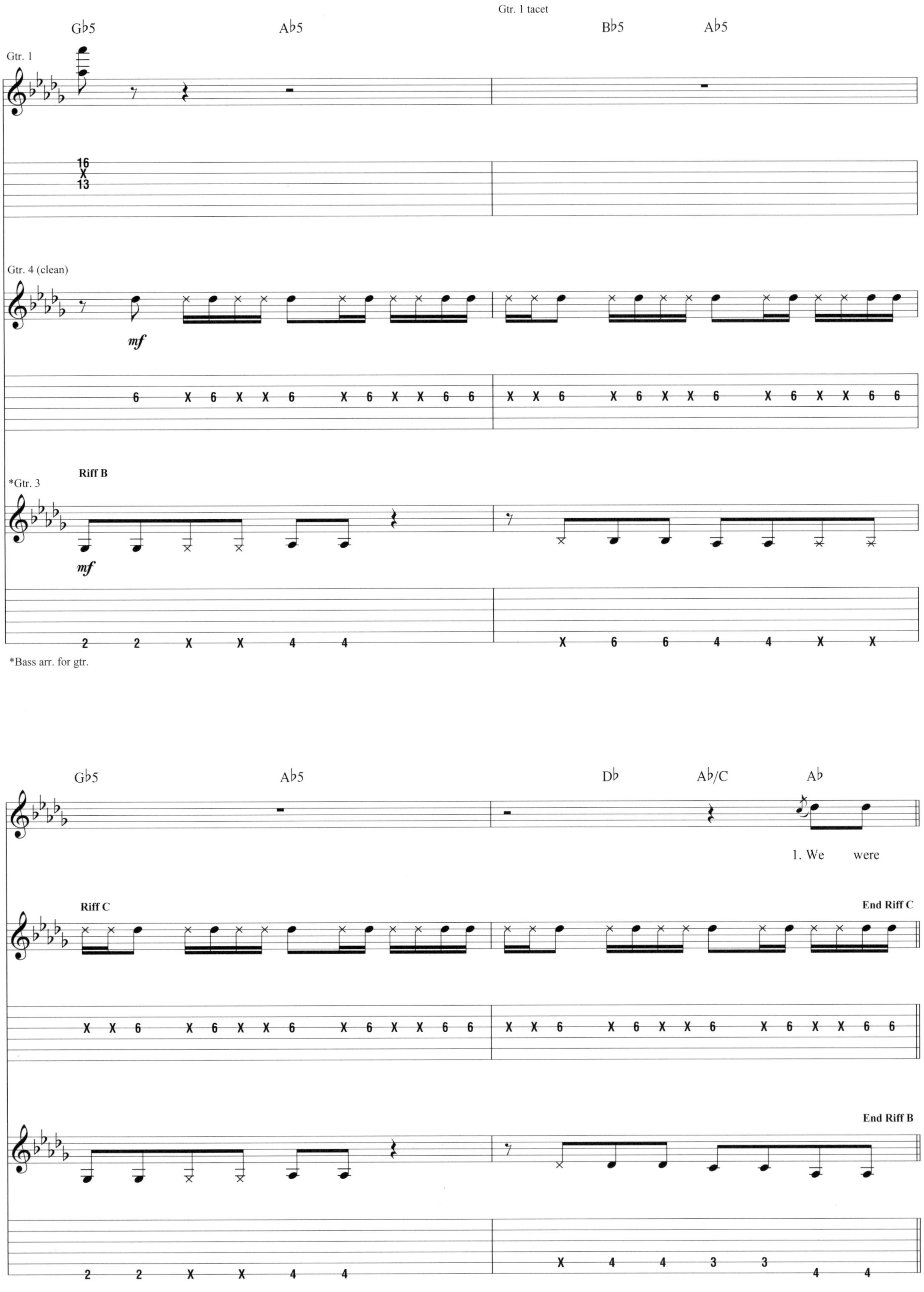

Gtr. 1 tacet

G♭5 A♭5 B♭5 A♭5

Gtr. 1

Gtr. 4 (clean)

mf

Riff B

*Gtr. 3

mf

*Bass arr. for gtr.

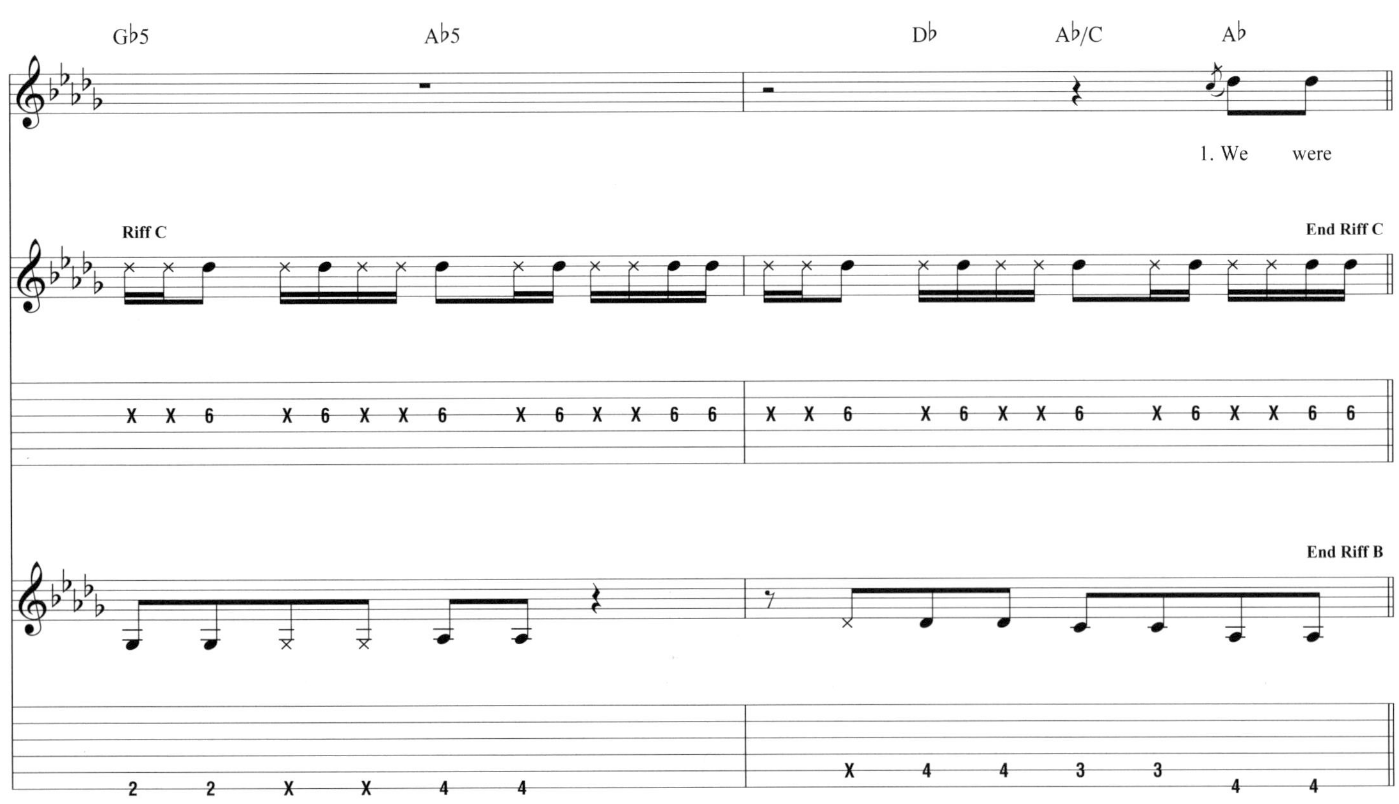

Verse
Gtr. 3: w/ Riff B (2 times)
Gtr. 4: w/ Riff C (3 times)
G♭5 A♭5 B♭5 A♭5 G♭5 A♭5
vic - tims of the night, the chem - i - cal phy - si - cal Kryp - to - nite.
dress and some beat up sneaks, my dis - co - tech Ju - li - ette teen - age dream.
D♭ A♭/C A♭ G♭5 A♭5 B♭5 A♭5
Help - less to the bass and fad - in' light. Oh, we were bound
I felt it in my chest as she looked at me. I knew we were bound
G♭5 A♭5 D♭ A♭/C A♭
to get to - geth - er, bound to get to - geth - er.
to be to - geth - er, bound to be to - geth - er.
Gtr. 4
Gtr. 5 (clean)
Gtr. 6 (dist.)

Pre-Chorus

Gtr. 4 tacet

Db/F Gb | Db Ab/C Ab Gb | Db/F Gb Ab

She took my arm, I don't know how it hap-pened. We took the floor and she said, ____ "Oh, don't you

Gtr. 5

Rhy. Fig. 2

End Rhy. Fig. 2

Gtr. 6

Harm.

𝄋 Chorus

Db Gbsus2 | Bbm7 Ab

dare look _ back, just keep your eyes on __ me." I said, "You're

*Chord symbols reflect overall harmony.

2.
G♭
Aw, come on, girl!
*Gtr. 7
f
*Synth arr. for gtr.
Gtrs. 5 & 6
Interlude
B♭5
D♭5
G♭5
A♭5
Gtr. 7
1/2
Riff E
Gtr. 5
End Riff E
Gtr. 6
Rhy. Fig. 4
End Rhy. Fig. 4

Gtr. 5: w/ Riff E (2 times)
Gtr. 6: w/ Rhy. Fig. 4 (2 times)

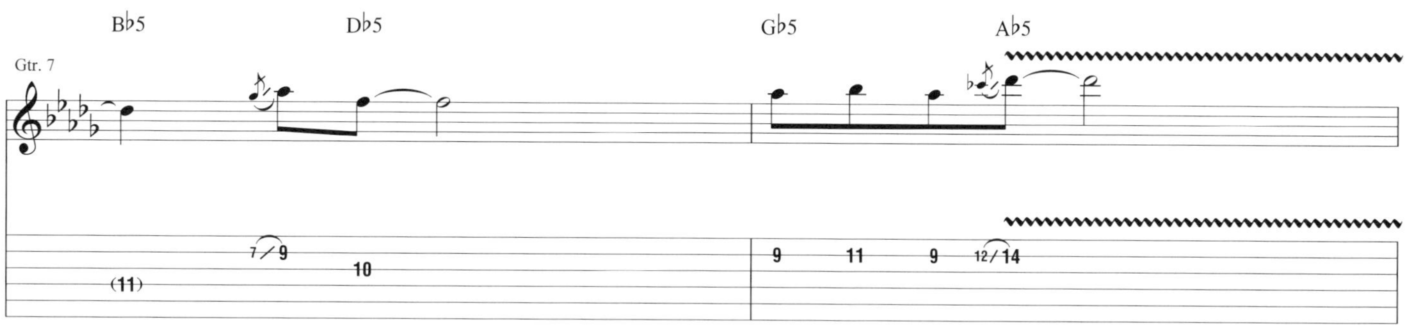

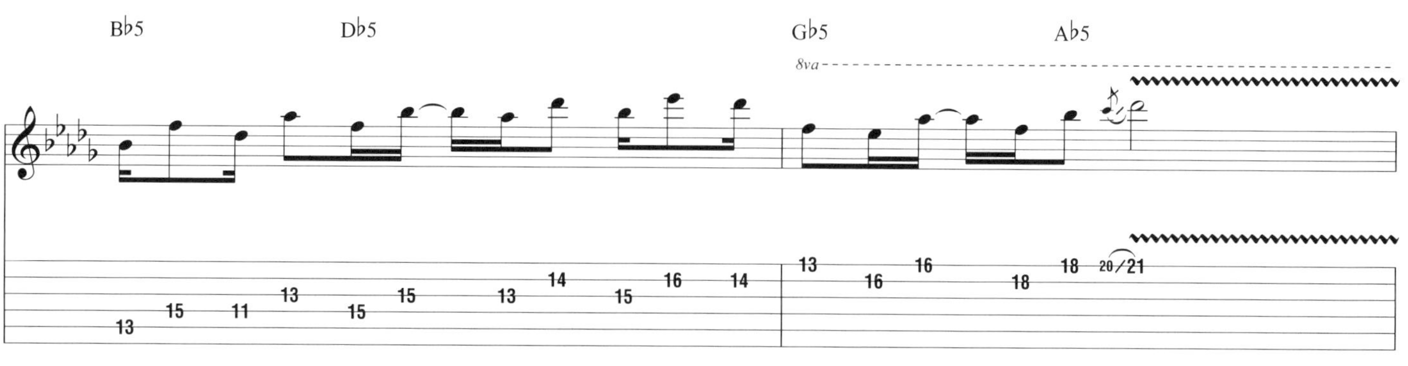

B♭5 D♭5 G♭5 A♭5

8va

Gtr. 7

let ring

Gtr. 5

1/4

Gtr. 6

Pre-Chorus
Gtr. 5: w/ Rhy. Fig. 2 (2 times)
Gtr. 7 tacet
D♭/F G♭ D♭ A♭/C A♭ G♭ D♭/F G♭ D♭ A♭/C A♭ G♭
Deep in her eyes, I think I see a fu - ture. I real - ize this is my last chance.
Gtr. 6
D♭/F G♭ D♭ A♭/C A♭ G♭ D♭/F G♭ A♭
She took my arm, I don't know how it hap - pened. We took the floor and she said,
Gtr. 5
Gtr. 6
Interlude
Gtr. 1: w/ Riff A (2 times)
Gtr. 2: w/ Rhy. Fig. 1 (2 times)
Gtrs. 5 & 6 tacet
D♭ D♭sus4 D♭ D♭sus2 D♭ D♭sus4 D♭ D♭sus2
"Oh, don't you
Chorus
Gtr. 1: w/ Riff A (3 1/2 times)
Gtr. 2: w/ Rhy. Fig. 1 (3 1/2 times)
D♭ D♭sus4 D♭ D♭sus2 D♭ D♭sus4 D♭ D♭sus2
dare look back, just keep your eyes on me." I said, "You're hold - in' back." She said, "Shut up and dance with me."

D♭ D♭sus4 D♭ D♭sus2 D♭ D♭sus4 N.C.

This wom - an is my des - ti - ny. She said, "Oo, hoo. Shut up and dance. Don't you

Coda

Gtrs. 2 & 6: w/ Rhy. Figs. 3 & 3A (2 times)
Gtr. 5: w/ Riff D

D♭ G♭sus2 B♭m7 A♭ D♭ G♭sus2 B♭m7 A♭

"Oo, hoo. Shut up and dance with me."

Gtr. 7

loco

1/2

B♭m7 D♭ G♭sus2 A♭

8va

Gtr. 7

let ring

Gtr. 5

1/4

Gtr. 2

Gtr. 6

from fun. - *Some Nights*

Some Nights

Words and Music by Jeff Bhasker, Andrew Dost, Jack Antonoff and Nate Ruess

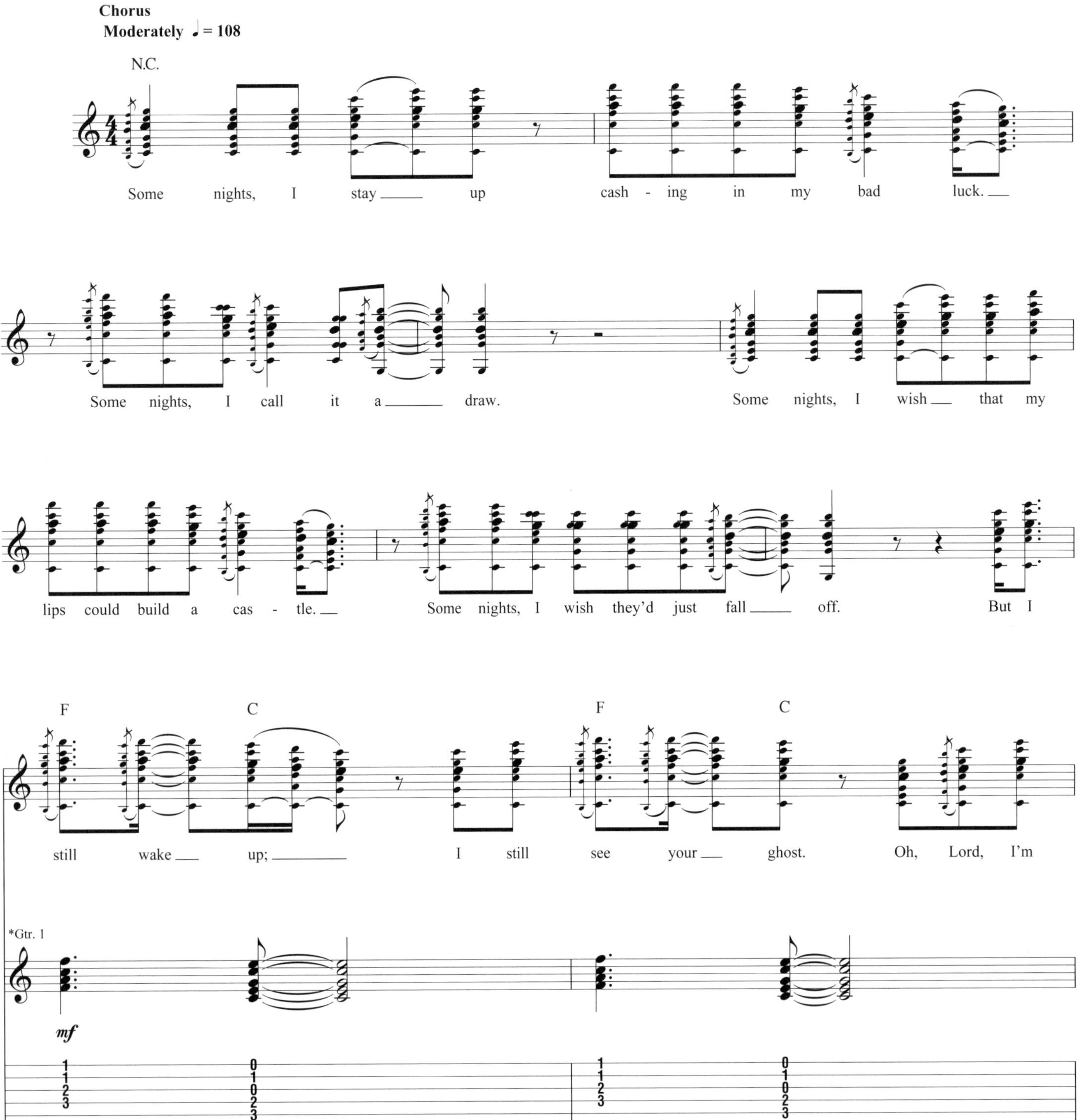

*Piano arr. for gtr.

F
C
G
still not sure what I stand for, oh.
Voc. Fig. 1
End Voc. Fig. 1
*(Oh.)
Voc. Fig. 2
(Whoa,
Gtr. 2 (clean)
mp
Gtr. 1
*Fade in.
Gtr. 2 tacet
F
C
F
C
Am
G
What do I stand for? What do I stand for? Most nights, I don't know an-y-
End Voc. Fig. 2
oh, oh, whoa.)
Gtr. 1
let ring
*T
let ring
T
*T = Thumb on 6th string

Interlude
F C F C F C G
more.
Voc. Fig. 3
(Oh, oh, whoa, oh, whoa, oh.
Rhy. Fig. 1
End Rhy. Fig. 1
let ring
F C F Fsus2 C F Fsus2 C G
1. So,
End Voc. Fig. 3
Oh, oh, whoa, oh, whoa, oh.)
Rhy. Fig. 2
End Rhy. Fig. 2
let ring
Verse
Bkgd. Voc.: w/ Voc. Fig. 3
Gtr. 1: w/ Rhy. Fig. 1 (1 3/4 times)
F C F C
this it it, boys; this is war. What are we wait - ing for?
Gtr. 3 (dist.)
mf
let ring

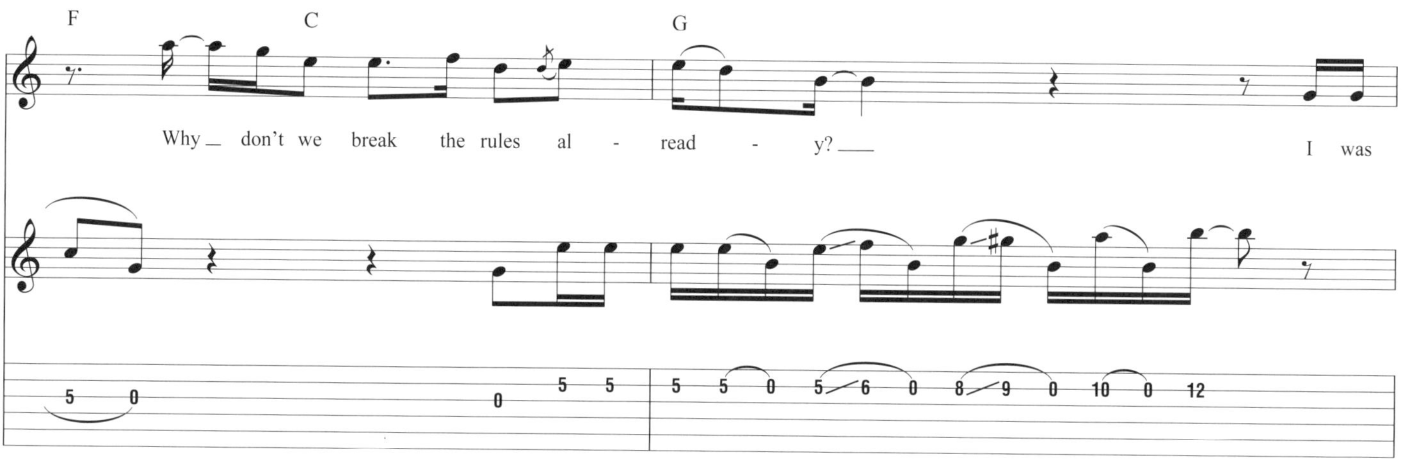
F C G
Why don't we break the rules al - read - y? I was

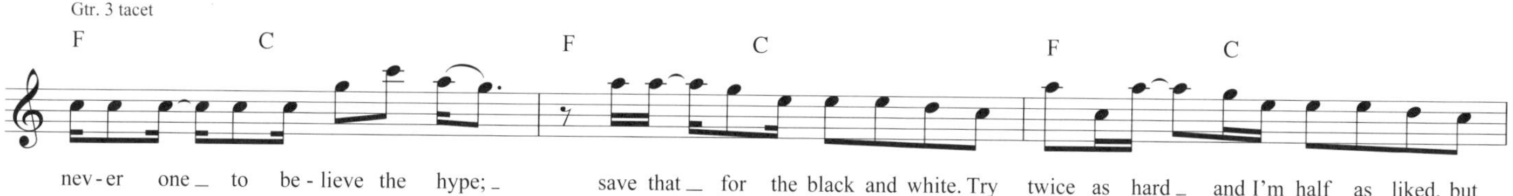
Gtr. 3 tacet
F C F C F C
nev - er one to be - lieve the hype; save that for the black and white. Try twice as hard and I'm half as liked, but

G
here they come a - gain to jack my style. That's al -
Gtr. 1
let ring

Pre-Chorus

Gtr. 1: w/ Rhy. Fig. 1
F C F C F C
right. I found a mar - tyr in my bed to - night. (She) stops my bones from won - der - ing

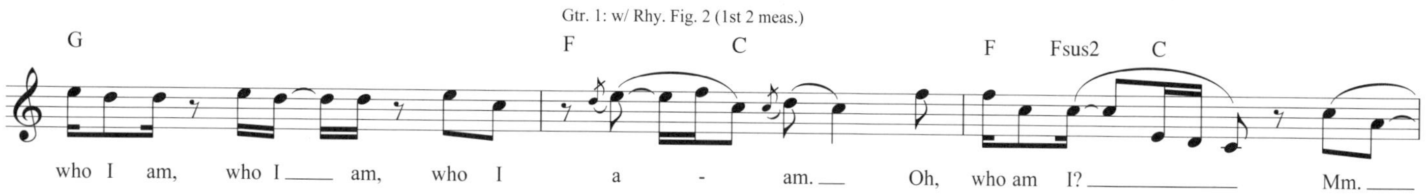
Gtr. 1: w/ Rhy. Fig. 2 (1st 2 meas.)
G F C F Fsus2 C
who I am, who I am, who I a - am. Oh, who am I? Mm.

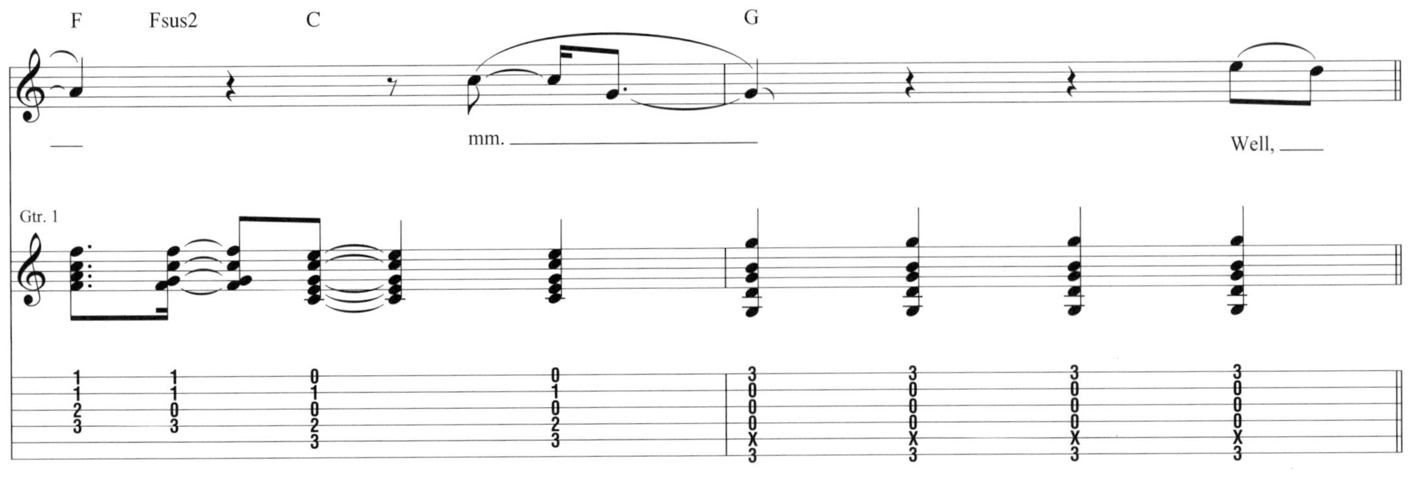

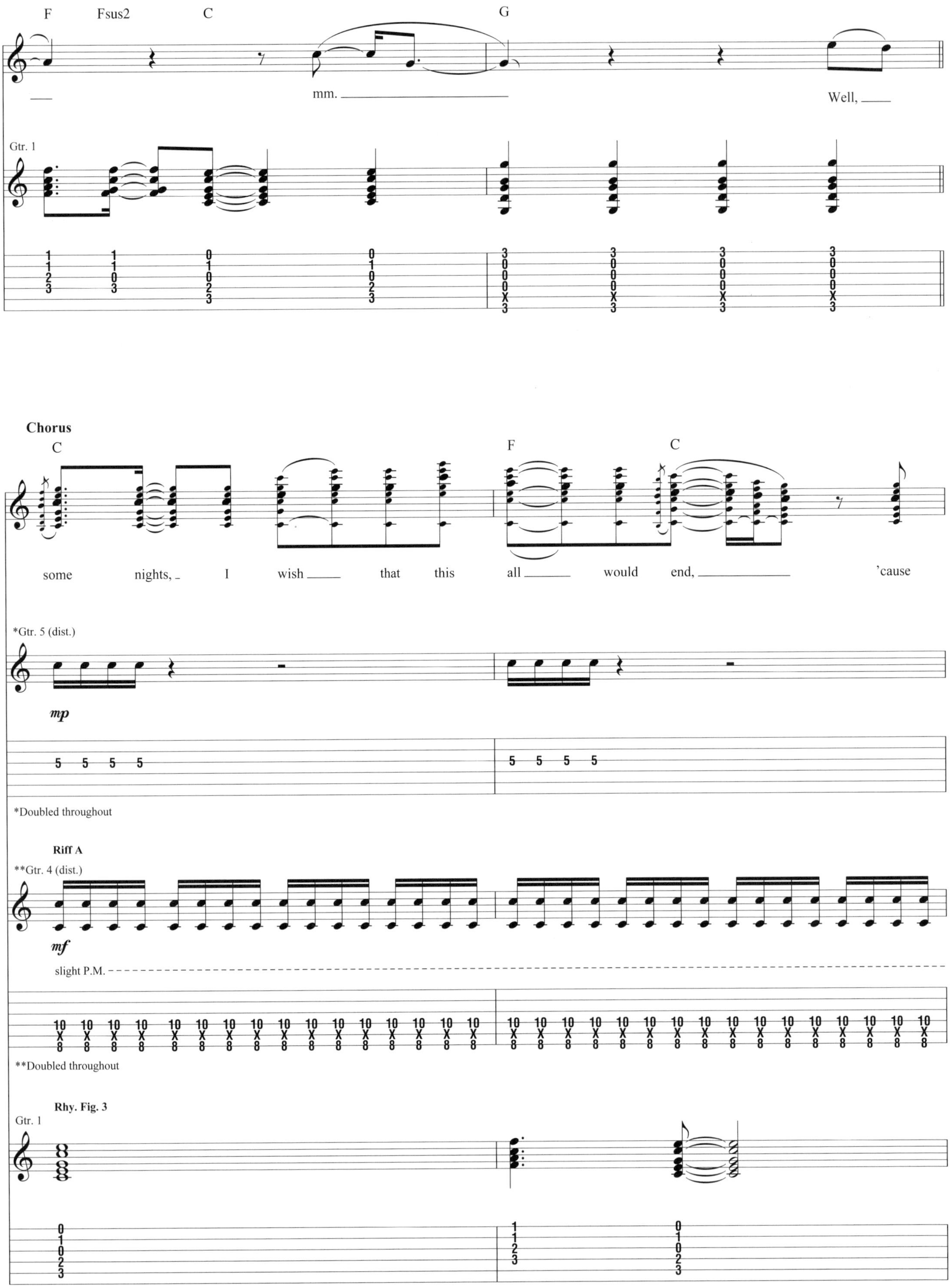

Chorus

C F C

some nights, I wish that this all would end, 'cause

*Gtr. 5 (dist.)

mp

*Doubled throughout

Riff A

**Gtr. 4 (dist.)

mf

slight P.M.

**Doubled throughout

Rhy. Fig. 3

Gtr. 1

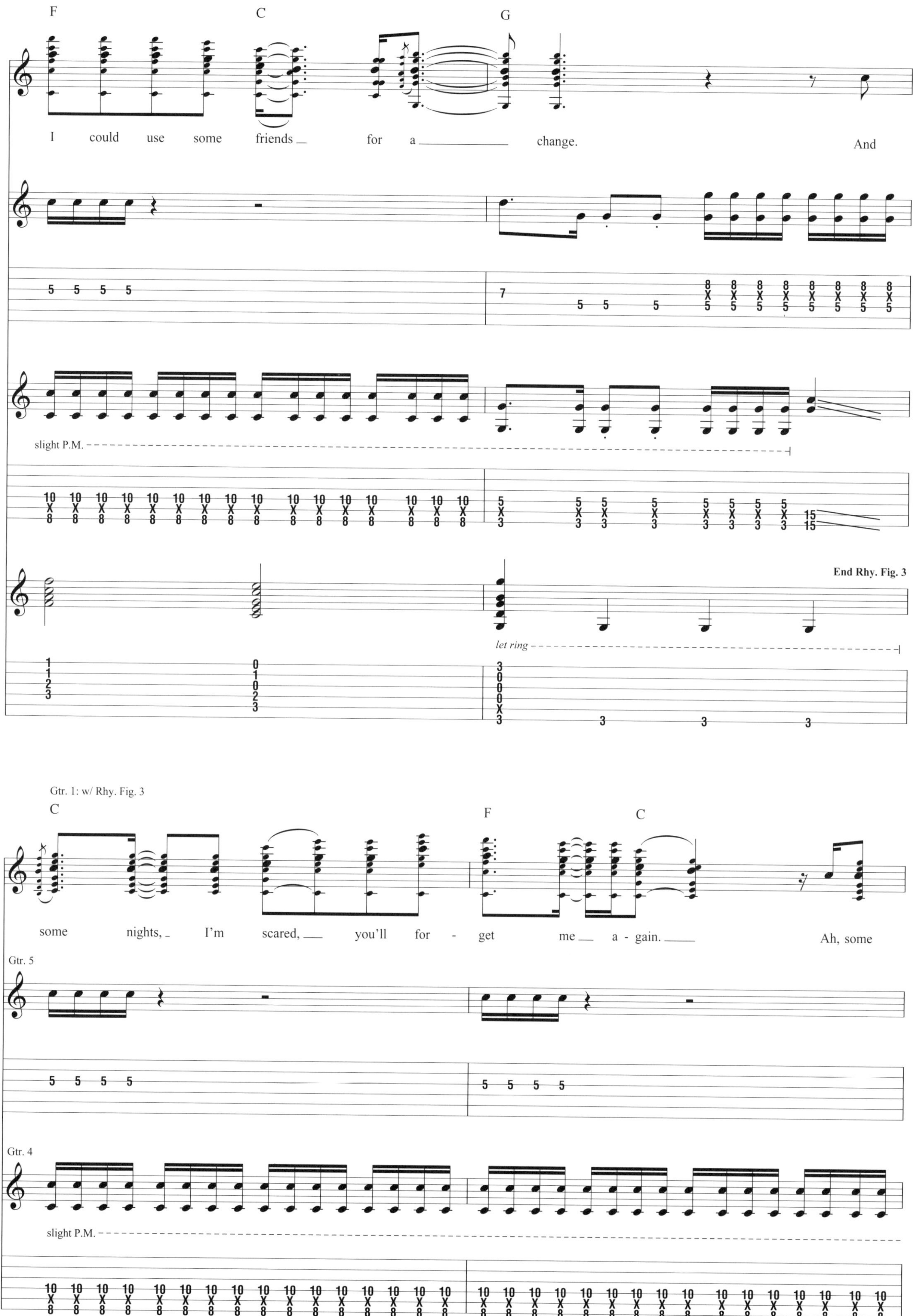
F
C
G
I could use some friends for a change.
And
slight P.M.
End Rhy. Fig. 3
let ring
Gtr. 1: w/ Rhy. Fig. 3
C
F
C
some nights, I'm scared, you'll for - get me a - gain.
Ah, some
Gtr. 5
Gtr. 4
slight P.M.

F
C
G
nights, I al - ways win.
But I
(I al - ways win.)
End Riff A
slight P.M.
Gtr. 1: w/ Rhy. Fig. 1
Gtr. 5 tacet
F
C
F
C
still wake up; I still see your ghost. Oh, Lord, I'm
*Gtr. 6 (dist.)
Riff B1
mf
*Doubled throughout
Gtr. 5
Riff B
Gtr. 4
slight P.M.

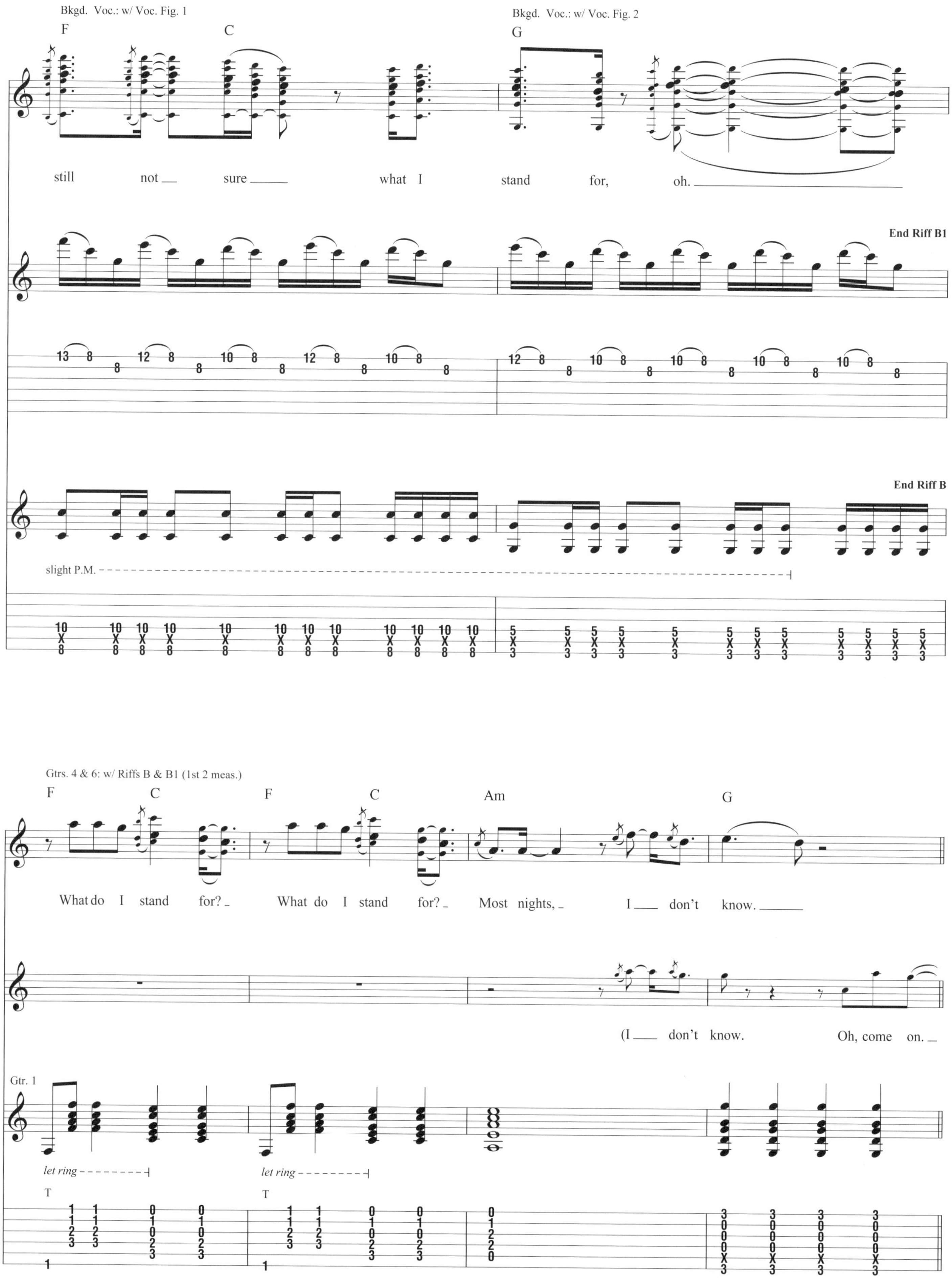

Bkgd. Voc.: w/ Voc. Fig. 1

F C

Bkgd. Voc.: w/ Voc. Fig. 2

G

still not sure what I stand for, oh.

End Riff B1

End Riff B

slight P.M.

Interlude
F
C
G
Spoken: So this is it.
I sold my soul for this.
Washed my hands of that for this?
I miss my mom and dad for this? No.
Oh, come on.)
(Na, na, na.
Na, na, na.
Na, na, na.
Rhy. Fig. 4
End Rhy. Fig. 4
Gtr. 1: w/ Rhy. Fig. 4 (2 times)
When I see stars, that's...
When I see stars, that's all they are.
When I hear songs,...
Come on.
...they sound like a swan. So come on.)
Na, na, na.
Na, na, na.
Na, na, na.
2. Well,
(Oh, come on!)
(Oh, come on.)
Oh, come on.)

Verse
Bkgd. Voc.: w/ Voc. Fig. 3
Gtr. 1: w/ Rhy. Fig. 1
F
C
F
C
that is it, guys; that is all. Five min - utes in and I'm bored a - gain.
F
C
G
Ten years of this, I'm not sure if an - y - bod - y un - der - stands. This
F
Fsus2
C
F
Fmaj7
C
one is not for the folks at home. Sor - ry to leave, Mom, I had to go.
Gtr. 1
let ring
F
Fadd♯4
C
G
Who the fuck wants to die a - lone, all dried up in the des - ert sun? My heart is
let ring
let ring

Bridge
F
C
breaking - ing for my sis - ter and the con that she called "love." And then I
G
Dm
look in - to my neph - ew's eyes. Man, you would-n't be - lieve
F
Dm
the most a - maz - ing things that can come from
G
some ter - ri - ble
let ring

Interlude

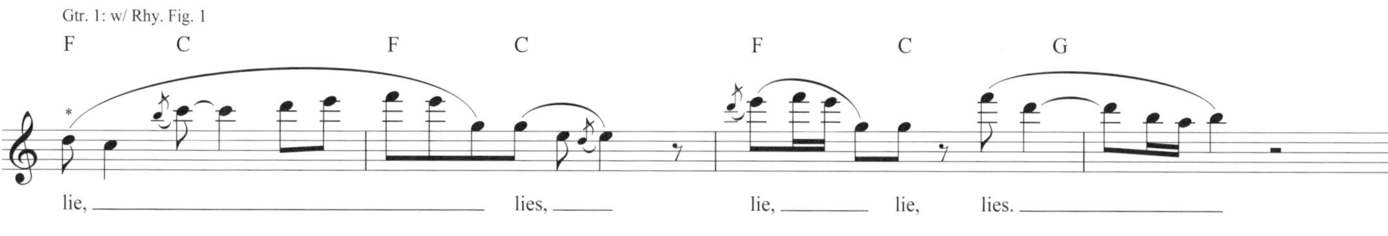

Interlude

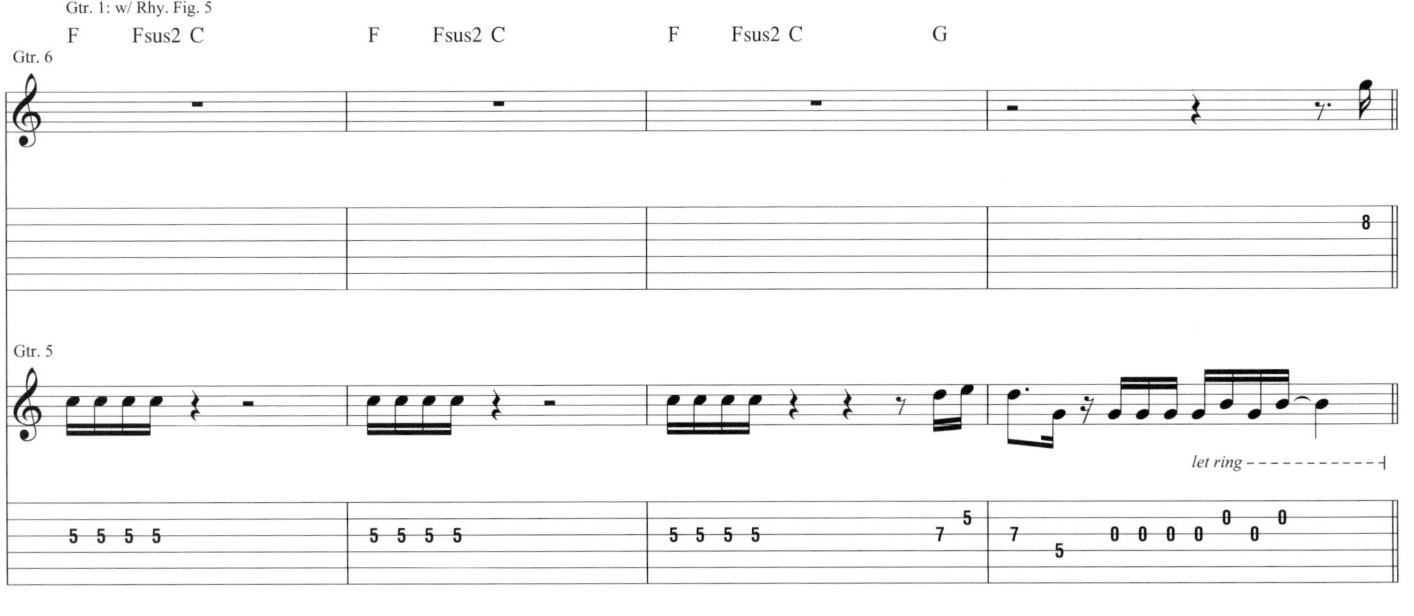

Outro

Gtr. 4: w/ Riff B (till fade)
Gtr. 5 tacet
Gtr. 6: w/ Riff B1 (1 3/4 times)

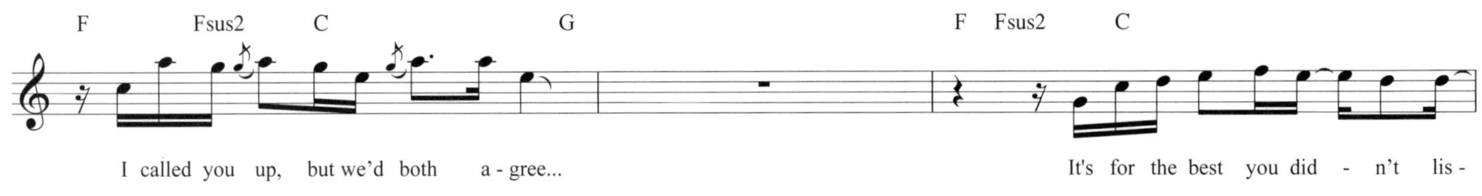

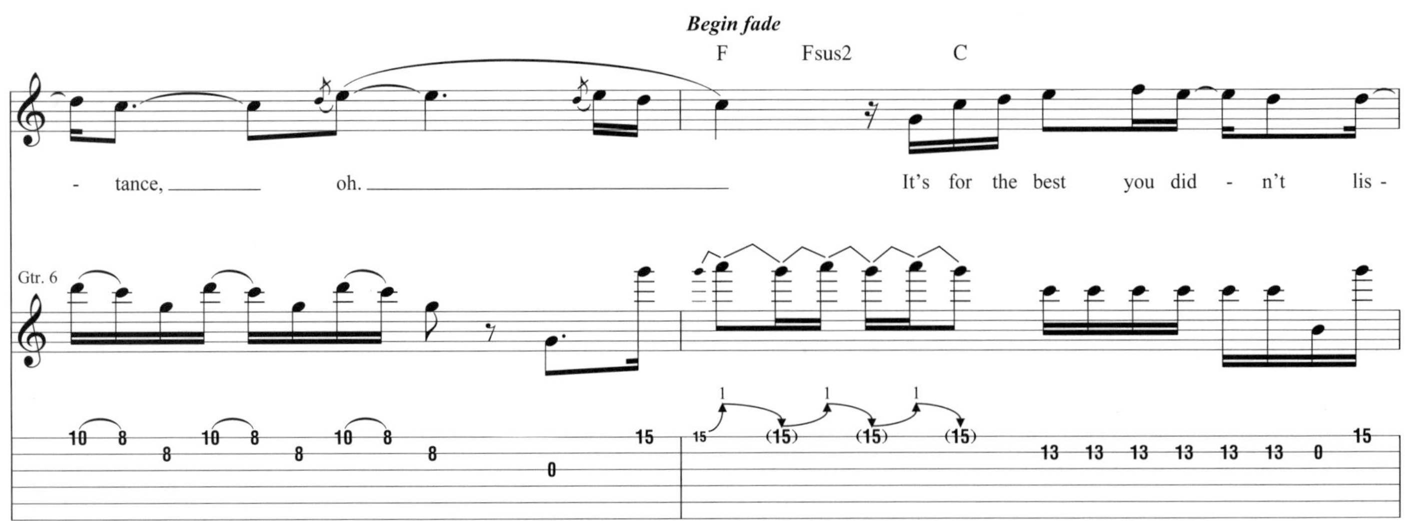

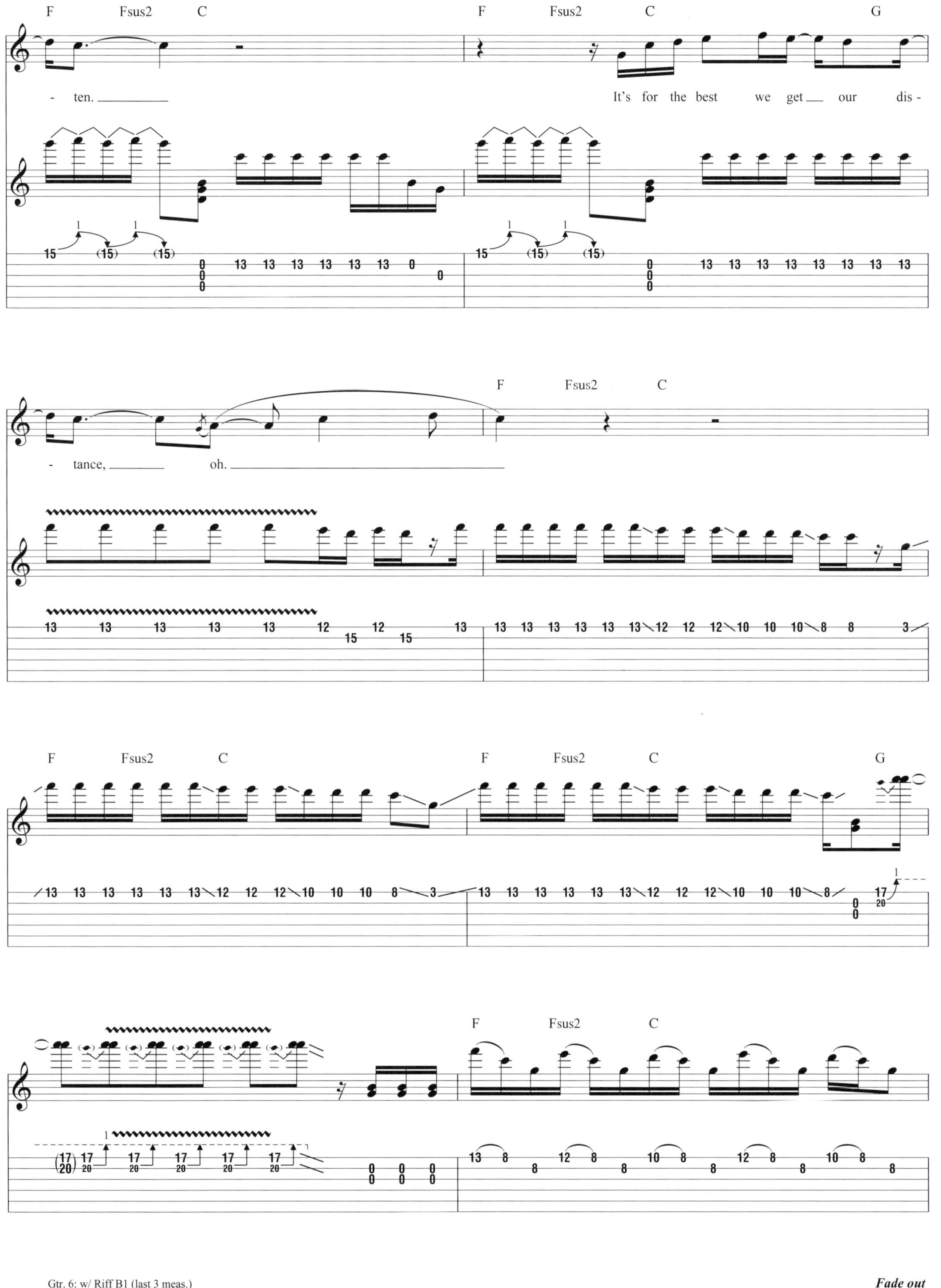
F Fsus2 C
F Fsus2 C G
- ten.
It's for the best we get our dis -
- tance,
oh.
F Fsus2 C
F Fsus2 C
F Fsus2 C G
F Fsus2 C
Gtr. 6: w/ Riff B1 (last 3 meas.)
Fade out
F Fsus2 C
F Fsus2 C G

from Gotye - *Making Mirrors*

Somebody That I Used to Know

Words and Music by Walter De Backer and Luiz Bonfa

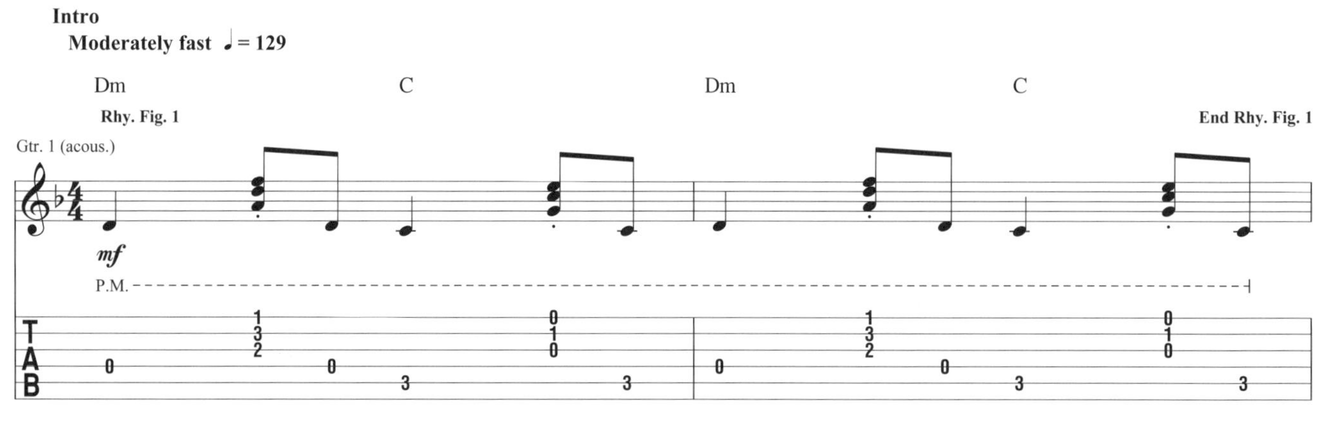

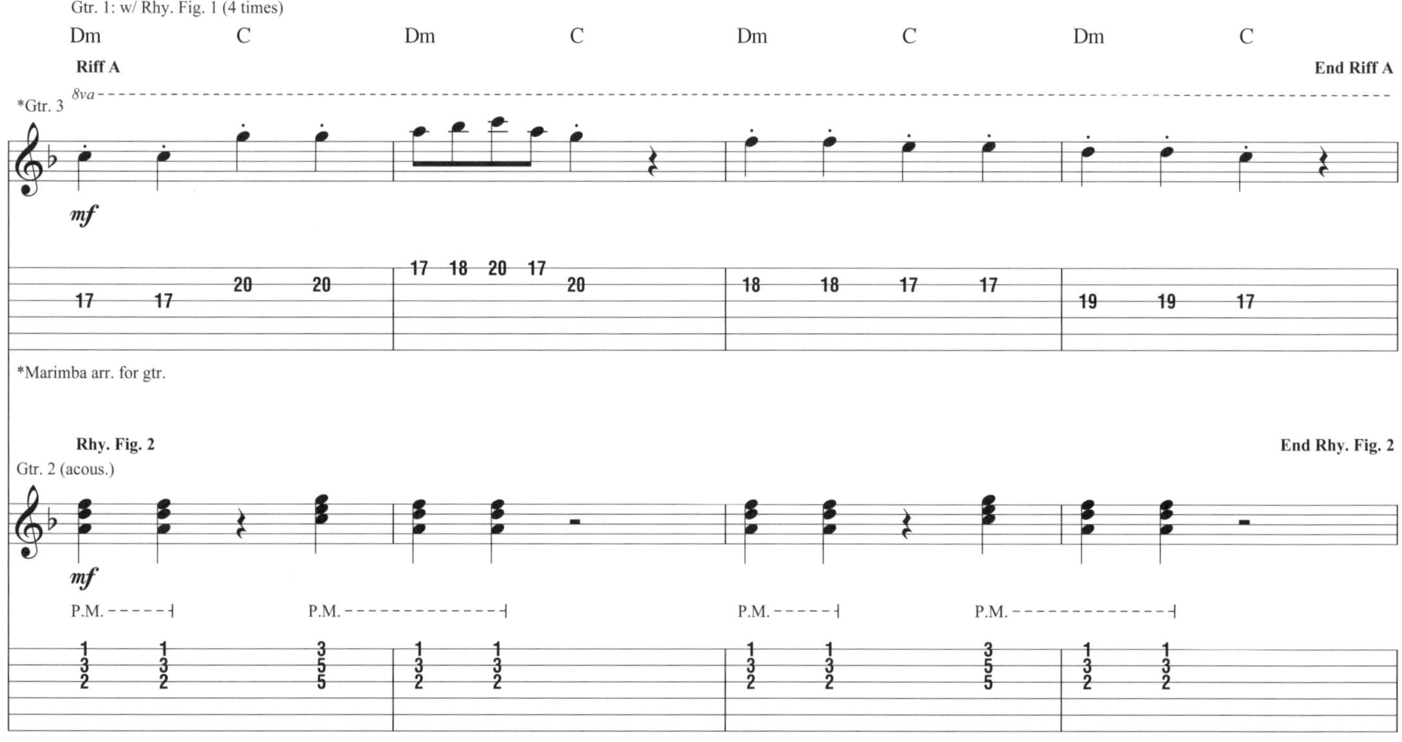

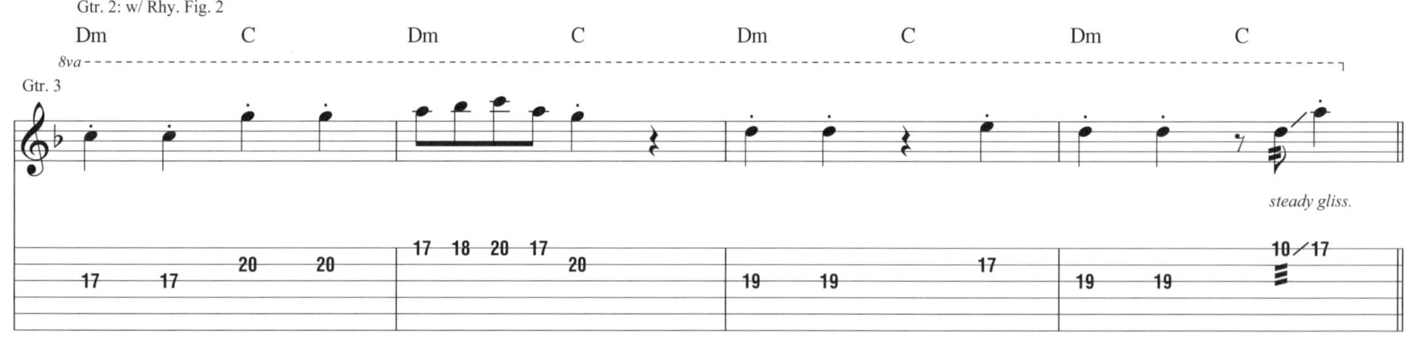

Verse
Gtr. 1: w/ Rhy. Fig. 1 (8 times)
Gtr. 3 tacet
Dm C Dm C Dm C Dm C
Male: 1. Now and then I think of when we were to - geth - er,
Dm C Dm C Dm C Dm C
like when you said you felt so hap - py you could die.
Dm C Dm C Dm C Dm C
Told my-self that you were right for me, but felt so lone - ly in your com - pa - ny.
Gtr. 2
P.M.
P.M.
Gtr. 2: w/ Rhy. Fig. 2
Dm C Dm C Dm C Dm C
But that was love and it's an ache I still re - mem - ber.
Interlude
Gtr. 1: w/ Rhy. Fig. 1 (4 times)
Gtr. 2: w/ Rhy. Fig. 2 (2 times)
Riff C
Dm C Dm C Dm C Dm C
*Gtr. 5 (elec.)
mf
w/ clean tone & tremolo
(cont. on bottom staff)
*Kybd. arr. for gtr.
Riff B
End Riff B
Gtr. 4 (elec.)
mp
w/ dist.

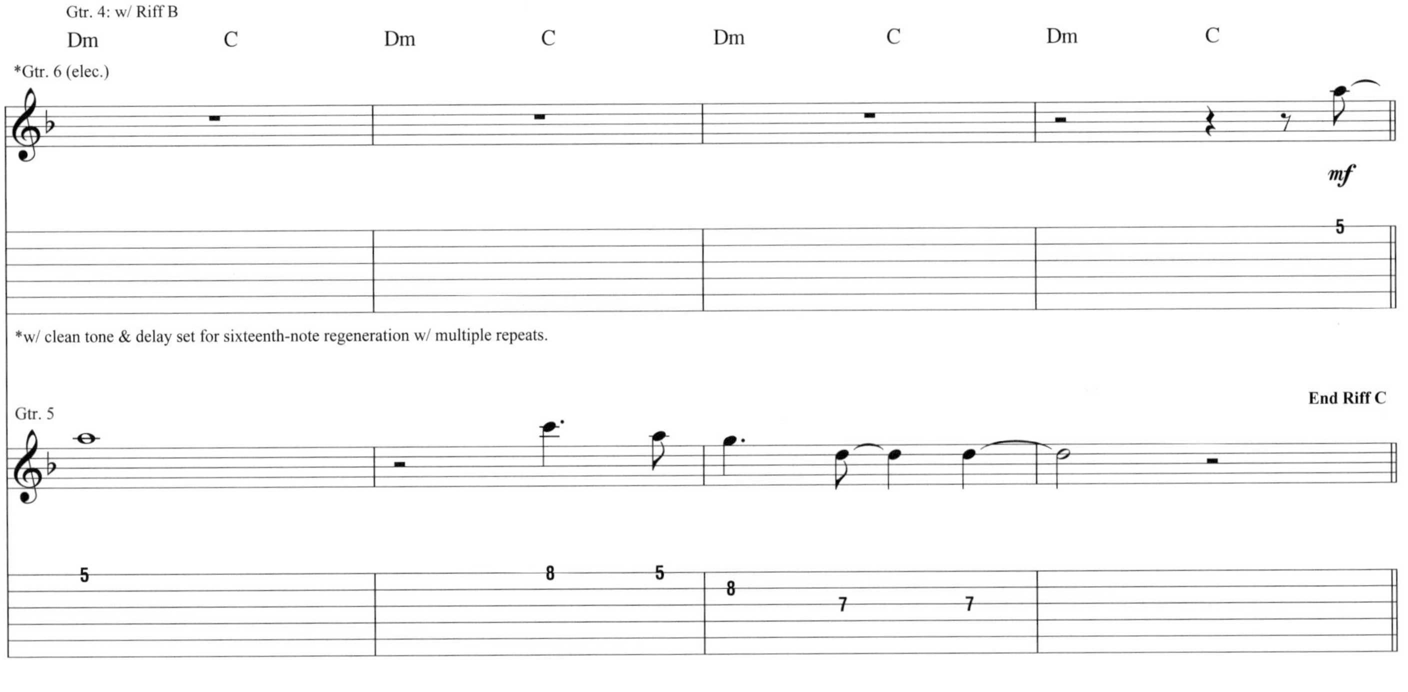
Gtr. 4: w/ Riff B
Dm C Dm C Dm C Dm C
*Gtr. 6 (elec.)
mf
*w/ clean tone & delay set for sixteenth-note regeneration w/ multiple repeats.
End Riff C
Gtr. 5

Verse
Gtr. 1: w/ Rhy. Fig. 1 (8 times)
Gtr. 2: w/ Rhy. Fig. 2 (3 1/2 times)
Gtr. 5 tacet
Dm C Dm C Dm C Dm C
2. You can get ad - dict - ed to a cer - tain kind of sad - ness,
Gtr. 6

Dm C Dm C Dm C Dm C
like res - ig - na - tion to the end, al - ways the end.
rake

Dm
C
So when we found that we could not make sense,
well, you said that we would still be friends.
let ring
Gtr. 6 tacet
But I'll ad - mit that I was glad it was o - ver.
Chorus
Dm
C
B♭
But you did - n't have to cut me off,
make out like it nev - er hap - pened and that we were noth -
Riff D
*Gtr. 7 (elec.)
8va
mf
w/ clean tone & tremolo
*Kybd. arr. for gtr.
Rhy. Fig. 3
End Rhy. Fig. 3
Gtr. 1
P.M.

Gtr. 1: w/ Rhy. Fig. 3 (5 times)
Dm C Bb C Dm C Bb C
ing. And I don't e - ven need your love, but you treat me like a stran - ger and that feels so rough.
End Riff D
8va
Gtr. 7
(20) 17 20 20 17 20 18 20
Dm C Bb C Dm C Bb C
No, you did-n't have to stooop so low, have your friends col-lect your rec-ords and then change your num-
Riff E
8va
(20) 17 20 20 17 18 17 20
Dm C Bb C Dm C Bb C
ber. I guess that I don't need that, though. Now you're just some-bod - y that I used to know.
End Riff E
8va
(20) 17 20 20 17 20 18 20
Gtr. 3: w/ Riff A
Gtr. 7: w/ Riff E (1st 4 meas.)
Dm C Bb C Dm C Bb C
Now you're just some-bod - y that I used to know.

Dm
C
B♭
C
Now you're just some - bod - y that I used to know.
Riff F1
8va
Gtr. 7
End Riff F1
Riff F
Gtr. 3
8va
steady gliss.
End Riff F
Interlude
Gtr. 1: w/ Rhy. Fig. 1 (4 times)
Gtr. 5: w/ Riff C
Gtr. 8 (acous.)
mf
P.M.
Verse
Gtr. 1: w/ Rhy. Fig. 1 (4 times)
Gtr. 8 tacet
Female: 2. Now and then I think of all the times you screwed me o - ver.
Gtr. 4
Riff G
End Riff G

Gtr. 4 tacet
Gtr. 4: w/ Riff G
Dm C Dm C Dm C Dm C
but had me be-liev-ing it was al - ways some-thing that I'd done.
Gtr. 5

Dm/C C Dm/C C Dm/C C Dm/C C
But I don't wan-na live that way, read-ing in - to ev-'ry word you say.
Riff H
End Riff H
Gtr. 5
Gtr. 1
P.M.

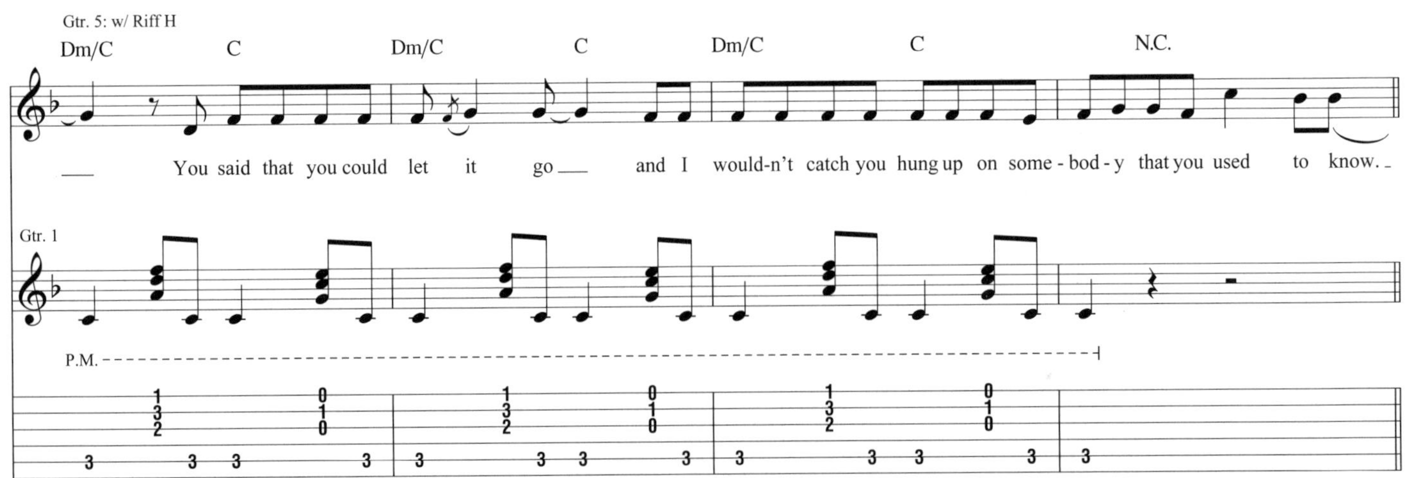
Gtr. 5: w/ Riff H
Dm/C C Dm/C C Dm/C C N.C.
You said that you could let it go and I would-n't catch you hung up on some-bod-y that you used to know.
Gtr. 1
P.M.

Chorus

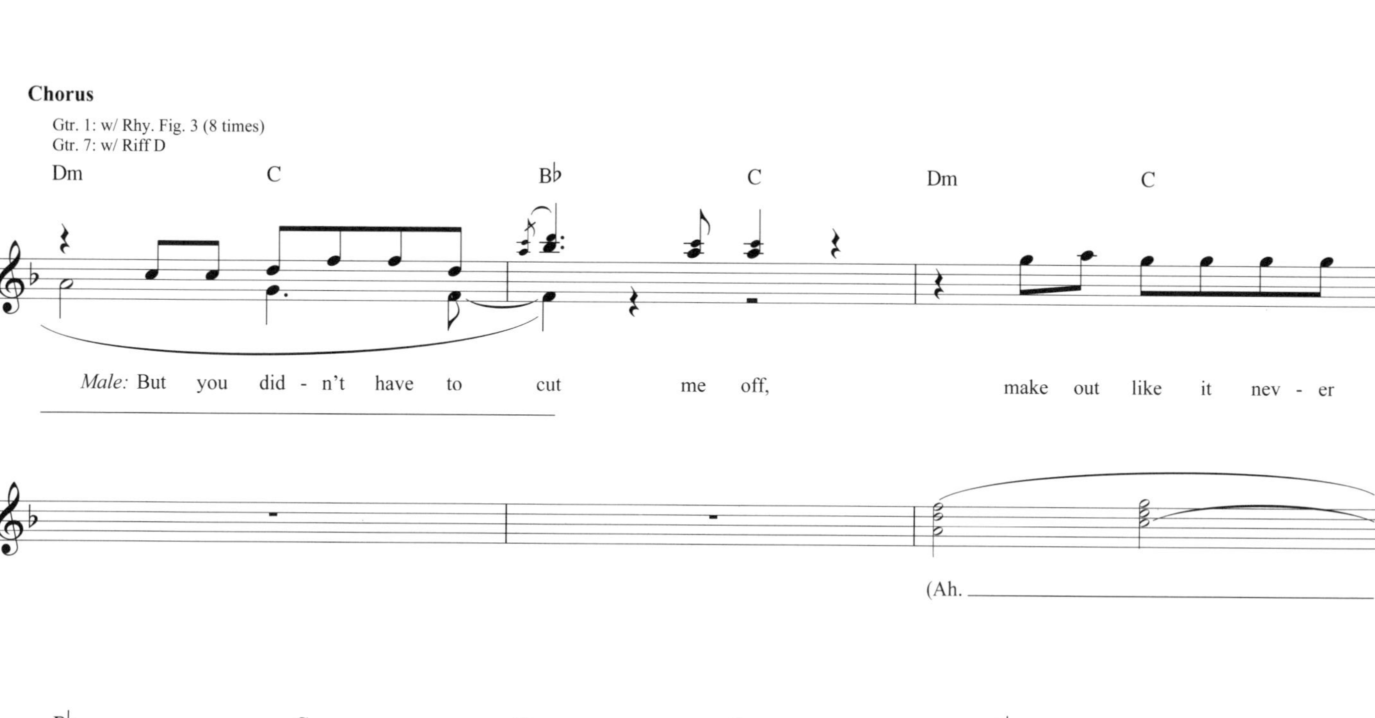
Gtr. 1: w/ Rhy. Fig. 3 (8 times)
Gtr. 7: w/ Riff D
Dm
C
B♭
C
Dm
C
Male: But you did - n't have to cut me off,
make out like it nev - er
(Ah.

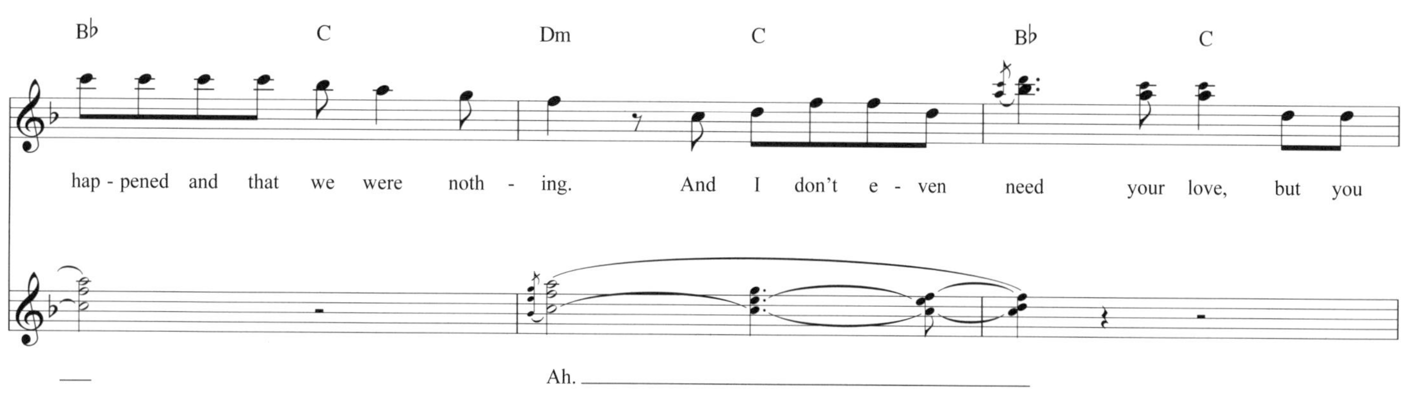
B♭
C
Dm
C
B♭
C
hap - pened and that we were noth - ing. And I don't e - ven need your love, but you
Ah.

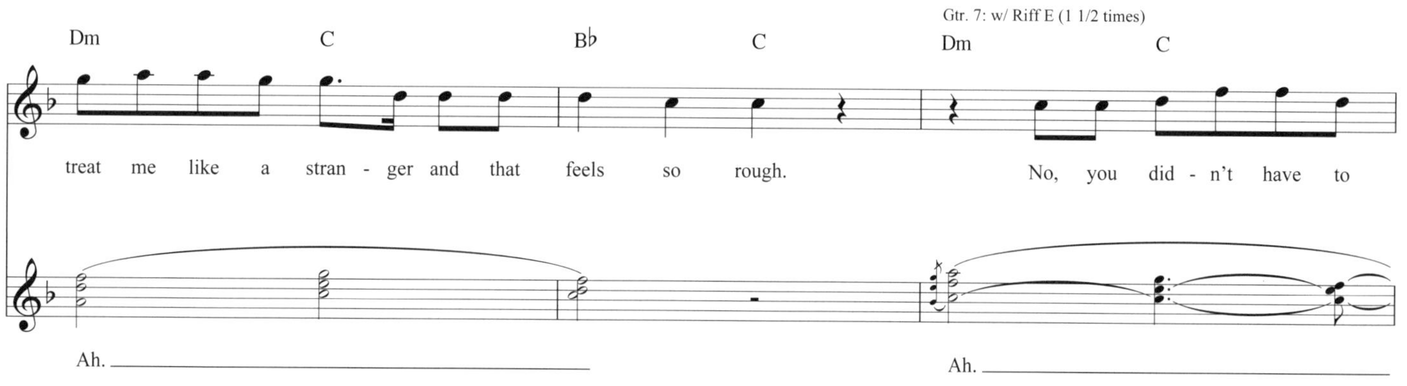
Gtr. 7: w/ Riff E (1 1/2 times)
Dm
C
B♭
C
Dm
C
treat me like a stran - ger and that feels so rough.
No, you did - n't have to
Ah.
Ah.

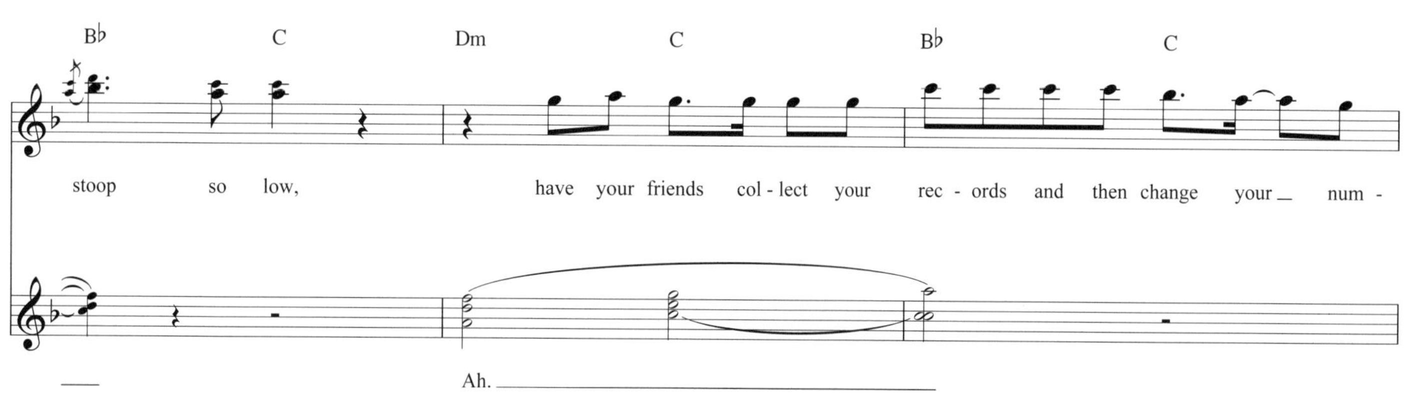
B♭
C
Dm
C
B♭
C
stoop so low,
have your friends col - lect your rec - ords and then change your num -
Ah.

Dm C Bb C Dm C Bb C
ber. I guess that I don't need that, though. Now you're just some-bod-y that I used to know.
Ah.
Some-bod-

Gtr. 3: w/ Riff A (3 times)
Dm C Bb C Dm C Bb C
Now you're just some-bod-y that I used to know.
y I used to know. Some-bod-y.
Some-bod-

Gtr. 7: w/ Riff F1
Dm C Bb C Dm C Bb C
Now you're just some-bod-y that I used to know.
y I used to know. Some-bod-y.

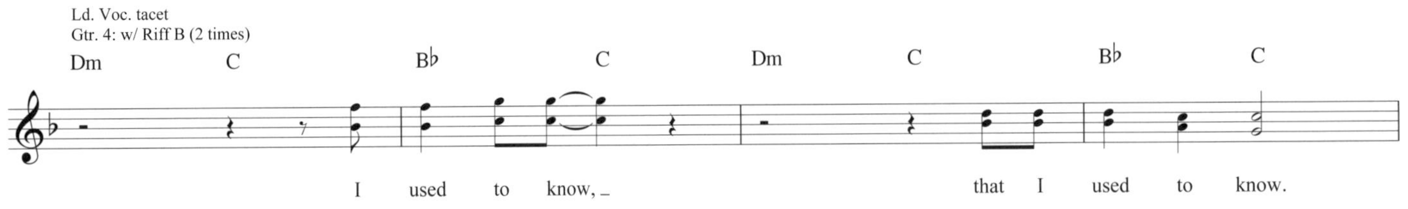
Ld. Voc. tacet
Gtr. 4: w/ Riff B (2 times)
Dm C Bb C Dm C Bb C
I used to know, that I used to know.

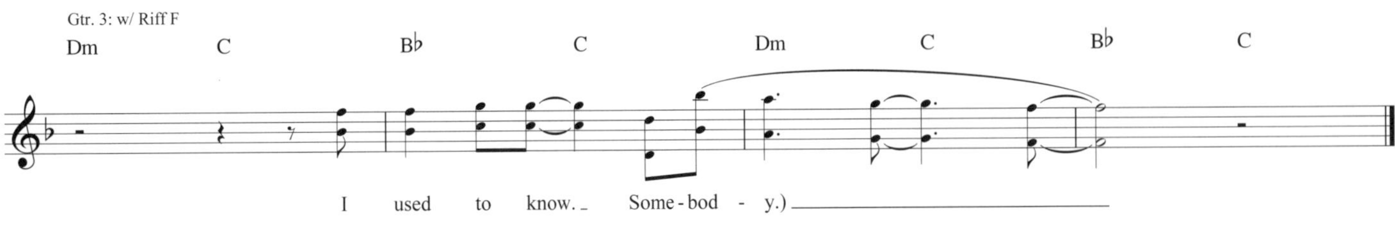
Gtr. 3: w/ Riff F
Dm C Bb C Dm C Bb C
I used to know. Some-bod-y.)

from Harry Styles - *Harry Styles*

Sweet Creature

Words and Music by Harry Styles and Thomas Hull

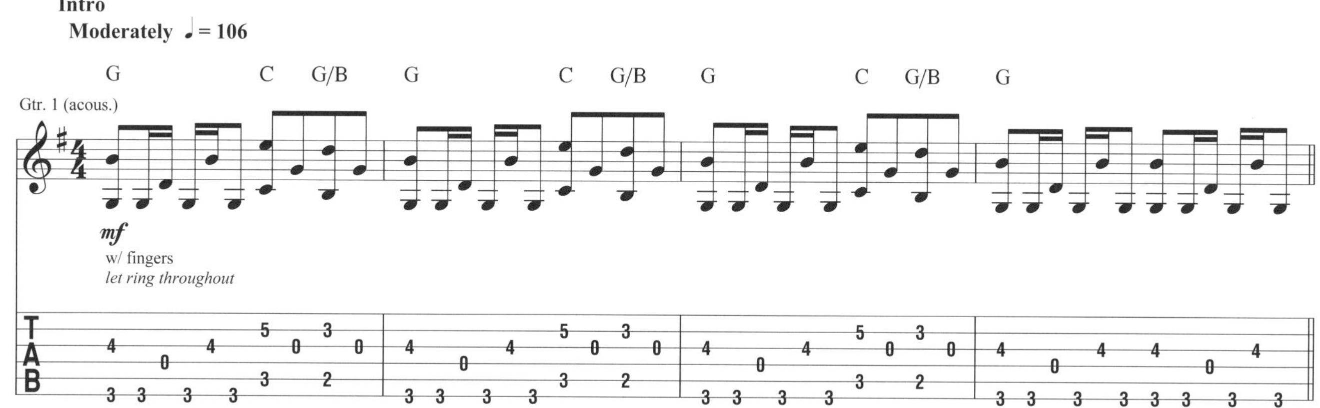

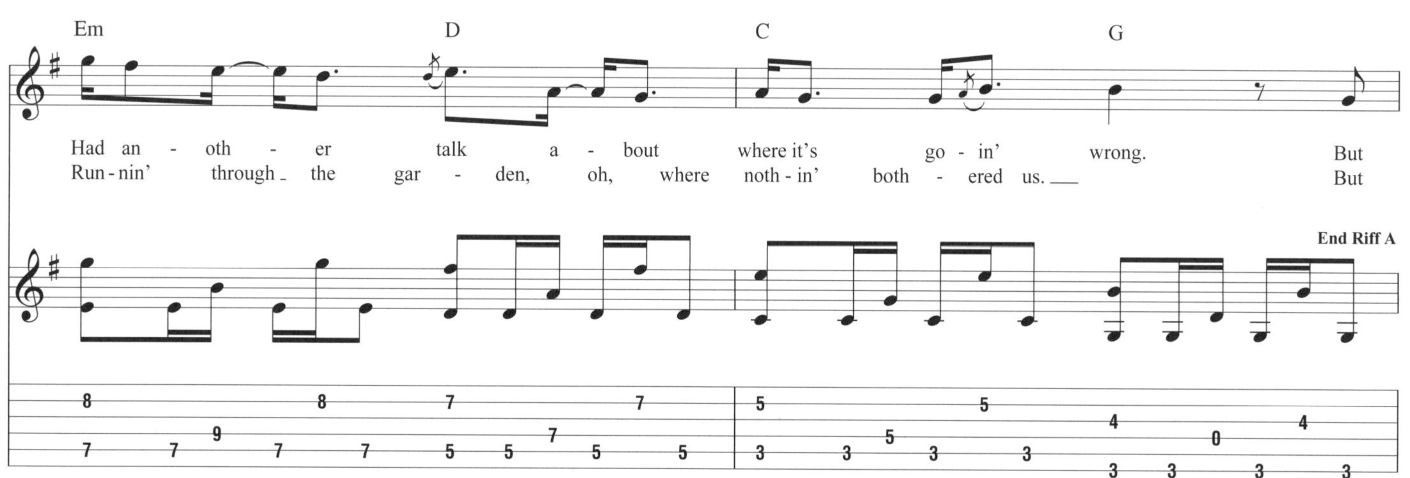

To Coda

Grtr. 1: w/ Riff A
C G/B G Em D C G
we're still young. We don't know where we're go - in', but we know where we be - long.
we're still young. I al - ways think a-bout you and how we don't speak e - nough.

Pre-Chorus
Am Em
Oh, we start - ed, two
Gtr. 1

G Dsus2
hearts in one home. It's

Am Em
hard when we ar - gue. We're both

G
D5/A
stub - born, I know.
But, oh,
*Lightly hit strings to produce a percussive sound.

Chorus
G Cadd2 G/B G Cadd2 G/B G Cadd2 G/B
sweet crea - ture, sweet crea - ture, where - ev -
Riff B

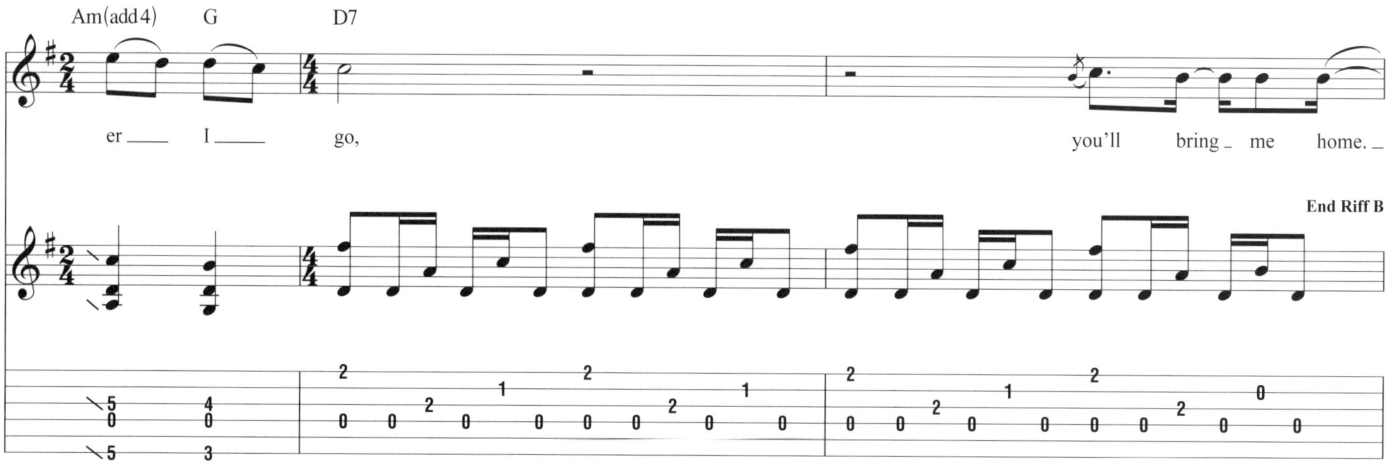
Am(add4) G D7
er I go,
you'll bring me home.
End Riff B

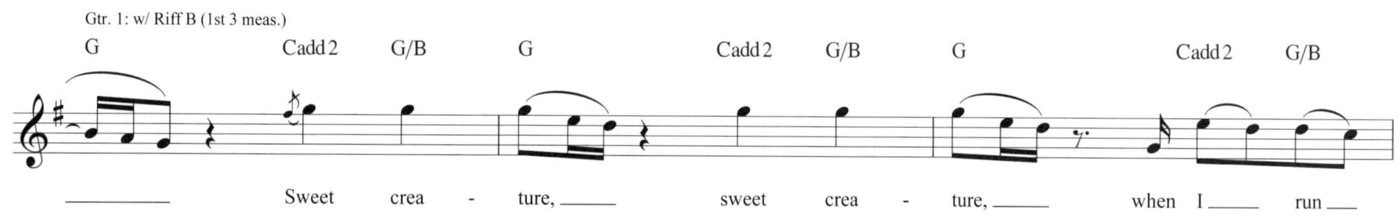
Gtr. 1: w/ Riff B (1st 3 meas.)
G Cadd2 G/B G Cadd2 G/B G Cadd2 G/B
Sweet crea - ture, sweet crea - ture, when I run

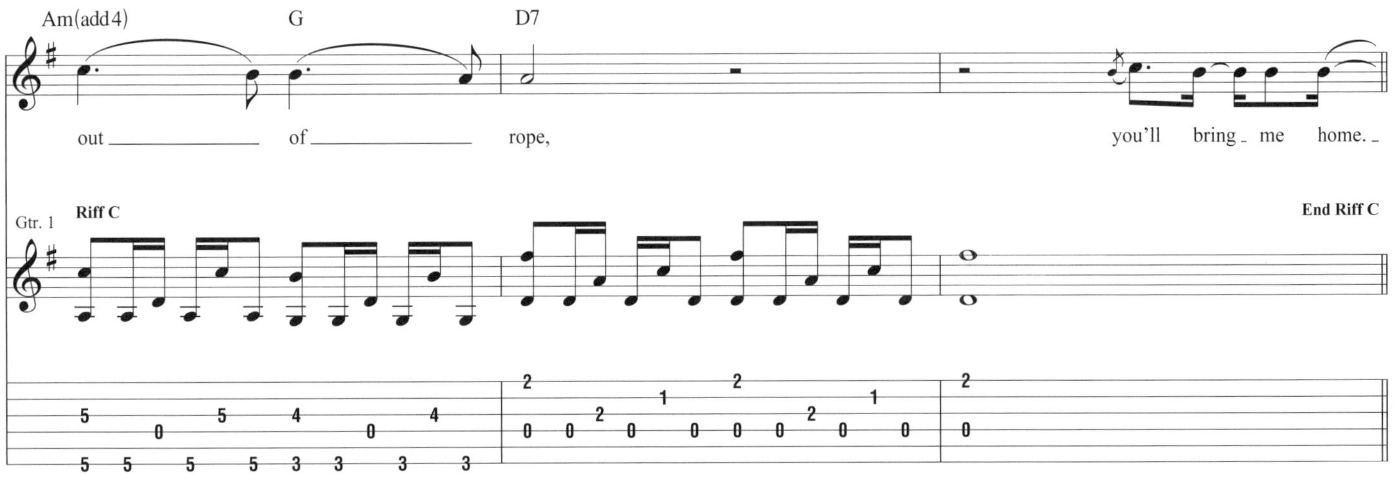

Interlude

D.S. al Coda

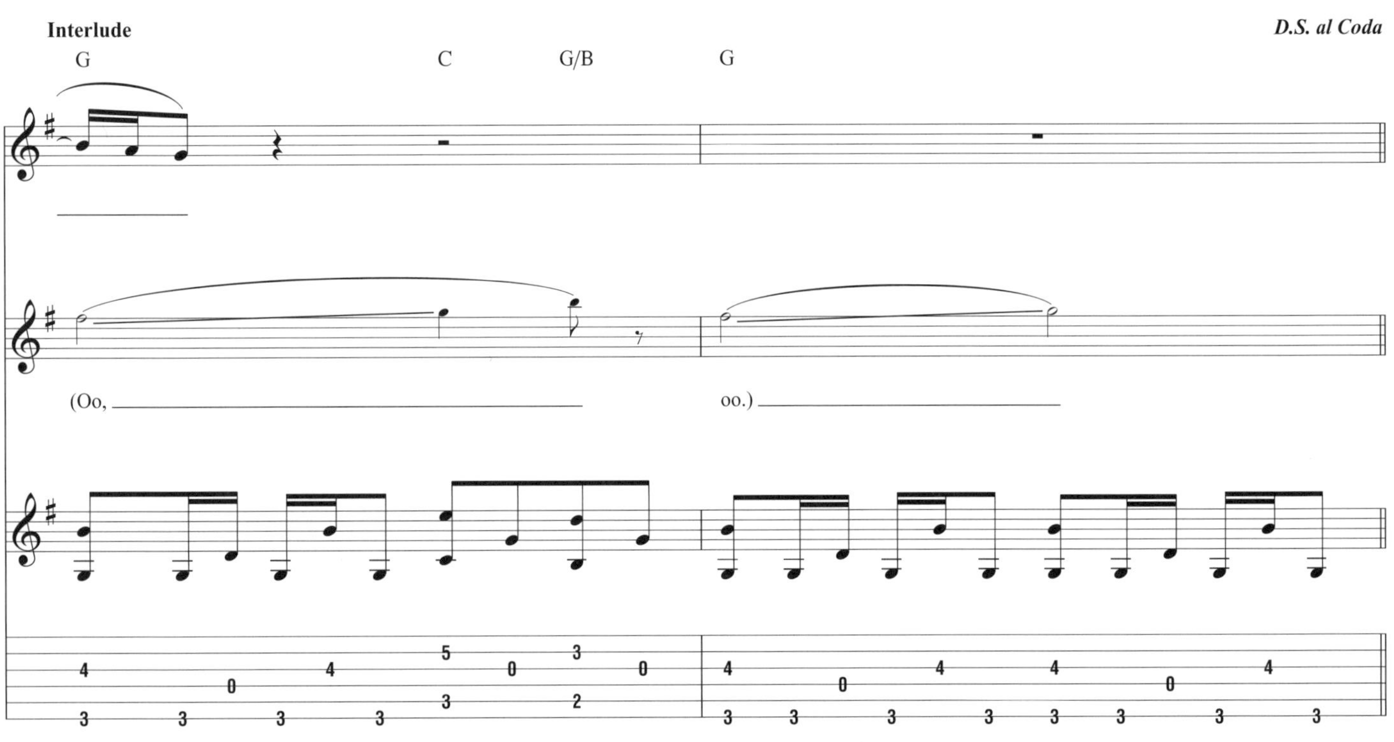

Coda

Pre-Chorus

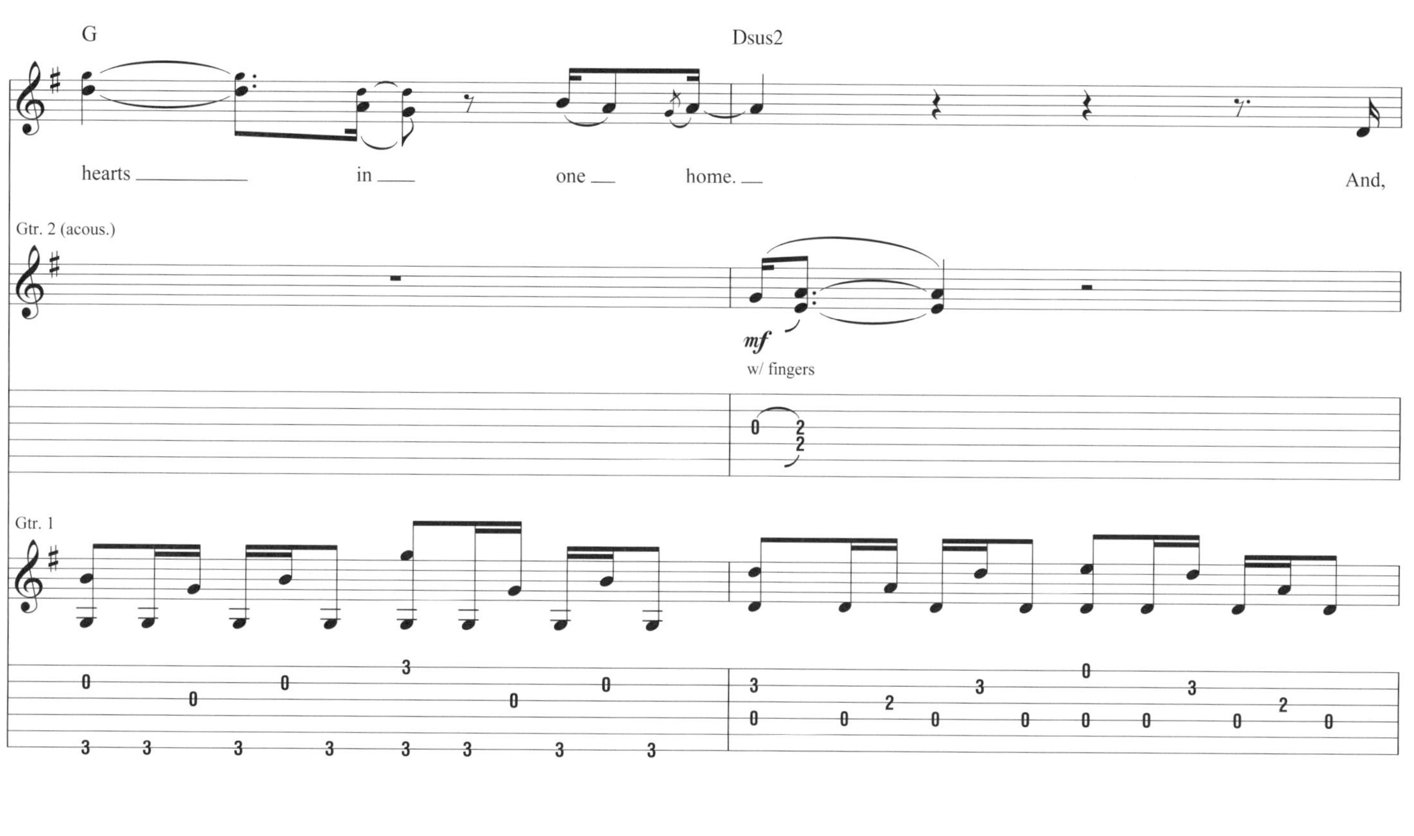
G
Dsus2
hearts in one home. And,
Gtr. 2 (acous.)
mf
w/ fingers
Gtr. 1

Gtr. 2 tacet
Am
Em
oh, it's hard, we ar - gue. We're both
Gtr. 1

G
D5/A
stub - born, I know. But, oh,

Chorus

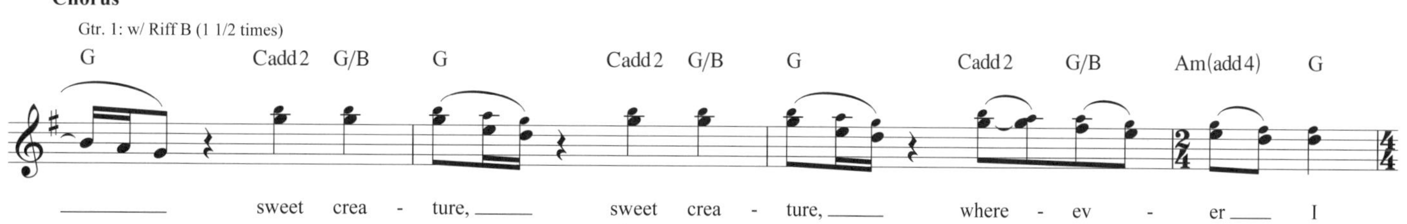
Gtr. 1: w/ Riff B (1 1/2 times)
G Cadd2 G/B G Cadd2 G/B G Cadd2 G/B Am(add4) G
sweet crea - ture, sweet crea - ture, where - ev - er I

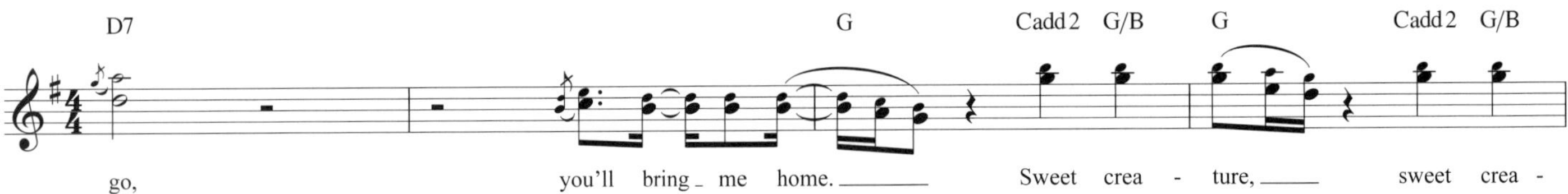
D7
G
Cadd2 G/B
G
Cadd2 G/B
go, you'll bring me home. Sweet crea - ture, sweet crea -

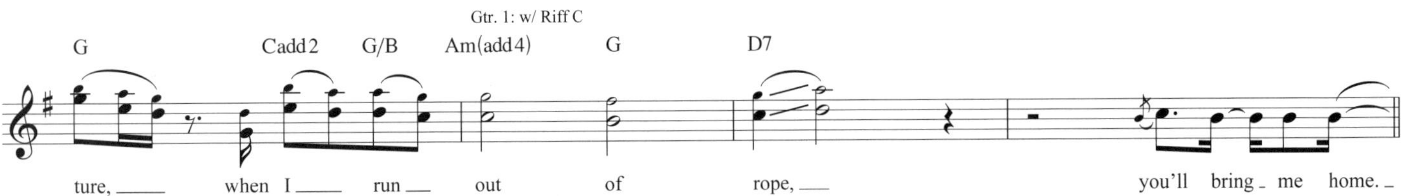
Gtr. 1: w/ Riff C
G
Cadd2 G/B
Am(add4)
G
D7
ture, when I run out of rope, you'll bring me home.

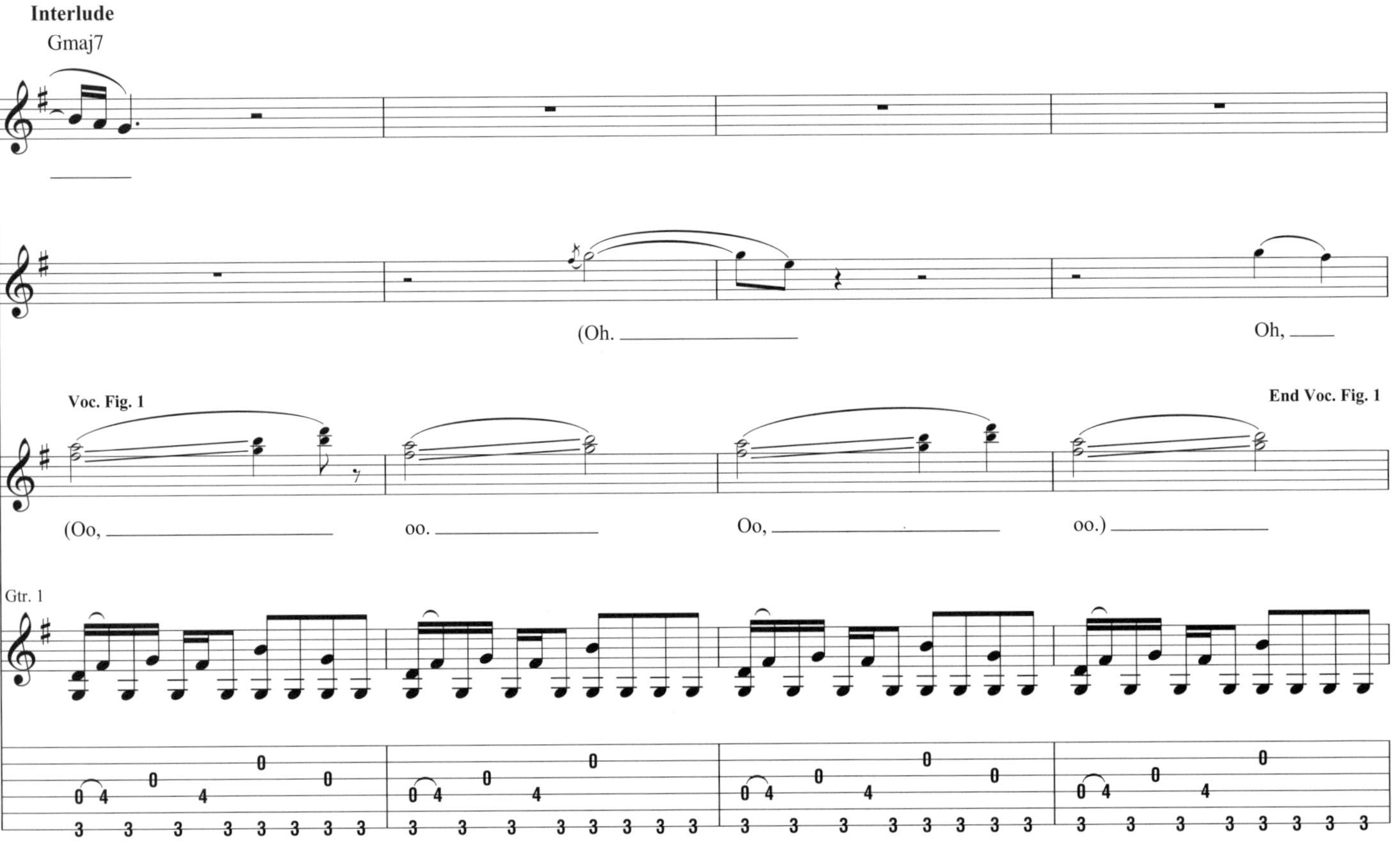
Interlude
Gmaj7
(Oh. Oh,
Voc. Fig. 1
End Voc. Fig. 1
(Oo, oo. Oo, oo.)
Gtr. 1

Bkgd. Voc.: w/ Voc. Fig. 1
Em(add9)
And,
oh. Oh.)

Pre-Chorus

*In a single downstroke, strike strings w/ backs of fingernails.

Chorus

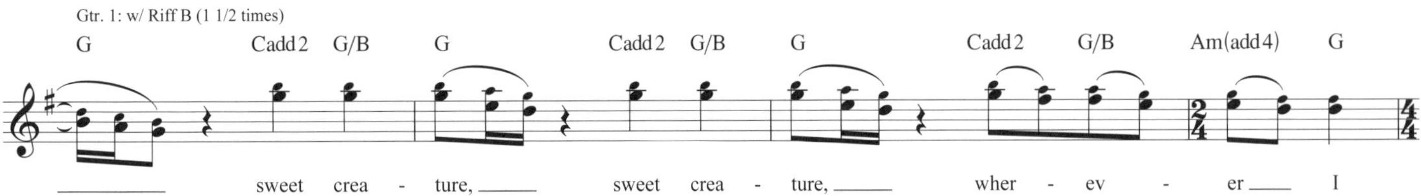

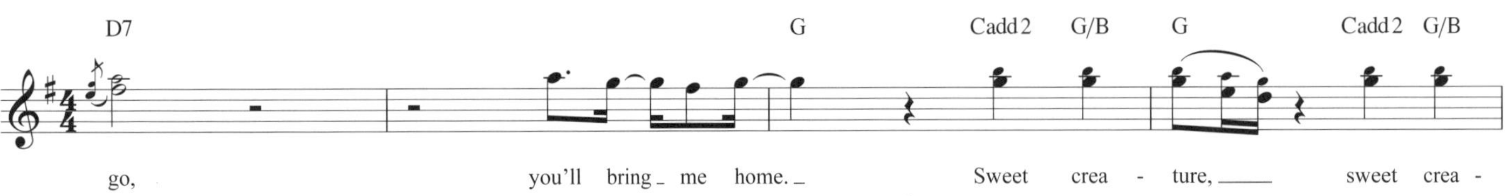

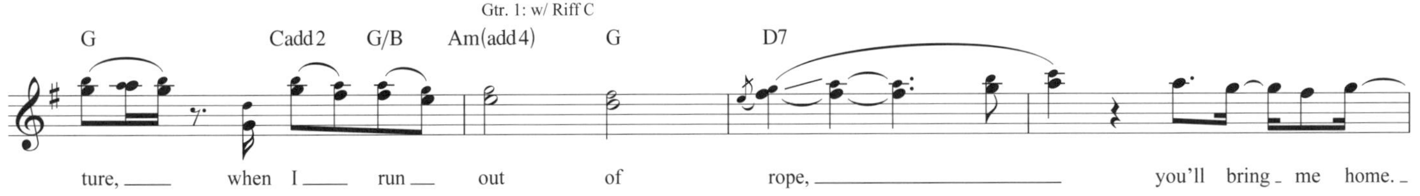

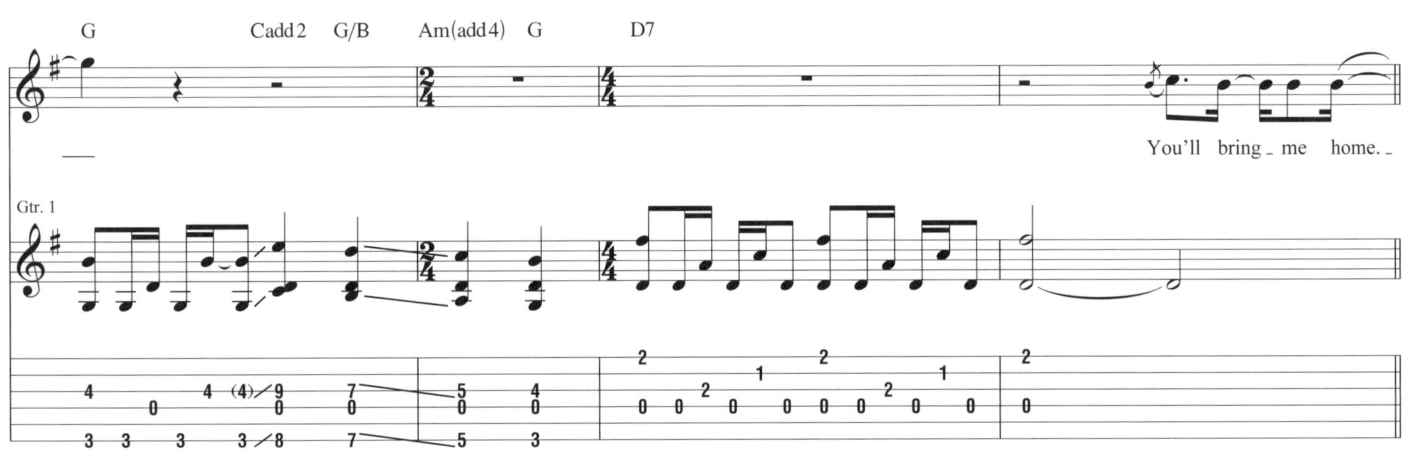

Outro

from Chris Stapleton - *Traveller*

Tennessee Whiskey

Words and Music by Dean Dillon and Linda Hargrove

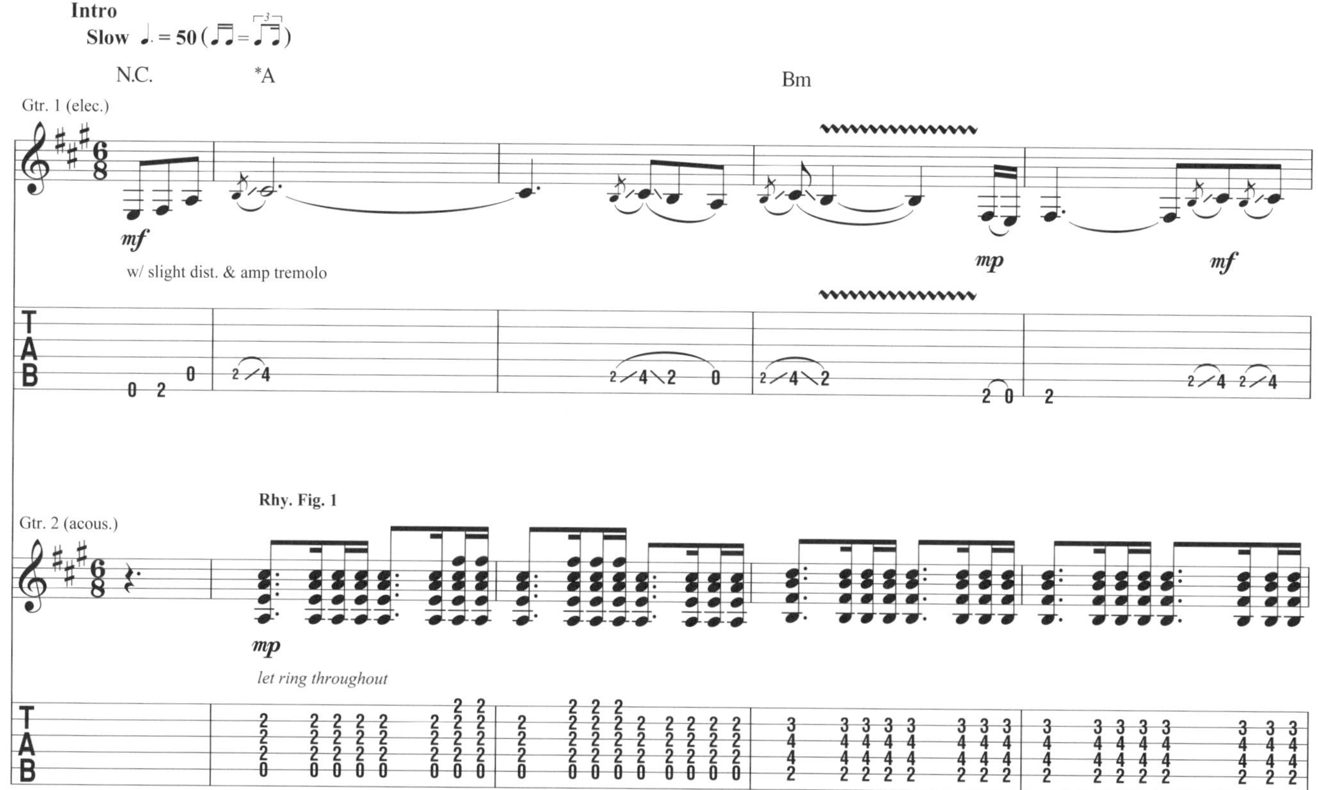

*Chord symbols reflect overall harmony.

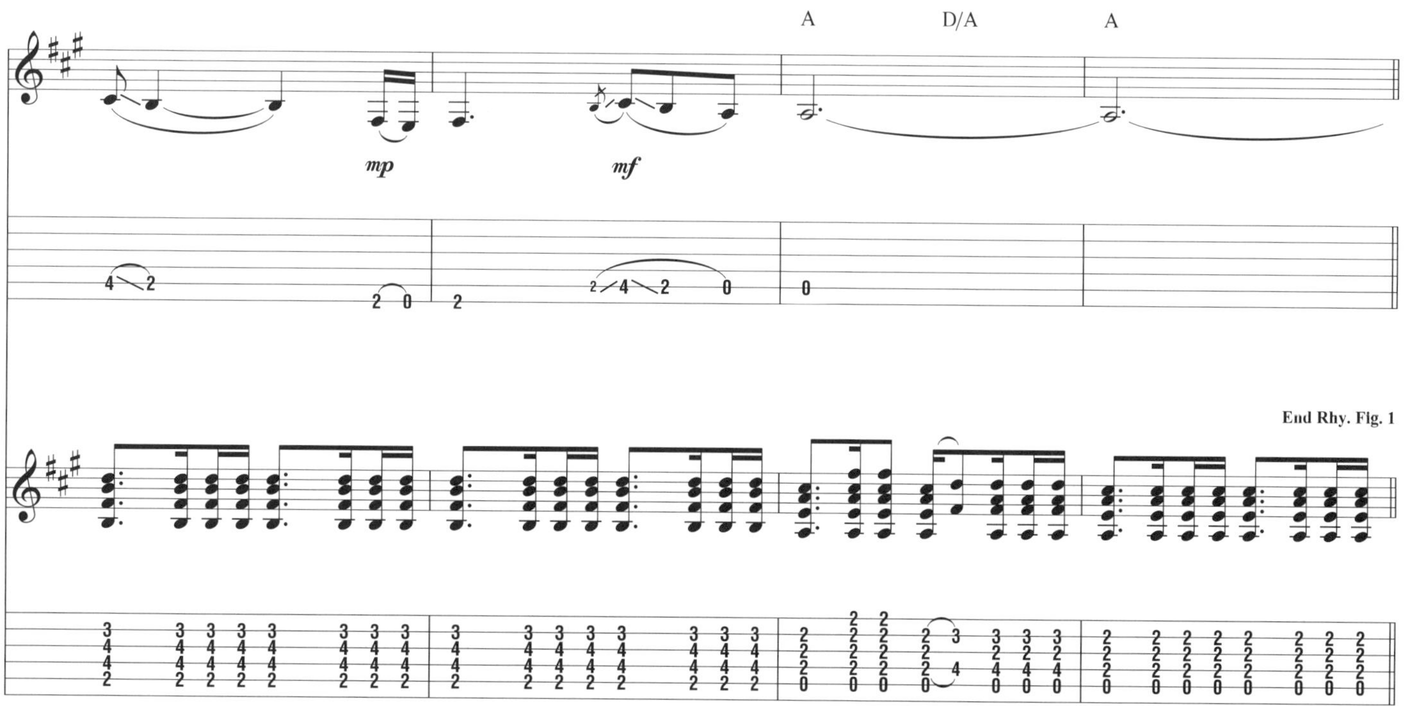

Verse

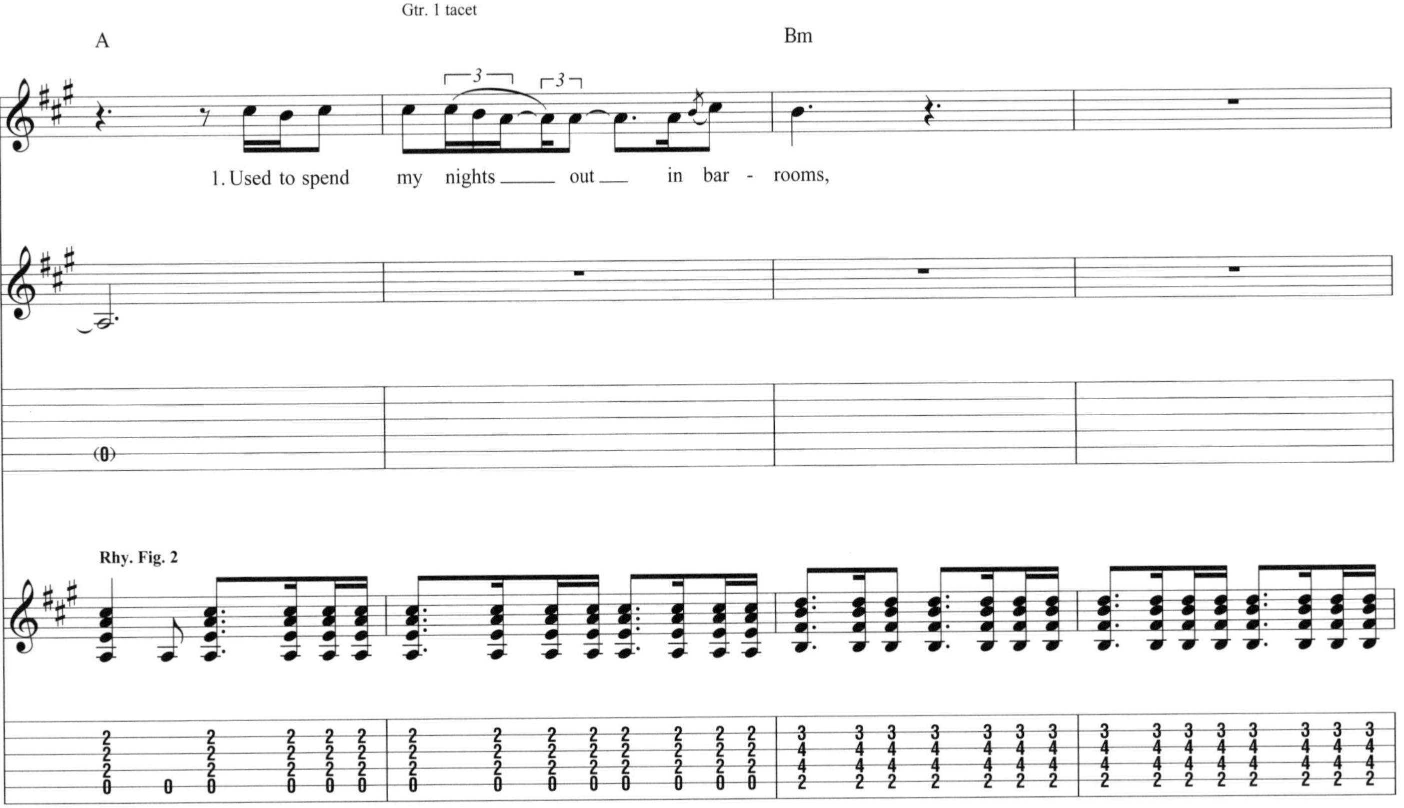
Gtr. 1 tacet
A
Bm
1. Used to spend my nights out in bar - rooms,
Rhy. Fig. 2

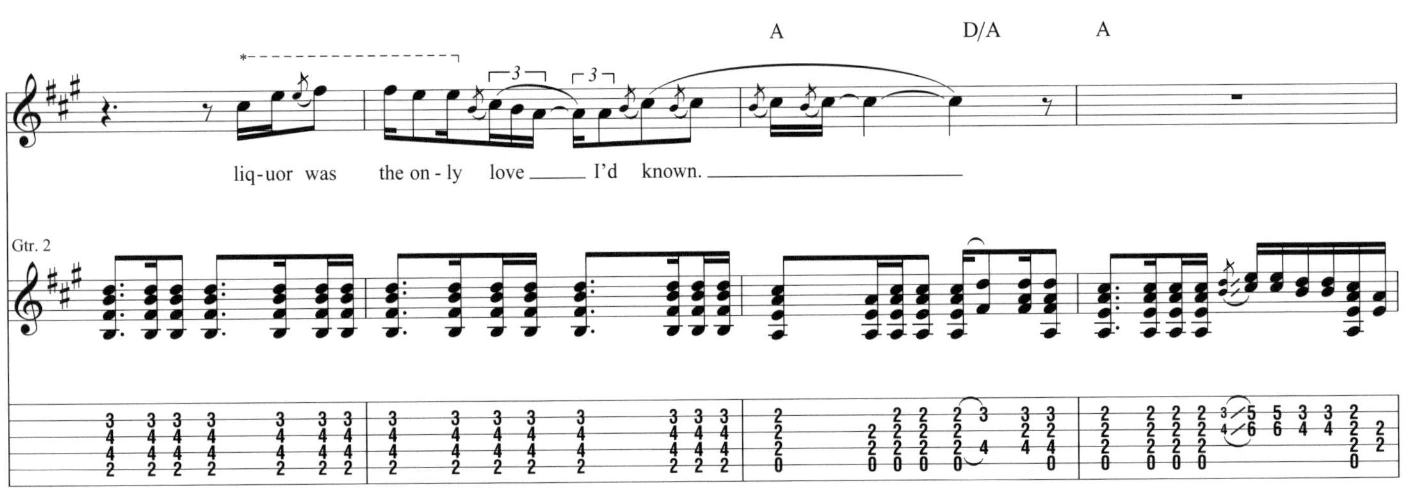
A
D/A
A
liq-uor was the on - ly love I'd known.
Gtr. 2
*Sung as even sixteenth-notes.

Bm
But you res-cued me from reach-ing for the bot - tom and brought me
End Rhy. Fig. 2
**As before
***As before

𝄋 Chorus

1st & 2nd times, Gtr. 2: w/ Rhy. Fig. 1 (2 times)
3rd time, Gtr. 2: w/ Rhy. Fig. 1 (1 7/8 times)

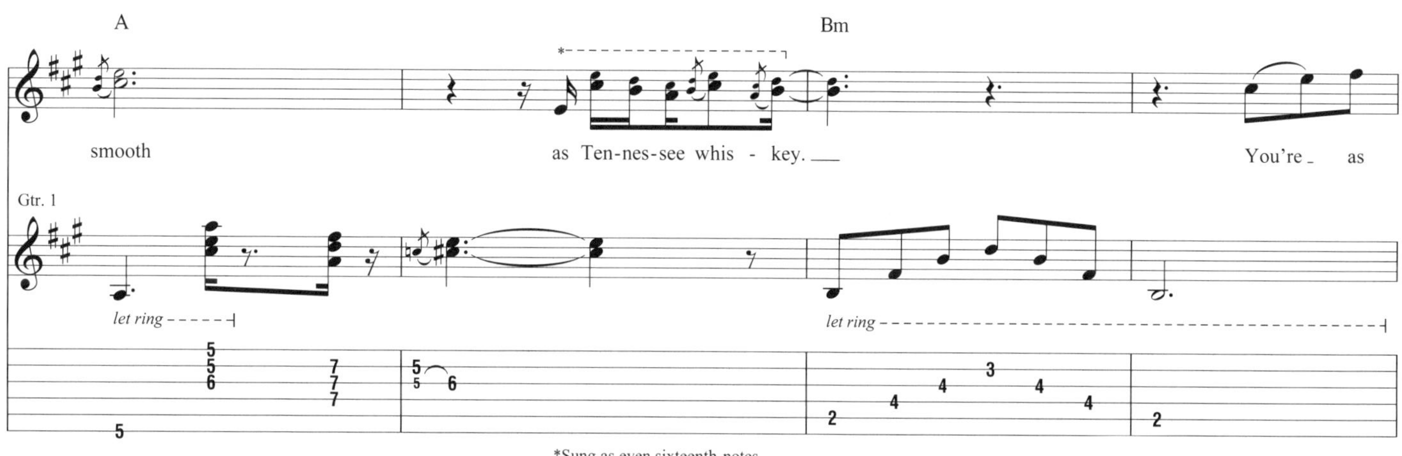

*Sung as even sixteenth-notes.

**As before

***As before

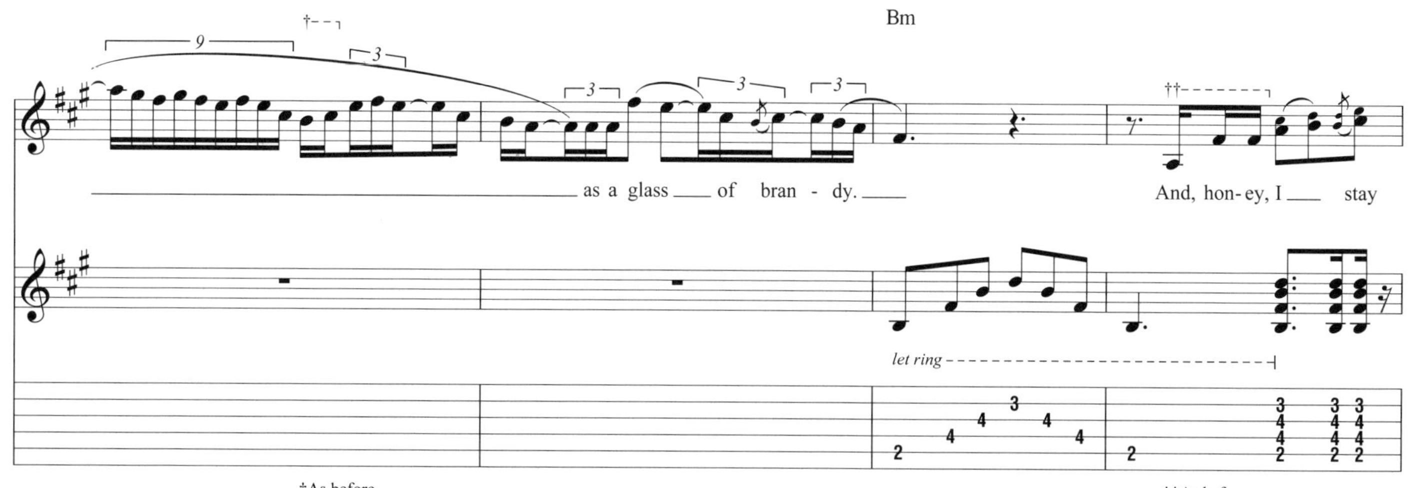

†As before

††As before

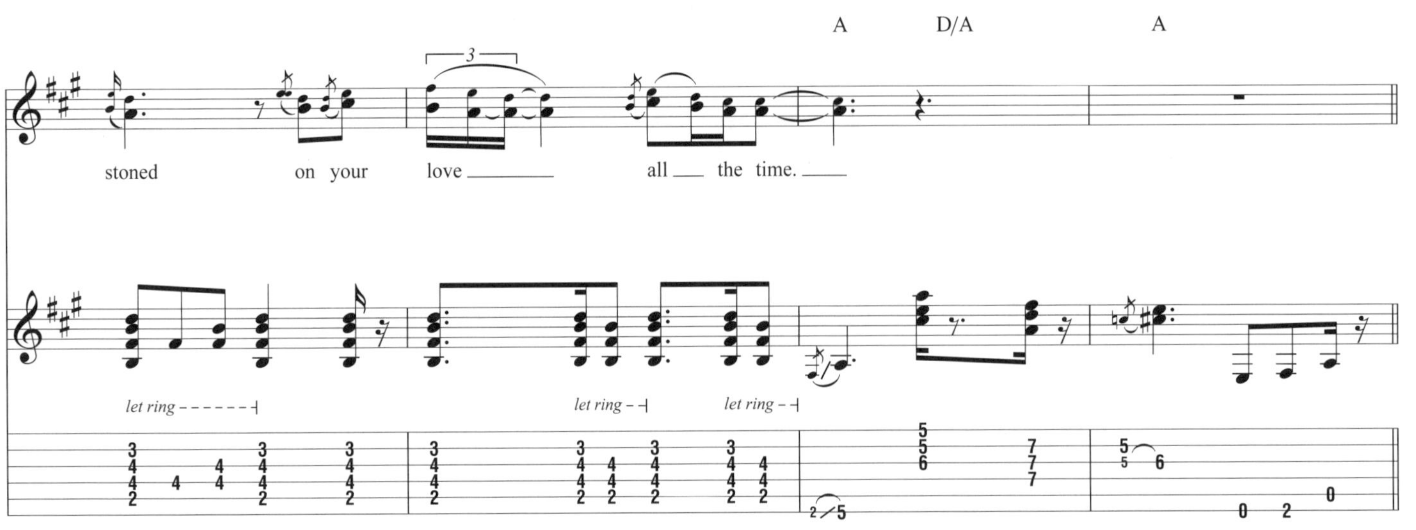

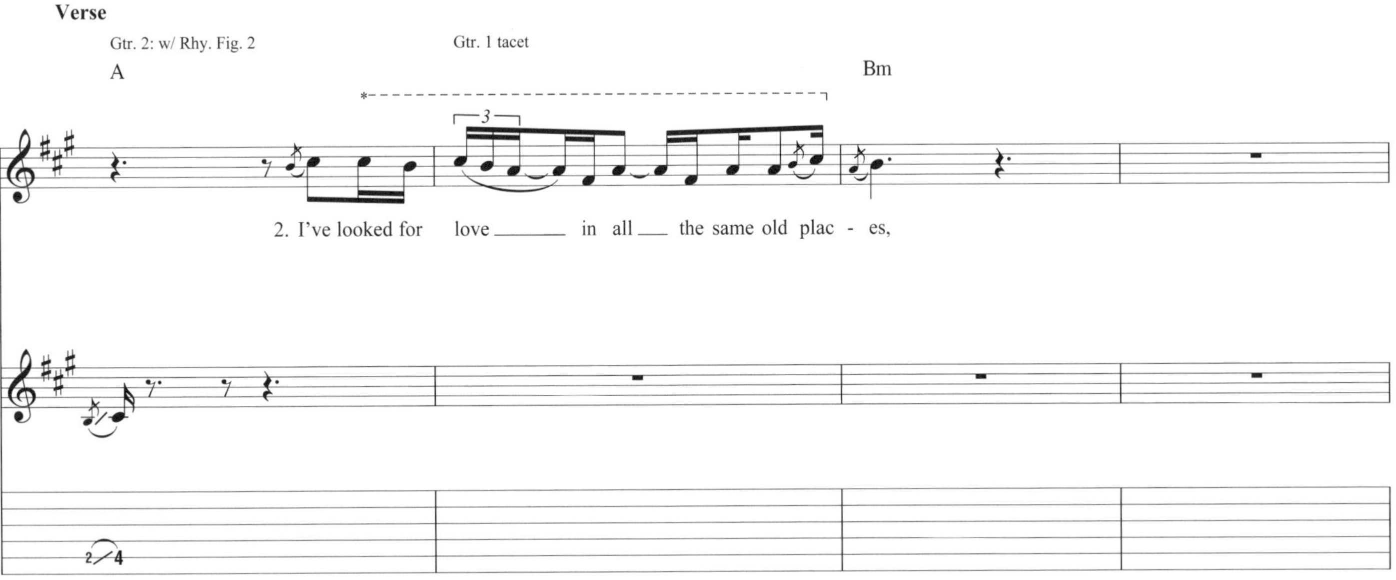

*Sung as even sixteenth-notes.

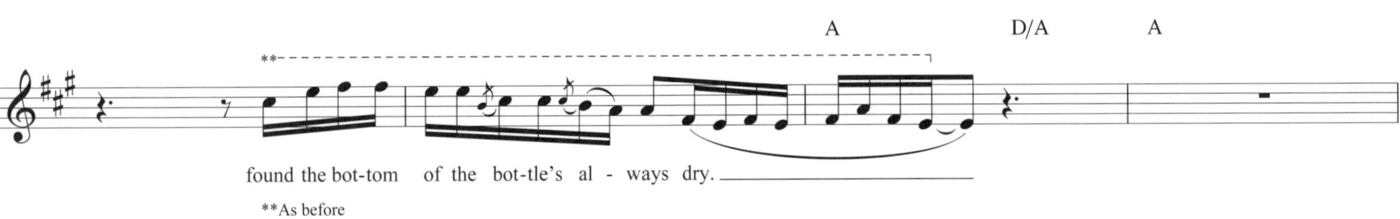

D.S. al Coda 1
A5
N.C.
A5
D/A
like your love to get me high.
And you're as
Gtr. 2

Coda 1

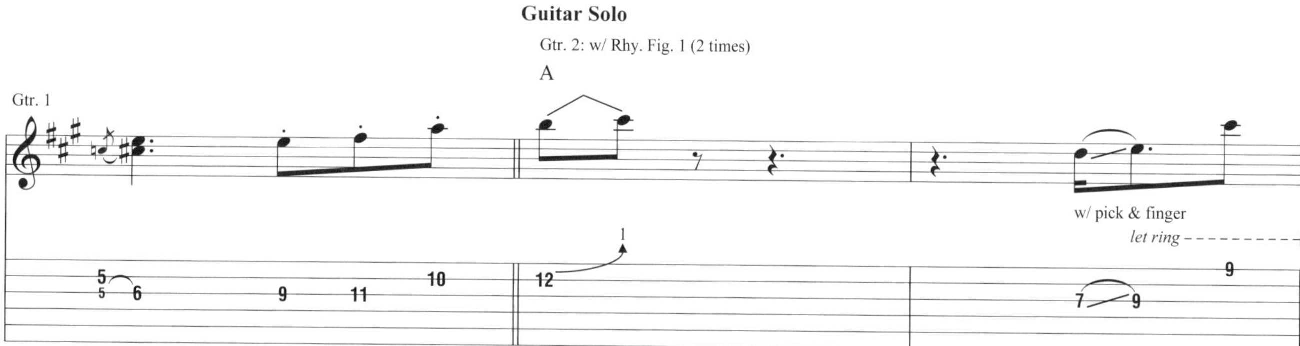
Guitar Solo
Gtr. 2: w/ Rhy. Fig. 1 (2 times)
A
Gtr. 1
w/ pick & finger
let ring

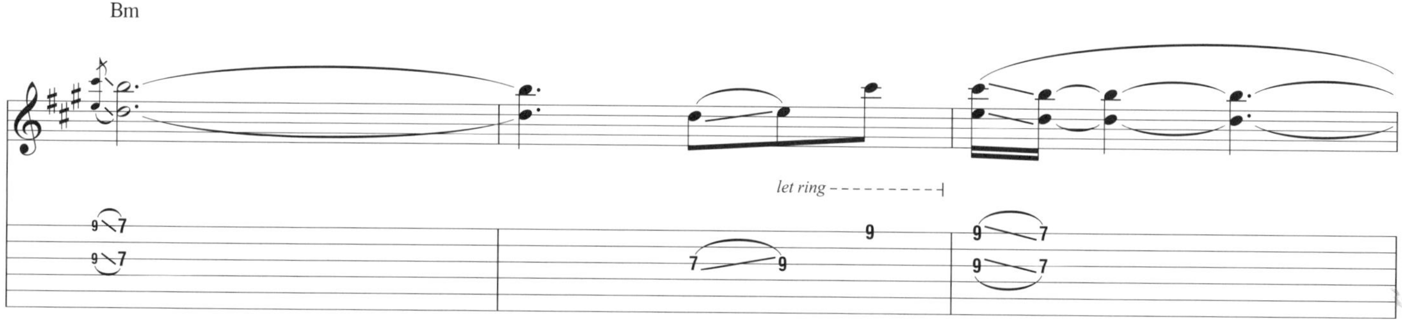
Bm
let ring

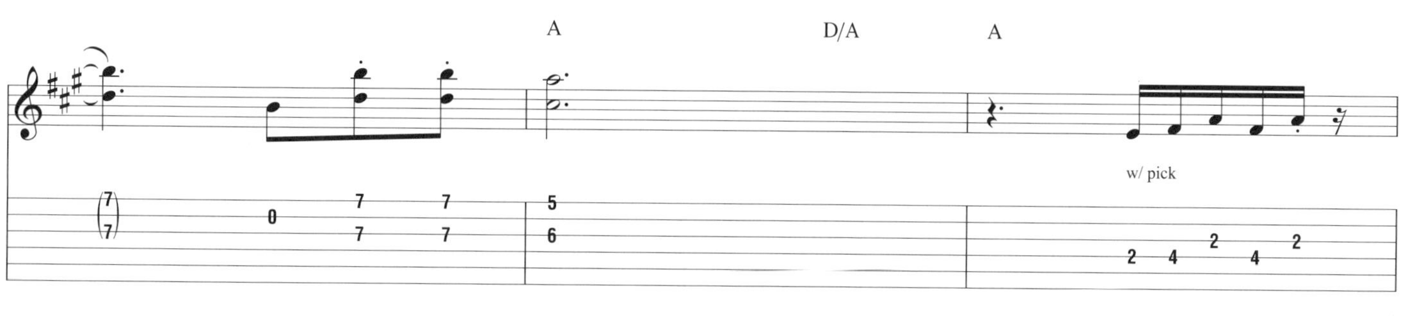
A
D/A
A
w/ pick

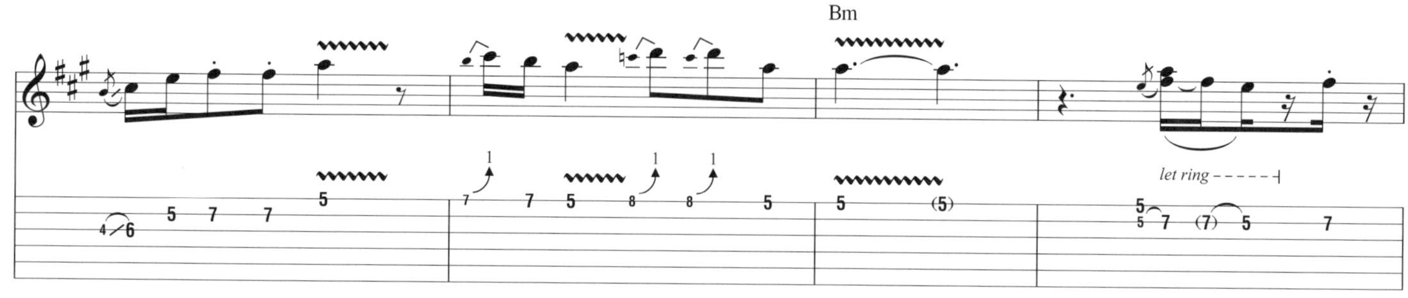
Bm
let ring

D.S. al Coda 2
A
D/A
A
You're as

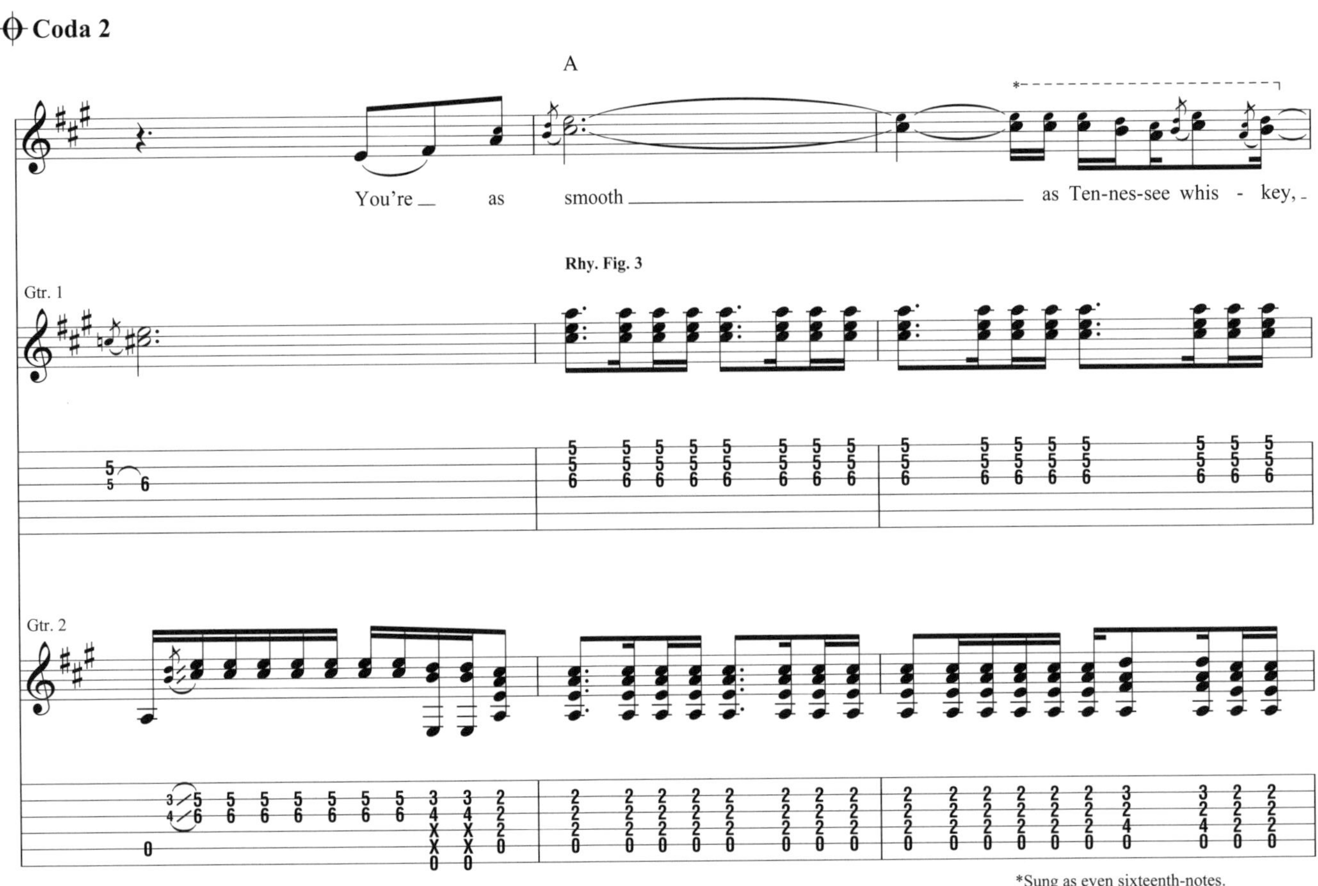
Coda 2
A
You're as smooth as Ten-nes-see whis - key,
Rhy. Fig. 3
Gtr. 1
Gtr. 2
*Sung as even sixteenth-notes.

Bm
Ten-nes-see whis - key,
End Rhy. Fig. 3
**Gtrs. 1 & 2
let ring
**Composite arrangement
***As before

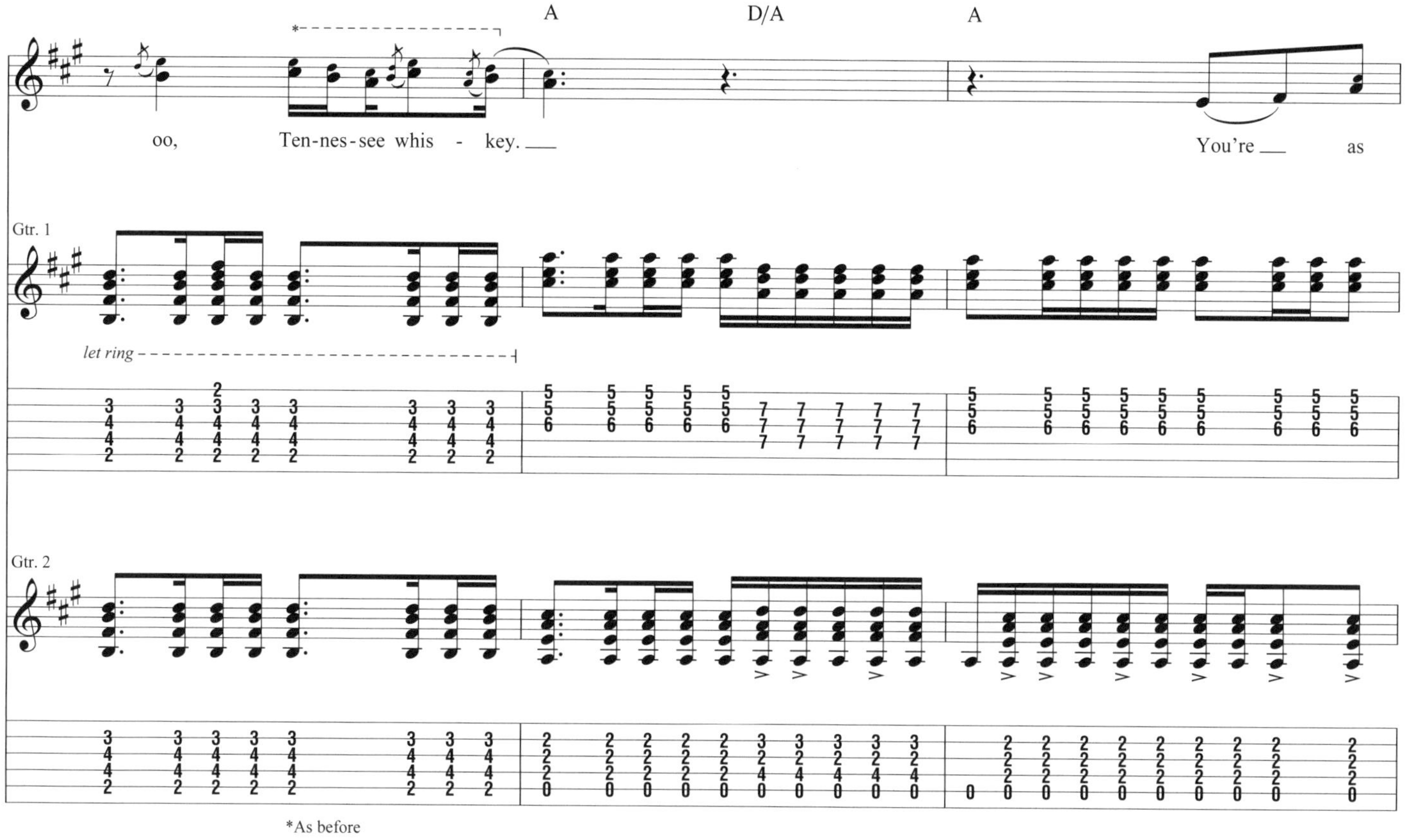
A
D/A
A
oo, Ten-nes-see whis - key.
You're as
Gtr. 1
let ring
Gtr. 2
*As before

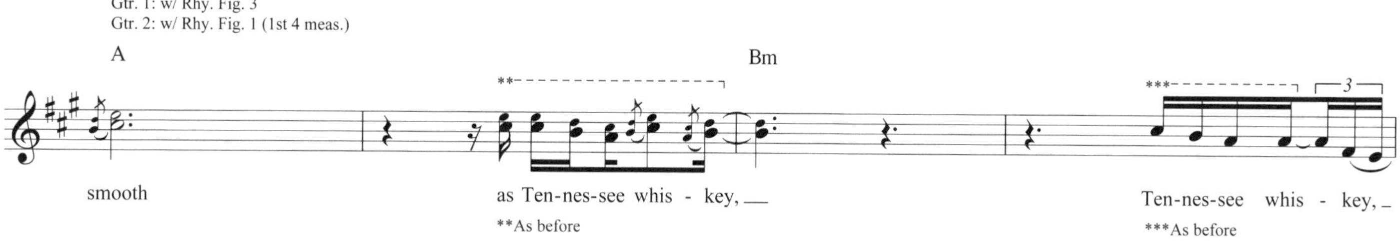
Gtr. 1: w/ Rhy. Fig. 3
Gtr. 2: w/ Rhy. Fig. 1 (1st 4 meas.)
A
Bm
smooth
as Ten-nes-see whis - key,
**As before
Ten-nes-see whis - key,
***As before

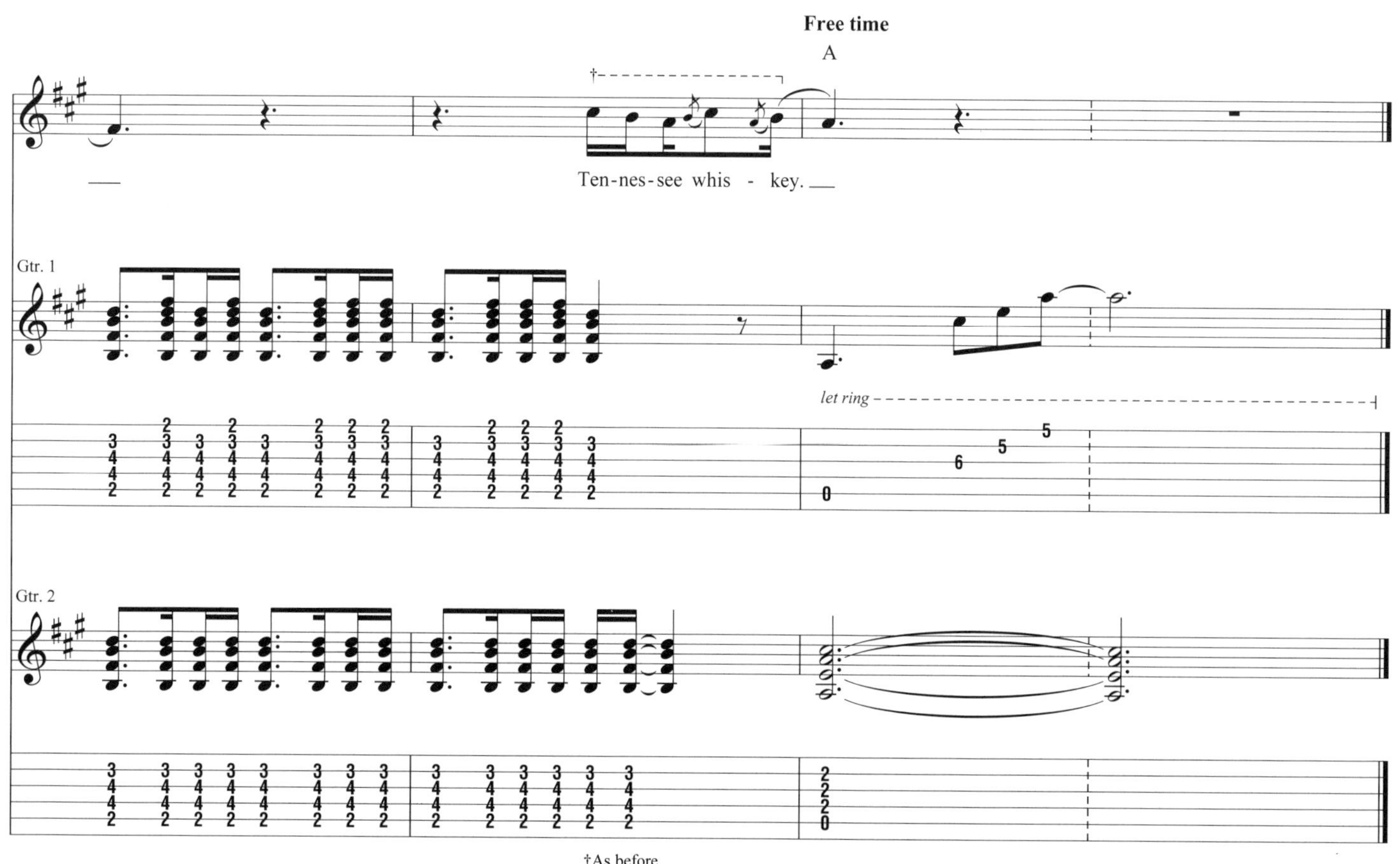
Free time
A
Ten-nes-see whis - key.
Gtr. 1
let ring
Gtr. 2
†As before

from Ed Sheeran - *X*

Thinking Out Loud

Words and Music by Ed Sheeran and Amy Wadge

D5
D/F♯
G5
A5
Will your eyes still smile from your cheeks? And, dar - ling, I
I know you will still love me the same. 'Cause, hon - ey, your
D5
D/F♯
G
A
mp
will be lov - ing you 'til we're sev - en - ty.
soul could nev - er grow old, it's ev - er - green.
D
D/F♯
G
A
And, ba - by, my
And, ba - by, your
D
D/F♯
G
A
heart could still fall as hard at twen - ty - three.
smile's for - ev - er in my mind and mem - o - ry.

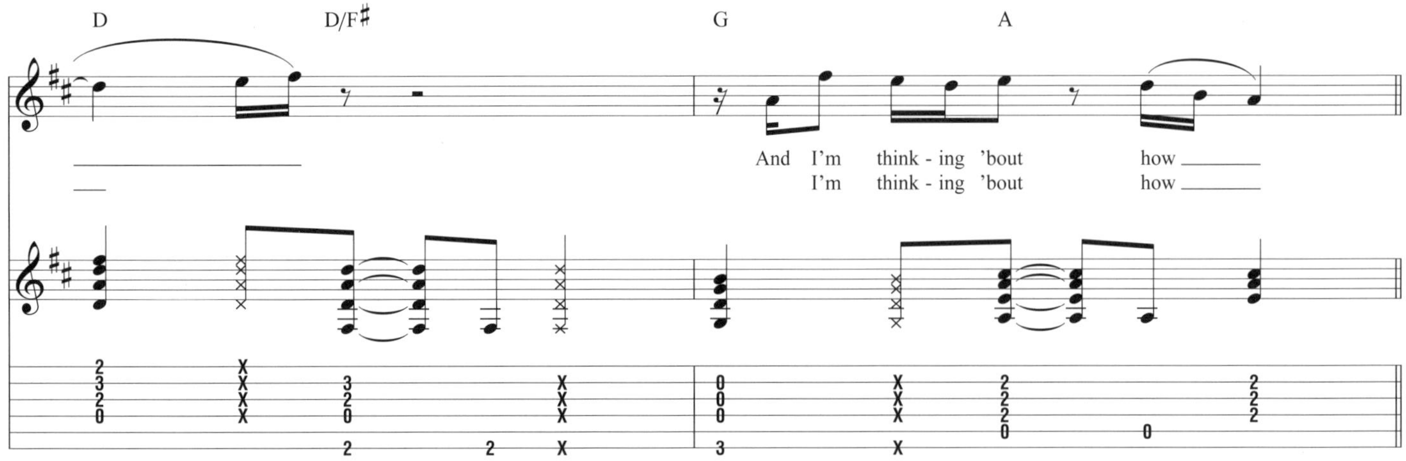

Pre-Chorus

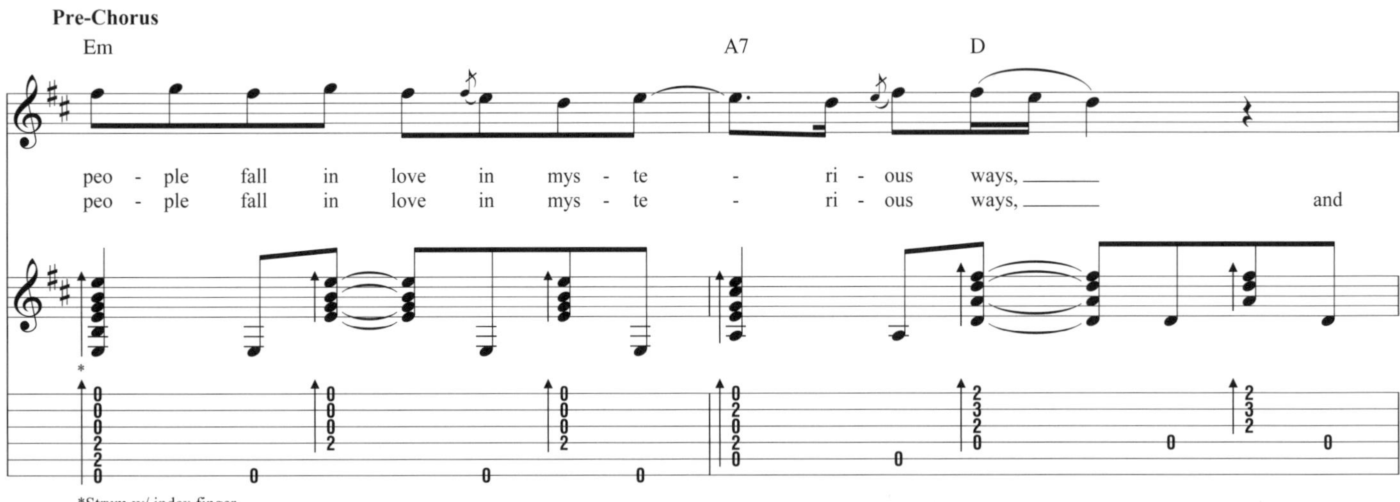

*Strum w/ index finger.

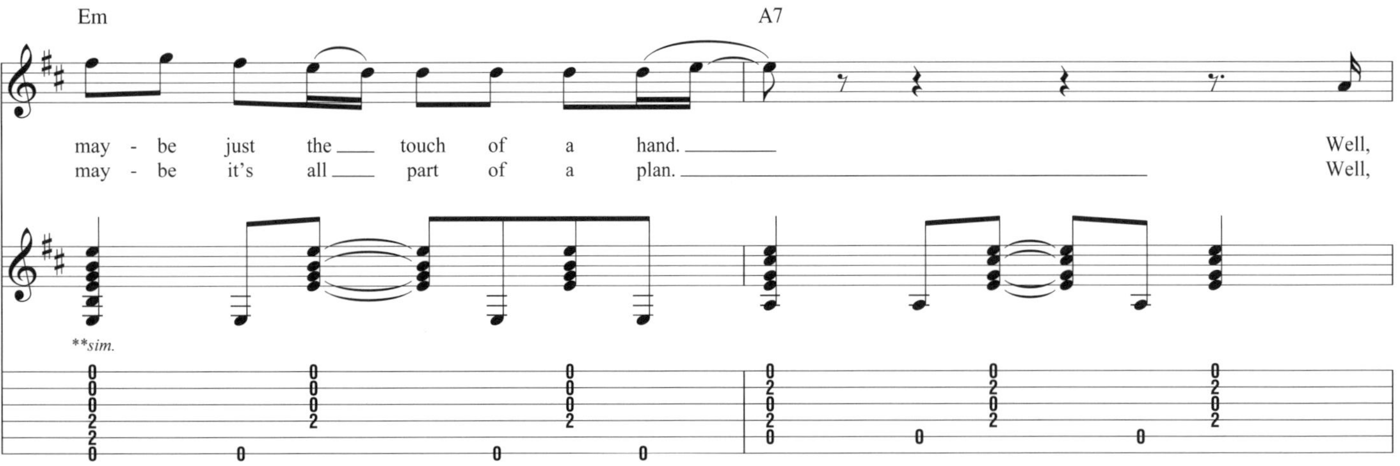

**All chords are strummed simile till end of Pre-Chorus.

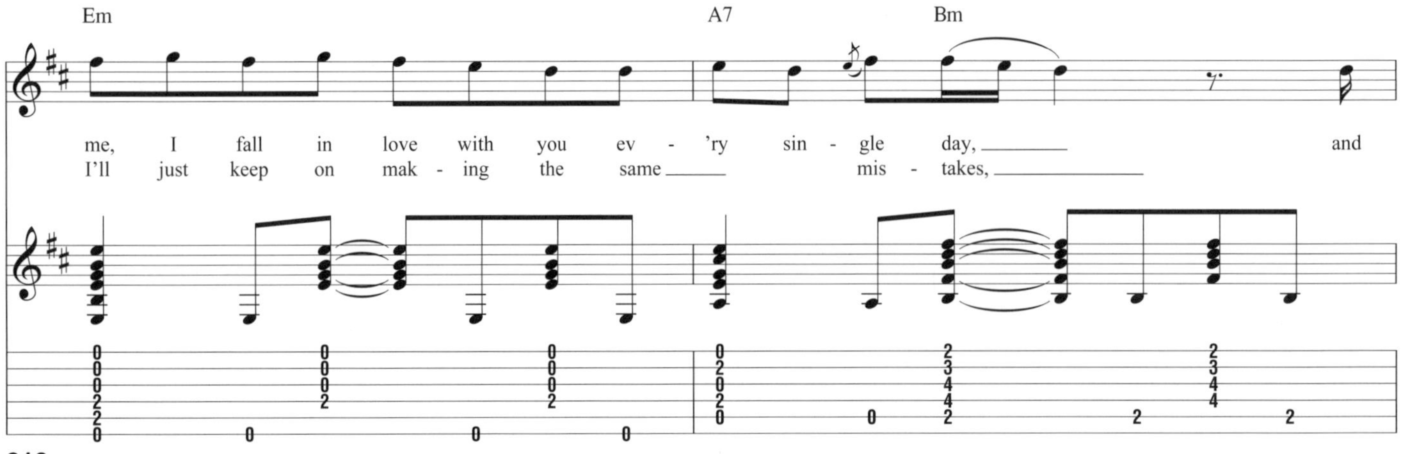

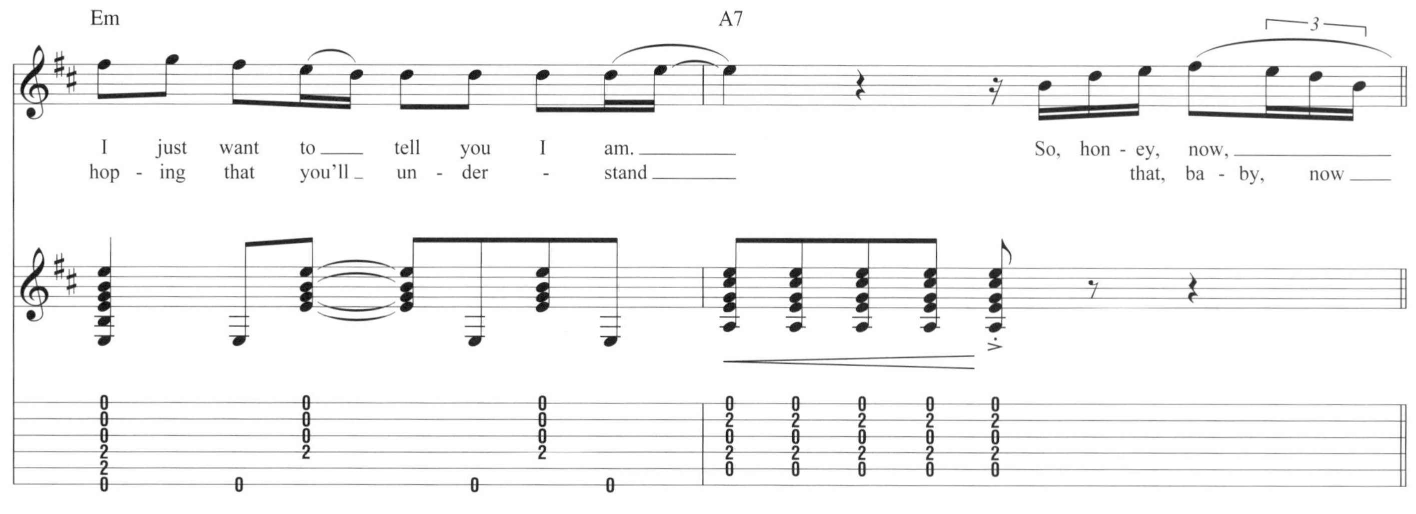
Em
A7
I just want to tell you I am.
So, hon - ey, now,
hop - ing that you'll un - der - stand
that, ba - by, now

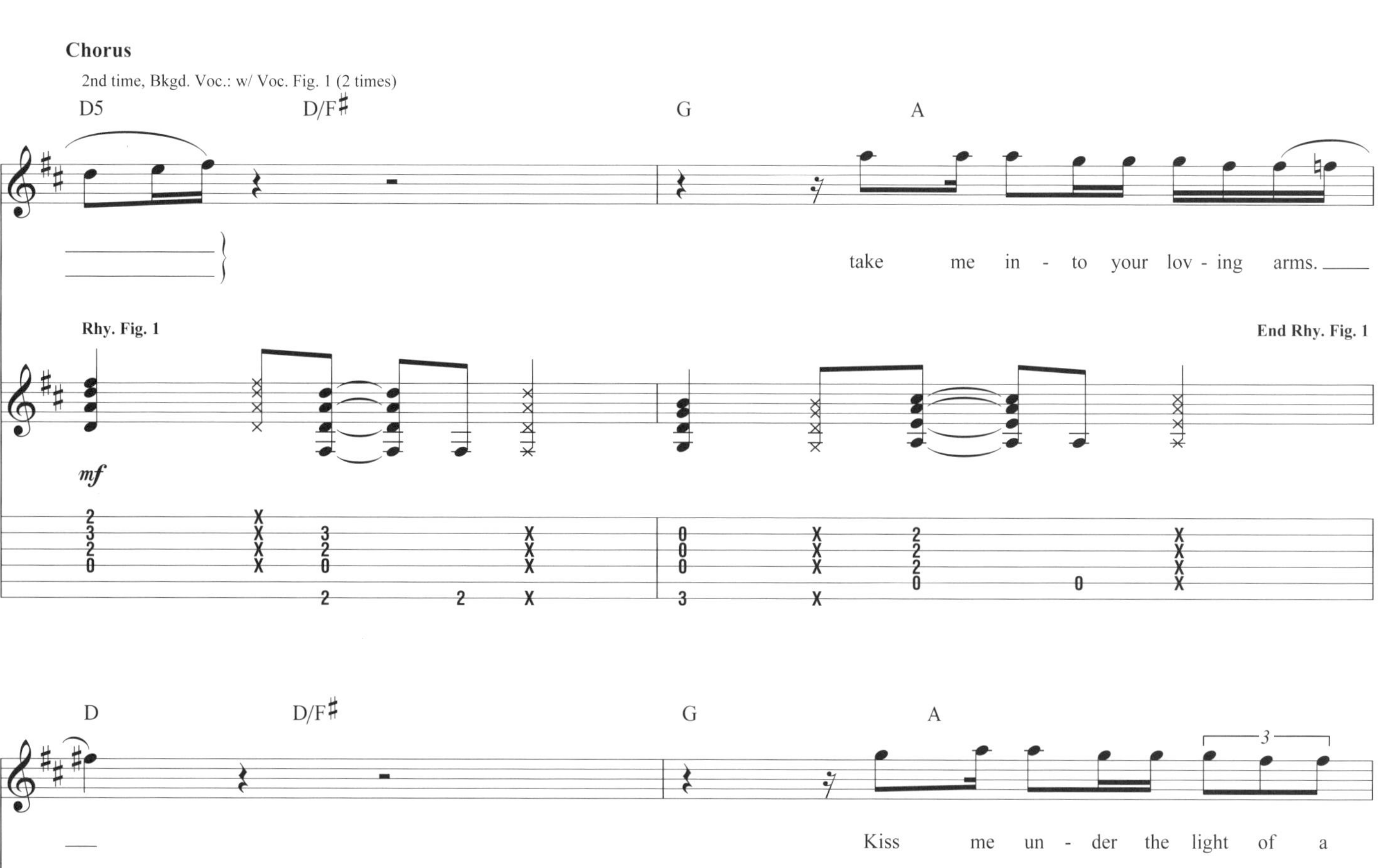
Chorus
2nd time, Bkgd. Voc.: w/ Voc. Fig. 1 (2 times)
D5
D/F♯
G
A
take me in - to your lov - ing arms.
Rhy. Fig. 1
End Rhy. Fig. 1
mf

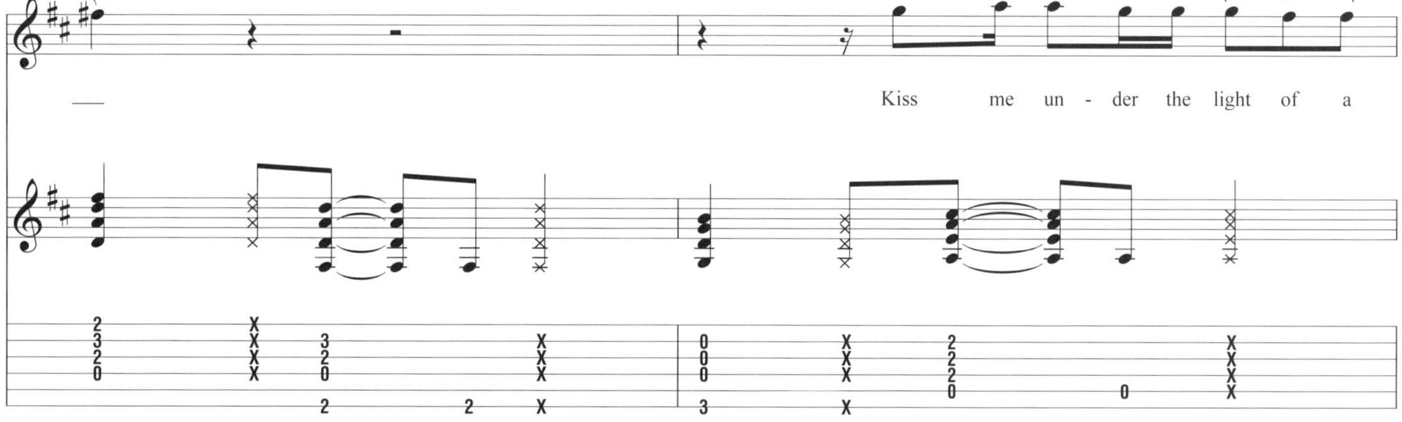
D
D/F♯
G
A
Kiss me un - der the light of a

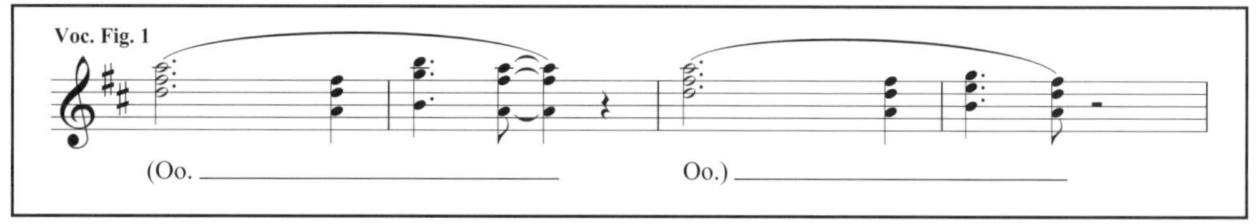
Voc. Fig. 1
(Oo.
Oo.)

D
D/F♯
G
A
D
D/F♯
thou - sand stars.
Place your head on my beat-ing heart.
I'm think-ing

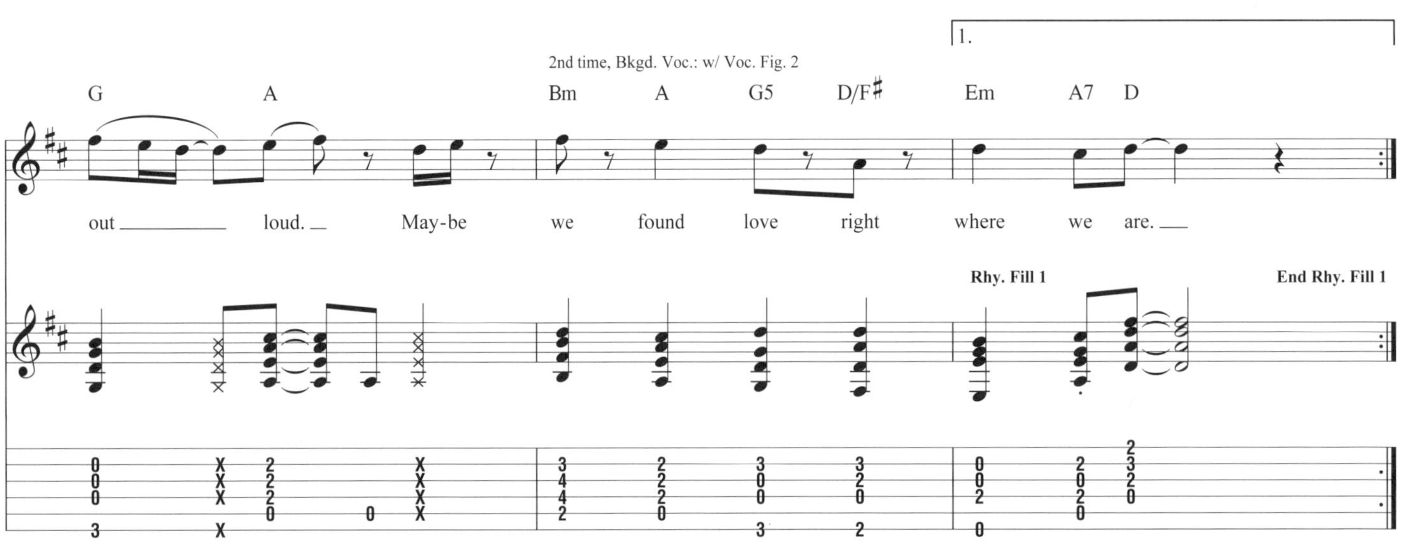
1.
2nd time, Bkgd. Voc.: w/ Voc. Fig. 2
G
A
Bm
A
G5
D/F♯
Em
A7
D
out loud. May-be we found love right where we are.
Rhy. Fill 1
End Rhy. Fill 1

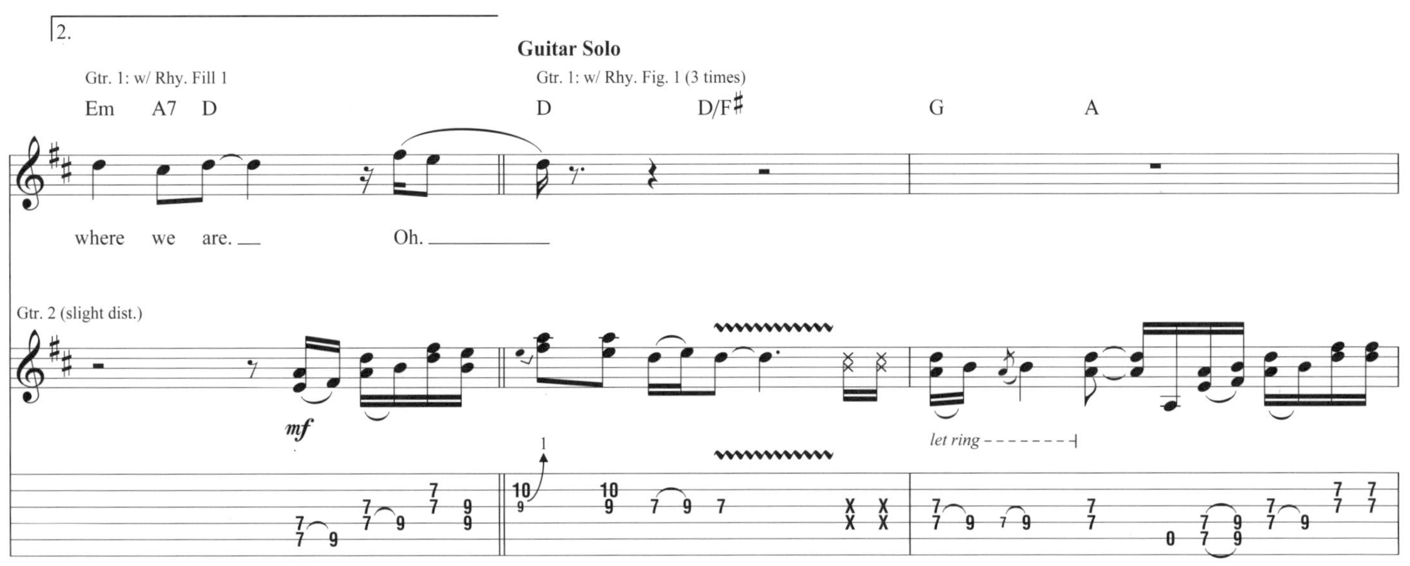
2.
Guitar Solo
Gtr. 1: w/ Rhy. Fill 1
Gtr. 1: w/ Rhy. Fig. 1 (3 times)
Em
A7
D
D
D/F♯
G
A
where we are. Oh.
Gtr. 2 (slight dist.)
mf
let ring

Voc. Fig. 2
(Oo.)

D
D/F♯
G
A
Oh, la, la, la, la, la, la, la, la, la, la, la, la.
D5
So, ba - by, now,
Gtr. 2
Gtr. 1
let ring
sim.
*Strum w/ index finger (as before).

Outro-Chorus

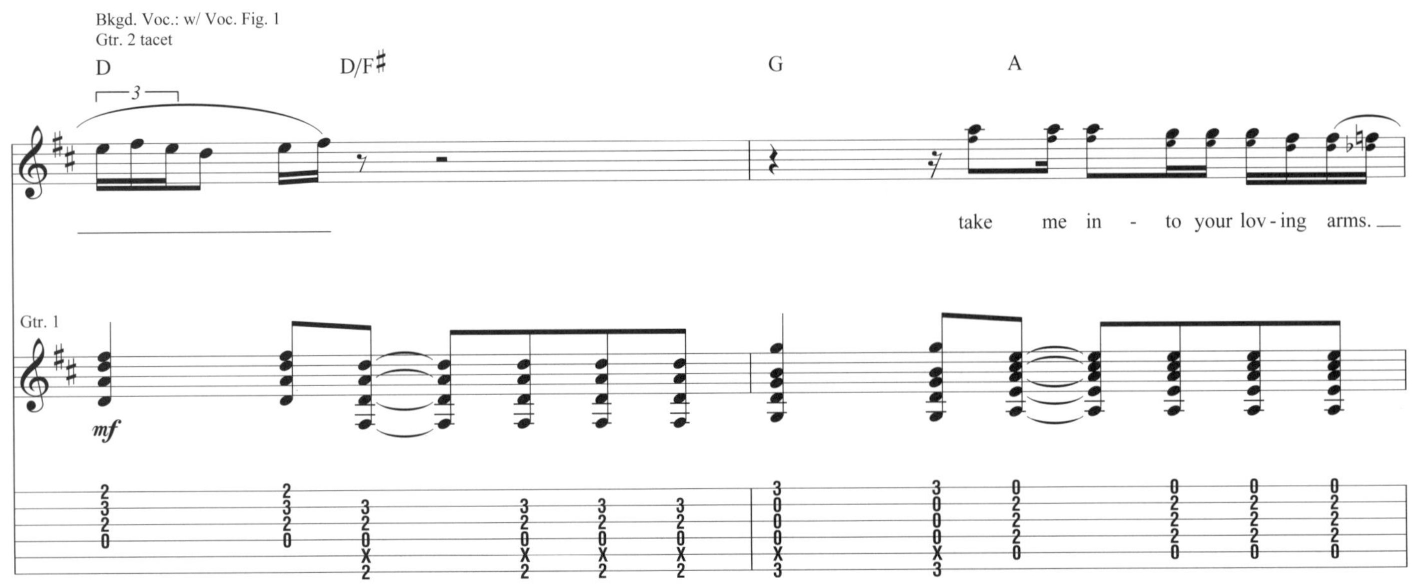

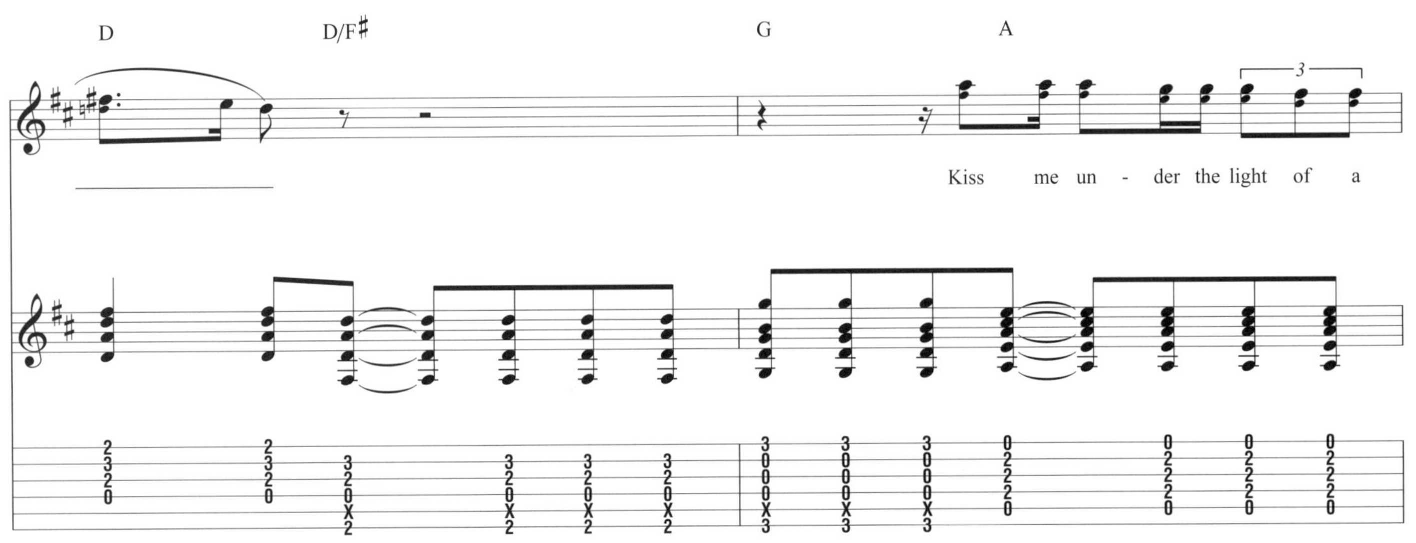

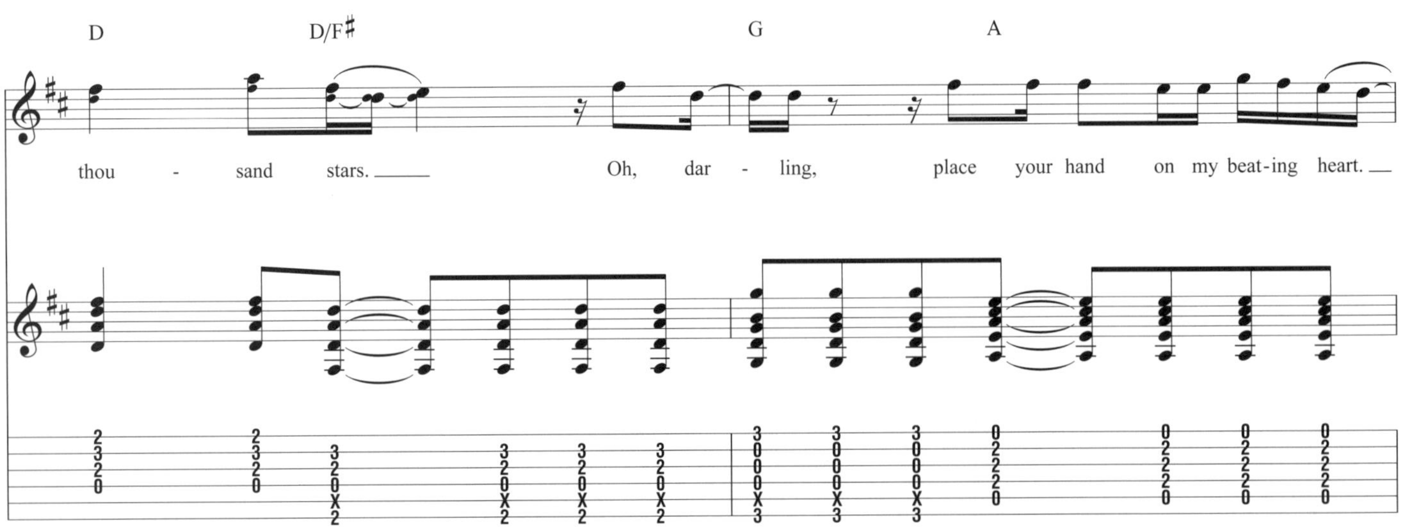

D
D/F♯
G
A
I'm think-ing out
loud
that may-be
Bm
A
G
D/F♯
Em
A7
D
we found love right where we are.
Oh, may-be
Bkgd. Voc.: w/ Voc. Fig. 1 (2 times)
Bm
A
G
D/F♯
Em
A7
D
we found love right where we are.
And
Bm
A
G
D/F♯
Em
A7
D
we found love right where we are.
mp
w/ fingers

from Mark Ronson - *Uptown Special*

Uptown Funk

Words and Music by Mark Ronson, Bruno Mars, Philip Lawrence, Jeff Bhasker, Devon Gallaspy, Nicholaus Williams, Lonnie Simmons, Ronnie Wilson, Charles Wilson, Rudolph Taylor and Robert Wilson

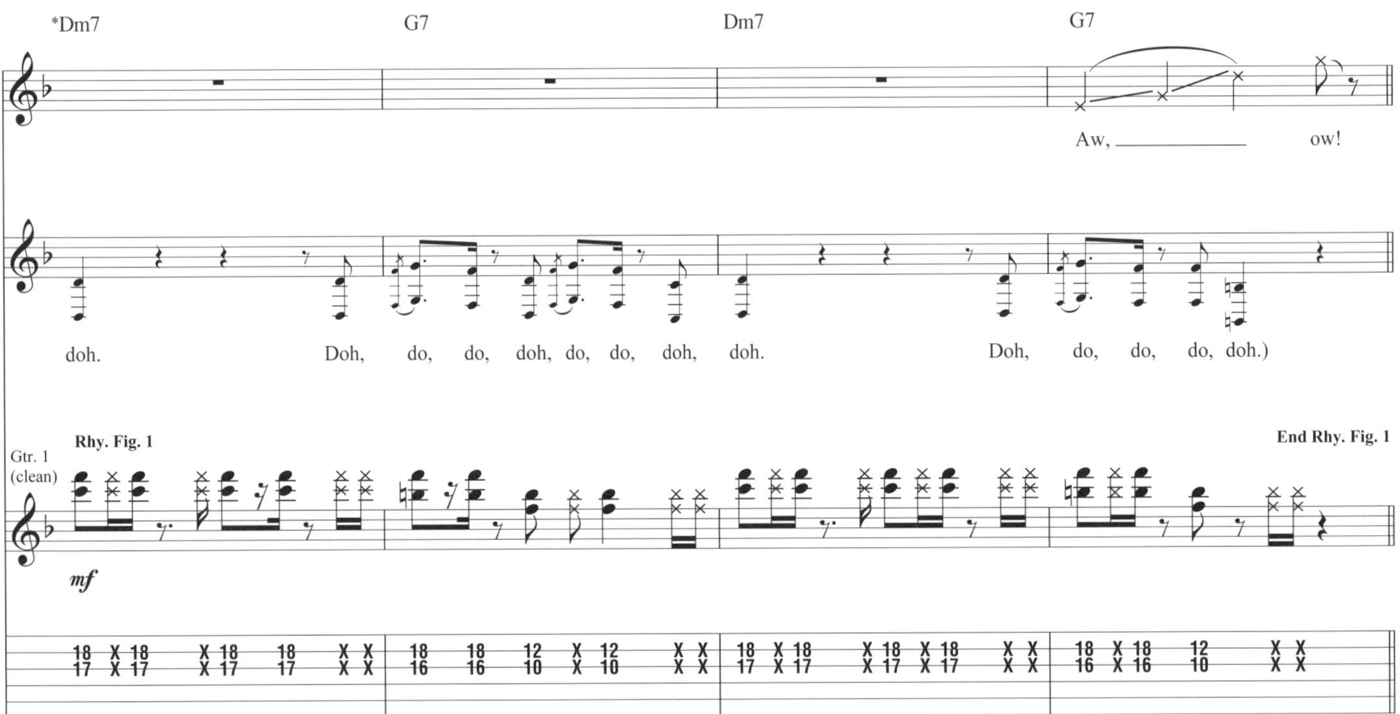

*Chord symbols reflect implied harmony.

2nd time, Gtr. 1: w/ Fill 1
good girls, straight mas - ter - piec - es. Styl - in', while in, liv - in' it up in the ci - ty. Got
Jul - i - o, get the stretch. Ride to Har - lem, Hol - ly - wood, Jack - son, Mis-sis-sip-pi. If we
Chucks on with Saint Lau - rent. Got - ta kiss my - self, I'm so pret - ty.
show up, we gon' show out. Smooth-er than a fresh jar of Skip-py.
I'm too
Pre-Chorus
*Dm7
G7
hot, uh, call the po - lice and the fire - man. I'm too
(Hot damn!
Voc Fig. 2
(Doh, doh, do, do, doh, do, do, doh,
Gtr. 1
Riff A
*Chord symbols reflect overall harmony.
Dm7
G7
hot, make a drag - on wan - na re - tire, man. I'm too
Hot damn!
doh. Doh, do, do, doh, do, do, doh,
End Riff A
Fill 1
Gtr. 1

Gtr. 1: w/ Riff A
Dm7
G7
Dm7
hot.
Hot damn!
Say my name, you know who I am. I'm too
hot.
Am I
Hot damn!)
doh.
Doh, do, do, doh, do, do, doh, doh.
Doh,
G7
Chorus
N.C.
bad 'bout that mon-ey? Break it down.
Girls hit you, hal-le-lu-jah.
Girls hit you, hal-le-lu-jah.
End Voc. Fig. 2
do, do, do, doh, doh, doh.
Oo,
oo,
Girls hit you, hal-le-lu-jah. 'Cause up-town funk gon' give it to ya.
'Cause
oo,
oo.)
('Cause up-town funk gon' give it to ya.
Gtr. 2 (clean)
mf
w/ talk box
5 6 7 8
Gtr. 2 tacet
up-town funk gon' give it to ya.
Sat-ur-day night and we in the spot.
Don't be-lieve me? Just watch.
Come on!
Sat-ur-day night and we in the spot.)
9 5 6 7 8 9 5 6

Interlude
Gtr. 1: w/ Rhy. Fig. 1 (2 times)
Gtr. 2 tacet
Dm7
G7
Dm7
G7
(Ha!)
Don't be - lieve _ me? Just watch, uh!
Voc Fig. 3
End Voc Fig. 3
(Doh, doh, do, do, doh, do, do, doh, doh. Doh, do, do, doh, do.)
Bkgd. Voc.: w/ Voc. Fig. 3
Dm7
G7
Dm7
G7
(Ha!)
Don't be - lieve _ me? Just watch, uh!
D7♯9
Don't be - lieve _ me? Just watch, uh. Don't be - lieve _ me? Just watch. ______
Gtr. 1
To Coda
Don't be - lieve _ me? Just watch. ______ Hey, hey, hey, ow! ______
Bridge
Bkgd. Voc.: w/ Voc. Fig. 1
N.C.
Spoken: 'Fore we leave, let me tell y'all a lit-tle some-thin'.

Bkgd. Voc.: w/ Voc. Fig. 2
Up - town funk you up, — up-town funk you up. — Up - town funk you up, — up-town funk you up. — Uh, I said
up - town funk you up, — up-town funk you up, — ah. Up - town funk you up, — up-town funk you up. — Come on,
Bkgd. Voc.: w/ Voc. Fig. 1 (1 3/4 times)
Dm7 G7 Dm7
dance. Jump on it. If you sex - y, — then flaunt it. If you freak - y, — then own it. Don't
Gtr. 1
8va
loco
Gtr. 3 (clean)
G7 Dm7 G7
brag a - bout – it, come show me. Come on, dance. Jump on it. If you sex - y, — then flaunt it. Well, it's

D.S. al Coda
(no repeat)
Dm7
Sat - ur - day night and we in the spot.
Don't be - lieve me? Just watch.
Come on!
18 18 18 18
17 17 17 17
17 17 17 17
18 18 18 18 18
17 17 17 17 17
17 17 17 17 17
18 18 X X
17 17 X X
17 17 X X
10 10 10 10 10 10 10 10 10 10 10
10 10 10 10 10 10 10 10 10 10 10
Coda
Outro
w/ Lead Voc. ad lib.
Gtr. 1: w/ Rhy. Fig. 1 (1 3/4 times)
Dm7
G7
Dm7
(Up - town funk you up,
up - town funk you up.
Up - town funk you up,
(Doh, doh, do, do, doh, do, do, doh, doh. Doh,
G7
Dm7
G7
up - town funk you up.
Up - town funk you up,
up - town funk you up.
do, do, doh. Doh, doh, do, do, doh, do, do, doh,
1.
2.
Dm7
Dm7
Up - town funk you up,
up - town funk you up.)
Up - town funk you up.)
Ah, ow!
doh.)
doh.)

from AVICII - *True*

Wake Me Up

Words and Music by Aloe Blacc, Tim Bergling and Michael Einziger

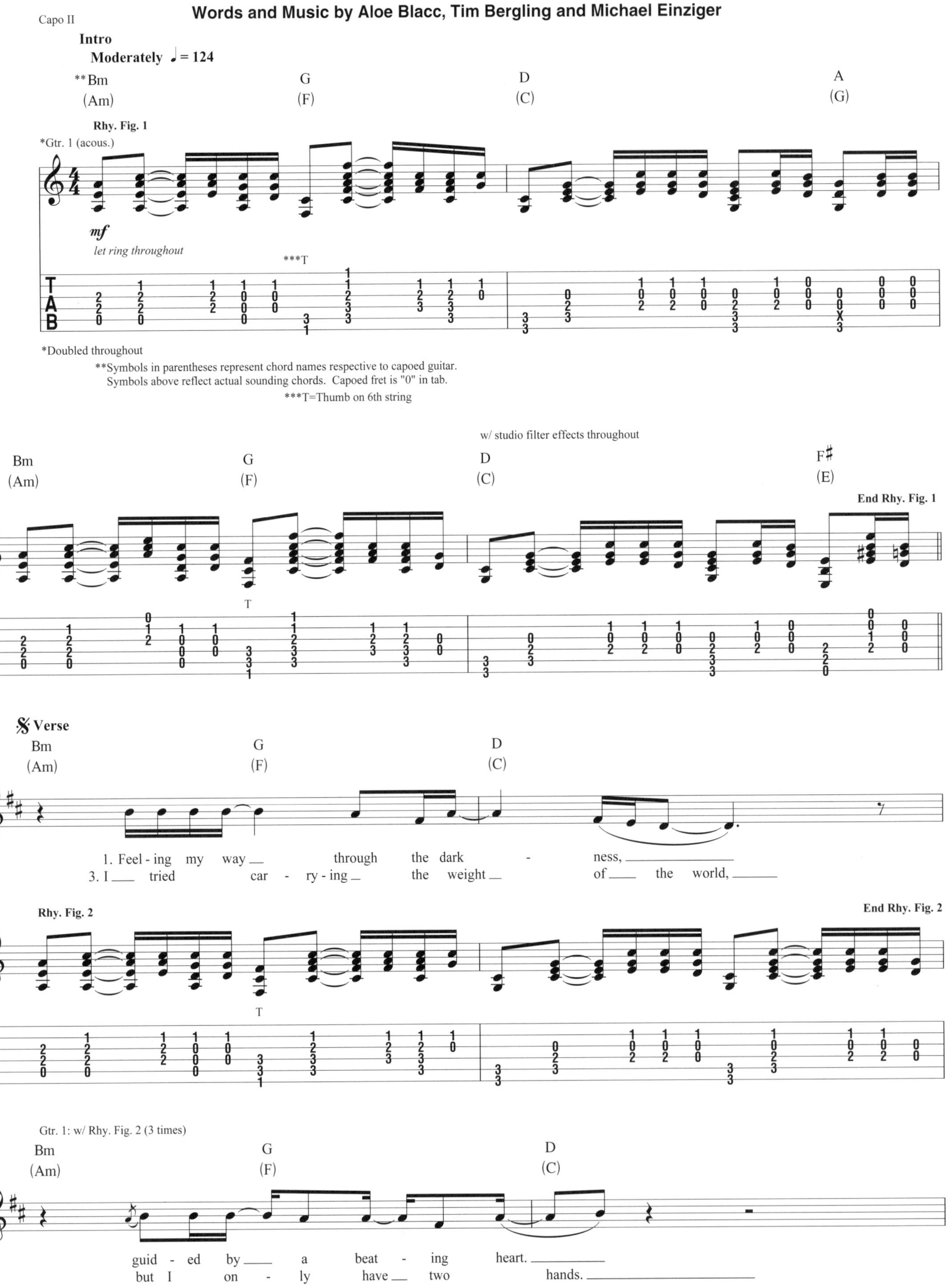

Capo II

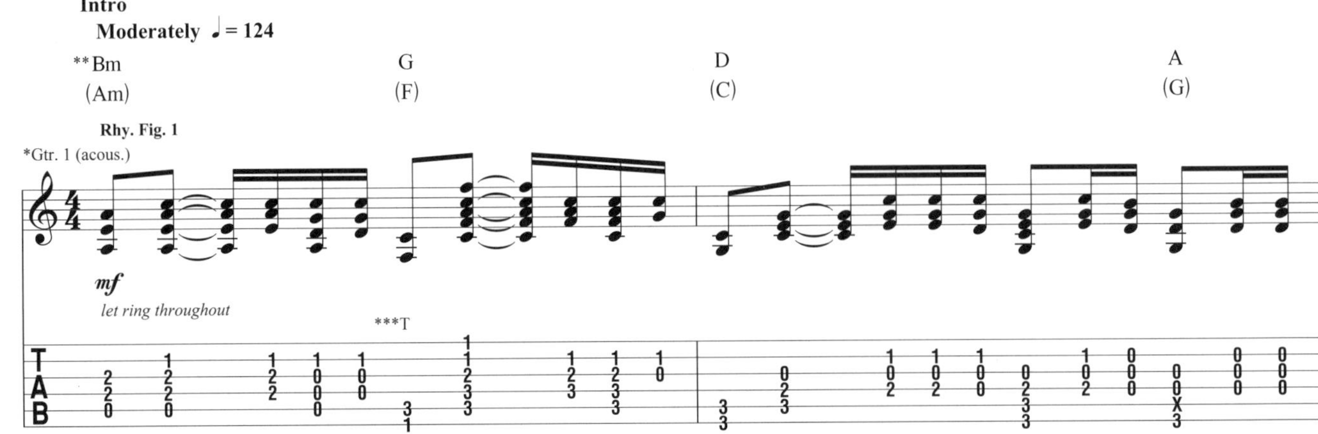

*Doubled throughout

**Symbols in parentheses represent chord names respective to capoed guitar. Symbols above reflect actual sounding chords. Capoed fret is "0" in tab.

***T=Thumb on 6th string

w/ studio filter effects throughout

Bm (Am) G (F) D (C) F♯ (E)

T

End Rhy. Fig. 1

Verse

Bm (Am) G (F) D (C)

1. Feel - ing my way __ through the dark - ness, __
3. I __ tried car - ry - ing __ the weight __ of __ the world, __

Rhy. Fig. 2

T

End Rhy. Fig. 2

Gtr. 1: w/ Rhy. Fig. 2 (3 times)

Bm (Am) G (F) D (C)

guid - ed by __ a beat - ing heart. __
but I on - ly have __ two hands. __

Bm (Am) G (F) D (C)
I can't tell where the jour - ney will end,
Hope I get the chance to trav - el the world,
Bm (Am) G (F) D (C)
but I know where to start.
but I don't have an - y plans.
Verse
Gtr. 1: w/ Rhy. Fig. 2 (4 times)
Bm (Am) G (F) D (C)
2. They tell me I'm too young to un - der - stand,
4. Wish that I could stay for - ev - er this young,
To Coda 1
Bm (Am) G (F) D (C)
they say I'm caught up in a dream.
not a - fraid to close my eyes.
Bm (Am) G (F) D (C)
Well, life will pass me by if I don't o - pen up my eyes.
Bm (Am) G (F) D (C)
Well, that's fine by me. So wake me
Chorus
Gtr. 1: w/ Rhy. Fig. 1 (3 1/2 times)
Bm (Am) G (F) D (C) A (G) Bm (Am) G (F)
up when it's all o - ver, when I'm wis - er and I'm old -

D (C) F♯ (E) Bm (Am) G (F) D (C) A (G)
- er. All this time I was find - ing my - self and I
Bm (Am) G (F) D (C) F♯ (E) Bm (Am) G (F)
did - n't know I was lost. So wake me up when it's all o -
D (C) A (G) Bm (Am) G (F) D (C) F♯ (E)
- ver, when I'm wis - er and I'm old - er. All this
Bm (Am) G (F) D (C) A (G)
time I was find - ing my - self and I
Bm (Am) G (F) D (C) N.C.
did - n't know I was lost.
Gtr. 2 (elec.)
Fill 1
End Fill 1
mf
w/ clean tone
Gtr. 3 (elec.)
Fill 1A
End Fill 1A
mf
w/ clean tone
Gtr. 1
T

Interlude
Gtr. 1: w/ Rhy. Fig. 1 (1 3/4 times)
Bm
(Am)
G
(F)
D
(C)
A
(G)
Riff A
End Riff A
Gtr. 2
Gtr. 3
Riff A1
End Riff A1
Gtrs. 2 & 3: w/ Riffs A & A1 (3 times)
F♯
(E)
N.C.
Gtr. 1: w/ Rhy. Fig. 1
Gtrs. 2 & 3: w/ Riffs A & A1 (2 times)
Play 3 times
To Coda 2
D.S. al Coda 1
Gtr. 1: w/ Rhy. Fig. 1
1st time, Gtrs. 2 & 3: w/ Riffs A & A1 (2 times)
2nd time, Gtrs. 2 & 3: w/ Riffs A & A1 (1 1/2 times)
Coda 1
Gtr. 1: w/ Rhy. Fig. 1 (1st 2 meas.)
Life's a game made for ev - 'ry - one

Bm (Am) G (F) D (C) N.C.
and love is the prize. So wake me
Rhy. Fill 1
End Rhy. Fill 1
Gtr. 1
Chorus
Gtr. 1: w/ Rhy. Fig. 1 (1 3/4 times)
Bm (Am) G (F) D (C) A (G) Bm (Am) G (F)
up when it's all o - ver, when I'm wis - er and I'm old -
D (C) F♯ (E) Bm (Am) G (F) D (C) A (G)
- er. All this time I was find - ing my - self and I
Gtr. 1: w/ Rhy. Fill 1
Gtr. 1: w/ Rhy. Fig. 1 (3 1/2 times)
Bm (Am) G (F) D (C) N.C. Bm (Am) G (F)
did - n't know I was lost. So wake me up when it's all o -
D (C) A (G) Bm (Am) G (F) D (C) F♯ (E)
- ver, when I'm wis - er and I'm old - er. All this
Bm (Am) G (F) D (C) A (G) Bm (Am) G (F)
time I was find - ing my - self, and I, I did-n't know I was lost.
Gtrs. 2 & 3: w/ Riffs A & A1 (1st meas., 7 times)
D (C) F♯ (E) Bm (Am) G (F) D (C) A (G)
I did-n't know I was lost.

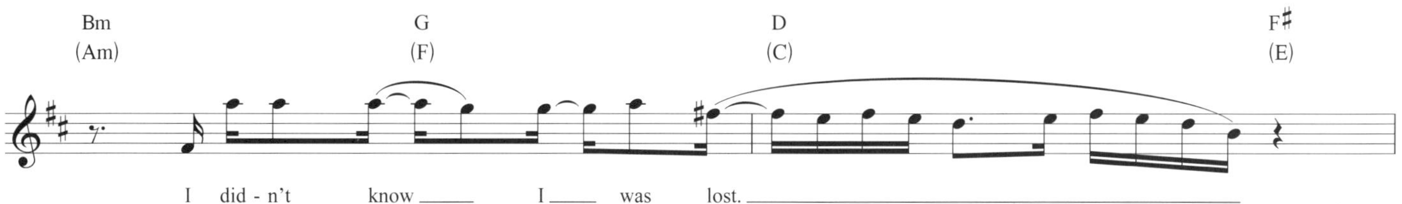
Bm
(Am)
G
(F)
D
(C)
F♯
(E)
I did - n't know I was lost.

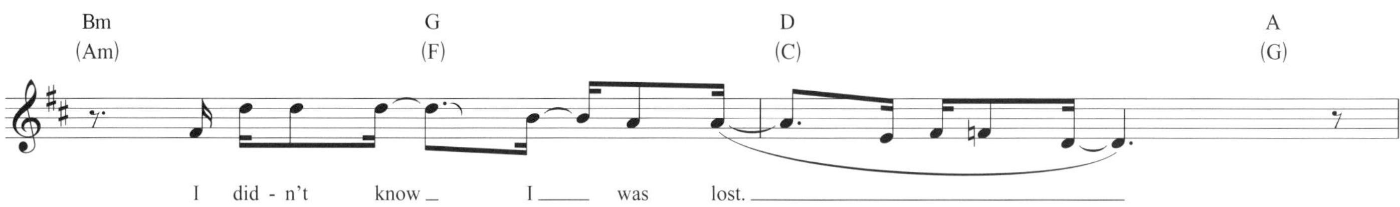
Bm
(Am)
G
(F)
D
(C)
A
(G)
I did - n't know I was lost.

D.S.S. al Coda 2
Gtrs. 2 & 3: w/ Fills 1 & 1A
Bm
(Am)
G
(F)
D
(C)
N.C.
I did - n't know.
Gtr. 1
*w/ echo set for halfnote regeneration w/ 2 repeats.

Coda 2

D
(C)
F♯
(E)
Bm
(Am)
N.C.
Gtr. 2
Gtr. 3

from One Direction - *Up All Night*

What Makes You Beautiful

Words and Music by Savan Kotecha, Rami Yacoub and Carl Falk

Pre-Chorus

Gtrs. 1 & 2 tacet

E A C♯5 B5 E A N.C.

Ev - 'ry-one else in the room can see __ it, ev - 'ry-one else but __ you, oo. __

Ba - by, you

Gtr. 2 (slight dist.)

Riff A

End Riff A

mp

Gtr. 1

Rhy. Fig. 2

End Rhy. Fig. 2

Chorus

E5 A5 B5 E5 A5 B5

light up __ my world like __ no - bod - y else. The way that you flip __ your hair gets __ me o - ver- whelmed. But when you

*Gtr. 3 (dist.)

mf

*Doubled throughout

E5 A5 C♯5 B5 E5 N.C.

smile at __ the ground, it __ ain't hard to tell __ you don't __ know, oh, oh, you don't know you're beau - ti - ful. __

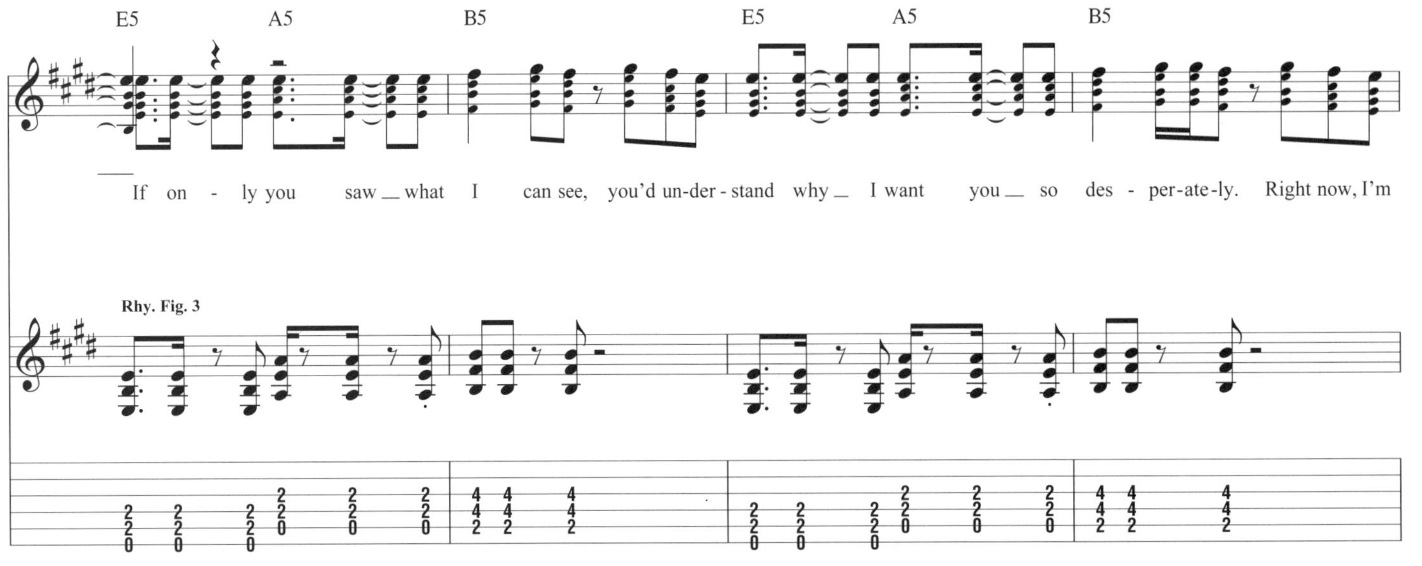

E5 A5 C♯5 B5 E5 A5

look - ing at you and I can't be - lieve you don't know, oh, oh,

Gtr. 2

Riff B

mf

9 11 13 12 14 12 13

Gtr. 4 (slight dist.)

Riff B1

mf

2 4 6 4 6 4 6

Gtr. 3

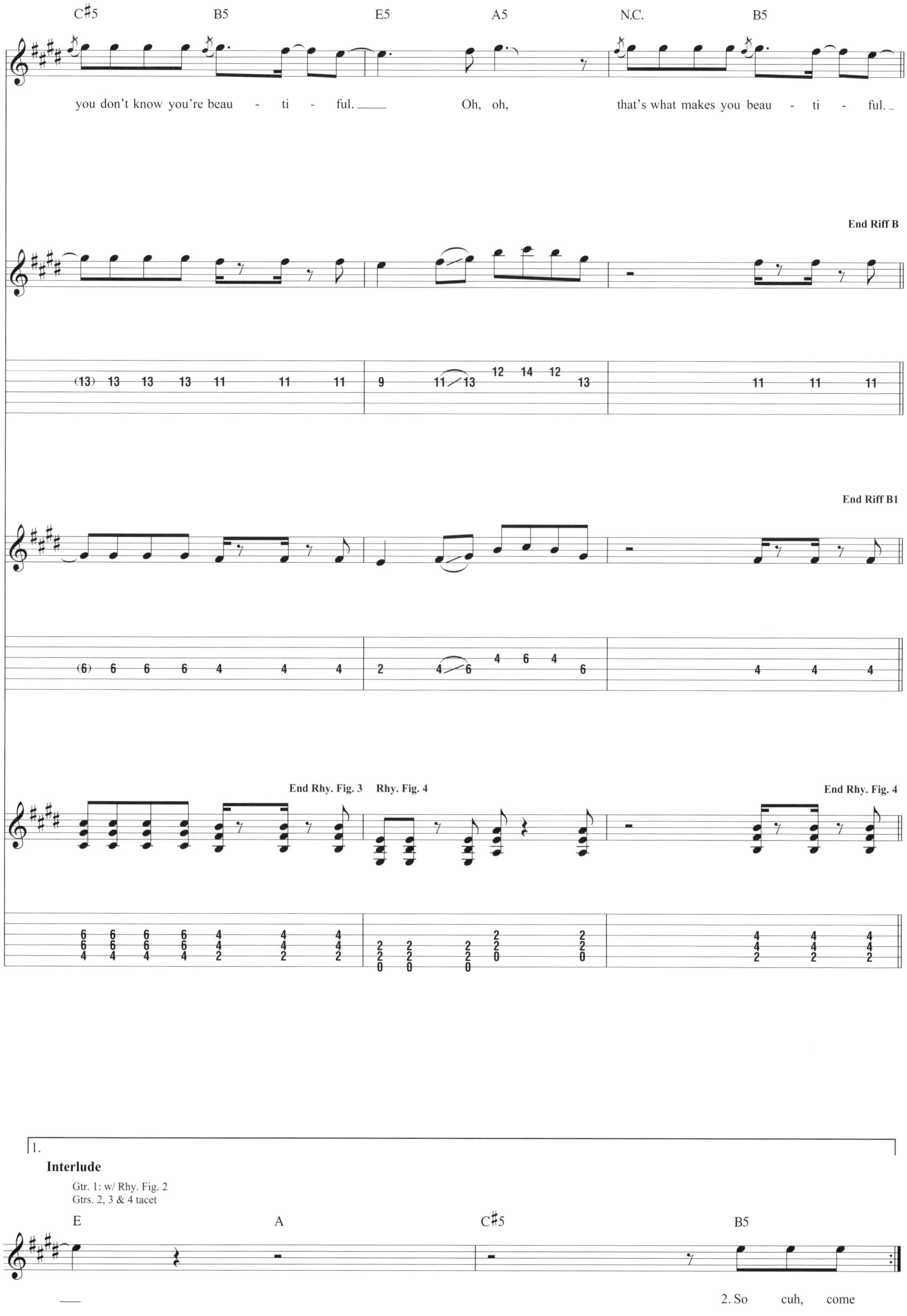

C♯5 B5 E5 A5 N.C. B5

you don't know you're beau - ti - ful. Oh, oh, that's what makes you beau - ti - ful.

End Riff B

End Riff B1

End Rhy. Fig. 3 Rhy. Fig. 4 End Rhy. Fig. 4

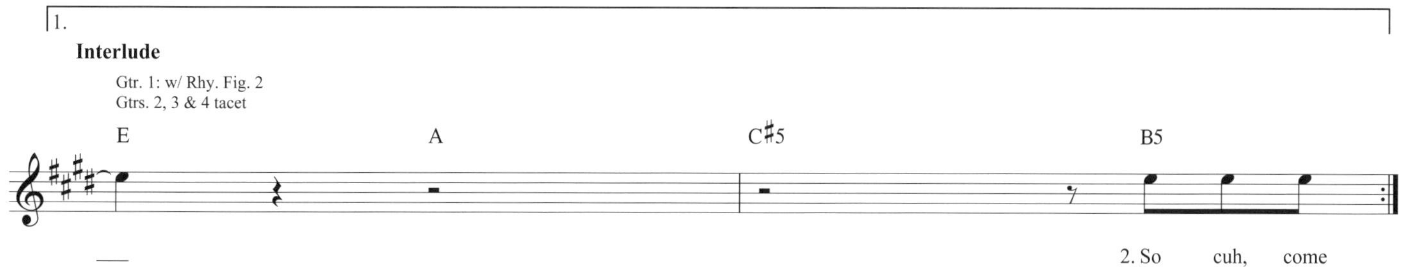

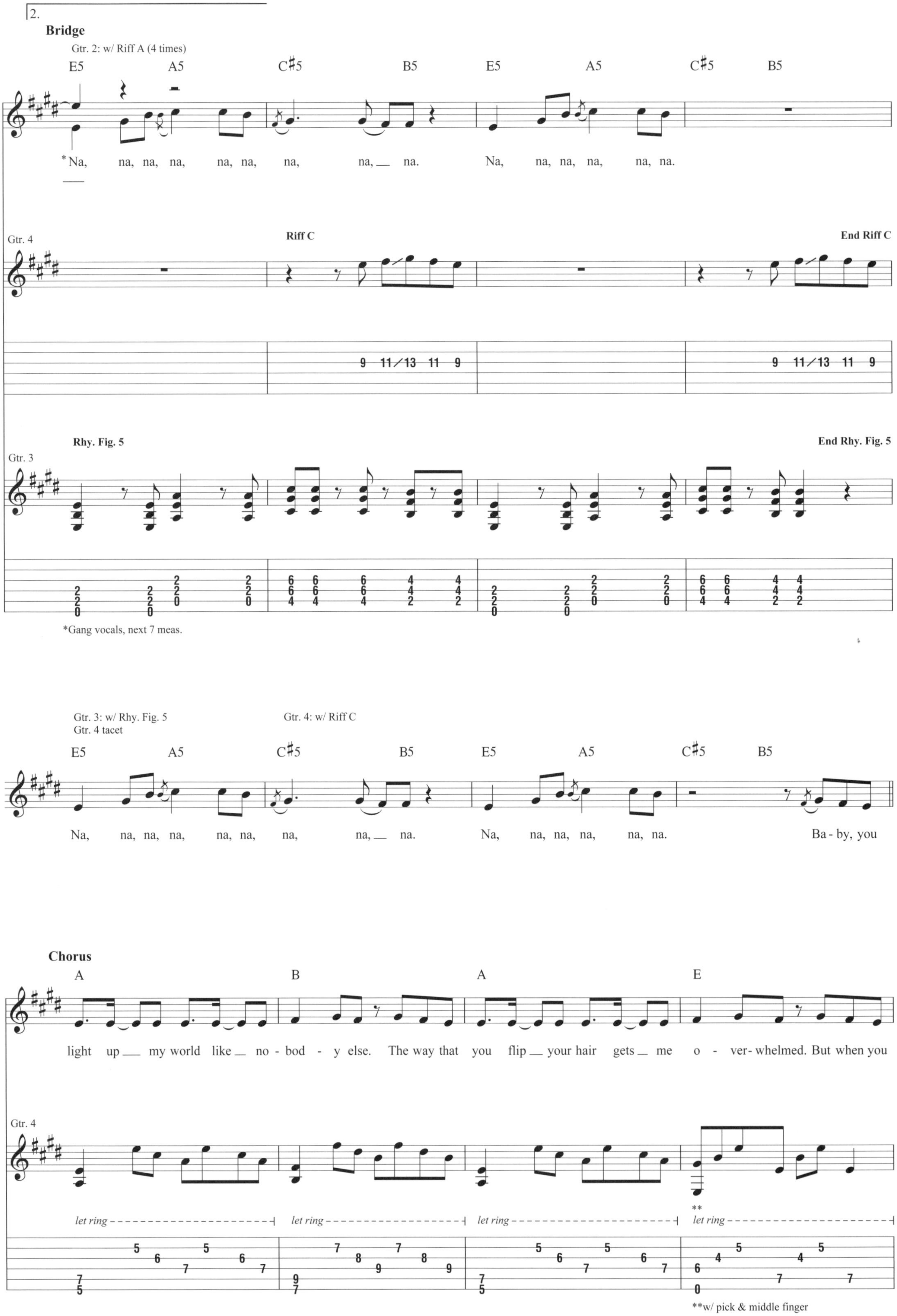

2.

Bridge

Gtr. 2: w/ Riff A (4 times)

E5 A5 C♯5 B5 E5 A5 C♯5 B5

*Na, na, na, na, na, na, na, na, __ na. Na, na, na, na, na, na.

Gtr. 4

Riff C

9 11/13 11 9

End Riff C

9 11/13 11 9

Rhy. Fig. 5

Gtr. 3

End Rhy. Fig. 5

*Gang vocals, next 7 meas.

A
B
C#m
*
smile at the ground it ain't hard to tell...
...you don't know, oh, oh, you don't know you're beau - ti - ful.
The way you
let ring
*Gang vocals, next 19 meas.

Chorus

Gtr. 3: w/ Rhy. Fig. 3 (2 times)
Gtr. 4 tacet
E5
A5
B5
light up my world like no - bod - y else. The way that you flip your hair gets me
Light up my world like no - bod - y else.
Uh.

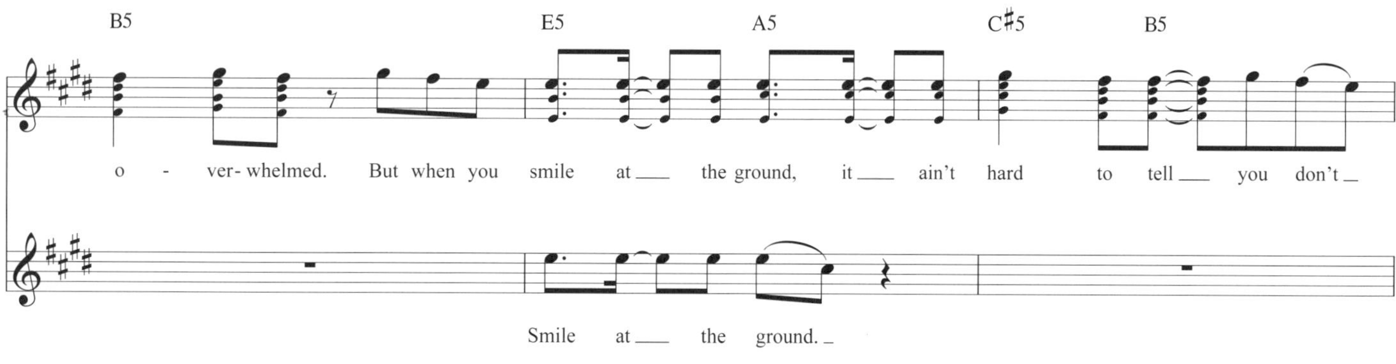
B5
E5
A5
C#5
o - ver- whelmed. But when you smile at the ground, it ain't hard to tell you don't
Smile at the ground.

Gtrs. 2 & 4: w/ Riffs B & B1 (1st 2 meas.)
E5
A5
C#5
B5
know, oh, oh, you don't know you're beau - ti - ful.
If on - ly you saw what
...ful.

B5
E5
A5
B5
I can see, you'd un - der - stand why I want you so des - per-ate - ly. Right now I'm
Des - per - ate - ly.

Gtrs. 2 & 4: w/ Riffs B & B1 (1st 2 meas.)
E5
A5
C♯5
B5
E5
A5
look - ing at you and I can't be - lieve you don't know, oh, oh,
You don't know.

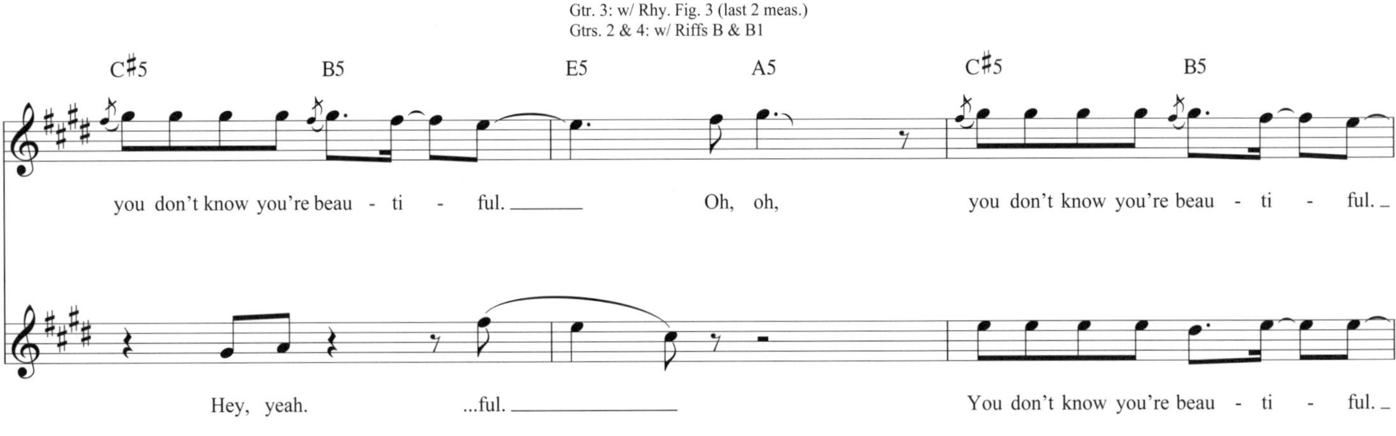
Gtr. 3: w/ Rhy. Fig. 3 (last 2 meas.)
Gtrs. 2 & 4: w/ Riffs B & B1
C♯5
B5
E5
A5
C♯5
B5
you don't know you're beau - ti - ful. Oh, oh, you don't know you're beau - ti - ful.
Hey, yeah. ...ful. You don't know you're beau - ti - ful.

Gtr. 3: w/ Rhy. Fig. 4
E5
A5
N.C.
B5
N.C.
Oh, oh, that's what makes you beau - ti - ful.

GUITAR NOTATION LEGEND

Guitar music can be notated three different ways: on a *musical staff*, in *tablature*, and in *rhythm slashes.*

RHYTHM SLASHES are written above the staff. Strum chords in the rhythm indicated. Use the chord diagrams found at the top of the first page of the transcription for the appropriate chord voicings. Round noteheads indicate single notes.

THE MUSICAL STAFF shows pitches and rhythms and is divided by bar lines into measures. Pitches are named after the first seven letters of the alphabet.

TABLATURE graphically represents the guitar fingerboard. Each horizontal line represents a string, and each number represents a fret.

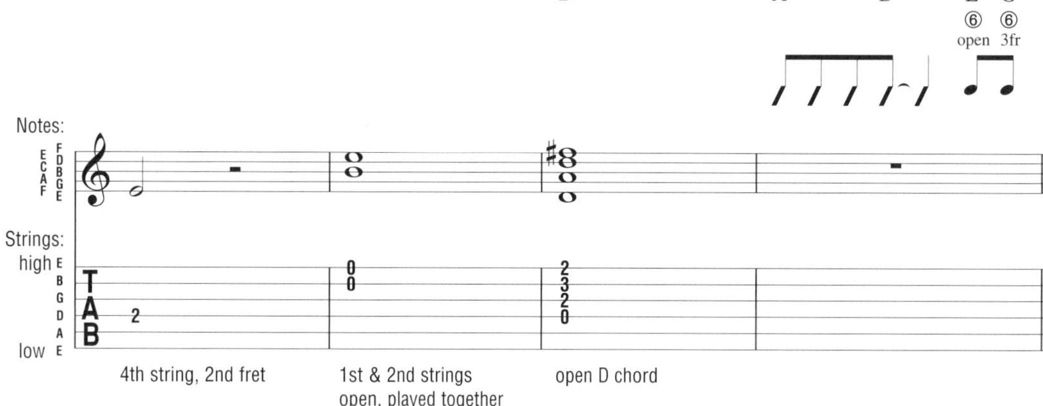

Definitions for Special Guitar Notation

HALF-STEP BEND: Strike the note and bend up 1/2 step.

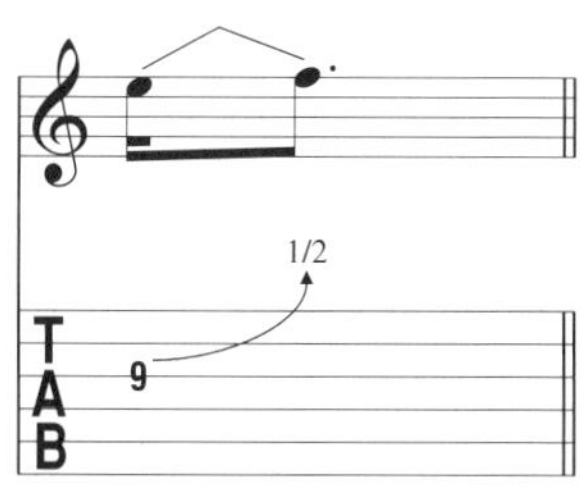

WHOLE-STEP BEND: Strike the note and bend up one step.

GRACE NOTE BEND: Strike the note and immediately bend up as indicated.

SLIGHT (MICROTONE) BEND: Strike the note and bend up 1/4 step.

BEND AND RELEASE: Strike the note and bend up as indicated, then release back to the original note. Only the first note is struck.

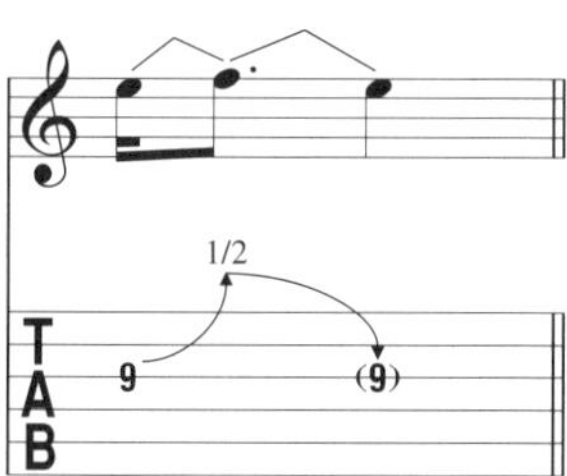
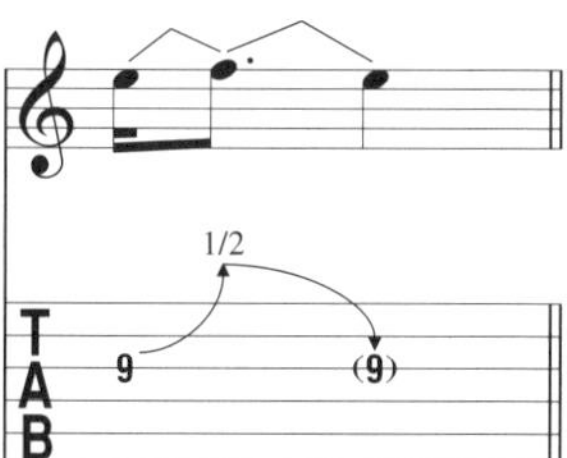

PRE-BEND: Bend the note as indicated, then strike it.

PRE-BEND AND RELEASE: Bend the note as indicated. Strike it and release the bend back to the original note.

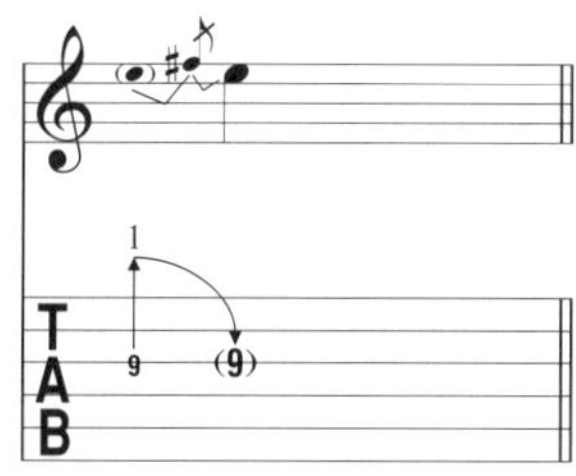

UNISON BEND: Strike the two notes simultaneously and bend the lower note up to the pitch of the higher.

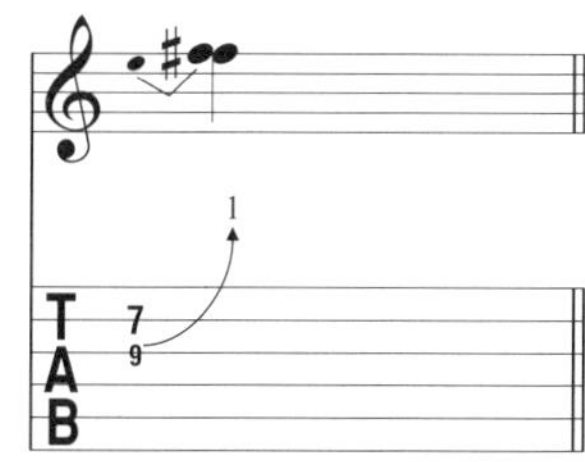

VIBRATO: The string is vibrated by rapidly bending and releasing the note with the fretting hand.

WIDE VIBRATO: The pitch is varied to a greater degree by vibrating with the fretting hand.

HAMMER-ON: Strike the first (lower) note with one finger, then sound the higher note (on the same string) with another finger by fretting it without picking.

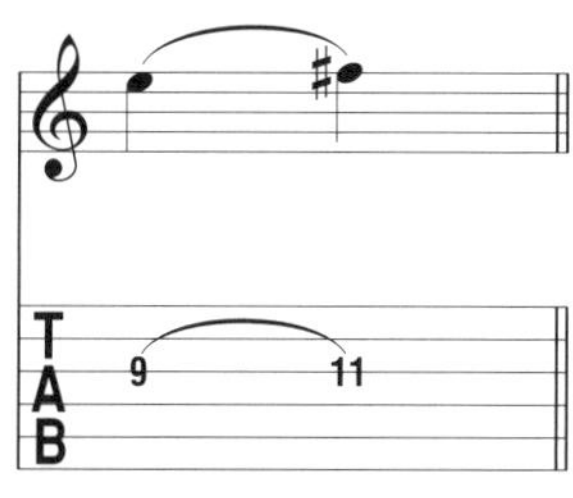

PULL-OFF: Place both fingers on the notes to be sounded. Strike the first note and without picking, pull the finger off to sound the second (lower) note.

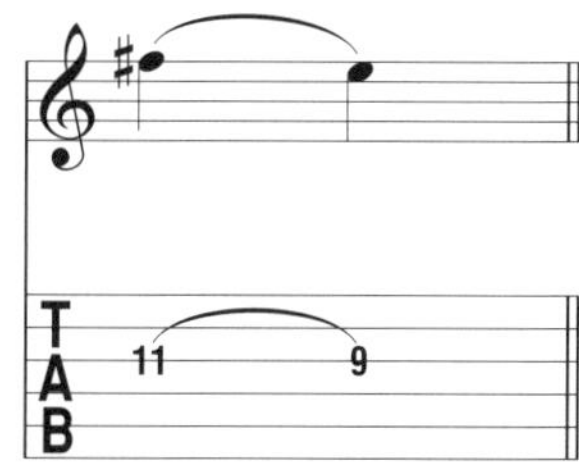

LEGATO SLIDE: Strike the first note and then slide the same fret-hand finger up or down to the second note. The second note is not struck.

SHIFT SLIDE: Same as legato slide, except the second note is struck.

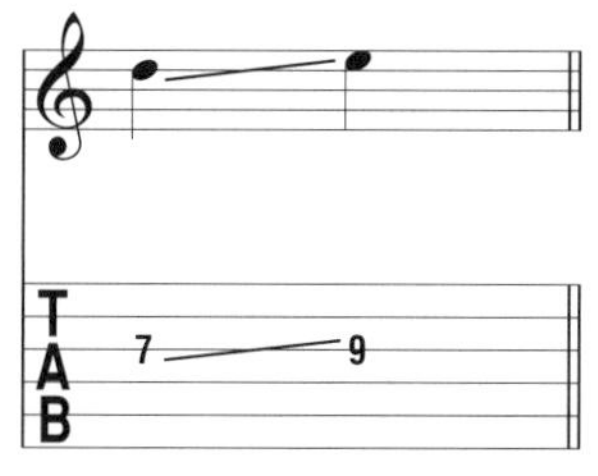

TRILL: Very rapidly alternate between the notes indicated by continuously hammering on and pulling off.

TAPPING: Hammer ("tap") the fret indicated with the pick-hand index or middle finger and pull off to the note fretted by the fret hand.

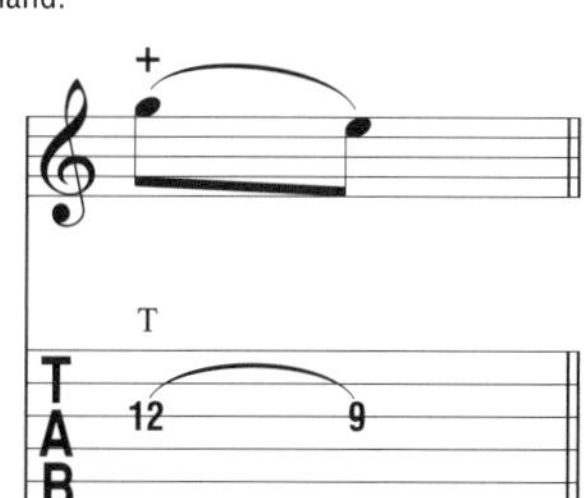

NATURAL HARMONIC: Strike the note while the fret-hand lightly touches the string directly over the fret indicated.

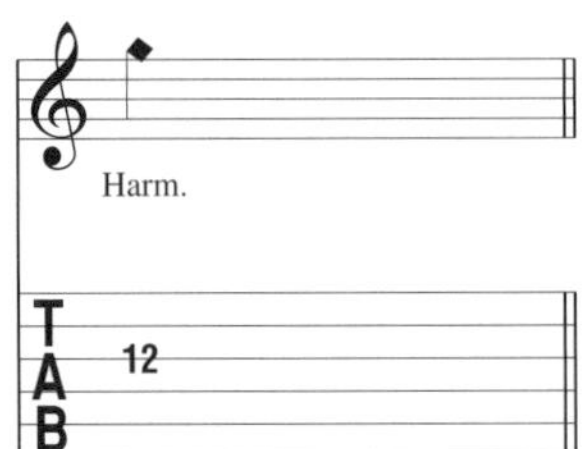

PINCH HARMONIC: The note is fretted normally and a harmonic is produced by adding the edge of the thumb or the tip of the index finger of the pick hand to the normal pick attack.

HARP HARMONIC: The note is fretted normally and a harmonic is produced by gently resting the pick hand's index finger directly above the indicated fret (in parentheses) while the pick hand's thumb or pick assists by plucking the appropriate string.

PICK SCRAPE: The edge of the pick is rubbed down (or up) the string, producing a scratchy sound.

MUFFLED STRINGS: A percussive sound is produced by laying the fret hand across the string(s) without depressing, and striking them with the pick hand.

PALM MUTING: The note is partially muted by the pick hand lightly touching the string(s) just before the bridge.

RAKE: Drag the pick across the strings indicated with a single motion.

TREMOLO PICKING: The note is picked as rapidly and continuously as possible.

ARPEGGIATE: Play the notes of the chord indicated by quickly rolling them from bottom to top.

VIBRATO BAR DIVE AND RETURN: The pitch of the note or chord is dropped a specified number of steps (in rhythm), then returned to the original pitch.

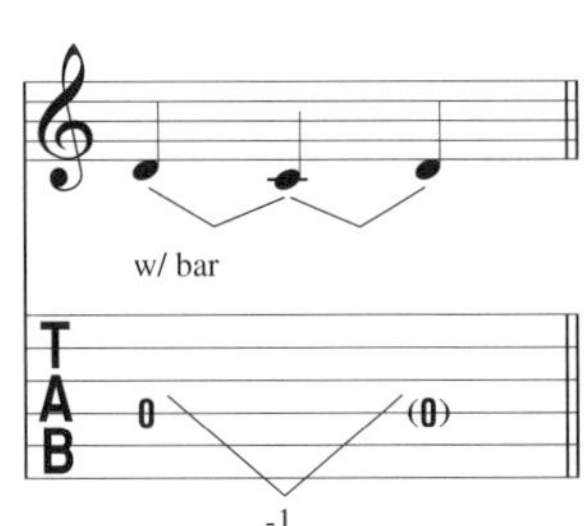

VIBRATO BAR SCOOP: Depress the bar just before striking the note, then quickly release the bar.

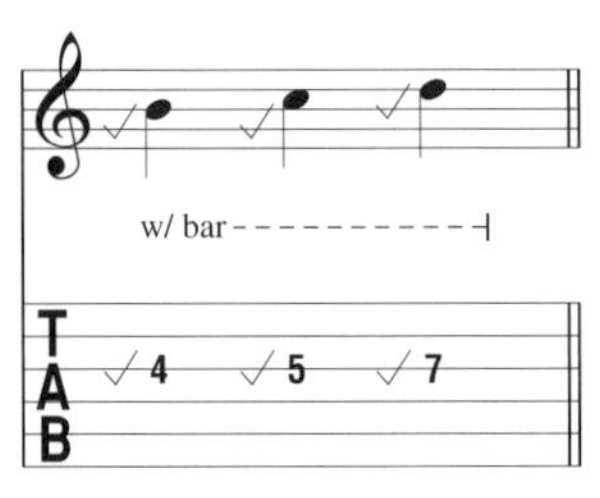

VIBRATO BAR DIP: Strike the note and then immediately drop a specified number of steps, then release back to the original pitch.

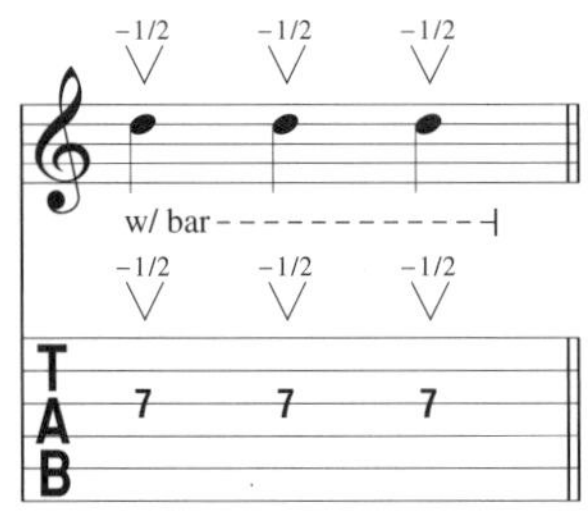

Additional Musical Definitions

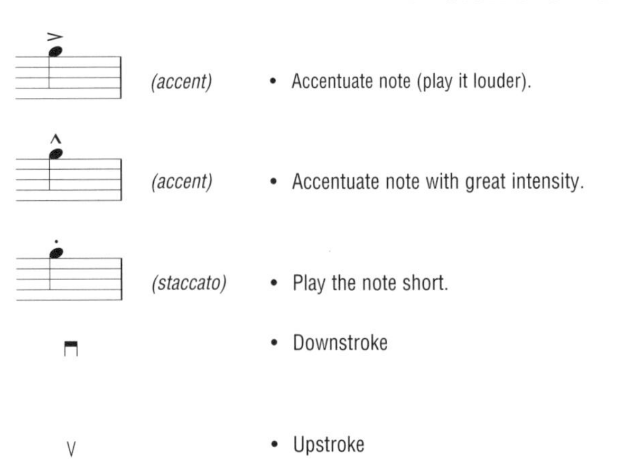

(accent) • Accentuate note (play it louder).

(accent) • Accentuate note with great intensity.

(staccato) • Play the note short.

• Downstroke

V • Upstroke

D.S. al Coda • Go back to the sign (𝄋), then play until the measure marked "***To Coda***," then skip to the section labelled "**Coda.**"

D.C. al Fine • Go back to the beginning of the song and play until the measure marked "***Fine***" (end).

Rhy. Fig. • Label used to recall a recurring accompaniment pattern (usually chordal).

Riff • Label used to recall composed, melodic lines (usually single notes) which recur.

Fill • Label used to identify a brief melodic figure which is to be inserted into the arrangement.

Rhy. Fill • A chordal version of a Fill.

tacet • Instrument is silent (drops out).

• Repeat measures between signs.

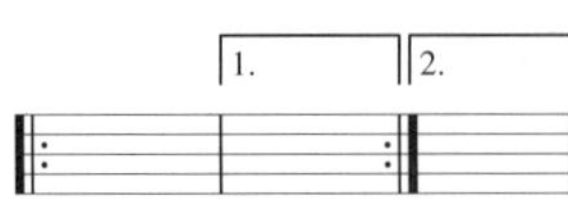

• When a repeated section has different endings, play the first ending only the first time and the second ending only the second time.

NOTE: Tablature numbers in parentheses mean:

1. The note is being sustained over a system (note in standard notation is tied), or
2. The note is sustained, but a new articulation (such as a hammer-on, pull-off, slide or vibrato) begins, or
3. The note is a barely audible "ghost" note (note in standard notation is also in parentheses).

HAL•LEONARD®

GUITAR PLAY-ALONG

AUDIO ACCESS INCLUDED

This series will help you play your favorite songs quickly and easily. Just follow the tab and listen to the audio to the hear how the guitar should sound, and then play along using the separate backing tracks. Audio files also include software to slow down the tempo without changing pitch. The melody and lyrics are included in the book so that you can sing or simply follow along. INCLUDES TAB

Volume	Item / Price
VOL. 1 – ROCK	00699570 / $16.99
VOL. 2 – ACOUSTIC	00699569 / $16.99
VOL. 3 – HARD ROCK	00699573 / $17.99
VOL. 4 – POP/ROCK	00298615 / $16.99
VOL. 6 – '90S ROCK	00699572 / $16.99
VOL. 7 – BLUES	00699575 / $17.99
VOL. 8 – ROCK	00699585 / $16.99
VOL. 9 – EASY ACOUSTIC SONGS	00151708 / $16.99
VOL. 10 – ACOUSTIC	00699586 / $16.95
VOL. 13 – FOLK ROCK	00699581 / $16.99
VOL. 14 – BLUES ROCK	00699582 / $16.99
VOL. 15 – R&B	00699583 / $16.99
VOL. 16 – JAZZ	00699584 / $15.95
VOL. 17 – COUNTRY	00699588 / $16.99
VOL. 18 – ACOUSTIC ROCK	00699577 / $15.95
VOL. 20 – ROCKABILLY	00699580 / $16.99
VOL. 21 – SANTANA	00174525 / $17.99
VOL. 22 – CHRISTMAS	00699600 / $15.99
VOL. 23 – SURF	00699635 / $15.99
VOL. 24 – ERIC CLAPTON	00699649 / $17.99
VOL. 25 – THE BEATLES	00198265 / $17.99
VOL. 26 – ELVIS PRESLEY	00699643 / $16.99
VOL. 27 – DAVID LEE ROTH	00699645 / $16.95
VOL. 28 – GREG KOCH	00699646 / $17.99
VOL. 29 – BOB SEGER	00699647 / $16.99
VOL. 30 – KISS	00699644 / $16.99
VOL. 32 – THE OFFSPRING	00699653 / $14.95
VOL. 33 – ACOUSTIC CLASSICS	00699656 / $17.99
VOL. 34 – CLASSIC ROCK	00699658 / $17.99
VOL. 35 – HAIR METAL	00699660 / $17.99
VOL. 36 – SOUTHERN ROCK	00699661 / $17.99
VOL. 37 – ACOUSTIC UNPLUGGED	00699662 / $22.99
VOL. 38 – BLUES	00699663 / $16.95
VOL. 39 – '80S METAL	00699664 / $16.99
VOL. 40 – INCUBUS	00699668 / $17.95
VOL. 41 – ERIC CLAPTON	00699669 / $17.99
VOL. 42 – COVER BAND HITS	00211597 / $16.99
VOL. 43 – LYNYRD SKYNYRD	00699681 / $17.99
VOL. 44 – JAZZ	00699689 / $16.99
VOL. 45 – TV THEMES	00699718 / $14.95
VOL. 46 – MAINSTREAM ROCK	00699722 / $16.95
VOL. 47 – HENDRIX SMASH HITS	00699723 / $19.99
VOL. 48 – AEROSMITH CLASSICS	00699724 / $17.99
VOL. 49 – STEVIE RAY VAUGHAN	00699725 / $17.99
VOL. 50 – VAN HALEN 1978-1984	00110269 / $17.99
VOL. 51 – ALTERNATIVE '90S	00699727 / $14.99
VOL. 52 – FUNK	00699728 / $15.99
VOL. 53 – DISCO	00699729 / $14.99
VOL. 54 – HEAVY METAL	00699730 / $16.99
VOL. 55 – POP METAL	00699731 / $14.95
VOL. 56 – FOO FIGHTERS	00699749 / $17.99
VOL. 59 – CHET ATKINS	00702347 / $16.99
VOL. 62 – CHRISTMAS CAROLS	00699798 / $12.95
VOL. 63 – CREEDENCE CLEARWATER REVIVAL	00699802 / $16.99
VOL. 64 – THE ULTIMATE OZZY OSBOURNE	00699803 / $17.99
VOL. 66 – THE ROLLING STONES	00699807 / $17.99
VOL. 67 – BLACK SABBATH	00699808 / $16.99
VOL. 68 – PINK FLOYD – DARK SIDE OF THE MOON	00699809 / $16.99
VOL. 73 – BLUESY ROCK	00699829 / $16.99
VOL. 74 – SIMPLE STRUMMING SONGS	00151706 / $19.99
VOL. 75 – TOM PETTY	00699882 / $16.99
VOL. 76 – COUNTRY HITS	00699884 / $16.99
VOL. 77 – BLUEGRASS	00699910 / $15.99
VOL. 78 – NIRVANA	00700132 / $16.99
VOL. 79 – NEIL YOUNG	00700133 / $24.99
VOL. 80 – ACOUSTIC ANTHOLOGY	00700175 / $19.95
VOL. 81 – ROCK ANTHOLOGY	00700176 / $22.99
VOL. 82 – EASY SONGS	00700177 / $16.99
VOL. 84 – STEELY DAN	00700200 / $17.99
VOL. 85 – THE POLICE	00700269 / $16.99
VOL. 86 – BOSTON	00700465 / $16.99
VOL. 87 – ACOUSTIC WOMEN	00700763 / $14.99
VOL. 89 – REGGAE	00700468 / $15.99
VOL. 90 – CLASSICAL POP	00700469 / $14.99
VOL. 91 – BLUES INSTRUMENTALS	00700505 / $17.99
VOL. 92 – EARLY ROCK INSTRUMENTALS	00700506 / $15.99
VOL. 93 – ROCK INSTRUMENTALS	00700507 / $16.99
VOL. 94 – SLOW BLUES	00700508 / $16.99
VOL. 95 – BLUES CLASSICS	00700509 / $15.99
VOL. 96 – BEST COUNTRY HITS	00211615 / $16.99
VOL. 97 – CHRISTMAS CLASSICS	00236542 / $14.99
VOL. 99 – ZZ TOP	00700762 / $16.99
VOL. 100 – B.B. KING	00700466 / $16.99
VOL. 101 – SONGS FOR BEGINNERS	00701917 / $14.99
VOL. 102 – CLASSIC PUNK	00700769 / $14.99
VOL. 103 – SWITCHFOOT	00700773 / $16.99
VOL. 104 – DUANE ALLMAN	00700846 / $16.99
VOL. 105 – LATIN	00700939 / $16.99
VOL. 106 – WEEZER	00700958 / $14.99
VOL. 107 – CREAM	00701069 / $16.99
VOL. 108 – THE WHO	00701053 / $16.99
VOL. 109 – STEVE MILLER	00701054 / $19.99
VOL. 110 – SLIDE GUITAR HITS	00701055 / $16.99
VOL. 111 – JOHN MELLENCAMP	00701056 / $14.99
VOL. 112 – QUEEN	00701052 / $16.99
VOL. 113 – JIM CROCE	00701058 / $17.99
VOL. 114 – BON JOVI	00701060 / $16.99
VOL. 115 – JOHNNY CASH	00701070 / $16.99
VOL. 116 – THE VENTURES	00701124 / $16.99
VOL. 117 – BRAD PAISLEY	00701224 / $16.99
VOL. 118 – ERIC JOHNSON	00701353 / $16.99
VOL. 119 – AC/DC CLASSICS	00701356 / $17.99
VOL. 120 – PROGRESSIVE ROCK	00701457 / $14.99
VOL. 121 – U2	00701508 / $16.99
VOL. 122 – CROSBY, STILLS & NASH	00701610 / $16.99
VOL. 123 – LENNON & MCCARTNEY ACOUSTIC	00701614 / $16.99
VOL. 125 – JEFF BECK	00701687 / $16.99
VOL. 126 – BOB MARLEY	00701701 / $16.99
VOL. 127 – 1970S ROCK	00701739 / $16.99
VOL. 128 – 1960S ROCK	00701740 / $14.99
VOL. 129 – MEGADETH	00701741 / $17.99
VOL. 130 – IRON MAIDEN	00701742 / $17.99
VOL. 131 – 1990S ROCK	00701743 / $14.99
VOL. 132 – COUNTRY ROCK	00701757 / $15.99
VOL. 133 – TAYLOR SWIFT	00701894 / $16.99
VOL. 134 – AVENGED SEVENFOLD	00701906 / $16.99
VOL. 135 – MINOR BLUES	00151350 / $17.99
VOL. 136 – GUITAR THEMES	00701922 / $14.99
VOL. 137 – IRISH TUNES	00701966 / $15.99
VOL. 138 – BLUEGRASS CLASSICS	00701967 / $16.99
VOL. 139 – GARY MOORE	00702370 / $16.99
VOL. 140 – MORE STEVIE RAY VAUGHAN	00702396 / $17.99
VOL. 141 – ACOUSTIC HITS	00702401 / $16.99
VOL. 142 – GEORGE HARRISON	00237697 / $17.99
VOL. 143 – SLASH	00702425 / $19.99
VOL. 144 – DJANGO REINHARDT	00702531 / $16.99
VOL. 145 – DEF LEPPARD	00702532 / $17.99
VOL. 146 – ROBERT JOHNSON	00702533 / $16.99
VOL. 147 – SIMON & GARFUNKEL	14041591 / $16.99
VOL. 148 – BOB DYLAN	14041592 / $16.99
VOL. 149 – AC/DC HITS	14041593 / $17.99
VOL. 150 – ZAKK WYLDE	02501717 / $16.99
VOL. 151 – J.S. BACH	02501730 / $16.99
VOL. 152 – JOE BONAMASSA	02501751 / $19.99
VOL. 153 – RED HOT CHILI PEPPERS	00702990 / $19.99
VOL. 155 – ERIC CLAPTON – FROM THE ALBUM UNPLUGGED	00703085 / $16.99
VOL. 156 – SLAYER	00703770 / $17.99
VOL. 157 – FLEETWOOD MAC	00101382 / $16.99
VOL. 159 – WES MONTGOMERY	00102593 / $19.99
VOL. 160 – T-BONE WALKER	00102641 / $17.99
VOL. 161 – THE EAGLES – ACOUSTIC	00102659 / $17.99
VOL. 162 – THE EAGLES HITS	00102667 / $17.99
VOL. 163 – PANTERA	00103036 / $17.99
VOL. 164 – VAN HALEN 1986-1995	00110270 / $17.99
VOL. 165 – GREEN DAY	00210343 / $17.99
VOL. 166 – MODERN BLUES	00700764 / $16.99
VOL. 167 – DREAM THEATER	00111938 / $24.99
VOL. 168 – KISS	00113421 / $17.99
VOL. 169 – TAYLOR SWIFT	00115982 / $16.99
VOL. 170 – THREE DAYS GRACE	00117337 / $16.99
VOL. 171 – JAMES BROWN	00117420 / $16.99
VOL. 172 – THE DOOBIE BROTHERS	00119670 / $16.99
VOL. 173 – TRANS-SIBERIAN ORCHESTRA	00119907 / $19.99
VOL. 174 – SCORPIONS	00122119 / $16.99
VOL. 175 – MICHAEL SCHENKER	00122127 / $17.99
VOL. 176 – BLUES BREAKERS WITH JOHN MAYALL & ERIC CLAPTON	00122132 / $19.99
VOL. 177 – ALBERT KING	00123271 / $16.99
VOL. 178 – JASON MRAZ	00124165 / $17.99
VOL. 179 – RAMONES	00127073 / $16.99
VOL. 180 – BRUNO MARS	00129706 / $16.99
VOL. 181 – JACK JOHNSON	00129854 / $16.99
VOL. 182 – SOUNDGARDEN	00138161 / $17.99
VOL. 183 – BUDDY GUY	00138240 / $17.99
VOL. 184 – KENNY WAYNE SHEPHERD	00138258 / $17.99
VOL. 185 – JOE SATRIANI	00139457 / $17.99
VOL. 186 – GRATEFUL DEAD	00139459 / $17.99
VOL. 187 – JOHN DENVER	00140839 / $17.99
VOL. 188 – MÖTLEY CRUE	00141145 / $17.99
VOL. 189 – JOHN MAYER	00144350 / $17.99
VOL. 190 – DEEP PURPLE	00146152 / $17.99
VOL. 191 – PINK FLOYD CLASSICS	00146164 / $17.99
VOL. 192 – JUDAS PRIEST	00151352 / $17.99
VOL. 193 – STEVE VAI	00156028 / $19.99
VOL. 195 – METALLICA: 1983-1988	00234291 / $19.99
VOL. 196 – METALLICA: 1991-2016	00234292 / $19.99

Prices, contents, and availability subject to change without notice.

Complete song lists available online.

www.halleonard.com

0719

AUTHENTIC TRANSCRIPTIONS WITH NOTES AND TABLATURE

GUITAR RECORDED VERSIONS®

Guitar Recorded Versions® are note-for-note transcriptions of guitar music taken directly off recordings. This series, one of the most popular in print today, features some of the greatest guitar players and groups from blues and rock to country and jazz.

Guitar Recorded Versions are transcribed by the best transcribers in the business. Every book contains notes and tablature unless otherwise marked. Visit **www.halleonard.com** for our complete selection.

14041344 The Definitive AC/DC Songbook $45.99
00690016 The Will Ackerman Collection $22.99
00690501 Bryan Adams – Greatest Hits $22.99
00690603 Aerosmith – O Yeah! (Ultimate Hits) $24.95
00690178 Alice in Chains – Acoustic $19.99
00694865 Alice in Chains – Dirt $19.99
00660225 Alice in Chains – Facelift $19.99
00694925 Alice in Chains – Jar of Flies/Sap $19.99
00690387 Alice in Chains – Nothing Safe: Best of the Box $19.95
00694932 Allman Brothers Band – Definitive Collection for Guitar Volume 1 $24.95
00694933 Allman Brothers Band – Definitive Collection for Guitar Volume 2 $24.99
00694934 Allman Brothers Band – Definitive Collection for Guitar Volume 3 $24.99
00690958 Duane Allman Guitar Anthology $24.99
00691071 Alter Bridge – AB III $22.99
00690945 Alter Bridge – Blackbird $22.99
00690755 Alter Bridge – One Day Remains $22.99
00123558 Arctic Monkeys – AM $24.99
00114564 As I Lay Dying – Awakened $22.99
00690158 Chet Atkins – Almost Alone $22.99
00694876 Chet Atkins – Contemporary Styles $19.95
00694878 Chet Atkins – Vintage Fingerstyle $19.99
00690609 Audioslave $22.99
00690884 Audioslave – Revelations $19.95
00690926 Avenged Sevenfold $24.99
00214869 Avenged Sevenfold – The Best of 2005-2013 $24.99
00690820 Avenged Sevenfold – City of Evil $24.95
00123216 Avenged Sevenfold – Hail to the King $22.99
00222486 Avenged Sevenfold – The Stage $24.99
00691065 Avenged Sevenfold – Waking the Fallen $22.99
00123140 The Avett Brothers Guitar Collection $22.99
00694918 Randy Bachman Collection $22.95
00690503 Beach Boys – Very Best of $19.99
00694929 Beatles: 1962-1966 $24.99
00694930 Beatles: 1967-1970 $24.99
00690489 Beatles – 1 $24.99
00694880 Beatles – Abbey Road $19.95
00691066 Beatles – Beatles for Sale $22.99
00690110 Beatles – Book 1 (White Album) $19.99
00690111 Beatles – Book 2 (White Album) $19.99
00690902 Beatles – The Capitol Albums, Volume 1 $24.99
00694832 Beatles – For Acoustic Guitar $24.99
00691031 Beatles – Help! $19.99
00690482 Beatles – Let It Be $19.99
00691067 Beatles – Meet the Beatles! $22.99
00691068 Beatles – Please Please Me $22.99
00694891 Beatles – Revolver $19.99
00694914 Beatles – Rubber Soul $22.99
00694863 Beatles – Sgt. Pepper's Lonely Hearts Club Band $22.99
00110193 Beatles – Tomorrow Never Knows $22.99
00691044 Jeff Beck – Best of Beck $24.99
00690632 Beck – Sea Change $19.95
00691041 Jeff Beck – Truth $19.99
00694884 Best of George Benson $22.99
00692385 Chuck Berry $22.99
00690835 Billy Talent $19.95
00690879 Billy Talent II $19.99
00147787 Best of the Black Crowes $19.99
00129737 The Black Keys – Turn Blue $22.99
00690149 Black Sabbath $16.99
00690901 Best of Black Sabbath $19.95
00691010 Black Sabbath – Heaven and Hell $22.99
00690148 Black Sabbath – Master of Reality $16.99
00690142 Black Sabbath – Paranoid $16.99
14042759 Black Sabbath – 13 $19.99
00692200 Black Sabbath – We Sold Our Soul for Rock 'N' Roll $22.99
00690389 blink-182 – Enema of the State $19.95
00690831 blink-182 – Greatest Hits $19.95
00691179 blink-182 – Neighborhoods $22.99
00148544 Michael Bloomfield Guitar Anthology $24.99
00690028 Blue Oyster Cult – Cult Classics $19.99
00286622 Bohemian Rhapsody $24.99
00691074 Bon Jovi – Greatest Hits $22.99
00158600 Joe Bonamassa – Blues of Desperation $22.99
00139086 Joe Bonamassa – Different Shades of Blue $22.99
00198117 Joe Bonamassa – Muddy Wolf at Red Rocks $24.99
00283540 Joe Bonamassa – Redemption $24.99
00160988 Bootleg Country Guitar Tabs $19.99
00690913 Boston $19.99
00690829 Boston Guitar Collection $24.99
00690491 Best of David Bowie $19.99
00690583 Box Car Racer $19.95
00691023 Breaking Benjamin – Dear Agony $22.99
00690873 Breaking Benjamin – Phobia $19.95
00141446 Best of Lenny Breau $19.99
00690451 Jeff Buckley Collection $24.99
00690957 Bullet for My Valentine – Scream Aim Fire $22.99
00119629 Bullet for My Valentine – Temper Temper $22.99
00690678 Best of Kenny Burrell $22.99
00691077 Cage the Elephant – Thank You, Happy Birthday $22.99
00691159 The Cars – Complete Greatest Hits $22.99
00690261 Carter Family Collection $19.99
00691079 Best of Johnny Cash $22.99
00690043 Best of Cheap Trick $19.95
00690171 Chicago – The Definitive Guitar Collection $24.99
00691011 Chimaira Guitar Collection $24.99
00690567 Charlie Christian – The Definitive Collection $19.95
00101916 Eric Church – Chief $22.99
00129545 The Civil Wars $19.99
00138731 Eric Clapton & Friends – The Breeze $22.99
00690590 Eric Clapton – Anthology $29.95
00692391 Best of Eric Clapton – 2nd Edition $22.95
00691055 Eric Clapton – Clapton $22.99
00690936 Eric Clapton – Complete Clapton $29.99
00690010 Eric Clapton – From the Cradle $22.99
00192383 Eric Clapton – I Still Do* $19.99
00690363 Eric Clapton – Just One Night $24.99
00694873 Eric Clapton – Timepieces $19.95
00694869 Eric Clapton – Unplugged $22.95
00690415 Clapton Chronicles – Best of Eric Clapton $19.99
00694896 John Mayall/Eric Clapton – Bluesbreakers $19.99
00690162 Best of the Clash $19.99
00690828 Coheed & Cambria – Good Apollo I'm Burning Star, IV, Vol. 1: From Fear Through the Eyes of Madness $19.95
00690806 Coldplay – X & Y $19.95
00690855 Best of Collective Soul $19.95
00141704 Jesse Cook – Works Vol. 1 $19.99
00691091 The Best of Alice Cooper $24.99
00694940 Counting Crows – August & Everything After $19.99
00127184 Best of Robert Cray $19.99
00694840 Cream – Disraeli Gears $24.99
00288787 Creed – Greatest Hits $22.99
00690819 Best of Creedence Clearwater Revival $24.99
00690648 The Very Best of Jim Croce $19.99
00690572 Steve Cropper – Soul Man $19.99
00690613 Best of Crosby, Stills & Nash $27.99
00699521 The Cure – Greatest Hits $24.99
00690637 Best of Dick Dale $19.95
00690822 Best of Alex De Grassi $19.95
00690967 Death Cab for Cutie – Narrow Stairs $22.99
00690289 Best of Deep Purple $19.99
00690288 Deep Purple – Machine Head $17.99
00690784 Best of Def Leppard $22.99
00694831 Derek and the Dominos – Layla & Other Assorted Love Songs $22.95
00692240 Bo Diddley – Guitar Solos by Fred Sokolow $19.99
00690384 Best of Ani DiFranco $19.95
00690979 Best of Dinosaur Jr. $19.99
00690833 Private Investigations – Best of Dire Straits and Mark Knopfler $24.99
00695382 Very Best of Dire Straits – Sultans of Swing $24.99
00122443 Dream Theater $24.99
00291164 Dream Theater – Distance Over Time $22.99
00160579 Dream Theater – Selections from The Astonishing $24.99
00278631 Eagles – Their Greatest Hits 1971-1975 $22.99
00278632 The Very Best of Eagles – Updated Edition $34.99
00690250 Best of Duane Eddy $17.99
00690909 Best of Tommy Emmanuel $24.99
00172824 Tommy Emmanuel – It's Never Too Late $22.99
00690555 Best of Melissa Etheridge $19.95
00690515 Extreme II – Pornograffitti $22.99
00150257 John Fahey – Guitar Anthology $19.99
00691009 Five Finger Death Punch $19.99
00690664 Best of Fleetwood Mac $22.99
00690870 Flyleaf $19.95
00691115 Foo Fighters – Wasting Light $22.99
00690805 Best of Robben Ford $24.99
00120220 Robben Ford – Guitar Anthology $24.99
00690842 Best of Peter Frampton $19.99
00694920 Best of Free $19.99
00694807 Danny Gatton – 88 Elmira St $22.99
00690438 Genesis Guitar Anthology $22.99
00120167 Godsmack $19.95
00212480 Green Day – Revolution Radio* $19.99
00113073 Green Day – Uno $21.99
00116846 Green Day – ¡Dos! $21.99
00118259 Green Day – ¡Tré! $21.99
00691190 Best of Peter Green $19.99
00287517 Greta Van Fleet – Anthem of the Peaceful Army $19.99
00287515 Greta Van Fleet – From the Fires $19.99
00690927 Patty Griffin – Children Running Through $19.95
00690591 Patty Griffin – Guitar Collection $19.95
00691027 Buddy Guy Anthology $24.99
00694854 Buddy Guy – Damn Right, I've Got the Blues $19.95
00690697 Best of Jim Hall $19.99
00690840 Ben Harper – Both Sides of the Gun $19.95
00691018 Ben Harper – Fight for Your Mind $22.99
00694798 George Harrison Anthology $22.99
00690841 Scott Henderson – Blues Guitar Collection $22.99
00692930 Jimi Hendrix – Are You Experienced? $24.99
00692931 Jimi Hendrix – Axis: Bold As Love $24.99
00690304 Jimi Hendrix – Band of Gypsys $24.99
00690608 Jimi Hendrix – Blue Wild Angel $24.95
00694944 Jimi Hendrix – Blues $24.99
00275044 Jimi Hendrix – Both Sides of the Sky $22.99
00692932 Jimi Hendrix – Electric Ladyland $24.95
00119619 Jimi Hendrix – People, Hell and Angels $22.99
00690602 Jimi Hendrix – Smash Hits $24.99
00691152 West Coast Seattle Boy: The Jimi Hendrix Anthology $29.99
00691332 Jimi Hendrix – Winterland (Highlights) $22.99
00690017 Jimi Hendrix – Woodstock $29.99
00690843 H.I.M. – Dark Light $19.95
00690869 Hinder – Extreme Behavior $19.95
00660029 Buddy Holly $22.99
00690793 John Lee Hooker Anthology $24.99
00694905 Howlin' Wolf $19.95
00690692 Very Best of Billy Idol $22.99
00121961 Imagine Dragons – Night Visions $22.99
00690688 Incubus – A Crow Left of the Murder $19.95
00690790 Iron Maiden Anthology $24.99
00691058 Iron Maiden – The Final Frontier $22.99
00200446 Iron Maiden – Guitar Tab $29.99
00690887 Iron Maiden – A Matter of Life and Death $24.95
00690730 Alan Jackson – Guitar Collection $22.99
00694938 Elmore James – Master Electric Slide Guitar $19.99
00690652 Best of Jane's Addiction $19.95